THE JEWS OF SPAIN

THE FREE PRESS
A Division of Macmillan, Inc.
NEW YORK
Maxwell Macmillan Canada
TORONTO
Maxwell Macmillan International
NEW YORK OXFORD SINGAPORE SYDNEY

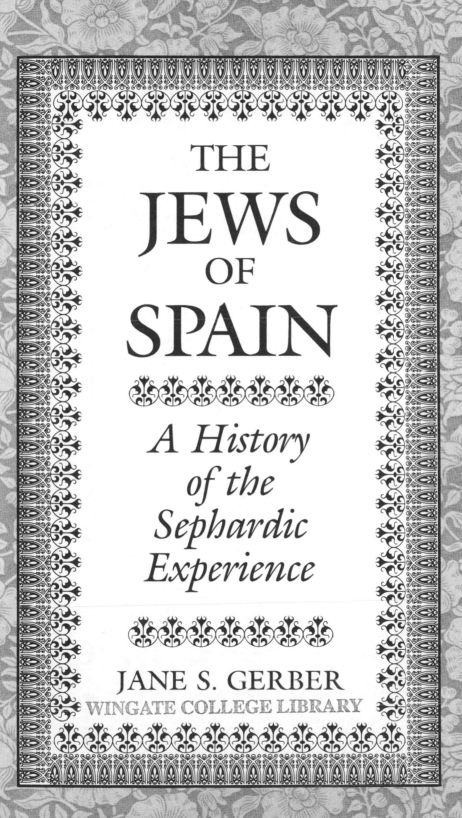

THE
JEWS
OF
SPAIN

*A History
of the
Sephardic
Experience*

JANE S. GERBER

The author gratefully acknowledges permission to reproduce printed and photographic material from the following sources:

American Jewish Historical Society, ASAP/Mike Ganor, Robert Attal, Beit Lohamei Haghetaot, Ben Zvi Institute, Beth Hatefutsoth, Bibliothèque Nationale Paris, Frédéric Brenner, Centre for the Study of Jews of Holland in Israel, Detroit Institute of Arts, Etan Dor-Shav, The Israel Museum, Jewish Historical Museum of Amsterdam, Jewish National and University Library, Leo Baeck Institute, Penguin Books, Photo MAS, Prado Museum, Tel Aviv Books, University of Alabama Press.

Jewish Publication Society of America, Philadelphia. Raymond Scheindlin, *Wine, Women, and Death* (1986) and *The Gazelle* (1991). Poems of Judah al-Harizi and Solomon ibn Gabirol, used by permission of the publisher.

Cornell University, Ithaca. Joseph F. O'Callaghan, *A History of Medieval Spain*. Copyright © 1975 by Cornell University. Three maps, used by permission of the publisher.

José Luis Lacave, Manel Armengol, and Francisco Ontañón, *Sefarad, Sefarad: La España Judía* (Barcelona: Comisión Quinto Centenario, 1987), p. 136, photograph No. I. Copyright © 1987 Lunweg Editores, S.A.

Archives of the U. Nahon Museum of Italian Jewish Art, Jerusalem. Two photographs, courtesy of the U. Nahon Museum.

Copyright © 1992 by Jane S. Gerber

The Free Press
A Division of Macmillan, Inc.
866 Third Avenue, New York, N.Y. 10022

Maxwell Macmillan Canada, Inc.
1200 Eglinton Avenue East
Suite 200
Don Mills, Ontario M3C 3N1

Macmillan, Inc. is part of the Maxwell Communication Group of Companies.

Printed in the United States of America

printing number
2   3   4   5   6   7   8   9   10

Library of Congress Cataloging-in-Publication Data

Gerber, Jane S.
    The Jews of Spain: a history of the Sephardic experience / Jane
S. Gerber
        p.   cm.
    Includes bibliographical references and index.
    ISBN 0-02-911573-6
    1. Jews—Spain—History.   2. Sephardim—History.   3. Spain—Ethnic
relations.   I. Title.
DS135.S7G47   1992
946'.004924—dc20   92-26941
                                                            CIP

Dedicated to the memory of
I. DAVID SATLOW
and
EDWARD GERBER

CONTENTS

PREFACE

Where are they, the hundred seventy and seven holy communities, overflowing with good, which once lived in Castile at ease and in contentment? How they were all destroyed in an instant, from the smallest to the biggest . . .

—Anonymous chronicle

The history of the Jews of Spain is a remarkable story that begins in the remote past and continues today. For more than a thousand years, Sepharad (the Hebrew word for Spain) was home to a large Jewish community noted for its richness and virtuosity. Summarily expelled in 1492 and forced into exile, their tragedy of expulsion marked the end of one critical phase of their history and the beginning of another. Indeed, in defiance of all logic and expectation, the expulsion of the Jews from Spain became an occasion for renewed creativity. Nor have five hundred years of wandering extinguished the identity of the Sephardic Jews, or diminished the proud memory of the dazzling civilization which they created on Spanish soil.

This book is intended to serve as an introduction and scholarly guide to that history. It is directed to the general reader who is interested in the history of the Jewish people and to the student for whom a one-volume overview is sorely needed. Specialists will recognize my debt to the pioneering studies of Ashtor, Baer, Beinart, G. Cohen, and Yerushalmi, as well as to the younger scholars pursuing new avenues of research today. Aside from the insights I have gained from my colleagues and students, I have been deeply impressed by several contemporary Sephardic leaders who, in the course of our friendship, have imparted to me the special sense of dignity and pride so integral to Sephardic Jews.

The daunting task of encompassing two thousand years of history

as rich as that of the Jews of Spain required difficult choices of selection
and omission. It is hoped that the necessary telescoping of events and
unavoidable condensation will not lead to distortions. In keeping the
debate of scholars to a minimum, I hope to present the saga of a unique
people in an easily accessible fashion.

I am especially grateful to the Maurice Amado Foundation for its
generous support of the photographic section of this book. Its dedica-
tion to the furtherance of Sephardic education has provided new impetus to the study of Sephardic civilization. To my editor, Adam
Bellow, I owe a special debt of gratitude for his probing questions,
sound judgment and superb advice. I am also grateful to Charles Flowers for his skilled editorial assistance. Finally, I can hardly imagine
having completed this project without the patience of my husband,
Roger, and the encouragement of my daughters, Dina, Debbie, and
Tamar.

Mishkenot Sha'ananim
Jerusalem
July 1992

INTRODUCTION
An Enigma of 1492

After the Spanish monarchs had expelled all the Jews from their kingdoms and
lands in January, in that same month they commissioned me to undertake the
voyage to India with a properly equipped fleet.

—Christopher Columbus

On the evening of August 2, 1492, two great dramas were simultaneously unfolding in Spain. In the port of Palos, three caravels under
the command of Christopher Columbus were undergoing final prepa-
rations for their historic journey of discovery. And throughout the
country, the nation's Jews were spending their last night on Spanish soil
after a sojourn that had lasted more than 1,500 years. The simultaneity
of these two events, which was noted by the explorer in his log, was not
accidental. The epochal meaning of his discovery may have eluded
Columbus during his lifetime, but the Jews well realized that they stood
on the threshold of a terrifying unknown that might yet mark the
beginnings of an age of redemption, or so they dared hope.

Five hundred years have elapsed since that summer when one of
the most brilliant collectivities in Jewish history was expelled from its
home, but its descendants, the Sephardim (from the Hebrew word
for Spain, *Sepharad*), continue today as one of the major branches of
the Jewish people. Deeply rooted in the Iberian peninsula since the
dawn of their dispersion, these Jews had fervently nurtured a love for
Spain and felt a deep loyalty to her language, regions, and traditions.
Long after their expulsion, this loyalty and some of the special characteristics of Spanish Jews born in Iberia would endure as a living
legacy of a medieval Golden Age. In fact, Spain had been considered
a second Jerusalem. At the same time, however, the effects of long

centuries of persecution on Iberian soil would also cling to the Sephardim like a shadow.

When King Ferdinand and Queen Isabella's decree of expulsion was promulgated on March 31, ordering the 300,000 Jews of Spain to leave within four months, the Sephardim reacted with shock and disbelief. (At Jewish request, an initial deadline of July 31 would be postponed to August 2 because of the holiday of Tisha B'av.) Surely, they felt, the prominence of their people in all walks of life, the sheer longevity of their communities (which had already survived centuries of uprisings, discrimination, and local pogroms), and the presence of so many Jews and Christians of Jewish ancestry (*conversos*) in the inner circles of the court, municipalities, and even the Catholic church could provide protection and avert the decree.

The biblical book of Obadiah itself spoke of "the exile of Jerusalem that was in Sepharad," and the Sephardim believed themselves to be descendants of Judaean royalty, tracing their lineage back to King David. For hundreds of years, theirs was a community of shared vitality and unbroken creativity, admired by all of world Jewry. Spanish Jews were especially proud of their long line of poets, whose secular as well as religious songs continued to be recited. Their philosophers had been influential even among the scholars of the West, their innovative grammarians had earned a lasting place as pioneers of the Hebrew language, and their mathematicians, scientists, and innumerable physicians had won acclaim. The resourcefulness and public service of Sephardic diplomats also filled the annals of many Muslim kingdoms. In fact, they had not just resided in Spain; they had co-existed side by side with Muslims and Christians, taking the notion of living together (*la convivencia*) with utmost seriousness.

But the harsh reality of expulsion was all too implacable, even as their two leading statesmen and community leaders, Abraham Seneor and Don Isaac Abrabanel, struggled throughout that tense spring to have the decree rescinded. Seneor, chief tax collector of Spain and *rab de la corte* (court rabbi), had served as the critical go-between in the betrothal of Ferdinand and Isabella, providing the funds for the precious gift that sealed the match. His assistant and eventual successor Abrabanel, although a relative newcomer to Spain, had earned respect in the highest political circles for his fiscal advice and was also considered to be one of the leading Jewish intellectuals of the day. The king was willing to listen to their pleas and even accepted a substantial bribe from Abrabanel, but the decision stood.

The vanished land of Sepharad provides one of the great themes of Jewish history, somewhat analogous to the destruction of the Temple and the Babylonian Exile. Yet it is not always clear to the observer precisely what Sepharad meant to the Jew. Was it a real or mythic place? Or was it a moment in time? Was it a memory of a fleeting era of song? Or was it the particular personality of the singer of that melody? Or did Sepharad connote a special sense of nobility? It was probably some combination of all of these elements. At the heart of Sephardic self-definition lies the memory of a Jewish Golden Age of philosophy, poetry, and science in tenth and eleventh century Andalusia that predates the Spanish Golden Age by 500 years. Sepharad also denotes the reality of a degree of integration unknown elsewhere in medieval times. Only in modern Germany and the United States have the surrounding cultures been as beckoning to the Jew.

Jewish historians agree that Sephardic Jewry as a unique, definable portion of world Jewry emerged from the fertile commingling of three civilizations in Iberia in medieval times. Jews had probably reached the westernmost edge of the Mediterranean in antiquity when the Second Temple still stood in Jerusalem. Thereafter, they remained within the cultural orbit of the Greco-Roman Jewish world for hundreds of years, enjoying a flourishing life on the peninsula. They were already an ancient, rooted community when Spain embraced Catholicism in the sixth century.

During the sixth and seventh centuries, the final years of Visigothic Christian rule and among the most turbulent in Jewish history, severe persecutions forced the community to disperse or go underground. But with the passing of the Christian Visigothic kingdom in 711, Spanish Jewish life slowly revived. Spain became part of a dynamic Muslim empire as well as a participant in Mediterranean Jewish civilization. Yet the country was never entirely subdued by Islam. Judaism flourished in an unusual, indeed unique, environment as one component of the medieval Iberian scene that included Muslims and Christians. It was precisely because of this interaction that special sparks and creative energies were generated. In all of medieval Europe, only in Spain were Jews not the sole minority in a homogeneous Christian state. Consequently, Jews experienced two overlords on one soil as Iberia remained home to all three faiths from 711 to 1492. Living side by side with Christians and Muslims, Jews shared the misfortunes and fortunes of both.

It is not accidental that Spain invented special words to denote Muslims who lived under Christian rule (*mudejar*) and Christians who lived under Islam (*mozarabs*) in recognition that these cultural boundaries were fluid. More than once, the Jews served as cultural intermediaries between the two realms, becoming permanently shaped by the pattern of oscillating control between Christendom and Islam.

Since the two major peninsular powers were locked in a battle that persisted for centuries, the atmosphere of "holy war" inevitably shaped the destiny of the Jews, who found themselves caught between the warring blocs. In this climate of continuous crusade and crisis, both Islam and Christendom were altered. Early flexibility and toleration in Islamic Andalusia soon gave way to intolerance and fanaticism, and Christian exclusivity (hegemonism) eventually replaced multiculturalism. The most drastic symptom of this change was the reappearance of the dreaded practice of forced conversion, which culminated in laws of racial purity, ghettoization, and expulsion.

The experience of Sephardim raises the issue of acculturation and assimilation as no other Jewish community has. For many centuries Jewish civilization borrowed freely from the surrounding Muslim culture. Even after Jews moved into Christian Spain, their interaction with the dominant culture persisted. When persecutions overwhelmed the Sephardim in 1391 and they were offered the choice of conversion or death, the numbers of converts outnumbered the considerable number of martyrs. The very novelty of this mass conversion, unique to Jewish experience, has induced scholars to seek causality in the high degree of acculturation attained by the Sephardim. Medieval commentators, especially, were fond of placing the blame for the breakdown of communal discipline upon Jewish acculturation, and some of the greatest modern Jewish historians, such as Itzhak Baer, have cited in addition the corrosive impact of Averroist philosophy and the cynicism of Spain's assimilated Jewish courtier class. But in the wave of mass conversions and the sharp communal conflicts, it was not just the philosophers who succumbed in the face of persecution.

Admittedly, in all of the great ages of Jewish history, Jews have freely borrowed ideas and institutions from the broader culture surrounding them, transforming these borrowings to create something both new and compatible with Judaism. When given a modicum of political freedom and tolerance, Jews have engaged in intensive prolonged dialogue with the civilizations of the world. A Jewish culture that did not adapt to new waves of thought would have become frozen in an ancient mold. To a large extent, then, the story of Jewish history is the story of creative cultural adaptation, and nowhere was this process more thoroughgoing than in Spain. Jewish encounters with Islam and Christianity were more profound and enduring, their fruits more varied and rich.

As it has been preserved and transmitted, Sephardic history in large part centers upon versatile personalities who were not ghettoized but mixed in the wider society with an unusual measure of confidence. Their familiarity with secular culture did not derive from living in a society that was welcoming and tolerant; like all medieval Jews, the Sephardim were often scorned by the majorities among whom they lived. Nevertheless, they exhibited a rare zeal to embrace the larger world around them, and indeed this openness to the broad intellectual currents of the wider society is one of the most pronounced Sephardic traits. Their experience also demonstrates the possibilities of minority cultural achievement even in times of tension and extreme pressure to conform.

It has been remarked that all great themes in world history have revolved around the idea of exile. Perhaps no people has been more keenly aware of the consequences of exile than the Jews, who have endowed their own experience with moral and theological dimensions. Jewish history has been played out in the shadow of an intense awareness of homelessness, coupled with a striving for ultimate redemption. The diaspora was seen as a history of waiting for redemption, not always patiently, and more than any other Jewry, Sephardic thinkers combed biblical sources in order to find clues to the date of the end of exile. Especially attuned to the pain of exile, they constantly sought remnants of Jewish sovereignty somewhere in the world and also raised innumerable false messiahs in this process of "pushing the end of days." Theirs was no ordinary yearning for redemption, and ultimately it broke all bounds in the seventeenth century, erupting in one of the most bizarre and destructive messianic movements in all of Jewish history. Sephardim believed in the imposter Sabbetai Zevi out of an explosive need to believe (see the end of chapter 6).

The Sephardic sense of incompleteness and loneliness in exile was paradoxical, however, for their exile in Sepharad was not only comfortable but not quite an exile. In the minds of her sons and daughters, Sepharad was a second Jerusalem. Expulsion from Spain, therefore, was as keenly lamented as was exile from the Holy Land. The sense of being *doubly exiled* gave Sephardic history both a new dynamism and a heightened sense of despair after 1492.

Still, no medieval Jew sang as poignantly of exile as did the Sephardic Jew. None argued as cogently about it, either, or spent as much time and effort calculating when that exile would end and redemption begin. The tension between rootedness and rootlessness, between Spain and Zion, gave the Sephardic diaspora a special coloration, for Zion was not only a future reality for them but an attainable destination. Each generation of Sephardim seems to have reestablished concrete links with the land of Israel through immigration of members of the community.

It is perhaps surprising that the expulsion from Spain should be considered in a class by itself in Jewish history, for it was only the last in a long line of expulsions that removed all Jews from western Europe by 1500 (with a few exceptions in Italy and Germany). The exclusion of Jews from England in 1290 left scarcely a ripple, and if the fourteenth-century expulsions from France and Germany were immortalized in dirge, they were not lamented as a wrenching departure. Only in the case of Spain was the plight of an exilic community construed as an exile within exile.

Historians must wonder why members of this one community retained such loyalty to a country that so brutally expelled them 500 years ago, proudly preserving the names of Iberian cities in their own names. What made the Sephardic experience different? How did Sephardic Jewry become a definable entity within world Jewry? Why did its diaspora remain distinctive in identity although not substantially distinctive in Jewish practice? There are no other instances in Jewish history of such a close and enduring identification of the Jews with a land outside the Holy Land. Jews have lived in every corner of the globe, yet only Sepharad has lent its name to a division of world Jewry. Even today, refugee Sephardic congregations in contemporary Canada call a new synagogue *kehillat anshei Castilia* (the congregation of the people of Castile), though it was established in the 1980s by emigrés from Israel whose ancestors have lived for centuries in Morocco and had last stepped on Castilian soil 500 years ago. Remarkably, during the turmoil of the early 1990s in Serbia, fifty-seven Sephardic Jews of Sarajevo sought to return, not to the land of Israel but to Spain, and successfully sought asylum from King Juan Carlos. The main division of world Jewry, the Ashkenazim, have never exhibited the same nostalgia and longing for a lost exile. Even their name is more vague. *Ashkenaz* does not refer to a clear association of Jews with a definable geographic unit. Rather, the term refers to a cultural complex that began in the Rhine-land in medieval times and stretched eastward. No country, not even modern Germany, ever held the same revered place in the consciousness of its Jewish residents as did Spain. Significantly, Sephardic identity with the country arose even before there was an entity known as Spain. By the eighth century, it was recognized that there was a separate Jewry in Iberia designated as Sephardic; Spain itself would not be-come a reality until the end of the Middle Ages when Granada was conquered, the Muslims were subdued, and her many kingdoms were united. When the great medieval scholar Moses Maimonides signed his letters as Moses ben Maimon ha-Sefaradi ("the Sephardic Jew") in the twelfth century, he expressed a reality that his readers undoubt-edly understood.

The Spanish element in the Sephardic identity, reflecting a special relationship with both Spain's Christian and Islamic culture, continued long after the ties with the country were severed. How strange it seems that Sephardim scattered in Turkey and Bulgaria, Curaçao and Pernam-buco, sang ballads about medieval Spanish knights and maidens in their medieval Spanish language, Ladino. Throughout the Turkish-speaking world, the conversation of Sephardic Jews, especially women, would be peppered with Spanish proverbs. The classical genres of Spanish oral literature would be preserved for centuries in the Balkans in *romances* as each important life-cycle event was marked by Jewish festivities rich in Spanish song. This portable folk culture was preserved in Ladino until it was brutally and decisively wiped out in Europe during World War II by the Holocaust and destruction of the Jews, including most Eu-ropean Sephardim. Retention of the Spanish language served to unite the Sephardic diaspora until the eve of its destruction.

A final feature distinguishing Sephardic history that recurs with surprising frequency is the notion of descent from royal and aristocratic lineage. Indeed, claims of noble ancestry cling to Sephardic history from their earliest myths of origin in Spain in Roman times. Such claims are unusual among Jews and may perhaps be related to the influence of ideas of honor, race, and lineage among their Hispanic neighbors. Sephardim remained aristocrats even in their exile, albeit aristocrats fallen on hard times.

Even today, Sephardic Jews pride themselves on their noble bearing and illustrious ancestry. Their sense of localism and "pedigree" is often reflected in meticulously detailed marriage contracts and family trees that trace generations of ancestors back to the medieval cities of Spain. The Sephardic self-perception of aristocracy has not always endeared them to other Jews nor it is easily comprehended.

Christopher Columbus arrived in Spain in 1484. The Inquisition had just been established in Castile, charged by the king and queen to ferret out the "heretics" who secretly engaged in Jewish practices. Jews and *conversos* were being subjected to the closest scrutiny as rumors and blackmail struck terror among thousands. In such circumstances, the arrival of Columbus, an inconspicuous visitor, evoked no comment.

In later centuries, both Spanish and Italian patriots have claimed him; but in fact the background of this obscure map maker and sea captain is extremely vague. He himself was always quite evasive about his origins, although he claimed to come from Genoa. In Spain he referred to himself as a foreigner (*extranjero*), but he kept his journals and made marginal notations in his books in Spanish, not Italian; his letters to his brother Bartholome and his son Diego were also written in Spanish, and he wrote Latin in a recognizably Spanish manner. Yet his Spanish was the language of the fourteenth century, and his characteristics seemed to suggest a Catalan background. Furthermore, although he made an elaborate show of his Christian piety, he always kept company with Jews and Muslims.

At first, his negotiations to obtain Ferdinand and Isabella's backing for an unprecedented *westward* voyage to India were unpromising. The kingdom of Castile was not in strong financial shape, for its treasury was depleted and whole provinces devastated by Ferdinand and Isabella's protracted war to reconquer Granada and reunify Spain under Christian ascendancy. Besides, the explorer's terms were much too high: he was demanding the titles of admiral as well as viceroy of all the realms he might discover and conquer, along with a tenth of their riches. Eventually, as the world knows, the royal couple would be convinced to support Columbus's proposal; what is less well known is how their decision was influenced by the intercession of powerful Jewish and *converso* courtiers who pressed his cause and gained agreement to most of his terms.

Even as these negotiations were taking place, the king and queen were drafting the historic decree of expulsion, apparently with the aid of courtiers in the inner circles of power. It was during the period between the drafting of the document and the public announcement that Abrabanel and Seneor had tried to have it revoked. Was there any coordination between Abrabanel's pleas and the enthusiastic petitions at court on behalf of Columbus? As it happens, the public announcement of the coming expulsion took place on the same day that Columbus was ordered to ready his fleet. Is it significant that a Jewish presence hovered so closely around this decisive voyage, or that so many of the principal actors at this court were involved in both affairs? And how had this obscure petitioner been able to obtain such powerful backing and make such influential friends at the center of power?

Somehow, Columbus had quickly established himself among the most prominent *converso* figures at court. In addition to Abrabanel, Seneor, Santangel, and Sanchez, Jewish converts who served the monarchy included Alfonso de la Caballeria, vice chancellor and political councillor of Aragon, and Juan Cabrero, the royal chamberlain. Evidently, these courtiers were still trusted and retained as faithful servants of the king and queen, even though the Inquisition hovered in the background.

Finance minister Luis de Santangel and Don Isaac Abrabanel were so enthusiastic about Columbus's voyage that they offered to advance the sum of five million maravedis as a loan to the king and queen to equip a fleet for the explorer, rejecting the queen's famously dramatic pledge of her own personal jewels to finance the trip. (Santangel probably got some of this money from his relative Gabriel Sanchez, the treasurer-general of Aragon, also a *converso,* but he apparently offered at least 17,000 ducats from his own purse.) Isabella accepted the loan, and Columbus's project was finally approved.

The initial obstacle to Columbus's trip, however, was not expense but the skepticism of the scientific *junta* that was assembled in Spain to scrutinize his proposal. After all, he had already been rebuffed by the Portuguese, who were then preeminent in exploration. Focused on the possibilities of the eastward routes, Lisbon was not interested in Columbus's schemes for sailing to India in the opposite direction.

Interestingly, cosmography, map-drawing, and astronomy at this time were almost exclusively Jewish occupations. For example, the work of the fourteenth-century Majorcan Jewish scientists Abraham Cresques, "Master of Maps and Compasses," and his son Yehuda, known as "the Compass Jew" or "Map Jew," were part of the intellectual baggage of all explorers. Their cartographic inventiveness was matched by Jewish technological advances, for the essential device used for determining the position of a vessel at sea, the quadrant, was known as the *quadrans Judaicus* after its Jewish inventor. It was used in conjunction with an improved astrolabe manufactured by two Jewish physicians of the Lisbon court, Masters Rodrigo and Joseph Vecinho. (The latter, a pupil of the famous Sephardic astronomer Abraham Zacuto who would later play an important role in Columbus's fortunes, was still attending King John of Portugal when the explorer arrived in Lisbon for the first time in the 1470s.) Finally, the preferred astronomical tables of the day, the Alfonsine Tables, had been prepared in Spanish for Alfonso the Wise in the thirteenth century by two Jewish court astronomers. Columbus was the proud possessor of his own copy.

Despite popular belief, by the 1480s all educated people knew that the earth was spherical. Yet many still doubted the technical feasibility of Columbus's proposal. The actual distance between the Azores, the most westward landfall known at the time, and the "eastern end of India" was unknown, thus rendering a westward voyage foolhardy at best. Columbus, relying on several miscalculations, was convinced that the ocean expanse he would have to cross was actually quite narrow and could be easily traversed by the day's oceangoing vessels. But his opponents in King John's scientific councils, choosing to reject his proposal in 1484, were more correct than he. His erroneous calculations put "India" more or less on the actual site of the North American continent.

When Columbus moved on to Spain with his schemes, he was immediately befriended by Diego de Deza, a prominent theologian of reputed *converso* background at the University of Salamanca as well as tutor to the heir-apparent, Prince Don Juan. When Deza summoned a conference of scientists to give the explorer a hearing, their doubts were dispelled by Zacuto himself, who probably taught at the university even though he was a practicing Jew. The outstanding astronomer of the day, he had produced the standard tables of the stars, moon, and sun in his *Almanac Perpetuum*. Originally composed in Hebrew but available also in Spanish and Latin, this work was used by Vasco da Gama as well as Columbus. In fact, Columbus believed it had rescued him more than once: in the most dramatic instance, he used the *Almanac* to predict an eclipse, thus quelling a mutiny within his ranks.

As early as 1487, Columbus had the backing of Seneor and Abrabanel and received a royal stipend. Does this connection with Jews prove, as some historians have argued, that the explorer shared their background? Such scholars have also noted the eager involvement of Santangel and of the prominent *converso* family of Alfonso de la Caballeria in backing the explorer. They wonder why Columbus sometimes dated his correspondence by Jewish reckoning from the date of the destruction of the Second Temple (*la casa secunda*) rather than by the birth of Christ. They also wonder about the strange cipher used in all of his letters to his son except the only one Diego was told to show to the Queen: it seems to resemble the Hebrew abbreviation for *beEzrat haShem* ("with the help of God") that is commonly found in Jewish correspondence. Even the explorer's signature, which he insisted his son use after his death, has been the subject of Jewish exegesis. Moreover, it is clear that he had an unusually strong interest in Jewish matters, which would be understandable and indeed common among *conversos* but definitely atypical for a Spanish Old Christian. Atypical, too, was his frequent use of Old Testament allusions to describe the hazards of his journey. Finally, his letter announcing his discovery was sent, not to the royal couple, but to the *conversos* Sanchez and Santangel. In a sense, this could be construed as the natural courtesy owed the latter for putting up his own money. But what is to be made of his exclamation in another letter?

> I am not the first admiral of my family. Let them give me the name they will, for, after all, David, a very wise King, kept ewes and lambs and later was made a King of Jerusalem, and I am the servant of the same Lord who raised David to that state.[2]

Moreover, six identifiable *conversos* were aboard the three vessels that left for the New World on the night of the expulsion of the Jews. Others might have been present as well, but it was typical for *conversos* to hide as much of their Jewish background as possible in order to evade the scrutiny of the Inquisition. Sanchez's nephew Rodrigo was included as fiscal inspector for the expedition. The translator Luis de Torres, who spoke Hebrew, Arabic, and Aramaic, had converted only a short time before. (He would become the first European to explore Cuba and would discover the Indians' use of tobacco.) Maestre Bernal, the apothecary, and Master Marco, the physician, were also *conversos*.

What lay behind these and similar connections? Perhaps Santangel, reeling from the devastation wreaked upon his family by the long arm of the Inquisition, was animated more by personal than by scientific motives to become involved in the voyage. Perhaps he shared the dream of many contemporaries that Columbus might find a kingdom of the Lost Tribes, a possible asylum for Jews far from the reaches of the Inquisition. Or perhaps the *conversos* and the explorer shared an obdurate attachment to some form of Judaism that has disappeared. The mystery cannot be solved.

Perhaps the explanation for the conspicuous involvement of so many Jews and *conversos* lies in the fact that Jews constituted some of the most educated segments of the population and took a lively interest in all scientific matters. Or, alternatively, they may simply have regarded his voyage as a promising business opportunity and hence agreed to underwrite the venture. Additionally, both Christians and Jews were intrigued by exotic stories which explorers circulated regarding the wealth and lure of lost kingdoms. These alone could account for the interest of so many Jews in Columbus's plans. Yet, with all the pressing issues of state confronting these *converso* ministers, it seems strange that so many of them were actively involved with plans for the voyage of an unknown adventurer whom many described as decidedly disagreeable. Unless, that is, he had managed to ignite their apocalyptic yearnings or offered concrete possibilities for refuge. Certainly no Jew, least of all a *converso* who had had a brush with the dreaded Inquisition, felt secure; and false hopes of messianic redemption, embellished by reports of distant kingdoms of the Lost Tribes of Israel, fired the imagination of thousands at this time.

Whether Columbus was an Italian of *converso* origin, a Spaniard, or a Jew will never be known, since his heirs—for unknown reasons—destroyed most of his private papers and other archival materials. But his dependence upon *conversos* and Jews for the initial commission to sail is a matter of record. These frightened courtiers had ample reason to encourage explorations in search of new kingdoms, particularly if they believed it possible that one of them could turn out to be the realm of the Lost Tribes.

Any potential benefits the Sephardim might have hoped to obtain from the voyage were never realized. By the time news of his great find reached the mainland, they had already been expelled. Some *conversos* did emigrate to the Americas during the 1500s, hoping to distance themselves from the Inquisition once and for all. However, such attempts were unsuccessful.

From the vantage point of Sephardic history, the most important individual who crossed the path of the explorer—and left a lasting mark on both the expedition and the Jews of Spain—was also the most representative of both his class and culture: Don Isaac Abrabanel. In the last months of frantic negotiations to rescue his community, Abrabanel was offered the choice of remaining in Spain, retaining his riches, and gaining further honors—if he converted. He chose instead to lead his people into exile with dignity. For centuries thereafter, his far-flung progeny in Turkey, Italy, Holland, Palestine, the American Northwest, and even Poland, from the humblest tailors to world-renowned musicians, have repeated the expression, *Basta mi nombre que es Abrabanel* (It is enough that I am named Abrabanel).

As a young man, Abrabanel worked with his father at the court of the Portuguese king Alfonso IV and also engaged in family business that extended beyond Iberia as far as Flanders. The king was a bibliophile who liked to surround himself with intellectuals and must have been impressed with Abrabanel, who published his first learned treatise in his twenties, a work that exhibited familiarity with Christian literature and several European languages. In 1471, the young scholar would be vividly confronted with the spectacle of Jewish despair: 250 Moroccan Jews captured in the Portuguese conquest of Arzila that year were brought into the country as slaves. Moved to action, Abrabanel traveled the countryside for six months, exhorting his brethren to redeem and rehabilitate their refugee co-religionists.

In 1483 he was forced to flee Lisbon for Spain, the victim of political machinations and court intrigue surrounding the succession to the throne. Leaving his fortune behind, he began his career anew in the service of Ferdinand of Aragon and soon achieved prominence and recouped his wealth. What drew him to the Spanish court? How did he serve Ferdinand and Isabella from 1484 through 1492, gaining ever more honors and greater prestige even as his community's fortunes were sinking? Was he attracted by an irresistible offer to reorganize the finances of the kingdom in order to pursue the war against Granada, or was he guided in his decision to reenter public service by the introduction of the Inquisition in Spain at this time? Did he hope to strengthen the monarchy's ability to counteract the anti-Jewish sentiments of the burghers, clergy, and feudal lords? Did he hope that his prominence would counteract the influence of hostile *conversos* at court? Did he feel a "calling" to leadership in the hour of his people's greatest need, based on his oft-proclaimed conviction that he was descended from the house of David?

We cannot know what motivated him, but it is surely suggestive that he had witnessed the expulsion of the Jews from Andalusia, seen the disastrous early trials of the Inquisition that wreaked havoc upon scores of secret Jews, and was familiar with the anxiety and impending destruction of the powerful Santangels. He was living in a time of mounting terror for the Jews.

The high point of his public career came in the spring of 1492, soon after he learned of the expulsion decree, when he tried unsuccessfully to prevail upon the monarchs to revoke the edict. Going into exile, he found refuge in the kingdom of Naples until 1494, when he was forced to flee yet again. During the last decade of his life he wrote unceasingly, once again combining the roles of communal leader, political activist, biblical commentator, and philosopher.

From our vantage point, it is obvious that 1492 marks the end of one spectacular chapter in the continuing odyssey of the Jewish people and the beginning of another. At least two routes of exile followed the expulsion: one ran directly eastward from Spain to the world of Islam, the other through Portugal to northern Europe. The larger group of exiles took the first, closing a circle that had begun with the Arab conquest of Iberia in the eighth century. This Spanish-speaking diaspora, which stretched from Morocco across North Africa to Egypt and Palestine, also included countless communities along the northern shores of the Mediterranean and up into the Balkans. Scarcely had these exiles planted new roots in the Ottoman Empire than dozens of outstanding rabbis, creative mystics, and towering legal figures like Samuel de Medina, Joseph Caro, Jacob Berab, Moses Cordovero, Jacob ibn Zur, David ibn Abi Zimra, and Solomon Alkabetz began to flourish. Sephardic craftsmen and skilled artisans enlivened the markets of the Near East while diplomats and courtiers like Don Joseph Nasi and Dona Gracia Mendes, Moses Hamon and the Picciottos, influenced the course of Ottoman diplomacy.

By the eighteenth century, this Asian and Africa diaspora, along with their host societies, entered an era of decline. An intellectual and demographic stagnation set in that was not arrested until the introduction of western ideas and technologies in the nineteenth century. Even as these ideas began to percolate down to all levels of Jewish society, the strong strain of mysticism so characteristic of post-expulsion Sephardic Jews remained prominent. Ladino- and Arabic-speaking, the Jews of Muslim lands more closely resembled the depressed state of their Muslim neighbors on the eve of the modern era than the phantoms of their glorious ancestors.

The second route of exile followed a more circuitous path. Sephardim who went northward generally began their wanderings in Portugal and only belatedly followed the path out of Iberia, usually as secret Jews or *marranos*. These Jews entered Europe in small numbers, forming secret communities in Holland, the Spanish-held Netherlands, and towns in southern France. Their arrival coincided with an era of major transformation on the Continent. By the seventeenth century the weight of economic gravity was shifting to the Atlantic. In England and Holland, the religious intolerance of the Reformation was yielding to a new mercantilist appreciation of the economic benefits that might accrue from toleration. Thus the Sephardim of western Europe would become pioneers and beneficiaries of a new age. With Amsterdam as its center, the Sephardic dispersion moved across the Atlantic to Brazil, Curaçao, Surinam, and New Amsterdam. These Portuguese-speaking merchants were distinguished by aristocratic bearing, a sense of pride, and a need to remain inconspicuous, born of the hazardous experience of having been crypto-Jews under the gaze of the Inquisition. Their diaspora produced great philosophers like Spinoza and multitalented personalities like the rabbi-printer Menasseh ben Israel or the economist Isaac Pinto. They could be found among the explorers of the Far East as well as at the frontiers of modern science and economic thought. Sephardic migrants would be the pioneering element in the resettlement of Jewish communities all over western Europe. They would also be the first Jews to arrive on North American shores in the 1650s.

The Sephardim retained their interest in secular culture even as their schools and communities were showing the first signs of decline. Ultimately, this Portuguese-speaking diaspora was engulfed either by the dominance of the Ashkenazim or, in Europe, by the forces of destruction that annihilated nearly all the Jews of Europe in our century. Very few survivors of the Western Sephardic diaspora can be found today, despite their tenacious attempts to retain their proud lineage.

Wherever they wandered after 1492, the Sephardim characteristically did not join the existing congregations of Israel but instead formed
their own synagogues and communities. This phenomenon had occurred previously in Jewish history when Babylonian Jews established
their own congregations in Palestine or Palestinian Jews had retained
separate institutions in Egypt. Usually, however, such separate identity
lasted only one or two generations, since the children and grandchil-
dren tended to discard traditional ways and settle down in their adopted
country. The case of the Sephardim was completely different, for more
than other Jews they remained loyal to their past. They were also more
contentious, forming splits even among themselves, and more unwilling to relinquish their cherished traditions. Finally, they also displayed
a tendency to overwhelm other Jewish communities and impose their
own ways, especially where they arrived in large numbers, as in Turkey
or Morocco.

Throughout much of the long history of the Jewish dispersion,
Sephardim were the largest group. Forming an absolute majority in
medieval times, they reached as high as 90 percent of the world Jewish population in the twelfth century. But by 1700 they comprised
only 50 percent, and their decline was steady thereafter. Living in increasingly depressed conditions in deteriorating Muslim societies,
Sephardic numbers remained constant or declined at precisely the moment that the Ashkenazic Jews of Europe began to experience a population explosion. By the twentieth century, an absolute reversal had
occurred: in 1930, Sephardim were less than 10 percent of world Jewry, or slightly more than one and a half million out of sixteen million. Most were Middle Eastern Jews, and thus their center of gravity
was decisively in the East.

After the Holocaust and the destruction of the European Jews, the
relative weight of Sephardim has once again shifted. Today, Sephardic
and Middle Eastern Jews comprise 25 percent of world Jewry and fully
60 percent of the state of Israel. Most observers, puzzled about how to
define the Sephardic world today, question the current tendency to
lump Sephardic Jews together with Jews from Muslim lands. This practice recognizes that the two communities are akin in liturgy and legal
traditions, in hundreds of years of coexistence, and in countless other
ways. The centuries during which most Sephardim have lived among
the Jews of the Islamic world have blurred the distinctive features that
once divided the Jews of Spain from their brethren. Joined by political
boundaries and shared intellectual traditions, Jews of North Africa, the

Near East, and Spain all came under the influence of the venerable rabbinic academies of Baghdad long before their peoples came together in exile.

After 1492, centuries of wandering muted the separate identity of Spain's Jewish offspring still further. The "exiles of Jerusalem who were in Sepharad" became the exiles of Sepharad in Djerba and Gibraltar, Belgrade and Valona, Cairo and Alexandria, Casablanca and Meknes. Neither the paths of their dispersion nor the process of cultural amalgamation have been predictable or easily comprehended. Especially today, the postwar Jewish world has witnessed remarkable, unpresaged change. Perhaps most extraordinary has been the return of Sephardic and Middle Eastern Jews to the land of Israel. Although that nation is most often associated with its socialist pioneers who came from eastern Europe, a large number of its contemporary leaders, artists, and builders are drawn from the Sephardic masses arriving after 1948.

Over the last generation perhaps one million Jews from Muslim lands have returned to Israel, becoming the majority today. In this old-new state the designations of Sephardim, Ashkenazim, and Middle Eastern Jews are increasingly a thing of the past. Attempts to unite these various exiles have been implicit in the process of nationbuilding.

Even as these groups come together, however, the lessons of the long, fascinating Sephardic story are compelling and significant. Overshadowed by the much larger and more familiar story of Ashkenazic Europe, the complete saga of a Jewry that spoke Judeo-Arabic, Judeo-Spanish, Catalan, Serbian, Turkish, Judeo-Tatar, or Marathi and were heirs to a glorious past in Valencia and Saragossa, Aragon and Aleppo, has yet to be fully told. Their journey was unparalleled, involving a continuous wrestling with the great cultures they confronted and a determination to keep alive the memory of Sepharad with the call to Jerusalem. For Don Isaac Abrabanel there was no mistaking the unique quality of his people as he departed with them from Spain:

> From the rising of the sun to its setting, from north to south, there never was such a chosen people [as the Jews of Spain] in beauty and pleasantness, and afterwards, there will never be another such people. God was with them, the children of Judea and Jerusalem, many and strong . . . a quiet and trusting people, a people filled with the blessing of God with no end to its treasures.[3]

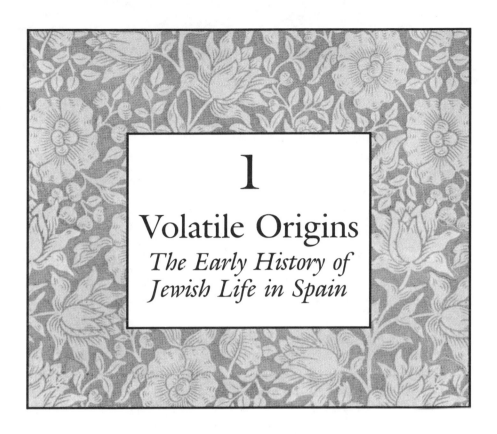

1
Volatile Origins
The Early History of Jewish Life in Spain

The exiles of Jerusalem who are in Sepharad will inherit the cities of the Negev.

—Obadiah I:20

The beginnings of Jewish life in Spain are cloaked in myth and legend. According to medieval Sephardic traditions, Jews reached the Iberian peninsula in biblical times. Thus the city of Tarshish toward which Jonah sailed in hopes of evading God's command was thought to be Tartessus, originally a Phoenician and later Carthaginian seaport on the Mediterranean coast. The tombstone of Adoniram, King Solomon's general, supposedly was unearthed in Murviedro. As early as the first century of the common era, the designation "Sepharad" mentioned in the biblical book of Obadiah was considered by Jewish teachers to be identical with *Ispamia* or Spain. One particular folk tradition has lasted virtually to the present day: the legend that some of ancient Jerusalem's aristocratic families, deported first by the Babylonians in 586 BCE and then again by the Roman conqueror Titus in 70 CE, resettled on the Spanish shore.

These and similar traditions attesting to the Sephardic community's biblical origins were probably a form of self-defense, for most of them emerged when anti-Semitism was intensified during the Christian reconquest of Muslim Spain. It was as if Spanish Jews were proclaiming that they could not be charged (as indeed they were) with "killing Christ," because they were nowhere near Palestine at the time of the crucifixion.

Still, these legends do not entirely violate historic truth. Migration of Jews throughout the Roman diaspora (c. 200 BCE–200 CE) was so widespread that the ancient Greek geographer Strabo reportedly exclaimed, "This people has already made its way into every city, and it is not easy to find any place in the habitable world which has not received this nation and in which it has not made its power felt" (Josephus, *Antiquities*, XIV, 115). More specifically, it is known that Jewish merchants and travelers followed the expansion of Phoenician and Syrian trading colonies all along the shores of the Mediterranean, certainly including the Iberian peninsula. Ships that brought wares from the East also invariably left Jewish settlers in their wake.

Somewhat contrary to popular belief, perhaps, Jews in the Roman diaspora flourished in some measure because the Empire recognized Judaism as a legal religion (*religio licita*). It was in Imperial Roman interests to permit a combination of religious toleration and measured ethnic, cultural self-government to the Jews since they constituted an important economic and cultural force throughout the Empire. Accordingly, Jews were treated as an autonomous, self-governing people and exempted from the obligation of recognizing the cult of the emperor. But this exemption also had a negative side since pagan Rome did not understand the exclusivist claims of a monotheistic faith and therefore assumed that the Jews were unpatriotic.

Rome also continued to recognize the Jewish cultural ties to their national homeland in Palestine even after the great Jewish revolts there in the first and second centuries. Thus, Jews from throughout the diaspora were permitted to send contributions to their political and cultural institutions in the Holy Land. This gesture had considerable symbolic and practical implications for such a far-flung dispersion, because deference to Palestinian religious leadership provided a sense of unity. At the same time, Jews ran their practical affairs on a day-to-day basis at the local level, each community being sovereign even though they all shared the same organizational patterns, adjusting them to meet local requirements. Congregations were typically autonomous even in the many cities in the Empire that had more than one. Throughout these early centuries, the Jewish population increased rapidly (in no small part, as a result of vigorous proselytizing). Ultimately, Jews would constitute 25 percent of the Roman population in the Eastern Mediterranean and ten percent in the Empire as a whole. According to some estimates, the total Jewish population at the beginning of the common era may have been eight million.

The movement westward began after Titus's destruction of Judea and was spurred on by Rome's brutal suppression of a revolt in Palestine in 135. As Jews fanned out to the further corners of the Mediterranean, Italy and Spain to the north, the African coast to the south, they built settlements that have left us such archaeological traces as ruins of synagogues, the underground burial caverns known as catacombs, and trilingual (Hebrew, Latin, Greek) tombstone inscriptions. One such tombstone dating from sixth-century Mérida confirms the proud claims of later Spanish Jews that they were descended from the "founding fathers" of the nation.

In the case of Spain, the archaeological record reveals clearly that Jews did not live as isolated individuals or families but as organized communities that, while cohesive and traditional, also received cultural cues from the surrounding milieu. Such acculturation is indicated, for example, in the great number of funerary inscriptions that are written only in Latin. At the same time, Spanish Jews remained connected to classic Judaism and faithful to their ancient beliefs, as shown by the occurrence of traditional Jewish symbols alongside many of these Latin inscriptions.

In fact, the Jewish concept of monotheism was spread to others with relative ease during the first centuries of the common era, setting the stage for the successful Christian evangelizing to follow. Typically, the proselytes of Judaism were strongly influenced by contact with established Jewish communities or their missionaries but did not necessarily become full-fledged converts. These so-called "God-fearers" (*sebomenoi*) did adopt some Jewish practices, however, making them receptive to subsequent Christian conversion. As the records of the early Church show, it was invariably true that wherever a Christian missionary appeared he found Jews already established. According to Christian tradition, Saint Paul preached in Spain. Well into the common era, Judaism remained an expansionist, proselytizing religion with a significant conversionist bent.

Hispania or *Ispamia* was one of the wealthiest provinces of the Empire. Its inhabitants, granted citizenship in 212 by the Emperor Caracalla, participated in a flourishing commerce: rich soil and mild climate made the province into Rome's granary, agriculture and livestock were cultivated throughout the peninsula, while Spanish horses were coveted in the Roman circuses for their swiftness and grace. In addition, a significant portion of the country's wealth came from minerals; its gold and silver mines, heavily dependent upon slave labor, provided a steady annual income to Rome.

At its height the Empire maintained a superb communications network that facilitated the transfer of information and interchange among such a widely dispersed people as the Jews. The great Roman highway, the Via Augusta, began in the capital and stretched 13,000 miles through Italy and Gaul to terminate at the port of Cádiz in southwestern Spain. Troops and goods moved easily along the ancillary routes that radiated out to the many towns of the peninsula.

The basic unit of administration was the municipality (*civitas*). The historian Pliny, who served as the procurator in Spain, describes 360 different towns in the province, all of them sharing a basically Roman appearance with their temples, arches, aqueducts, and amphitheaters. Even today, remnants of these ancient public works can still be seen, such as the aqueducts in Segovia and Tarragona, the amphitheater in Tarragona, and the bridges of Mérida and Salamanca. One measure of the tranquillity of the province is that only one Roman legion had to be stationed there to keep Spain within the Empire.

So long as Rome was tolerant and prosperous, Jewish life flourished. Archaeological remains all along the Spanish coast attest to the density of Jewish settlement in this period. Early Church councils indicate that Jews mixed freely among their neighbors and were generally regarded with favor. The works of pagan writers suggest that attitudes toward Jews varied according to social class; some admired Jews for their "temperance, wisdom, courage, and justice"[1] while others resented what they perceived as clannishness because of the Jews' refusal to recognize the pagan gods.

Deterioration of Jewish life in Spain began in the fifth century, when the Roman Empire converted to Christianity under the Emperor Constantine. For one thing, the Jewish population declined throughout the Mediterranean region as the Empire became increasingly chaotic and lawless. The conditions that had been critical to Spain's prosperity were breaking down. Beginning in the third century, for example, the small freeholds were progressively being absorbed by the great landed estates. The invasions of various German tribes from western Europe merely accelerated a trend to ruralization as the *latifundia* of Roman times continued to grow through confiscation, a symptom of the general lawlessness and breakdown in imperial rule. As the cities declined, trade diminished and industrial production was reduced to essential items. Naturally, Jews suffered along with the rest of the population as gold and silver were drained to the East, onerous tolls were introduced, the road system disintegrated, and the overall economy declined.

More importantly, of course, a confrontation between the new state religion and Judaism was inevitable: Christianity defined itself as the successor to its older (and, as is often said, rival) sibling in the divine drama. Conversion to Judaism became a capital crime. This competition for converts from among the same pagan population provides part of the background for early Spanish ecclesiastical legislation against the Jews.

Even before the Empire converted to Christianity, the vexing problem of the status of the Jews was the subject of a historic ecclesiastical council convened in Elvira in the year 306. Participants were especially concerned about the close social relations between neighboring Christians and Jews. Evidently, the Jewish community was a substantial and influential presence, and some rabbis were held in alarmingly high esteem by many Christians. In Canon 49 of the Council of Elvira, the Christian believer is given specific instructions on this issue:

It seems appropriate to warn farmers not to permit that their fruits, which they receive from God as a gift of grace, be blessed by Jews so that our blessing should not appear as worthless and despised; if anyone continues to act in such a manner despite our prohibition, he will be driven away from the Church.

The council was even more exclusionary in another decree (Canon 50):

If any of the priests or believers eats his meal with a Jew, we decide that he does not participate in the communion so that he atones.[2]

Precisely because Jews were still an influential force in Spain, the Elvira Council deemed it necessary to insulate Christian believers from the seductions of Judaism by derogating both its tenets and its leaders. Restrictions were imposed to limit opportunities for social interaction between the two faiths; Christians were specifically warned not to ask rabbis to bless their fields. In short, the work of this council typified an emergent body of legislation designed to isolate Jews from the larger community throughout the Empire while hammering out a doctrine that defined and affirmed the lowly place of Judaism in history.

Perhaps surprisingly, the historical separation of Christianity from Judaism, with its profound consequences for Jewish communal life, was a long and complex process. After all, the Church had emerged directly out of the synagogue in the first century, and Christianity would never totally disassociate itself from its Jewish origins. On the contrary, Christian apologists argued the supremacy of their belief over Judaism by making recourse to promises and predictions in the Hebrew scriptures. In a sense, then, early Christians could be said to have defined themselves in terms of the religion they rejected.

Consequently, Church thinkers could not simply dismiss Judaism out of hand. Their most troubling challenge was the enigmatic perseverance of the Jewish people after the advent of Jesus had made their religion obsolete. A partial solution was to reinterpret selected ancient Hebraic texts, yet even then the Church had to retain many Jewish elements, unable either to abandon or acknowledge their origin. Another tactic was to regard Judaism as a *perfidia*, or perversion of the true faith.

Therefore, the appropriation and reinterpretation of the scriptures, a process which began with Paul's career in the first century, was focused on working out an earthly role for Jews to play that would be consistent with the essential Christian message. Church thinkers reinterpreted the scriptures to become proof texts of the basic, two-edged doctrine: Christian election, Jewish obsolescence. Out of obstinacy and perverseness, the Jews refused to understand the shared scriptures "properly," blind to the validations of Christianity there and the proof that their belief had been superseded. But even as Christians and Jews disagreed about the true meanings of the ancient texts, it was Scripture that linked them.

How should the bearers of the old tradition be treated so that they would not pose a "threat" to the fledgling new faith? In other words, what purpose should Jews serve in the new Christian world order?

A fateful rationale was devised from the doctrine of Christian supersession: the Jews would be preserved because their veneration of the Old Testament bore witness to the truth of Christianity. At the same time, they would be tolerated only minimally, so that their debased state itself would provide visible proof of their "rejection" by God. Their misery would also demonstrate what would befall those who did not accept Jesus as the Messiah. In addition, the maligning of Judaism would serve to enhance the self-esteem of Christians. Finally, the doctrine implied that strenuous efforts should be made so that a saving remnant of the Jewish people would "see the light," since their conversion was to presage or accompany the Second Coming.

The paradoxes of a doctrine that simultaneously advocated toleration and discrimination, preservation and persecution, conversion and persuasion, would plague the Jews for centuries. Modern scholars have collectively labeled these contradictions "the teaching of contempt." Its legacy was an enormous edifice, built over several centuries, that provided much of the material from which theological anti-Semitism in Western civilization evolved.[3]

After Constantine's conversion, attacks against Jews were no longer solely verbal, confined to council deliberations and doctrinal disputes. Even though the status of Judaism as a lawful religion was not formally revoked, those in positions of authority in the state now shared the increasingly hostile ecclesiastical attitude. The pen of the bishops began to guide the hand of the emperors, and the currents of anti-Semitism in the early Church formed a powerful partnership with the pagan anti-Semitic legacy. Assaults upon the person and property of Jews followed as a matter of course, and their situation began a long decline toward the medieval position: the Jew as pariah and demon. It was not possible, after all, for the simple folk and lower clergy to discern the doctrinal nuance between preserving the Jews and humiliating them, all the while praying for their conversion though asserting that conversion should not be forced. For the man in the street, derogation and persecution frequently won out over theological subtlety.

In 409, Spain was overrun by three different Germanic tribes—the Suevi, Vandals, and the Alani—who all, but especially the Vandals, ravaged the countryside. A few years later, yet a fourth tribe, the Visigoths, drove out the Vandals and established themselves in Spain, in the process destroying many of the Roman institutions on such ideological grounds as, for example, the contention that the public baths encouraged softness and effeminacy.

The Visigoths constituted an ethnically and religiously alien element in their new domain. A small group of German-speaking warriors and herdsmen never exceeding 200,000, they practiced Arianism, a form of Christianity that did not recognize the Trinity. Yet they ruled over something like eight million Latin-speaking trinitarian Catholics, most of them farmers. In such circumstances, it was useful to tolerate Jews, who could either mediate between the foreign elite and the indigenous majority or serve as a convenient ally, when the occasion arose.

The several centuries of Jewish life under Visigothic rule are among the most obscure in all of Jewish history. We do know that when the Germans arrived, they found a Jewish population that was well integrated and in fact formed an influential part of society. Initially, Jewish life did not undergo drastic change as a result of the invasion. The patterns of Jewish autonomy established in Roman times continued to be respected. Local communities were led by elders, sometimes including women. The synagogues supported schools, the community was allowed to own property, and Jewish legal traditions were so well established that local Jewish courts were able to adjudicate in most instances. The community leadership played a strong role in regulating all aspects of daily life: it was empowered by tradition to supervise such economic activities as controlling prices, regulating wages, and regulating the markets, including the use of weights and measures. In addition, each community had a highly organized network of self-help and welfare institutions, each administered by a special committee: the public kitchen (*tamhui*), a chest for the needy, funds for orphans, dowries for indigent brides, and resources for the ransoming of Jewish captives. In sum, the community was capable of withstanding a variety of strains from external sources and buttressing its members even in extremely adverse conditions.[4]

Under the Visigoths, the Jews of Spain presented a varied economic profile and worked in a wide range of occupations. Some held ranking posts in the government or the army; others were recruited and organized for garrison service; still others continued to hold senatorial rank. Many Jews possessed landed wealth, perhaps using slaves to till the land.

We should pause for a moment to discuss the issue of Jewish slaveholding, which would prove to be a recurrent thorn in the side of both ecclesiastical and lay leaders in Visigothic times—not because either authority had any special moral scruples but because the practice challenged accepted notions of Jewish subservience and also became a prime means of proselytism to Judaism. Precisely because the institution of slavery among the Jews touched a vital nerve in the Christian-Jewish contest for converts in these early centuries, it has been the subject of lengthy discussion and much controversy. Later, in medieval times, Jews were rarely slaveholders, although in the ninth century they did play a role in the extensive Muslim slave trade in the pagan Slavic lands. They never became involved, on the other hand, in the slave trade in Africa, which was dominated in the Middle Ages by the Arabs at first and then by the Turks. Neither Christian nor Muslim objected to slavery in itself; the landholdings of the Church were worked extensively by slaves throughout the Middle Ages, and Islamic civil bureaucracies and military rulers both relied heavily on slaves. Chiefly, Jewish slaveholding inspired a voluminous polemical literature because it posed a special kind of religious threat. Under Judaic law, which detailed a solicitude for slaves that was unparalleled in other civilizations, the Jewish slaveholder was subject to certain obligations that made his religion an attractive and available option for his slave. The master was obliged to permit his slaves to rest on the Sabbath. Non-Jews working in a Jewish home were considered to be part of the household and to be treated with respect and kindness. In many cases, a kind of semiconversion of slaves occurred, in which some Judaic practices were observed. Further, it was a prime duty of Jews to ransom all Jews from servitude, for the holding of Jewish slaves was declared to be illegal in the Talmud (*Baba Batra* f.8). Therefore, the slave who converted was immediately freed. Such conversions became quite commonplace since the Talmud prohibited Jews from keeping uncircumcised slaves. (See Babyl. Talmud, *Gittin* 8a–9a, 11b–15a, 37b–45a, 46b–47a.)

The *Shulhan Aruch*, the late medieval Jewish legal code, has this to say of slavery (Yoreh Deah, 267,27):

> Mercy is the mark of piety and no man may load his slave with a grievous yoke. No non-Jewish slave may be oppressed: he must receive a portion from every dainty that his master eats: he must not be bullied nor scornfully entreated; but must be addressed gently, and his reply heard with courtesy.

Slaves were not only given positions of trust in the household but were also allowed to do business on their own account. Some are included on the lists of larger donors to charity or as owners of boats. In Muslim lands, one of the last rites of a dying Jew was the freeing of his household servant. Moreover, it was forbidden for a female slave to work in a Jewish household in the absence of another female or if a female member of the household objected to her presence. By contrast, the Islamic slaveholder was entitled to engage in sexual relations with his female slaves.[5]

Church authorities became extremely concerned about the practice of Jews owning Christian or pagan slaves. For one thing, it was not uncommon for Christians to offer themselves as collateral for loans. Also, a debtor might default on his loan and became dependent upon, or even enslaved to, a Jew. It was partly for these reasons that in the sixth century Pope Gregory the Great explicitly expressed his concern to the various monarchs of the West that pagan or Christian slaves might convert to Judaism.

The Visigothic German invaders set up the political center of their new kingdom at Toledo, but in fact held little dominion outside the city walls. Undisciplined and strife-ridden from the outset, the Visigoths never established a principle of succession and orderly dynastic rule. During the several hundred years of their reign, the country was in a state of almost continuous political turmoil if not anarchy. In contrast to the earlier centuries of stability, the Visigothic era was a time of mounting anti-Jewish legislation.

The single institution the Germanic outsiders managed to control was the Church. The Visigothic monarchs appointed bishops, structured dioceses, and convened the clerical councils in Toledo that enacted legislation on behalf of the Church's "welfare." This relationship began when, in 587, King Reccared I converted to Catholicism and Bishop Leander of Seville reportedly declared, "Now we are one nation." The Visigothic elite would be absorbed into the rest of the nation, but the Jews would be left as the only "alien" element in Spain.

This is the real implication of the conversion of the Visigoths. Although religiously united at the top, the state remained deeply divided politically and at the grassroots level. The eighteen kings who ruled from King Recarred's conversion until the Arab conquest of Spain in 711 represented at least fifteen different families. Seven of these monarchs were deposed or murdered, and numerous pretenders or usurpers simply took over parts of Spain, minting coins in their own name.[6]

Perhaps, as some have suggested, the monarchy's desire to win over the clerical party was responsible for their sudden turn toward active persecution of the Jews. We cannot really say with certainty what motivated this change in policy, but one thing is unmistakably clear: the two centuries of Visigothic persecutions following Recarred's conversion comprise one of the darkest periods in Jewish history and ominously portend future Spanish policies toward the Jews.

Almost immediately, the newly Catholic King Reccared convened the first Council of Toledo in order to win endorsement for his decrees to "regulate" relations between Christians and Jews. This overtly ecclesiastical assembly and its successors would often be led by the ruling monarch rather than by the titular head of the Spanish Church, the bishop of Seville. Typically, canons enacted by a council were confirmed by the king, thus becoming the law of the land, but they also entered the annals of the Church. By that route the anti-Jewish laws of Visigothic Spain, having been absorbed into Canon Law, served as legal precedents in other parts of Europe, even though they had been specifically devised to address local conditions or suit the whims of Spanish royalty.

In the language of a constitution issued by Reccared, one aim of the new legislation was to limit Jewish influence on Christians.[7] In other words, the Elvira decree to this effect promulgated three centuries earlier had had only limited success, for Jews were still integrated in Spanish society. Dismayed by this source of both Christian attrition and resulting Jewish strength, the Church joined with King Reccared to bring Jewish slaveholding to an end. The monarch decreed that all slaves held by Jews should be handed over forthwith to Christian slaveholders (a measure that not only weakened the minority community but also guaranteed that they could no longer participate in agriculture). In the same exclusionary vein, the death sentence was instituted for any Jew found proselytizing. But conversion of Christian slaves to Judaism was only part of the perceived problem. Clerics and kings, engaging the broader issue of Jews exercising any authority at all over Christians, became determined to make the Jews' worldly position conform to the lowly status assigned them in Church doctrine. Thus, they were forbidden to intermarry or to hold public office.

In 613, King Sisebut issued a radical decree at the Third Toledan Council that called for the forced conversion of all Jews. Any Jew who refused baptism would be given one hundred lashes and, if still resistant, would be banished and deprived of all property. Not only did he affirm the proscription on slaveholding; he also forbade Jews to hire Christian workers. Sisebut confirmed his predecessor's death penalty for Jewish proselytism and required that any Christians who had converted should either revert or be publicly flogged and enslaved.

Some clerics, notably Isidore of Seville, reprimanded the king for this decree, but not on humanitarian grounds. Like Pope Gregory the Great (590–604), who had condemned forced conversions in a famous letter to the bishops of Arles and Marseilles in 591 but had also lauded Reccared for the rest of his anti-Jewish legislation, they objected that such conversions could not possibly produce genuine believers. Even so, Sisebut's decree was permitted to stand. The results were devastating. Jewish children were wrested from their parents, who were legally prohibited from fleeing the country. Church and state joined together in supervising the forced conversions. The convert who received the sacraments of the Church was not permitted to revert to Judaism; punishment for lapses was severe. It seems likely that as many as 90,000 Jews were converted under the terms of Sisebut's decree, while uncounted thousands more were able to escape. Thus began a century of forced conversion and martyrdom. Council followed upon council, issuing anti-Jewish decrees with increasing ferocity.

As Gregory wisely foresaw, however, forced conversions were often *pro forma*. Many Jews continued to practice their ancient religion in secret, thus ensuring that "crypto-Judaism" would be a long-standing problem on Spanish soil. (Medieval Spain would learn little from the failures of its Visigothic past in using forced conversion as an instrument of public policy.) Clearly, religious coercion would neither assure conformity nor resolve the country's political rifts. Certainly, the population at large drew distinctions; converts were automatically suspect, and Christians began ferreting out crypto-Judaic practices and informing on the practitioners. Such peculiar designations as "baptized Jews" and "non-baptized Jews" entered the national lexicon along with the novel racial conception of Old and New Christians. The latter were not allowed the slightest doubts about their new faith; wavering or lukewarm converts were threatened with expulsion from Spain by the Eighth Council of Toledo. These seventh-century persecutions, which clearly foreshadowed the drastic policies of the Inquisition, seem indicative of a uniquely Spanish racial interpretation of the question, "Who is a Jew?" in the ancient and medieval worlds.

Outbursts of intolerance were by no means limited to Spain. In the first quarter of the seventh century, when Byzantine and Persian military forces confronted each other in a series of bloody campaigns in Syria and Palestine, Jews in Palestine sided with the Persians. Possibly in reprisal, Byzantium's Emperor Heraclius decreed a forced conversion of his Empire's Jews in 632. In Langobard, Italy, in 661, persecution also took the form of forced baptism, and some twenty years after Sisebut's decree, the Jews of Merovingian France met the same fate as well. Whether or not these drastic measures were related to the larger context of sweeping Muslim victories in the Near East is not clear, but it is significant that in these early centuries the fate of forced converts was already assuming especially tragic forms in Spain. In this vein, the Visigoths promoted the concept of a unitary Iberian kingdom that ideally combined political with religious unity. The rulers of the Christian kingdom of Asturias-Leon in the north of Spain would preserve this ideal of unity and reconquest through the Middle Ages.

On the other hand, the Visigothic anti-Jewish laws were repeated with such regularity in the successive Toledan councils that one suspects they were implemented sporadically and were only temporarily successful. We can discern a recurrent cycle. A persecutory king would be deposed, then the Jews who had fled (especially those in neighboring Morocco or Narbonne, France) would return. Harsh measures would be relaxed for a time, only to be eventually affirmed yet again by a subsequent ruler. These cycles succeeded each other with astonishing frequency as civil wars and royal conspiracies tore Spain apart.

A glance at the rapidly changing succession of the Visigothic rulers juxtaposed with the major anti-Jewish decrees[8] suggests the political motivation behind many of the peaks of repression:

Visigoth King		Assassinated/Deposed	Anti-Jewish Decree
Reccared I	586–601		**
Liuva II	601–603	*	
Witteric	603–10	*	
Gundemar	610–12		
Sisebut	612–20		**
Suinthila	621–31	*	
Sisenand	631–36		**
Chintilla	636–40		**
Tulga	640–42	*	
Chindasuith	642–53		**
Reccessuinth	649–72		**
Wamba	672–80	*	
Erwig	680–87		**
Egica	687–702	*	**
Witiza	702–10		
Achila	710?–13?		
Roderick	710–11		

In 680, King Erwig gained the throne only after a particularly brutal battle for succession. Typically, he unleashed a fresh spate of anti-Jewish legislation, including twenty-eight different laws in the first two months of his reign. At first, the themes were familiar—for example, Jews were given one year to have themselves baptized or face the consequences. His predecessor, King Recessuinth, had referred to the Jews as a "contagious pestilence"; Erwig not only coined the term *Judaeorum pestis* (the plague of Jews) but was soon advocating the extermination of the Jews. He appealed to the Twelfth Council of Toledo to rise up against "the leprosy of Jewish corruption." By 694, the Jews were finally pushed to the edge of revolt, but their plans were thwarted by informers. Infuriated by this failed attempt at insurrection, the Toledan Councils now declared all Jews to be slaves, ordered their goods confiscated, and bound their children under the age of seven over to Christian slavemasters to be raised as Catholics.

Visigothic Spain contributed a novel feature to the sordid history of persecution of the Jews. The forced converts were compelled to renounce their faith and pledge their devotion to Christianity in extraordinarily elaborate oaths of abjuration. They had to vow to have no further contact with practicing Jews or participate in any Jewish festivals. Instead, they promised to present themselves before priests at church services during all Jewish and Christian festivals and there eat pork and other foods specifically forbidden under Jewish law. The penalties for breaking these macabre pledges included death by burning or stoning, or confiscation of all property and sale into permanent slavery. The cruel forced oaths were characterized by a disdainful tone toward Judaism; for example, the convert had to declare his traditional religion to be a "superstition" or the "vomit of my former error."[9] (These and similar phrases were appropriated from Pope Gregory's 591 letter spelling out the dangers of forced baptism.) King Erwig, who would reign until 687, added the requirement that all business transactions between Jews and Christians begin with the Lord's Prayer and consumption of a dish of pork. No convert could travel without the permission of his parish priest. An additional method of undermining and demoralizing the Jews was to force attendance at lectures and sermons. To help assure implementation of his policy, Erwig ordered bishops to denounce any colleague who did not comply fully.

Outside Spain, events were occurring that undoubtedly influenced the nature and severity of these repressions, for religious extremism was becoming the rule rather than the exception elsewhere in the Mediterranean world. The war of 610 between Christian Byzantium and Persia provoked violent anti-Christian measures in the Persian-controlled East. Jews welcomed the Persian forces as liberators from their Byzantine persecutors in Antioch and elsewhere. In Palestine, the Jews formed a potent military force alongside the Persians, who captured Jerusalem in 614 and are said to have deported 37,000 of its inhabitants. Rumors immediately circulated that Jews were involved in these actions and probably filtered back to the West, further exacerbating Christian-Jewish relations in Spain.

No sooner did the Persian menace subside in the East than the new faith of Islam burst forth from the Arabian Peninsula, swept through the ancient Mediterranean provinces of the Byzantine Empire, and threatened proud Constantinople itself, Byzantium's capital. As the

Muslim armies spread westward across North Africa, Spanish Jews were seeking asylum in Morocco. Undoubtedly, the Visigothic monarchs in Spain at the end of the seventh century made a political connection between the distant and increasingly powerful enemy that could not be touched and the increasingly vulnerable "enemy" at home. Since many Jews had "defected" to the Muslim stronghold, in other words, they were fair game.

Yet another excuse for exacerbating persecution of the Jews was the series of natural disasters that afflicted Spain from the beginning of the century, leaving its agriculture and economy in a shambles. Bad harvests, plagues of locusts, and famine reduced the population by half during Erwig's relatively brief reign, producing an atmosphere of hysteria in which conspiracy theories flourished. Eventually, the country literally lay in ruins, its commerce strangled, irrigation systems destroyed, and cities decimated.

Ironically in this chaotic time, an actual conspiracy of certain Visigothic princes turned out to be far more devastating for their kingdom than any of the imaginary conspiracies attributed to the Jews. With disputes raging over the succession to the Visigothic throne, the heirs of King Witiza (702–10), aided by the Byzantine governor of the Moroccan coastal outpost of Ceuta, opened the gates of Spain to a small Arab force. Later legends embroidered the story of the fall of Visigothic Spain with a romantic subplot: the governor seeking revenge for Visigothic King Roderick's seduction of his beautiful daughter. In truth, the regime fell as a result of the combined forces of internal collapse and the passivity of the Hispanic masses weary of Visigothic domination and continued instability.

Although historians have traditionally depicted the invasion of Spain as almost an accident or an afterthought to the conquest of Morocco, it is more accurate to consider it as one more victory in an ever-widening circle of a century-long process of Islamic expansion. Undoubtedly, the Arabs had heard rumors of Spain's great riches and initially sent their small reconnaissance party across the Straits—400 troops commanded by an Arab general named Tarifa—to find out the truth. Instead of untold wealth, they discovered widespread discontent and found themselves welcomed as liberators by the warring sons of

Witiza, the tired city dwellers, and the persecuted Jews. After Tarifa's initial foray revealed that the peninsula was ripe for conquest, a much larger force of Berbers under Tariq ibn Ziyad invaded in 711 and Visigothic resistance swiftly collapsed. Some defiance continued at the purely local level, but within four years almost all of Spain had capitulated. In such a short period of time and with very few troops at their disposal, the Muslims had moved into the heart of Europe, beginning an occupation that would continue for nearly 800 years.

The Muslim armies arriving from North Africa marched under the banner of a religion only a century old. When its founder, the prophet Muhammed, died in 632, the movement was confined within the borders of Arabia; but within the next few decades victorious Muslim armies subdued the Persian Empire and much of Byzantium with cyclonic speed. By the beginning of the eighth century, this new Islamic empire extended from the shores of the Atlantic in the West to the Indian Ocean and China in the East, and its armies stood at the portals of Europe, soon to occupy Sicily as well as Iberia. In fact, this relentless advance would not be stopped until 732 at Poitiers, France (the Battle of Tours), where the Muslims would be defeated by Frankish warriors under Charles Martel. Subsequent expeditions into France through the western Pyrenees were also repulsed, leading the Muslims to give up attempting to advance in this direction.

At the same time, Muslims were suffering reverses in northwest Spain. The exploits of the Christian prince Pelayo and his bands of rugged mountaineers in Galicia have inspired many highly embellished stories that have entered the lore of Spain, but in fact he was successful in retaining large portions of territory, thus providing a base for the ultimate Christian reconquest. Under the leadership of the King of Asturias, Alfonso I (739–57), much of northwest Spain and Portugal was reconquered and proclaimed heir to the Visigothic legacy. This continuing presence of an independent Christian enclave in the mountainous north served as a constant challenge and later rallying point against Islam's domination of the peninsula.

The conquest of Spain was achieved during a period of heady expansion and with seeming invincibility. Yet, it was not only the speed of the Arab conquests but the permanence of their effects that was truly astonishing. The ever-expanding waves of military occupation introduced the faith of Islam and its Arabic language, engulfing and ultimately supplanting the ancient Greek, Latin, Syriac, and Aramaic-speaking cultures and empires. Finally, when the dust settled, the characteristic Muslim sense of an extended community (*umma*) descended over the entire Mediterranean and a new era began.

Tariq's conquest of Spain, far from being part of an integrated plan of territorial expansion, was almost serendipitous. His original invading force of 12,000 was very small, yet, according to Arab chronicles, city after city meekly capitulated as these North African Berbers (perhaps including as few as seven Arabs) drove deeper into Spain. These chronicles, which provide richly detailed accounts of the *jihad*, portray both victories and setbacks with surprising accuracy. From them we learn that Christians usually fled their towns, leaving the gates unguarded; few but Jews remained behind. The invaders gathered them together into principal cities or fortresses, frequently leaving these almost vacant cities in the hands of Jewish patrols, who acted as the local militia and guarded the gates, while they continued their advance. The Arab chronicles of these events are almost contemporaneous with the conquests and are consistent with what we know about the confusion and conspiracies in Spain at the time, as well as with the standard Arab military tactic of rapidly pressing a forward advance while utilizing non-Muslims as a rear guard. Undoubtedly, the Jews cooperated because they regarded these invaders as liberators. They did not, however, invite the Islamic forces to invade or work to deliver Spain to them. These charges were circulated by Christians in the Middle Ages, a revision of history reflecting two complementary themes: the explanation of Spain's fall to Islam as the consequence of Jewish treachery, and the tendency to portray Jews in the worst possible light in terms of stereotypes based upon Gospel accounts of Jewish "betrayals" in the first century.

But the historical truth is unmistakable. By 715, a full-scale invasion of Berbers and Arabs had conquered all of Spain except for the mountainous areas in the northwest, which they skirted in their eagerness to proceed further north into France. In addition to Arabs and Berbers, the mixed and internally divided conquerors included tribesmen from Syria, Egypt, and Yemen, fortune seekers and adventurers, merchants and purveyors. Most, of course, sought little more than booty and self-aggrandizement, but the Berbers who engineered the triumph would not be given their fair share of the rewards. In accordance with the custom of Muslim conquerors, land was not equally divided: the few Arabs who participated in the invasions seized the choicest fertile plains and valleys, and the disgruntled Berber majority were allotted the inferior rocky hillsides. An economic division between the two groups developed, governed by a garrison-like polity. Soon after the conquest, the Arab minority was augmented by elite Arab forces brought in from the East, thus forming a dominant upper class that controlled the economy and the state bureaucracy. Yet they were divided by the same rivalries and tribal factions that plagued Arab rule at the other end of the Mediterranean. The challenge was thus to maintain a delicate balance. Each group staked its claim: the Arabians in the Guadalquivir valley, the Syrians in Granada, the Egyptians in Murcia, and the Berbers in the hill country of Andalusia as well as the high plains of central Spain and Extremadura. In none of these territories did they form a clear majority, nor was Christian Spain entirely subdued. (This would take generations to achieve and was never really completed.) At first, the Muslim state was governed by a highly decentralized authority, an eminently practical course for a society characterized by deep cultural and social cleavages. These traditional divisions were buttressed by Spain's mountainous geography, which isolated and regionalized the peninsula. Small wonder that centralization and unification did not occur until the ninth century. Even then, it had to be fostered by Muslim administrators who consciously adopted a policy based upon statecraft practices in the East.

Another distinctive feature of the Muslim conquest was the small number of the indigenous Spanish population who initially converted to Islam. Mass conversion did not occur until the ninth century. In general, converts became a Muslim underclass. Meanwhile, Christians continued to live willingly in areas controlled by the Arab invaders, who called them *Musta'rib* (*mozarabs* in Castilian), just as many Muslims would later choose to live under the victorious returning Christians (*mudejar* in Castillian). Much of the vigor of social relations in medieval Spain derived from this rich ethnic diversity. For all groups, religious affiliation was the primary reference point, defining ethnicity as well. Linguistic diversity was quite common; as far as we can tell, it was an accepted part of the landscape. Paradoxically, this extraordinary heterogeneity—"old" and "new" Muslims, Jews and Christians, Berbers

and Arabs, Yemeni Arabs and Syrian Arabs—accounts in no small measure for both the chronic instability of Muslim Spain and its remarkable
intellectual ferment.

The invasion promptly set off a wave of Jewish immigration to the
newly conquered province known as Andalusia. These Jews were now
able to reunite with relatives who fled in the last decades of Visigothic
persecution and immediately improve their position. Many returned
from refuge in Morocco on the heels of the Muslim armies. Significantly, the migration of Jews (as well as Muslims) back and forth across
the narrow straits separating Europe from Africa would become a constant feature of life in medieval Spain, in part because of deliberate
government policy. Thus in 740, when the Berbers living in the northern cities of Spain revolted because they felt cheated in the allocation of
the spoils of conquest, Damascus sent an army of 27,000 warriors to
suppress them. Once victorious, these Syrian Arabs refused to leave,
adding one more element to the country's ethnic diversity. Still other
foreigners, Muslim and Jew, were attracted by the lure of the pacified
country. Elsewhere in the Islamic world, it was not uncommon for
Jewish merchants and suppliers from many lands to follow the Muslim
conquerors and form the nuclei of new Jewish communities, even as far
as the Gobi Desert and China. By the tenth century, when Andalusia
had established her reputation as a thriving intellectual center, she became a magnet for scholars who in turn attracted further Jewish and
Muslim immigration.

The dynamism of the Muslim conquests was born of a self-
confidence rooted in religious belief and their record of worldly success.
United by Islam and the Arabic language, the disparate Muslim forces
were imbued with a sense that they held the truth and had a duty to
bring it to the rest of mankind. The worldview behind their *jihad* was
relatively simple. The world was divided into two main parts: conquered territory, called the House of Islam (*dar el-Islam*). and territory
still to be conquered, called the House of War (*dar el-Harb*) Ideally, the
House of Islam was one unified community; waging war for the sake of
Islam was a pillar of faith accorded the highest religious merit: the
believer who died in battle with the infidel was a martyr who would
enjoy ample rewards in Paradise.

It followed that the world was not regarded in territorial or linguistic terms; in fact, some Muslim countries remained nameless until
the twentieth century. Rather, religion was the yardstick for classifying
and differentiating groups, relegating Judaism and Christianity to an

inferior status in the Muslim scheme of things. Yet it was something of a privileged status, too, since these two groups alone were in the House of Truce (*dar al-sulh*) or Covenant (*dar el-Ahd*). Under Islamic legal theory, all religious minorities who were not monotheists had to choose between Islam and death. But the existence of monotheistic Judaism and Christianity was accepted and given a niche, however uncomfortable, in Muslim society. Muhammed himself, as a merchant in Mecca and lawmaker in Medina, had interacted with Jews in commerce and politics and had much to say about them, based on his experiences. His utterances, incorporated both in the Koran and in the collections of oral traditions known as *Hadith*, were the authoritative source of reference for all believing Muslims, providing the fundamental guidelines for behavior between the two groups.

But the legal status of the Jews under Islam was never static, based as it was upon diverse traditions that emerged in a vast territorial expanse over a period of several hundred years. The Muslim empire was never one entity but rather a dynamic human reality composed of different languages, people, cultures, and regimes. It was most open to the talents and self-expression of other peoples, especially if they were monotheistic, during its period of greatest unity, about 800 to 1200. After 1100, as the Muslim world started to fragment and became prey to various feudal and military dynasties, the status of Jews declined steadily, with only a brief respite during the sixteenth-century Ottoman renaissance. From the earliest years of Muhammed's movement, the eastern periphery of the Muslim world tended to be harsher to Jews and Christians than the west, the heterodox Shi'ite regimes there even more so than the Arab and Sunni regimes. In contrast, the conquerors of Spain were the most lenient in all Islam, especially during the first centuries of their rule.

To some extent, this passionate new religion defined itself in opposition to its two predecessors.[10] To rebut those who believed in the divinity of Jesus, for example, the Koran describes God as "unique, alone, He does not beget and is not begotten, none is equal to him." At the same time, Judaism and Christianity both were recognized as kindred, if inferior, faiths also based on revelations. The continuing existence of these separate monotheistic faiths was (and is) justified in a single verse in the Koran:

Say, O believers! I shall not worship what you worship. You do not worship what I worship. I am not a worshipper of what you have

worshipped, and you are not worshippers of what I have worshipped.
To you, your religion. To me, my religion. (Sura 109)

Judaism received the special attention of Muslim theologians because Muhammed had encountered many Jews during his career in
Arabia. In the course of hammering out his new faith, in fact, he had
engaged in many verbal exchanges with the substantial and articulate
Jewish community in Arabia, especially the vital group in the Medina
oasis. (By contrast, there was only a limited Christian presence in the
Arabian peninsula.) Muhammed drew upon many elements of Judaism
in the development of his doctrines, including the fast, the concept of
charity as an obligation, the content and direction of prayer, and a
myriad of details concerning daily human conduct. In fact, he conveyed
his religious message to the Jews of Medina, having come to regard
himself as the pinnacle and seal of all of the ancient biblical prophecies,
and offered them his leadership. He contended that the Koran contained the true revelation that Jews and Christians fail to follow. When
the Medina Jews rejected him out of hand, he was struck to the core.
First he angrily confronted them in debates whose echoes are preserved
in the Koran, vividly excoriating them as corrupters of Scripture and
enemies of Islam. But polemics soon gave way to military campaigns
that brought terrible consequences to all Arabian Jews, though some
were treated differently from others. Where politically expedient and
militarily feasible, Muhammed did not hesitate to expel some Jewish
tribes from Arabia entirely or to decapitate all male members of others.
Those "infidels" who survived were required to submit to Muslim supremacy and pay tribute. The Prophet drew a distinction between those
Jews with whom he was willing to contract treaties, deeming them
descendants of Abraham who had been granted a partial revelation, and
those who had to be subjugated because they were an ignoble people
with a rebellious, malevolent spirit.

Muhammed officially accorded a low level of toleration to Jews, as
to Christians, but the relative tolerance or intolerance of Islam toward
these two faiths has been the subject of lively controversy since the
nineteenth century. European Jewish scholars, frustrated with the slow
progress of Jewish emancipation in their own place and time, tended
to romanticize and embellish whatever benevolence could be seen in
Muslim religious tolerance, but others have emphasized the harsher
aspects of Islamic attitudes. It has been frequently pointed out that
Muhammed recognized the validity of Judaism and Christianity be-

cause both possessed written revelations, but the Islamic approach to toleration refined in the Muslim schools of law during the first centuries of the movement is quite unlike Western Lockean notions of freedom.[11] Classical Islamic legal theory holds that the possessors of Scripture, or *Ahl al-Kitab*, should be opposed until they surrender. Thereafter, the imposition of payment of tribute in the form of discriminatory taxes (the *djizya* was a poll tax, the *haradj* was a tax on produce from the land) was only one of several obligatory signs of humiliation, but these special non-Muslims were also to be protected (hence the term *Ahl ed-dhimma*, "protected people"). In other words, subjugated Jews and Christians were permitted to reside in the House of Islam with certain limitations placed upon them. The Koran is quite clear on this point:

> Fight against such as those who have been given the Scripture and believe not in Allah nor in the Last Day, and forbid not that which Allah hath forbidden by his messenger and follow not the religion of truth, until they pay the tribute readily, being brought low. (Sura 9:29).

Elsewhere, the Koran characterizes the lot of non-Muslims as "humiliation and wretchedness," since they are "visited with wrath from Allah" (Sura 2:61).

The distinctive nature of Islamic toleration is further elaborated in one of the earliest Muslim legal handbooks, Abu Yusuf's eighth-century classic *Kitab al-Kharadj* (Book of Taxes). This scholar's unique approach joins symbols and practices of toleration with signs of humiliation; in other words, the Jews and Christians should indeed pay the special taxes and be humbled, in accord with the Koran, but should also be permitted to worship their own tradition. He warns:

> If you take the poll tax from them, you have no claim on them or rights over them. . . . Therefore, place a poll tax upon them and do not enslave them and do not let the Muslims oppose them or harm them or devour their property except as permitted.[12]

In addition to fiscal exploitation, Abu Yusuf lists numerous other measures to differentiate Jews and Christians (*dhimmis*) from Muslims. These "marks of distinguishing" or "marks of recognition," which also served to provide tangible proof of the bearer's inferiority, included clothing of a special color, distinctive (and sometimes ludicrous) footwear and headgear, restrictions upon the use of animals, prohibitions against walking in certain areas, and limitations upon choice of occupation. All forms of worship were to be inconspicuous in order to avoid giving offense to Muslims; in addition, there were limitations on the size of synagogues and churches, no new synagogues could be built, and older religious structures could not be repaired. Over the course of time, these discriminatory laws assumed outrageous forms, especially in Iran and Yemen from the seventeenth century onward.[13]

Collectively, the restrictions on *dhimmis* were known as the Pact of Umar, but it should be noted that these regulations were not followed in all places at all times. Indeed, in Muslim Spain, they were usually more honored in the breach. Arab pragmatism coupled with the circumstances of rapid conquest called for the utilization of minorities, a circumstance that tended to inspire a sense of optimism among the Sephardim. (When the situation reversed, they could be plunged into despair.) For example, there was a proliferation of new synagogues, Jews commonly wore lavish clothing and adopted Muslim patronyms, and, as we shall see later, there was an influential Jewish general and vizier in the person of Samuel ibn Nagrela. Still, when the discrepancy between theory and practice became too great—that is, when Jews waxed too powerful or enjoyed too many rights—there was always the danger that Muslim reformers would insist upon a restoration of stringent dress codes and other onerous and humiliating restrictions. The Pact of Umar provided a potential source of inspiration for such fundamentalist leaders and religious reformers as the eleventh-century Almoravids and twelfth-century Almohade rulers who imposed anti-Jewish restrictions during times of religious fervor or social stress. It was partly as a result of the application of the harsher codes of Islam that Jews began their wholesale exodus from Muslim Spain in those two centuries.

In general, however, the "protected status" of *dhimmi* offered the Jews of Spain several important freedoms: they could freely practice their faith, they could nurture their religious and communal institutions, they were permitted to engage in a wide variety of professions, and they could settle more or less where they chose and move freely throughout

Muslim territories, except in the Arabian peninsula. Compared to these essential privileges, disabilities involving social status and prestige were minor. In fact, the blend of religious guarantees with subtle discriminations did not strike Jews as particularly menacing, especially in relation to the conditions they had faced in Visigothic Spain or in Byzantium. In other words, the comparatively mild limitations of Islamic Spain held out great promise for Jewish settlement.

But despite the euphoria of the first centuries of the Islamic movement, when it seemed as if the entire world might soon convert to the true faith, Spain would never be entirely won. Although the country was formally annexed to the Umayyad caliphate in 713–14, local autonomy prevailed in practice since it always took several months for the caliph's commands to reach this province from Damascus, 2,500 miles distant. As we have seen, the rapid conquest was followed by a slow consolidation of Muslim power. Relations between warring Spanish factions were exacerbated when troops sent from Damascus to quell Berber insurrections refused to leave after doing their job, and the non-Muslim population seethed under a succession of unpopular Berber and Arab governors. While the conquerors quarreled over the division of their booty, Jews and Christians were in charge of many administrative tasks.

The continuing cultural confrontations among Jews, Muslims, and Christians were enacted in the presence of the Islamic south and the unconquered Christian north. Ostensibly formed by the Duero River and demarcated by a line of castles, this border was both physical and mental. In actual fact and in apprehension, the Christian kingdoms—Leon, Navarre, Asturias—never ceased to be an irridentist threat. Consequently, Muslim rulers tended to rely upon the economic and administrative talents and services of Jews more than Muhammed's discriminatory ideology had anticipated or intended.

In the middle of the eighth century, a violent coup d'état in Damascus drove the last Umayyad caliph from power, and the caliphate was moved to Baghdad. A lone survivor, 'Abd ar-Rahman I, evaded the massacre in Syria and escaped to Spain, where he was able to re-establish the Umayyads as an emirate or princedom in Córdoba in 756. He and his successors immediately began pacifying a divided country by setting up a strong army and bureaucracy. Driven also by the desire to equal the splendor of their rivals in Baghdad and other foes, they would ensure that Persian traditions of statecraft and social life, art and architecture, that dominated Abbasid political institutions in Baghdad, would soon flower abundantly, as would new forms of cultural expression.

No Jewish inhabitant of eighth-century Spain could possibly have anticipated the remarkable consequences for their community. Now, after the horrors of Visigothic rule and the uncertain beginnings of Muslim-Jewish relations, they were about to embark upon a new and vibrant chapter in their history. Just as the Muslims of Al-Andalus or Andalusia were poised to emerge as a distinctive unit within the larger Islamic community that surrounded the Mediterranean, so the Jews of Spain were about to become, in the fullest sense, the distinctive grouping known as Sephardim.

2

The Birth of Sepharad

From the Muslim Conquest to the Caliphate of Córdoba

In the days of Hasdai the Nasi they began to chirp, and in the days of Samuel the Nagid they sang out loud.

—Abraham ibn Daud, *Sefer ha-Qabbalah*

A German nun visiting Córdoba in the tenth century was moved to exclaim that the city represented "the majesty and adornment of the world, the wondrous capital . . . radiating in affluence of all earthly blessings." Even a contemporary Muslim, Ibn Hawkal, who was deeply familiar with the splendors of medieval Islam, remarked that neither in Syria nor in Egypt nor in all the countries of North Africa could a comparable city be found. As was apparent to these observers and indeed all visitors, a brilliant era was dawning in Spain. Forever afterward, the tenth and eleventh centuries would be remembered by Jews as the nation's "Golden Age," an epoch in which they enjoyed unusual political power and could participate actively in the dominant culture. No less cherished in Islamic memory, the period gave rise to the legend that when Allah was creating the world, Andalusia asked for five things: clear skies, a sea well stocked with all manner of fish, trees laden with every species of fruit, beautiful women, and a just government. Allah agreed to every one of these requests but the last, having decided that if all were granted Andalusia would rival Paradise.

Christians, too, found the city an especially inviting place to live in the tenth century, but for Christian Spaniards, it is the sixteenth century—the period of Christian ascendancy—that is recalled as the country's Golden Age. From the political point of view, Spaniards usually view the reign of the Catholic monarchs (1479–1516) as the era of their greatest achievements, while foreigners tend to regard the age of Charles V and Philip II (1516–98) in this light. But the *Siglo de Oro* of Spanish arts and literature that includes Cervantes, Lope de Vega, Calderón, El Greco, Velásquez, and Murillo begins somewhat later and continues into the seventeenth century. The differing Jewish, Muslim, and Christian concepts of a golden age reflect the more fundamental differences in the ways that the three groups view their historical experience in Iberia.

'Abd ar-Rahman I had originally chosen Córdoba as the Andalusian capital because of its central location and the fertility of the surrounding countryside, making it a natural market for all branches of agriculture. By the 900s it had reached its zenith, becoming home to at least 100,000 inhabitants of various nationalities and ethnic backgrounds. (According to some Arab geographers, the total could have risen as high as half a million.) It boasted 700 mosques and perhaps as many as 3,000 public baths within the city limits, paved and illuminated streets, indoor plumbing in luxurious homes, and countless villas dotting the banks of the Guadalquivir. The air was filled with the humming of 5,000 looms weaving silk and brocades, with the cascading of waters over the brightly colored ceramic-tiled basins of its innumerable fountains and reflecting pools. Perhaps because of their desert origins, the Muslims were especially appreciative of water as well as landscaping that used tropical trees to provide shade and frame dramatic views. Twenty-eight suburbs, alive with thriving markets, fanned out to the expansive out-skirts of the city. Nowhere else in all of Europe could such splendor and sophistication be found.

Córdoba's sparkling cultural life was enriched by seventy libraries, with the caliph's library alone reportedly stocking 400,000 volumes. Recognized as a center of medicine and technology, the city also housed numerous observatories. Consciously imitating Baghdad, the first several Umayyad princes were more esthetes than bureaucrats, importing talented architects and scientists from the East and establishing schools to translate classical works into Arabic. Energetically pursuing a policy of city building and the patronage of culture in the broadest sense, they built palaces as well as mosques, endowed hospitals and hospices. The foundations of Córdoba's legendary splendor in the tenth century were laid enthusiastically by the series of rulers who established the city as the imperial seat of the Islamic empire in the West: 'Abd ar-Rahman I (756–88), 'Abd ar-Rahman II (822–52), 'Abd ar-Rahman III (912–61), and al-Hakam II (961–76).

Córdoba's great mosque was an architectural gem that rivaled in size and beauty the most famous religious monuments in the Islamic heartland. The cinnamon-colored exterior, stark and understated, stood in sharp contrast to a rich interior with an elaborately carved wooden ceiling, enameled and gilded doors, and geometrically subtle tilework. Illuminating the vast inner spaces were 4,000 lamps filled with per-fumed oil and 300 candelabra partially constructed from the church bells of the cathedral of Santiago. Ornamentation included Koranic quotes in elaborate Arabic script, vegetal motifs sculpted in the capitols of endless rows of columns, and intricate abstract leaf-scroll patterns derived from Arabic calligraphy. This grand mosque was repeatedly enlarged under the Umayyads in order to house the constantly increas-ing number of worshippers in the city. Not only did it set the pattern for Islamic art in Spain, it also served as a source of inspiration and imitation for synagogue architecture.

The embellishment of Córdoba reached a peak in the tenth century when 'Abd ar-Rahman III began building a new imperial enclave to honor his favorite concubine, Zahra. At Madinat az-Zahra, a colossal undertaking that created an economic boom in the city, more than 13,000 household attendants, including jesters and poets, would vie with diplomats and courtiers for the attention and favor of the ruler. Their machinations took place in a 400-room palace constructed from tons of marble and semiprecious stones sent from Constantinople as the gift of Leo IV, the Byzantine emperor. Arab accounts describe this lavish enclave only in superlatives, but it is as difficult to distinguish accurate description from hyperbole as it probably was at that time to distinguish between the authentic and the ornamental. The site took twenty years to complete, requiring the labor of some 8,000 workers aided by 1,000 mules, but was used only briefly before being destroyed by more puritanical Muslim forces in the eleventh century.

Yet the memorable brilliance of Golden Age Córdoba had not been achieved overnight. It took the Umayyads some time to consolidate their rule and organize their territory after an initial, and prolonged, period of discord and turbulence. In the beginning, Christians or Mozarabs (Christians who lived in Muslim Spain), smarting under the discriminatory Islamic regulations, sent frequent appeals to neighboring Christian rulers to intervene on their behalf. Some of these princes, keeping a constant eye on the internal discord in al-Andalus, were not loath to foment revolt there. Christian converts to Islam, the *muwalladun*, saw little chance of gaining access to positions of power, since the new Arab aristocracy treated them with suspicion and contempt. It seemed as if the Jews alone made no irredentist claims and had no foreign protectors who might step in to help them.

Despite these early strains however, the state grew in affluence, its wealth based upon a diversified economy that combined agriculture, industry, and trade. Soon after the original conquest, the Muslim invaders had begun restoring and improving the ancient Roman irrigation canals and aqueducts, which had fallen into disuse. They also introduced profitable new crops from the East such as citrus fruits, bananas, figs, cinnamon, and almonds. To supply the growing demand for conspicuous consumption, cash crops like cotton, silk, flax, and wool were added as well. The peasants who grew this produce would be predominantly non-Muslims, and thus subject to discriminatory taxes, but the economic inducements to till the soil were still considerable.

It has been observed that conquerors often deliberately settle in a place that reminds them of home, or if possible refashion the subjugated country to resemble their own. Apparently, the Umayyads longed for the Levant, establishing in Spain the same trees, plants, and food crops their forefathers had cultivated in Syria, and serving the same traditional foods on their tables. The wholesale importation of Syrian styles of living produced an extensive Syrianization, as it were, of the entire Andalusian countryside. Seville, which became known as Hims al-Andalus, strove to model itself on Damascus, the Syrian capital.[1]

Under the Umayyads, Andalusia's lively cities emerged as centers of industry whose markets overflowed with staples and luxuries from Italy, North Africa, Egypt, and even further east, alongside colorful displays of such local goods of recent invention as lead crystal, especially fine leather, fine locally produced silk (*Kurtubi* in contemporary Hebrew sources), crimson Shadhuna silk (produced near Seville in the town of that name), ivory carvings, and luster-glazed ceramics. With all their religiosity, Muslim legal authorities were not ascetics; in fact, the abundant display of these luxuries was regarded as a natural human indulgence, and the enjoyment of worldly goods was condoned. According to an old Arab proverb, when Allah bestows favors on man, he wants them shown off. Elaborate attire was justified by the saying, "Squander on your back, and save on your belly."

Jewish tastes mirrored those of the Muslims, and Spanish silks dyed brilliantly in many colors were especially prized. As the luxury commerce thrived, gold and silver circulated throughout the country, and agriculture, always the backbone of its economy, flourished. And even in the face of the Islamic prohibitions against consumption of alcohol, vintners from the Córdoba countryside brought their wines to eager customers in the city.

The description of this cornucopia of riches given by the tenth-century Jewish statesman Hasdai ibn Shaprut is convincingly detailed:

> The land is rich, abounding in rivers, springs, and aqueducts; a land of corn, oil and wine, of fruits and all manner of delicacies; it has pleasure-gardens and orchards, fruitful trees of every kind, including the leaves of the trees upon which the silkworm feeds. . . . There are also found among us mountains . . . with veins of sulphur, porphyry, marble and crystal. Merchants congregate in it and traffickers from the ends of the earth . . . bringing spices, precious stones, splendid wares for kings and princes and all the desirable things of Egypt. Our king has collected very large treasures of silver, gold, precious things, and valuables such as no king has ever collected. His yearly revenue is about 100,000 gold pieces, the greater part of which is derived from the merchants who come hither from various countries and islands.[2]

The Jews of Spain participated in this prosperity as part of the larger economic universe, a virtual free-trade zone established by Muslim control of the Mediterranean world. The unity of the Mediterranean under Islam in a *Pax Islamica* is somewhat reminiscent of its ancient unity under the *Pax Romana* of the first and second centuries. Political boundaries within the Muslim orbit were not barriers to trade and an economic unity prevailed.

Trade was fundamental to Islamic life from the outset, in large part because Muhammed had been a merchant. According to Muslim (but not Jewish) tradition, Abraham's son Ishmael, the forefather of Islam, was a textile merchant. The quasi-global economy of Islam eventually stretched from Iberia to the Indian Ocean as ideas and men, goods and armies, moved freely between East and West. Mobility was facilitated by early oral Islamic tradition, which regarded travel for the sake of knowledge (*rihla* or *talab el-ilm*) as a venerable and pious activity that might even assure entry into Paradise. According to one source, the Prophet himself said, "Those who go out in search of knowledge will be in the path of God until they return" (al-Tirmidhi, *Sunan,* 39:2). Or, as the traditional phrase put it, "In mobility there is blessing" (*f'il haraka baraka*). (In the Talmud, too, travel for the sake of learning was commanded.).

Not surprisingly, Arabic travel literature increased during the eighth and ninth centuries, expanding the available knowledge of routes and of the remote areas of the explored world. As Muslims departed Spain to study at the feet of famous scholars in North Africa, Cairo, and Persia, Sephardic intellectuals traveled to such academies of learning as Kairouan on the Tunisian coast, and the revered Yeshivot of Sura, and Pumbeditha in Baghdad. Medieval Jewish documents spanning almost a thousand years, preserved in the treasure trove known as the Cairo Geniza, show how natural it was for Jews to be on the move.[3] Their religious persuasion was no barrier to travel, and the surrounding culture helped revive and reinforce the ancient Talmudic custom of traveling in order to learn. The Geniza documents note quite casually the frequency with which Jews also moved between Spain and Sicily, Aden and the Indian Ocean, for the sake of contracting marriages for their offspring or establishing new branches of business. Evidently, it was not even unusual to make several journeys from Spain to India during one's lifetime. Jews preferred to travel by sea, because one did not desecrate the Sabbath by gaining mileage on the water; the requirement of halting a land caravan for a day could be extremely expensive. Moreover, the Muslims had made the sea routes eminently safer by constructing lighthouses along the shores and introducing new, improved naval vessels; even so, ships in this era stayed fairly close to shore, and in winter, when tides were tricky, traders took the land routes. A medieval Jewish merchant might well own a home in Iberia and another elsewhere, perhaps in Morocco or in the Near East. Thus was fashioned an overarching culture and cosmopolitan community that shared many features, exchanging new tastes and technologies along with goods and services.

The storehouse of thousands of commercial and personal papers discovered in the Cairo Geniza indicates how remarkably free travel was in the medieval Mediterranean world. The concept of law was personal, not territorial, and a person was judged according to the law of his religious community. Geniza letters are oblivious to political boundaries as Jewish merchant families moved back and forth between rival kingdoms. To be sure, there were customs stations everywhere, but both Christian and Muslim powers seemed intent upon preserving a free-trade community in the Mediterranean. Maimonides remarks casually in a *responsum* that Jews were regular passengers on boats commuting between Seville and Alexandria.

Serious studies of this era have pointed out that the learned merchant was the standard-bearer of medieval Islamic civilization. The Muslim pilgrim's standard wish was "May your *hajj* be accepted, your sin be forgiven, and your merchandise not remain unsold." Jews drew freely from this intellectual and commercial climate as a large and influential merchant class began to rise all over the Middle East in the eighth and ninth centuries. Jewish, Muslim, and Christian mercantile families dealt with each other in partnerships, and "formal friendships" characterized business relationships. These bonds of friendship were solidified by marriages concluded between families all over the Mediterranean and the Indian Ocean route. The family was considered the ideal form of business partnership, with ties of blood superseding ties of marriage.

The Geniza collection includes over 300 letters to and from the Tunisian Jewish merchant-scholar Nahrai ben Nissim, a regular commuter between Tunisia and Egypt in the eleventh century. His transactions over the course of a fifty-year career (1045–96) involved merchandise from Spain, North Africa, Sicily, Egypt, Syria, and India. His extremely diversified trade included almost all the staples and luxuries of the commercial world of his day: flax and silk, olive oil and spices, metals and books, jewels and chemicals, food and hides. His detailed surviving accounts reveal a man of exceptional organizational and intellectual abilities who worked in partnership with a variety of experts, but it appears that such versatility in trade was an exception. Usually, leading merchants worked closely with others who specialized in one item of commerce. The remarkable Nahrai was also a talented scholar who was honored by his peers in Egypt, Palestine, and North Africa.

The international trader is a familiar figure in the Geniza correspondence, for merchants were practically commuters and would casually remark about the ordinariness of long-distance trips, although a spirit of adventure also permeates many of their letters. Such business travel was commonplace in part because merchants felt they had to protect their merchandise, in part because they believed that "one who is present sees what one who is absent cannot see."[4] Although the rhythm of life in all Jewish communities was determined by the religious calendar, it was also shaped by the comings and goings of their itinerant merchants. As one of the Geniza correspondents writes, "The synagogue is desolate, for the Maghrebis have left."

From a ninth-century Arabic account, *Kitab el-Masalik wa'l Mamalik* (*The Book of the Roads and Kingdoms*), we learn incidentally of the remarkable commercial activities of the Radhanites, a Jewish firm whose operations may have been based in Spain or southern France. Their name may derive from the Persian "knower of the way." Very little is known about them other than the Arabic description of their routes and merchandise, from which we learn that their trade stretched across several continents with branches in many ports and commercial outposts. Their representatives followed four distinct land and sea routes. One went northward through Europe via Prague, Bulgaria, and the land of the Khazars. Two proceeded along the Mediterranean littoral and ended in Iran and Iraq (the trip from Córdoba to Baghdad normally took a year). The fourth went by sea and land all the way to China. Generally speaking, most of the commercial agents of the Radhanites went only part of a route, making trades with colleagues who had accumulated merchandise on an adjacent leg of the whole route.

Factors specific to medieval Jewry helped the Radhanites acquire monopolies. For example, Muslims were excluded from European markets, and Christians were virtually barred from Islamic waters; only Jews could travel as commercial agents in both realms. In addition, like all Jews, the Radhanites could be assured of hospitality among co-religionists dispersed all along their transcontinental route through North Africa and Asia as well as in the European hinterlands.

The naturalness with which the medieval Jew engaged in commerce over long distances should not obscure the fact that considerable peril was involved. Geniza letters are replete with allusions to the hazards of nature and the merchants' sense of gratitude to God for deliverance from danger. In anticipation of the ever-present threats of piracy, banditry, and assaults by the crew, merchant ships tended to sail in convoys. Frequently, such phrases as "We arrived safely in Alexandria for God protected us from pirates" appear in the Geniza letters. Piracy, which colored all aspects of sea commerce, was a part of the continuing holy war between Islam and Christendom and was especially active near Byzantine shores and in the Eastern Mediterranean in the eleventh century. So well known and feared was the pirates' nest off the coast of Libya that merchants would write their families in relief as soon as they passed by safely.

Jews captured by pirates could count on ransom and rescue by fellow Jews in the area when they were brought to a slave market, generally deprived of all possessions including the clothes on their back. Repeatedly, communities in Cairo and especially Alexandria were summoned to redeem men and women from the hands of pirates. One fragment indicates how the Jews in Cairo were burdened with frequent requests for ransom and had to organize collections in other communities:

> We turn to you today on behalf of a captive woman who has been brought from Byzantium. We ransomed her for 24 dinars besides the government tax. You sent us 12 dinars; we have paid the remainder and the tax. Soon afterwards sailors brought two other prisoners, one of them a fine young man possessing knowledge of the Torah, the other a boy of about ten. When we saw them in the hands of the pirates, and how they beat and frightened them before our own eyes, we had pity on them and guaranteed their ransom. We had hardly settled this, when another ship arrived carrying many prisoners. Among them a physician and his wife. Thus we are again in difficulties and distress. And our strength is overstrained, as the taxes are heavy and the times critical . . .[5]

Several other factors also helped establish Jewish prominence in international commerce (and benefited the Radhanite monopolies). Jewish multilingualism, a reflection of their complex history, facilitated trade with other national groups. Traders used Hebrew, Arabic, Persian, and Greek as well as "the language of Franks, Andalusians, and Slavs." At the same time, Hebrew was understood in educated Jewish circles the world over, giving them a kind of *lingua franca* not only for trade but also for religious and intellectual discourse. Sometimes, for example, merchants would return to Spain with letters from the rabbinic scholars of Baghdad or Palestine, typically responses to questions about ritual. The excited Sephardic community would gather for a public reading and celebration. Finally, merchants also benefited from the uniform legal code of the Talmud, which was recognized as binding for all Jews, regardless of country of residence.

The operations of the Radhanites are fairly representative of trends in Mediterranean trade in this period. Luxury goods from the Islamic heartland—e.g., textiles and metalwork produced in Spain, Cairo, or Kairouan—were exchanged in the Orient for spices and exotic substances like musk from China, in the West for raw materials such as the fur and timber of Christian Europe. (Spain's demand for raw materials increased in response to the burgeoning economy and ambitious construction programs of the Umayyads.) The Radhanites brought incense for churches in the West and also introduced Europe to the use of sofas and mattresses as well as ancient medicinal plants. Slaves figured prominently on the bills of sale in the area of the Crimea, the very word "slave" deriving from "Slav." By the late Middle Ages, the Slavic lands were, along with the Nordic lands, the last outposts of paganism in Europe and were therefore regarded as the most desirable arena for the Muslim slave trade. Slaves were needed for agriculture, for domestic service in the caliphal household, and for harems and royal guards, and were one of the few commodities that Byzantium could export to the Islamic world.

Despite its fame, Córdoba was never the sole seat of Andalusian culture. Comparatively small but dazzling centers of Islamic civilization, consciously imitating the capital, emerged also in Seville, Granada, Málaga, and Lucena. They competed for talent in an atmosphere of rivalry that redounded to the benefit of poetry and science, if not always to political stability. When Córdoba was sacked by the Almoravids in the eleventh century, Seville became Andalusia's leading urban center. (Nevertheless, Córdoba would remain a major center of Jewish life into the fourteenth century, as can be seen from the magnificence of its synagogue at this late date.) When Seville in turn was taken by Christian forces in 1248, Granada assumed the role of cultural and political center of the progressively contracting Muslim kingdom until it finally fell in 1492.

These Islamic cities did not have citizens in the modern sense. Each was an island that held separate peoples, tribes, and communities, with many foreigners coming and going, adding to the complex mix. Organizationally weak, their urban markets nonetheless dominated the surrounding regions. Most major towns were located on the sites of former Roman settlements but had been revived and redesigned along the pattern of cities throughout the Muslim world. Such public areas as the markets and the mosque were centrally located; communal activities were held in these open spaces, often around a tiled fountain. Otherwise, the streets were generally quite narrow and serpentine, with numerous cul-de-sacs. Shops were concentrated in specific districts according to what they produced or sold. Typically, residences lined winding streets that followed the natural slope of the terrain to allow for drainage through a channel in the middle of the adjacent valley. Main thoroughfares were unnamed, but the small alleys were named for the people who lived there. Behind austere undecorated walls, the private homes, built around airy patios, were luxurious to the point of opulence. The central fountain or pool of the patio garden was usually surrounded by flower beds and columns of stylized palm trees with birds and arabesque foliage carved in the boughs. Perhaps stone statuary of lions or deer stood beside the pool. Poets, in particular, enjoyed the artificial order created by these settings, which were often the site of poetry readings and celebrations.[6] They and their middle-class merchant patrons disported themselves in surroundings not unlike the famous Lions' Court built several centuries later in the Alhambra fortress at Granada. In fact, some historians suggest that the cluster of ornamental statuary there originally belonged to an eleventh-century Jewish courtier from the city, Joseph ibn Nagrela.

As we have seen, Jewish residence in many of the urban jewels of Andalusia predated the Muslim conquests. As the towns expanded, so did the Jewish population. But no exclusively Jewish neighborhoods existed in the cities and towns of the Golden Age, even though areas of Jewish residential concentration were common. Generally speaking, Jews preferred to reside in walled neighborhoods with gates that could be barred for security; the blocks of houses in such a cul-de-sac were often protected by a guard who would make his rounds at night with dogs and a lantern. Before the Muslim conquest, the Jewish quarter of Córdoba had been confined to a southwestern neighborhood near the city wall, but it was moved and enlarged in the tenth century. Jewish residence became so conspicuous near the city's northern gate, in fact, that Arab historians of the Middle Ages called it *Bab el-Yahud,* the Gate of the Jews. Christians seem to have lived alongside Muslims in areas of mixed residence in Córdoba, but elsewhere (Valencia, for example) they congregated in separate neighborhoods, as the Berbers did in Granada and Saragossa. In sum, the practice of residential segregation in medieval Muslim times was not necessarily discriminatory but rather a time-honored trait typical of Middle Eastern patterns of city dwelling.

Córdoba's highly developed Jewish community would be matched and then surpassed by the Sephardic Jewish community of Seville in the eleventh century. There, too, they resided in more than one district, playing an important role in the transformation of the city into a regional center of culture after the sack of the capital. Because the Guadalquivir became wide enough near Seville to allow oceangoing vessels to dock there, the city would emerge as a principal focal point of overseas commerce; from the ninth century onward, silk weaving and metalwork were important sources of income. The Jews of Seville were especially active in both foreign trade and the textile industry; they were intellectually active, too, as we know from their tenth-century correspondence with Saadiah Gaon of Baghdad, then the foremost scholar in the Jewish world. Questions of proper Jewish burial, issues of marriage, inheritance, and divorce, and uncertainty regarding interpretations of law constituted the heart of the correspondence. When the sage rose to prominence, traditional scholarship in Spain was in its early formative stages. Even after the Christian reconquest of the city, Jews remained a significant force in local affairs, as can be inferred from the inclusion of Hebrew in the multilingual epitaph of Ferdinand III in the royal chapel of the cathedral of Seville as late as 1279.

Before the ascendancy of Córdoba and its magnetic appeal to Andalusian Jewry, the spiritual center of Jewish intellectual life in the region had been Lucena. Well into the Middle Ages, Jews formed a substantial majority of the population living in the fortified inner city. But in the tenth century and afterward, the alumni of the town's rabbinical academy generally went to Córdoba to pursue their intellectual and worldly careers. Even so, they remained proud of their training in

Lucena, boasting that it was the first Spanish Jewish intellectual center to correspond with the prestigious academies of Jewish learning in Iraq. No less important, Lucena is remembered in tradition as a "city of song," where the Hebrew language and its poetry were lovingly cultivated. In the eleventh and twelfth centuries, the town's rabbinical academy, whose renowned and beloved teachers included Isaac ibn Ghiyyat, Isaac al-Fasi, and Joseph ibn Megash, introduced a new curriculum that would serve as the model of Sephardic learning for generations.[7]

There was also a large Jewish community in Granada, the chief city of eastern Andalusia. In fact, according to some medieval legends, the city had been founded by Jews after the destruction of the first Temple of Jerusalem and the beginning of the Babylonian Captivity. Because of its large and dynamic Jewish population, the tenth-century Arab historian Ahmed ar-Razi called it "Granada of the Jews." By 1066, the ibn Nagrelas, a family of Sephardic courtiers, were so powerful that envious Muslims became enraged at what they considered to be the arrogation of too much power by Jews and rose up, causing widespread destruction and Jewish flight. Moses ibn Ezra, one of the exiles, was among the city's most talented Hebrew poets and would nostalgically lament the demise of "beautiful Granada land" in his wanderings. Yet Jews remained in the city even after the persecutions and continued to participate in all aspects of life until its fall in 1492.

Other cities with strong, influential Jewish communities included Calatayud, its very name derived from the Arabic *Kalaat el-Yahud* (quarter of the Jews) and Mérida, from which many Sephardic families proudly claimed their origin. According to tradition, it was the first Spanish city founded by the Jerusalem exiles, making it the home of a special nobility and ancient aristocracy. Toledo, too, was an important center of Jewish life throughout the Visigothic and Muslim periods, retaining its premier position in both Jewish life and Castilian politics practically until the eve of the final expulsion of the Jews from Spain. Though always overshadowed by Córdoba, which would ever be regarded as their intellectual home, the Sephardic communities of the smaller cities with their mini-courts began to emerge with individual clarity in the ninth and tenth centuries. In the eleventh century, as they effectively replaced Córdoba, all of these independent Spanish kingdoms housed a Jewish courtier class along with a Jewish artistic circle that mirrored the court life of the fallen capital. But Spanish Jews did not confine themselves to these so-called royal cities of

Spain. They could also be found in organized urban concentrations, with their own residential area and scientific, artistic, and intellectual circles, in Barcelona, Saragossa, Tarragona, Valencia, and many other localities; and many also worked the land as vintners, farmers, and cultivators of grain.

Andalusia's prosperity percolated down to the Jewish and Christian middle classes in the ninth and tenth centuries, and they were able to share fully the Muslims' taste for acquiring luxury goods and decorative arts. In the Geniza trove, dowry lists from widely dispersed Mediterranean communities reveal that the Sephardic bourgeoisie accumulated expensively brocaded textiles, wall hangings, tapestries, and elaborate carpets from Egypt and Persia. Household inventories of merchants show that they owned private libraries that included medical and ethical texts.

A much more important indication of Sephardic assimilation, however, is the role of Jews as cultural intermediaries, a role that would in fact typify their position in Spain. They were well equipped to arbitrate between the mutually exclusive and hostile worlds of Christianity and Islam precisely because they lived in the heartland of Islam as well as on the Iberian peninsula, in Europe as well as in Africa, and never became totally parochial to any given place.

Eventually, individual Jewish personalities would become distinguished in this role. When the ninth-century emirs al-Hakam II and 'Abd ar-Rahman II decided to adopt the administrative practices of the Abbasids in Baghdad, one Jewish intermediary was particularly influential. Abu al-Nasr Mansur, music master for the latter ruler's court at Córdoba, was inspired to introduce sweeping innovations by importing one of Baghdad's virtuoso entertainers, a certain Ziryab. The newcomer's mandate to "civilize" the still backward Hispanics by teaching them Abbasid arts and manners was tantamount to a cultural revolution. Although Ziryab was potentially a rival, the Jewish musician convinced 'Abd ar-Rahman II to set him up in grand style and give him free reign to serve as the arbiter of taste. The foreigner soon won the confidence of the monarch, even enjoying special access to the royal private chambers through a secret passageway.

Not content merely to establish a music conservatory for the youth of the court and introduce innovative new musical instruments, Ziryab composed and taught music himself to the most talented women in the royal harem. He reformed etiquette (thus revolutionizing daily life) by introducing a set order to meals: soup, fish, main meat courses and fowl, sweets. Insisting upon the use of tableclothes as well as cutlery, he redesigned the wooden spoon in order to bring some refinement to the gluttonous table manners of the wealthy. In the same vein, he established glass factories to produce fine crystal goblets that were soon famous beyond Córdoba. Ziryab's influence extended to personal hygiene and fashion, for he introduced perfumes, cosmetics, depilatories, and toothpaste, set the vogue in hairstyles, prescribed separate wardrobes for summer and winter, and altered protocol to match the Persian customs of the luxurious Abbasid court. Not least, this innovator brought in astrologers from India and Jewish doctors from Iraq and North Africa. In sum, Ziryab's reforms would set the tone of Cordoban court life for something like thirty-five years and be disseminated quickly among the lesser kingdoms of Andalusia as well.

Political intrigues, too, were a fact of daily life in the courts of Spain, where there was no principle of orderly succession to power. Harems were large, and each of the wives pressed the claims of her son, while each rival advisor became enmeshed in the domestic quarrels and manumitted slaves rose up to take advantage of the palace rivalries and factionalism. Jewish translators and physicians employed in the palace could also become involved in the conspiracies. The rise to power of Samuel ibn Nagrela, refugee from Córdoba to Málaga and subsequently to Granada, was based upon his skills as a tax collector, his gifts as a writer, and, not least, his luck in backing a successful contender for the throne. Hostilities between the Berbers from North Africa and the Andalusians opened the doors of the courts to many ambitious politicians. Ibn Nagrela was briefly imprisoned in 1020 as a result of political intrigue but catapulted to the highest political position in Granada in the 1030s as a result of political adroitness. The stakes in these political intrigues were extremely high: a life of privilege or violent death, imprisonment or great fortune.

In Muslim Spain, in fact, individuals played a special role in the process of launching and then sustaining the era that became a Golden Age for the Sephardim. Historians of the Jews have been especially intrigued with the problem of defining and explaining such rare periods. How does such a golden era begin? What are its distinguishing hallmarks, and what brings it to an end? Obviously, the absence of persecution alone is not the defining factor.

One tantalizing line of investigation is the possible role played by the host culture in the emergence and articulation of new Jewish cultural forms. For instance, do Jews need to live in an interesting milieu in order to be culturally creative themselves? How absorbent must the minority culture be to partake fully of the culture of the majority? Of course, it is impossible to answer these questions fully without reference to the elusive process of cultural borrowing and adaptation in general. But it can certainly be said that a distinctive factor in Spain was the large number of unusually gifted Jewish individuals who succeeded in negotiating the process of cultural borrowing in a fashion all their own.

In the corridors of power of the dazzling courts of Andalusia, the wiliest and most talented courtiers—be they Muslim, Jew, or Christian—set the tone of an era. There could have been no Golden Age for the Jews of medieval Spain without the involvement of outstanding Sephardim in the government and its bureaucracy. But the notion of a golden age includes more than politics and administration. In Córdoba, Lucena, and Granada, for example, there was an exceptional flowering of Hebrew poetry, only one indication that this unique period in the history of Jews must be understood as a combination of political, artistic, intellectual, and social elements.[8]

In 929 'Abd ar-Rahman III proclaimed himself caliph of Córdoba and set out to pacify the warring Muslim factions on the peninsula in order to create a unified kingdom. In his view, one way to accomplish this aim was to make peace with Christians by offering them the opportunity to participate in affairs of state and by granting them religious freedom. His conciliatory attitude toward minorities, combined with his active encouragement of arts and commerce, ushered in a reign of tranquillity and affluence. His servants, who included Berbers, Arabs, manumitted slaves, Christians, and Jews, were adroitly exploited and balanced one against the other.

'Abd ar-Rahman III loved the ceremonial aspects of the caliphal office. In the somewhat inaccessible suburb of Córdoba known as Madinat az-Zahra he established a lavish court where he surrounded himself with a wide circle of men of means and taste, along with a host of craftsmen, skilled artisans, storytellers, jugglers and other entertainers, bookkeepers, gardeners, jewelers, and, of course, poets. A talented Jew or Christian might gain entrée through the recommendation of a Muslim friend connected with the court. A manumitted slave from Africa or

Eastern Europe could also rise, if he or she possessed special talents or was befriended by the "right" patron. Although no talent was rejected, Jews tended to have the skills considered especially useful to the new caliph.

An island of tolerance in the tenth century, the caliphate of Córboda was especially inviting to Jews because they confronted sporadic forced conversions in the Byzantine Empire and occasional outbursts of fundamentalist antagonism from Muslim rulers in the East. In North Africa, too, the consolidation of Fatimid rule was accompanied initially by warfare and tribal devastations.

Political power in Spain at this time was not broken down simply into Christian and Muslim blocs, for 'Abd ar-Rahman III's self-proclaimed caliphate presented a direct challenge to the established Abbasid caliphate in Baghdad, which viewed his actions as usurpation of power and overt rebellion. Muslim politics were further complicated by the emergence of the Fatimids in 909 in North Africa, a Shi'ite dynasty whose conquest of Egypt and Palestine in 969 destabilized the Mediterranean. The rivalry of these three great Islamic empires, each claiming legitimacy as the rightful heir to the mantel of Muhammed (the office of caliph being technically the successor to the Prophet), was mirrored in the rivalry of the European Christian powers of Byzantium and the Holy Roman Empire. The entire geopolitical situation induced 'Abd ar-Rahman III to turn his gaze toward Byzantium, the natural enemy of both the Abbasid and the Fatimid dynasties because of their geographical proximity, but he also had to remain wary of the movements of the Christian kings in the north of Spain. Upon his death in 961, his son al-Hakam II (961–76) continued the policy of expanding the power of the Andalusian kingdom while also supporting the arts.

Diplomatic missions flowed in and out of the lavish complex of palaces at Madinat az-Zahra amidst vivid trappings of power in luxuriously appointed quarters. At one point, reportedly, 'Abd ar-Rahman III lined the four-mile path to his palace from the city with soldiers to receive a delegation, while richly attired attendants waited at the gates. If an ambassador was not to his liking, the hapless diplomat might be kept waiting to present his credentials for as long as three years. His dealings with Germans, Catalans, Byzantines, Castilians, and rulers of smaller principalities called for multilingual talents and diplomatic aplomb.

The first mention of Jewish participation in the Umayyad caliph's court occurs in connection with diplomatic exchanges between 'Abd ar-Rahman and the emperor of Byzantium, Constantine VII Porphyrogenitus. Even prior to the emergence of Hasdai ibn Shaprut as a courtier in Córdoba, the Jews had equipped themselves to engage in new public roles.

The Sephardic courtiers of the Golden Age shared a cultural orientation and political ethos with the ruling Muslims. Their humanistic education was exceedingly broad, including a remarkable variety of subjects from astronomy to astrology, geometry to optics, calligraphy to rhetoric, philology to metrics. A client who sought advice from a Jewish physician would find himself speaking with a poet, philosopher, and linguist as well. The interdenominational court physicians regularly produced translations, a task that typically involved invention and commentary. A special emphasis on the arts and foreign tongues mirrored the prevailing Arab cultural mores that judged a man by his literary skills as well as his social graces. But as Sephardic fathers prepared their sons for their new roles in tenth-century Spanish society, cosmopolitanism and the secular sciences were not sufficient to assure the ambitious young courtiers a respected position in the Jewish community or, for that matter, in Jewish history. It was also essential to complete rigorous schooling in the Hebraic tradition, including the Bible and Midrash, Hebrew language study, the Talmud, and codes and commentaries. Although the secular and religious curricula were certainly disparate, one of the Sephardic intellectual's distinctive characteristics was an ability to blend these separate academic traditions, while bearing himself with sophistication and speaking with dignified eloquence. In actual fact, these courtier-intellectuals constituted only a small minority of the Jewish community, but because they were able to play multiple roles at court and articulately set down their (sometimes egoistic) autobiographies, they have shaped the way in which Sephardic history developed, was preserved, and is now perceived.

To some extent, the history of the Jews in Muslim Spain is indeed a history of the forceful, versatile personalities who charismatically dominated the Jewish communities while at the same time managing to negotiate their way in Gentile society. These multitalented individuals self-consciously integrated Jewish traditions with Arabic and Islamic culture in order to create something dynamically new. In fact, the Jewish people would not again experience such a thoroughgoing synthesis of Judaic culture with foreign elements until the modern era. As we shall see in detail later, poetry was the principal medium through which this process occurred, primarily in the Hebrew language, in a short but brilliant period of poetic innovation (950–1150). In addition, philosophy, mathematics, and the sciences provided fruitful opportunities for Jewish creativity and cultural borrowing.

It has often been remarked that Arab society has a special attachment to its language; poetry, in particular, is held in high esteem. In Andalusia, perfection in the use of Arabic was not only a prerequisite for public service, but refinement in diction and expression to the point of affectation, especially in court circles, was an avenue for rapid advancement. For the Arab, in fact, nuances of speech and ornamental expression were extraordinarily prized, and Muslim society exhibited a passion for eloquence, delighting especially in decorative details or arcane phrases that originated in the pre-Islamic period known as the *Jahiliya*. In addition, educated people were expected to be at home in a broad curriculum, derived from the ancient Greek classics, that had come to Spain from the East sometime in the ninth century.

No doubt understanding the implications for political success, the Sephardim quickly adapted this new curriculum to their own needs and also adopted some of the subtleties of Arabic. Indeed, since Jews had long emphasized the verbal over the visual or pictorial, they probably felt a special affinity for the Muslim's preference for language over image. Both groups rigorously (and comfortably, since religion was not an issue) studied the rhymed pronouncements and huge linguistic reservoir of the pre-Islamic bards. One generation of Jews learned Arab rhetoric, and their sons, to a remarkable degree, perfected and adopted the language as their own. Most of the philosophic and scientific classics composed by Sephardic scholars until the twelfth century, including some of the most profoundly Jewish texts, were written in Arabic.

The unusual reverence given the Arabic language by both Muslim and Jew cannot be overestimated. To the followers of the Prophet, the exceptional virtuosity of the language was proof of divine favor; to be specific, they believed (then and now) that the excellence of the Arabic in the Koran was proof of the perfection of Islam itself. The case for the cultural superiority of Arabic was made forthrightly in the eleventh century by al-Tha'alibi (d. 1038):

> Whoever loves the Prophet loves the Arabs, and whoever loves the Arabs loves the Arabic language in which the best of books was revealed. . . . Whomsoever God has guided to Islam . . . believes that Muhammed is the best of prophets . . . that the Arabs are the best of peoples . . . and that the Arabic language is the best of languages.[9]

Such flaunting of the alleged excellence of the Arabic language occurred often in verbal jousts at the Umayyad courts of medieval Spain. Not surprisingly, the Sephardic reaction was first to assert and explore the special qualities of Hebrew, but Jewish courtiers also engaged vigorously in the linguistic pyrotechnics displayed by the more gifted and inventive of the Muslim poets and elocutionists. Such inventiveness often led to glibness; many court activities were extremely superficial if not frivolous, and life at the center of Andalusian power frequently verged on the decadent. Later generations of Sephardic courtiers, in fact, would elegantly rue the laxity of their lives at court, but it is impossible to determine how far from the accepted code of Jewish decorum they actually strayed and how much their expression of remorse is simply a literary convention.[10]

To the medieval Jewish chronicler Abraham ibn Daud, the cultural renaissance of his people was embodied in two men, Hasdai the Nasi and Samuel the Nagid. The golden age was perhaps a century longer than the period spanned by their lives, the 950s through the 1050s, but they are indeed apt examples, for each vividly illustrates the amalgam of politics and poetry, worldliness and piety, Judaism and Islamic taste, that was unique to Spanish Jewry.

Hasdai (the Nasi) ibn Shaprut (915–70) was certainly not the first medieval Jew to become prominent in public life. Several Jewish figures also emerged from obscurity in Iraq at about the same time. But Hasdai is the first courtier Jew whose life we know in great detail and whose role was so central in launching a cultural movement that became identical with a new era.[11]

Ibn Shaprut was the scion of a learned family. His father Isaac, who hailed from Jaén in Eastern Andalusia, migrated to Córdoba before his son's birth, probably attracted by the intellectual and economic opportunities offered by this burgeoning cultural center. Wealthy, pious, and philanthropic, in his adopted city the elder ibn Shaprut endowed a synagogue and reportedly subsidized Jewish scholars. In keeping with the customs of his class, he provided his son with private tutors in Hebraic studies and languages. The young man also studied Latin with Christian clergy, as well as Romance, a Latin dialect that was the predecessor of Castilian and was spoken by many Christians and Muslims.

It was ibn Shaprut's singular medical skills, notably his discoveries of antidotes for poisons, that first gained him the attention of 'Abd ar-Rahman III and his courtiers. In the ongoing palace conspiracies, countless princes, whether in power or aspiring to the throne, fell victim to the poisons of the scheming harem members. In the early 940s, when the young scholar was barely thirty years old, he won many friends in the royal household with his rediscovery of an ancient compound, theriaca, that was considered to be effective not only against poisoning but also against jaundice, snakebites, impotence, and the plague. Overnight, he joined the council of doctors who customarily served the rulers.

Trusted physicians were often appointed to administrative posts; in this traditional fashion, Hasdai embarked upon his political career and quickly made a mark for himself, particularly in dealing with customs revenues. One position led to another as he gained the caliph's confidence, for the gratitude of 'Abd ar-Rahman proved to be as large as his colossal architectural ambitions and his need for money to fulfill them. Before long, the ruler appointed him head of the Jewish community, a position known as *nasi* (prince) among the Jews, and eventually he was entrusted with sensitive diplomatic negotiations on behalf of the caliphate. Because the occasional alliances Muslim rulers formed with Christian power could irritate the sensibilities and provoke the animosity of the Islamic religious establishment, it was not uncommon to make discreet use of Jews or Christians as diplomats. Jews were preferable, of course, since they had no natural alliances with Córdoba's Christian rivals and therefore posed no political threat.

Like other men of his class, whether Jewish, Muslim, or Christian, Hasdai surrounded himself with cultivated spirits and young, gifted talent; support of such talent was considered to be a mark of quality. Soirées in the courtier's presence or home were scintillating affairs. Fathers exhorted their sons, as no doubt Hasdai's father had, to make their way among the learned, to tend to the poor without fee, to seek the company of poets, and to write with elegance and learning. Hasdai and his colleagues among the emerging Sephardic leadership have been described as "worldly Orthodox Jews, who were as chic in Arab tastes as they were fastidious in their Jewish ones." In a phrase, they combined "Torah, Greek wisdom, and poetry."[12]

Hasdai ibn Shaprut was able to benefit enormously from an extraordinary diplomatic opportunity. In the late 940s, the interests of the Christian emperor of Byzantium, Constantine VII, began to coincide with those of the Cordoban caliphate. The Abbasids of Baghdad, from whom Spain wanted to be completely independent, were attacking the Byzantine Empire. In addition, both Constantine and 'Abd ar-Rahman showed a special interest in the arts and sciences and were equally unaffected by the traditional theological inhibitions that kept Christendom and Islam apart. Their common intellectual interests were complemented by their shared antagonism toward the caliph of Baghdad, in keeping with the old Arab adage, "The enemies of my enemies are my friends." In opening their diplomatic negotiations with each other, however, they had to confront the problem of finding someone who could conduct delicate conversations between a Christian and a Muslim power in this era of warring faiths. Because of his substantial gifts as a translator and negotiator, ibn Shaprut rose from relative obscurity to prominence in the sensitive negotiations between Spain and Byzantium.

His first task was a matter of translation. Typically, the diplomatic delegations of Europe, especially Byzantium, would be welcomed to Madinat az-Zahra with great ceremony, including the declamation of poetry composed for the occasion, and the exchange of valuable gifts such as exotic animals, exquisite fabrics, and important books. One exceptional gift from Constantine, however, a rare first-century Greek manuscript by Dioscorides, posed a problem. *De Materia Medica,* considered to be a classic textbook for pharmacology, was not entirely unknown in Spain, having been translated into Arabic in Baghdad in the ninth century. But the translation was so flawed that many of the herbs and remedies described were unidentifiable. Because none of the caliph's court translators knew Greek, ar-Rahman asked the emperor to send help, whereupon a certain Nicholas, a monk learned in Greek and Latin, was dispatched from Constantinople forthwith. Hasdai was part of an ecumenical team of translators appointed to work with this Byzantine, including a Greek-speaking Sicilian Arab and five Andalusian Muslims. Nicholas translated from the Greek to Latin, Hasdai rendered the Latin into Arabic. Previously, medical students had been forced either to travel to Baghdad for their scientific training or to learn from instructors imported from the East. Because the Cordoban courtier-rabbi was successful in translating the prized medical work, the caliphate now began to function as an independent scientific center, and Hasdai's reputation grew enormously: not merely because he had demonstrated linguistic skill but because his achievement furthered Spain's autonomy, a cultural as well as political aim that was important to both Muslims and Jews.

Thereafter, Hasdai would be entrusted with several challenging diplomatic assignments that involved the Christian kingdoms to the north, like Burgundy or Léon, and also the German emperor Otto I (936–73). In his role as statesman, Hasdai reveals the other face of the Sephardic Jewish courtier: his continuing sense of responsibility to the Jewish community. He and his like saw themselves as heirs to such biblical personalities as Joseph, Daniel, and Esther, all of whom had worked in foreign courts for the welfare of their fellow Jews. In turn, Hasdai's career became the prototype of Sephardic leadership for subsequent generations; court influence, political connections, and aristocratic bearing were to be considered admirable only when used in the combined role of courtier-defender to accomplish "the great good for Israel." Patronage of Jewish learning was part of this amalgam.

Records show, for example, that when Hasdai went abroad on a diplomatic mission to conduct state affairs he would inquire about the welfare of beleaguered Jewish communities at every opportunity. Given his reputation, Jews would write to describe their plight, confident that they could rely upon his assistance. From surviving letters, we learn that the Jews of southern Italy were threatened with religious persecution and that the government banned and confiscated their books. In addition, scholars were arrested for teaching Judaism and several were in danger of execution. Sketchy accounts also reveal that the Byzantine emperor Romanus I Lekapenos, who ruled from 919 to 944, introduced sweeping anti-Jewish measures in his realm. In defense of Byzantine Jewry, ibn Shaprut wrote two letters to Empress Helena and had them delivered by 'Abd ar-Rahman's envoy in 948, presumably having gained the caliph's permission to dispatch personal mail with an official diplomatic envoy. In one strongly worded letter to the empress, who was the real power behind the throne, he reminded her that his Islamic monarch was tolerant of the numerous Christians in Spain. In a separate incident, he also undertook a defense of the Jews of Toulouse. Apparently, they were forced to offer thirty pounds of wax for church candles annually and present this special tax at the cathedral gate on Easter Eve, a requirement that was clearly provocative. In addition, as each Jew made his offering, the bishop would respond with a resounding slap. We do not know from the surviving correspondence whether or not ibn Shaprut was successful in having these humiliating ceremonies eliminated, but the very existence of a "prince of Israel" in Islamic Spain was seen far and wide as proof and consolation that God had not abandoned his people.

Above all else, however, it was ibn Shaprut's elegant Hebrew correspondence with Joseph, king of the Khazars, that would be lovingly preserved by the Jews in Spain and circulated for centuries because it so poignantly expressed his exemplary personal qualities. The Khazars were nomadic Turkish tribes who had wandered for centuries in the inaccessible Central Asian region where Byzantine and Muslim borders met. By the seventh century, their kingdom had spread to the Crimea and encompassed several cities that contained Jewish, Muslim, and Christian settlers. During waves of Byzantine persecution in the eighth century, the Khazars had more than once given refuge to Jews. In fact, finding themselves caught between the warring armies of Byzantium and Islam and pressed by both regimes to convert, the Khazars converted to Judaism themselves some time in the eighth century. By the ninth century, Khazaria covered much of Russia in a vast area between the Caucasus, the Caspian Sea, the Volga, and the Dnieper.

News of this sovereign Jewish kingdom filtered back to the West, arousing hopes and yearnings among Jews there, who had often smarted under the taunts that their dispersion and impotence were proof of rejection by God. At the very least, existence of the Khazar state nurtured Jewish feelings of self-esteem. As Hasdai himself confessed to Joseph, the Khazar king, "We have been cast down from our glory and have nothing to reply when they say daily unto us, 'Every other people has its kingdom, but of yours there is no memorial on the earth.' " He had been moved to address his royal co-religionist with joy: "Blessed be the Lord of Israel, who has not left us without a kinsman as defender nor suffered the tribes of Israel to be without an independent kingdom."[13]

On a more "practical" level, Hasdai asked Joseph whether he possessed secret knowledge of when the Jewish dispersion would end and all Jews be gathered together by their Messiah and reconstituted as a nation in the land of Israel. This query was neither casual nor unusual. During the Middle Ages the Jews in Muslim lands, particularly the Sephardim, repeatedly searched for facts or clues to help them calculate the date of the Messiah's coming and the end of Jewish exile. Messianic speculation of this nature engaged some of the best minds in Spain, including such leading Jewish figures in subsequent centuries as Solomon ibn Gabirol, Abraham ibn Daud, Abraham bar Hiyya, Judah ha-Levi, Moses Maimonides, Moses ibn Ezra, and Isaac Abrabanel.[14] These yearnings were often channeled into poetry, sometimes into quasi-political movements that involved armed uprisings to bring an end to statelessness and hasten the redemption. The activists produced false messiahs with some regularity. Of course, the failure of each movement would exacerbate dependency, but the expectancy and longings of the masses were not destroyed. The mere knowledge of the Khazar autonomy provided a consolation of sorts.

Before Hasdai began his correspondence with King Joseph, he had found his curiosity mounting as travelers brought back information about the unlikely kingdom. When Byzantine diplomats visited in Córdoba, he questioned them intensely. He decided to send his own emissary, Isaac bar Nathan, to Khazaria in the summer of 946. But the Byzantines were afraid that Córdoba might enter into a diplomatic relationship with a northern neighbor that was hostile and aggressive to the Christian empire, and they refused his request to provide Isaac with a ship and let him proceed northward from Constantinople. Isaac was able to obtain a detailed description of the Khazar kingdom, however, from a Khazar Jew he met in Constantinople. Subsequently, Hasdai wrote a letter of introduction to King Joseph that eventually reached Khazaria by a circuitous route through the Balkans and Eastern Europe. In his reply, the Khazar ruler explained in detail the disputations between Muslim, Christian, and Jew that had led to the nation's adoption of a synchretistic form of Judaism. He could supply no secret knowledge about the date of redemption but shared Hasdai's messianic yearnings. The two men corresponded as one royal officer to another, with Hasdai proudly describing his exalted position as well as that of all Jews in Spain.

And indeed, at home, this successful diplomat was bringing about an astonishing change within his own community. Until his ascendancy, Andalusian Jews had typically turned to Baghdad's rabbinic scholars for instruction and guidance, much as Islamic Spain, despite political rivalry with the Abbasid dynasty, still turned to the East for cultural leadership. The acknowledgement of the preeminence of the *gaonim,* or intellectual leaders of the Eastern rabbinical academies (the Yeshivot of Sura, and Pumbeditha in Baghdad), as the ultimate interpreters of Jewish law for the entire diaspora was part of a continuous tradition of Jewish learning in Iraq stretching back hundreds of years to the creation of the Babylonian Talmud. Traveling merchants took donations to the academies for their upkeep and also brought along questions about the application of Jewish law to various life situations.

But, with Hasdai playing a central role, the Andalusian Jewish community entered a new era of independence and cultural autonomy

in the tenth century. First, he actively patronized scholars and founded
an academy of learning in Córdoba under the direction of the immigrant scholar, Moses ben Hanoch. When the Sura Talmudic academy
was temporarily closed, he procured its library, ensuring that the Jews
of Andalusia would become less dependent on the East for religious
guidance. No longer, for example, did they have to ask Baghdad to
determine the Judaic calendar. In establishing this new cultural autonomy, Hasdai drew heavily upon the model of Babylonia, just as 'Abd
ar-Rahman drew upon the Abbasids. Still, Sephardic leadership was not
merely a reflection of Muslim attitudes but a result of the process of
Jewish maturation in Spain, even though some parallels with Baghdad
may have been intended. For example, Hasdai's civil authority within
the Jewish community of Córdoba was not unlike that of the Jewish
"civil leader" (*exilarch* or *rosh ha-golah*) in the Abbasid capital; similarly,
religious authority for the Sephardim was the province of the *Rosh
Yeshiva* (Moses ben Hanoch, in Hasdai's day), a position something
like that of the Babylonian *gaon*. Even so, the analogy between Spain
and Baghdad should not be overemphasized, since Hasdai's career as
courtier-rabbi was quite unlike any leadership role in the East.[15]

Once news of the intellectual ferment in Córdoba began to circulate, gifted scholars from North Africa and Egypt followed in the footsteps of the artisans and merchants who had earlier come to Spain to
seek their fortune. It is worth mentioning that some of them would find
Hasdai a mercurial patron. Although he enjoyed the competition
among the poets and was duly flattered by their praise, he was capable
of suddenly turning against a favorite and dismissing him in disgrace, or
worse. He reportedly not only discarded his secretary Menahem ibn
Saruq in favor of a newcomer from North Africa, Dunash ben Labrat,
but also had the hapless poet thrown into prison.

Such power in the hands of a Sephardic courtier reaches its apogee in
the career of Samuel ibn Nagrela (993–1055), known as Samuel the
Nagid. He rose to the highest position of state, an astonishing achievement even in the tenth- and eleventh-century Spain that temporarily
lowered the boundaries between Jew, Muslim, and Christian. An accomplished statesman who probably attained the position of vizier in
the Kingdom of Granada, ibn Nagrela exhibited the standard multi-

plicity of talents—gifted Hebrew poet and patron of poets, biblical commentator and exegete philosopher. But his most impressive feats were performed as the leader of Muslim armies.

An unconventional man living in unusual times, he would win power in part because of the special conditions connected with the downfall of Córdoba. 'Abd ar-Rahman III's immediate successor, Al-Hakam II (961–76), was able to continue the great caliph's political and cultural policies until his death. But then Andalusia was engulfed by the Arab political instability that marked each moment of succession. Eventually, over thirty petty Muslim kingdoms (the-so-called party kingdoms) would emerge. From the perspective of Jewish history, this fragmentation of Muslim power and continuing internecine warfare had two important results. On the one hand, opportunities for Sephardic courtiers increased dramatically. The proliferation of overnight kings, insecure and sensibly fearful of relying upon the loyalty of their own ministers or relatives, turned to Jews to further their political aims. Since each of these minor courts had its own system of patronage, there was a wide array of openings available to the courtier-rabbis. On the other hand, the growing disorder encouraged Christian attempts to reconquer Spain, thus fanning the flames of Islamic fundamentalism. Consequently, Jews were increasingly caught between what they called the forces of Edom (Christianity) and Ishmael (Islam). Especially after the fall of Toledo to the Christians in 1085, Jewish intellectuals and *bon vivants* of the Muslim courts began to feel estranged and vulnerable, even as they continued their privileged lives under the returning Catholic princes.

Only against this background can we fully understand the meteoric career of Samuel ibn Nagrela. Born in Córdoba in 993, he was educated both by his father and by the son of the revered *Rosh Yeshivah* Moses ben Hanoch. He imbibed the family tradition of descent from the nobility of Mérida and from ancient Levites who were poets in the Temple of Jerusalem; throughout his life, in fact, he would show particular pride in this aristocratic lineage, claiming direct descent from King David. So gifted in rabbinics that he tried his hand at serious Talmudic scholarship while still young, he also trained in the classical curriculum of the courtiers, including ancient sciences and Arab poetics. Undoubtedly, he drew inspiration from the career of Hasdai ibn Shaprut, who had died only a generation before and whose achievements were recalled in detail in the Jewish community of Córdoba.

Young Nagrela's precocity apparently also extended to Islamic theology, for he is reported to have met and exchanged views with ibn Hazm, greatest of the Spanish Muslim theologians. On one occasion, they vigorously debated the concept of "the chosen," with the Jewish youth confidently arguing the traditional biblical view of Israel's special relationship with God. Such interfaith dialogues were not approved by official Muslim religious circles or by the ideology of Islam, but because of the relaxed religiosity and tolerance that still characterized the last years of the Cordoban caliphate, they were probably not uncommon. Even so, they surely required a great deal of assurance on the part of the Jewish participant.

In 1013, when Nagrela was just twenty years old, the caliphate of Córdoba dissolved. The breakup of Andalusia had begun four years before when Berbers, along with former Slavs known as Saqaliba and "Andalusians" (i.e., all Muslims of Arab and Iberian stock), tore the country apart in internecine warfare. In the process, a Berber force sacked and destroyed Córdoba, massacring its inhabitants, pillaging the city, and burning the palace complex to the ground. The unity of the peninsula was sundered as the three groups parceled out the country into rival kingdoms. One group of Berbers, known as the Hammudids, controlled the southern coast up to Granada, ruling Málaga and Algeciras. A rival Berber dynasty, the Zirids, took control of Granada. But of the several Andalusian dynasties, the Abbadids of Seville were the strongest, eventually taking Córdoba. Seville would remain the most brilliant successor to Córdoba until its reconquest by the Christians in 1248. The frequent clashes involving these so-called "party kings" gave the Christian princes in the north the opportunity to begin their reconquest. The Nagrela family fled to Granada, where Samuel's remarkable epistolary and calligraphic skills reportedly attracted the attention of a minister to King Habbus, the town's Berber ruler. This tale of "discovery," however, bears the fanciful hallmarks of Islamic legend. It is much more likely that Nagrela attracted the king's notice by saving him from conspirators plotting a coup d'état. Later, by supporting a successful contender for the throne named Badis, he would rise to the highest political position in Granada. A proud man sumptuously attired in silks for his court appearances, Nagrela wielded his considerable power with intelligence and prudence.

But his lofty position in the Muslim state was inherently dangerous, for it conflicted with both the letter and spirit of traditional Islam. For a Jew to be accepted as physician or financier or diplomat was one thing; a Jewish vizier was another matter entirely. Roundly cursing the "miserable worms" who opposed him, Nagrela was forced out of office in 1020 under obscure circumstances, then brought back to power when the political tides turned. Still, he did not lose his characteristic self-confidence. He would write poetry proclaiming his nobility and comparing his feats on the battlefield with those of ancient biblical heroes. Such poems were composed during the heat of actual battle, as he led the armies of Granada from 1038 to 1056. Unusually for a medieval Jew, he was evidently thrilled by the experience of warfare, dwelling often upon the personal satisfaction he received from military success and graphically evoking the ferocity of Arab and Berber warriors.

It was not only the novelty of his political power, military prowess, and battle poetry that assured Nagrela fame among Spanish Jews, however, for he was also an accomplished Talmudic scholar and polemicist. A generous patron to some of the leading Hebrew poets and students of Torah in his day, he purchased many important books for Spain, reinforcing the country's growing cultural independence by assuring that copies were made for several communities and individual scholars. The first known owner of a great private library, he was important in establishing the Sephardic tradition of placing value on fine books. In addition, his endowments supported learning in Iraq, the Maghreb, Sicily, and Egypt, as well as the Jewish academies in Palestine.

It is difficult to determine precisely what led to the downfall of Nagrela and his family. One factor may have been the escalation of his debates with his Muslim interlocutor, ibn Hazm. In one particularly audacious treatise, Nagrela pointed out numerous inconsistencies and contradictions in the Koran; Ibn Hazm responded with a brilliant counterdefense, attacking similar weaknesses in the Bible and taunting the Jews for their loss of sovereignty and temporal power. When the daring Nagrela parried by pointing to the continuous line of Jewish grandees in Baghdad and Spain, his Islamic opponent thundered that not only should the arrogance of this Jew be condemned and his name blotted out, but that the king who had elevated him should also be eliminated. He warned Badis to "stay far away from these impure, evil-smelling, unclean people, upon whom God has inflicted curse and malediction, contempt and abasement, infamy, ire, degradation and vileness as upon no other people." These words of the sage inspired others. Around 1066, the Muslim polemicist Abu Ishaq wrote a fierce tirade against Joseph ibn Nagrela and condemned the king "who has chosen an infidel as a secretary," thus enabling the Jews of Granada to become "great and proud and arrogant."[16] He exhorts his co-religionists to rise up against

Nagrela and the entire Sephardic community, defending such an action as legitimate since the Jews had broken their contractual arrangement with the Muslim community by seizing excessive power.

For all his wisdom and experience, Samuel ibn Nagrela seems not to have understood that mounting religiosity among the Muslims was making his situation increasingly perilous. Writing criticism of the Koran or leading the armies of Islam into battle did not suit the limitations on a Jew's position in the Muslim world as laid down in the days of the Prophet. Moreover, this *nagid* (head of the Jewish community) of the Jews lived ostentatiously on a hilltop commanding a view of the River Vega, hosting banquets and salons, winefests and witty encounters between Jewish and Muslim court favorites. His exalted position brought a fresh influx of Jews into Granada, while he continued to move freely (though protesting deep personal misgivings) in the charmed political circles of the vulgar Berber princes who held power. The Muslim masses were not captivated. They saw an infidel strutting on the battlefield with sword unsheathed, wearing ornamental robes embroidered with Koranic verses. How little Nagrela understood their resentment became clear when he bequeathed his title, rank, and position to his less able son Joseph. Muslim precept was usually much harsher than practice, but that harshness could be easily invoked with a shift in the political wind, and Andalusian tolerance eventually wore thin, with calamitous results. In 1066 thousands of Jews in Granada were slaughtered, the Nagrela family was toppled, and Jewish prominence throughout the numerous party kingdoms was quashed.

These petty kingdoms themselves would last only until 1091, but in their brief existence these "turbaned Italian republics" had produced a flourishing culture, even as they battled with each other to replace the defunct caliphate of Córdoba. Meanwhile, the Christian reconquest went forward. When Toledo fell in 1085, the prince of Seville sought assistance from the Almoravid kingdom of Morocco, a choice that was particularly unfortunate for non-Muslims. Indeed, the Almoravid ruler, Yusuf ibn Tashufin (1090–1106), would temporarily succeed in reuniting Andalusia under one crown, but his devotion to the ascetic Malikite form of Islam spelled the end of the hedonistic culture of the Golden Age. The easygoing interaction of Muslims with Jews and Christians was one of the first casualties. In addition, Islamic judges now set a serious public tone, and stricter enforcement of Koranic principles accompanied a strong opposition to *belles lettres* and the entire Andalusian secular cultural enterprise. As life became more restrictive for both Jews and Christians, they began to migrate to Christian Spain. The Golden Age thus began drawing to a close decades before 1147, when the invasion of the zealously fundamentalist Almohad Muslims from North Africa would set off a wave of pogroms and spur Jewish flight. Yet before this annihilation of Jewish life in medieval Muslim Spain, the Sephardim produced an outpouring of Hebrew secular and religious poetry unmatched in any other previous period of Jewish history.

3

The Golden Era

The Emergence of Sephardic Civilization

They mingled among the nations and learned their ways.

—Psalms 106:35

In the spring of 1140 Judah Halevi, renouncing the "good life," bid farewell to Spain. His decision caused astonishment. The darling of the court, he was at the peak of his poetic and philosophical powers and the height of his career, his every poem eagerly awaited and recited by Jews throughout the nation's Muslim and Christian realms. Having embraced Andalusian culture and attained a position that included royal favors as well as fame, he renounced everything in order to return to the land of Israel, supposedly to weep amid the ruins of Zion. In some ways, Halevi's surprising decision signals the end of an era, but it was not wholly inconsistent with the complex, paradoxical personality of this singular character of the Golden Age.

Seven years after Halevi's departure from Spain, the Andalusian experiment of Muslim-Jewish symbiosis ended abruptly with the invasion of a zealous fundamentalist dynasty from North Africa, the Almohades. The youthful Moses Maimonides and his family were forced to become refugees at this time, drifting from one Andalusian city to the next. But Halevi had not been clairvoyant: his flight reflected the pressures upon courtier Jews caught between Jewish loyalties and the attractions of Arab culture.

Judah Halevi was born in Tudela, the northernmost outpost of Muslim rule, in 1075. Reared in the Andalusian Judeo-Arabic cultural tradition, he received his Hebrew education from Isaac Alfasi in Lucena, then became secretary to the great scholar's illustrious successor, Joseph ibn Migash. For a while, he lived in Seville and Granada, savoring the pleasures of Muslim culture, but his budding career coincided with the fall of Toledo to the Christians in 1085 and the conquest of Granada by the Almoravids in 1090. The Jews of Spain found themselves attacked by all of the warring powers in their recurrent battles on the peninsula. In 1096 the Christian-Muslim conflict reverberated throughout the Mediterranean as Europe's Christians set out to recapture the Holy Land from Islam. Halevi, a sensitive artist, could not avoid confronting the historical events swirling around him.

His life marks the zenith of the Golden Age but also reflects the Jewish community's subsequent rejection of its ideals. Until the age of fifty, Halevi was the consummate courtier—*bon vivant,* court doctor in Córdoba, respected communal leader, patron of talents. He wrote poems in almost every genre then fashionable, leaving an enormous *oeuvre* that is integral to the Sephardic and Ashkenazic prayerbooks. His gifts were first discovered during a literary evening when, as an unknown youth, he exhibited a genius for poetic improvisation before the assembly of leisured, educated gentlemen. This successful debut led to lifelong friendship with the Granadan poet, Moses ibn Ezra. Throughout his brilliant career, Halevi remained close to the royal court, whether in Spain or later in Egypt and was regarded as the "quintessence and embodiment" of Andalusia, but he described himself as deeply divided, a man "whose life is Spain and whose destination is Jerusalem." This paradox requires a closer look at the place of the poet in the Jewish cultural revolution in Spain.[1]

The poetic revolution that symbolizes the era began inconspicuously even before Hasdai ibn Shaprut invited Jewish talent from North Africa and the Near East to join the coterie of literati who adorned his private "court." At the end of the ninth century, experiments in prosody produced a new form of poetry that lay somewhere between classical Hebrew and Arabic meter. Such seemingly "literary" developments actually excited the imagination of the larger society; at social gatherings, Jews heatedly debated fine points of philology. By Hasdai's day, a breakthrough in Hebrew poetic form occurred as a result of the professional rivalry between two gifted poets in his service, Dunash ben Labrat and Menahem ibn Saruq. In their venomous exchanges Dunash daringly introduced Arabic rhymes and meter into Hebrew, thereby inventing tools that could be used for a poetic revolution. New forms would open the way for new poetic content, a process aided by the kinship between the two languages.

Poetry in the ancient Hebrew tradition, especially in the Bible (which served as the model for all subsequent poetry), had neither meter or rhyme, relying instead for poetic effect upon the use of parallelism. Postbiblical Hebrew poetry, at least the examples Jews chose to preserve before the Golden Age in Spain, was written in this prefixed mold of accepted conventions and earmarked for designated places in the liturgy. The new poetry that emerged in tenth-century Córdoba, however, utilized Arab forms that derived from the pre-Islamic literary tradition. One was the *muwashshah,* a strophic verse form consisting of five or six stanzas and a final couplet, written either in the colloquial tongue or in Romance. Another form adopted for Jewish secular and liturgical purposes was known as the *zajal.* These prosodic innovations were more radical than might at first appear, for the Arab forms were associated with popular street tunes, love songs, and drinking songs. But the Islamic motifs and conventions were soon refashioned by the Sephardic poets and interwoven with Hebrew, especially biblical, traditions, producing a new poetry remarkable both for its brilliant adaptation of Arab themes and skillful interlacing of philosophical and scientific concepts. Not only Jewish secular poetry but also religious works were dramatically transformed and flourished in this atmosphere of cultural borrowing.[2]

Poetry would become the finest expression of the two centuries of Golden Age culture, but almost as remarkable were the achievements in Arab philosophy, medicine, science, music, song, dance, and the visual arts. In addition, despite its elitism, the amalgam of power, poetry, philosophy, and science touched several classes outside the courts, not just the powerful. A casual tourist traversing the lanes of Seville, Granada, or Málaga could delight in the sounds of the strumming of a lute accompanying a Hebrew song, possibly mixed with the muffled laughter of an inebriated group of nocturnal revelers. In countless courtyards, along the verdant river banks, or beside bubbling fountains in shaded patios, middle-class Sephardic men would be singing of the vagaries of friendship, the beauty of women or young men, the idleness of youth, and the continuing exile of the Jews. The secular themes of their Hebrew and Arabic songs would be repeated in similar social settings among their Muslim and Christian neighbors, in Arabic and Romance. A society of professional poets was emerging, and their verses were recited in courts, salons, on the streets, and at exclusive parties. Surprisingly, their poems were also declaimed in the synagogues and on the battlefield.

Andalusia was not alone in encouraging this flowering of poetry, for the Jewish consumers of the new culture comprised an international class of merchants and craftsmen so well-grounded in Hebrew that they could appreciate the allusive cleverness of a newly coined phrase or rhyme. In Baghdad, Kairouan, Muslim Sicily, or Cairo, poetic entertainment was also a part of leisure activity; as works traveled from city to city, a poem that struck the fancy of worshippers might be incorporated into the local liturgy. Research in the Hebrew language had, in fact, been born in Baghdad and North Africa, where linguistics and grammar were considered integral to a Jewish education. Ironically, then, the medieval Arab city became the venue of a new linguistic and poetic sensibility in the Judaic tradition.

In this environment, any Jew pretending to good breeding was expected to learn Arabic linguistics, too. But Spain stood above other Muslim cultural centers because of the sheer volume and intensity of its literary outpouring, as well as the participation of virtuosos from all three major religions. Andalusian Jews consciously set their minds to mastering the Arab cultural curriculum of grammar, poetics, and science through disciplined study. (A parallel situation would have been inconceivable in Christian Europe, for Latin culture was considered indistinguishable from the Church and thus completely beyond the pale for Jews.)

The popularity, not to say omnipresence, of poetry in the daily life of Andalusia is almost staggering. A poem would be dispatched by the poet on perfumed stationery; the recipient might have it read aloud to the accompaniment of music. The secretaries to statesmen were expected not only to compose official correspondence in artistically formed script but also to dash off poems for special occasions. Statesmen themselves might produce government documents, such as passports, in rhymed prose. Now that elegance in the use of language was not considered the exclusive preserve of the Muslim, any practitioner of rhetoric could gain access to the seat of power, as did Hasdai ibn Shaprut and Samuel ibn Nagrela. (It should be stressed that Jews did not discover how to write poetry because of Arab influence; they had been writing communal poetry for at least half a millennium. Rather, the Hebrew poets in Spain were the first to confront and manipulate a literary tradition not their own.)

Professional poets, dependent upon the whims of their patrons, often wrote panegyrics as well as special poems for family occasions. A disproportionate number of patrons, of course, were courtiers who were also men of learning, and they were influential in the careers of many poets. The writer was expected to act as his sponsor's official secretary and public relations official, ever alert to prepare poems that would enhance the reputation of the patron or demolish his foes. (Predictably, a number of such works suffer from excessive exaggeration and flattery.) Not infrequently, posterity knows the patron only through the efforts of the poet, as with Yequtiel ibn Hassan, a courtier in Saragossa who has survived obscurity solely because of his encouragement of the great poetic genius, Solomon ibn Gabirol. When Yequtiel was murdered, his protégé was forced to flee, but composed a moving elegy to the magnanimity of his deceased sponsor and protector, as we will see later in this chapter. Gabirol, like many other poets, would serve several masters in his short life (1020–57?).

When paper was introduced into the Islamic world in the ninth century by Chinese merchants, books became more affordable and readily available throughout the West. The appearance in Spain of Jewish classics from the great centers of learning in Baghdad helped the local community assert its religious and cultural independence from the East. Both ibn Shaprut and ibn Nagrela actively acquired books from abroad for this purpose. As is clear from the property lists of the Cairo Geniza, where such books are set down as prized possessions, the scholar-merchant was a common figure in the Egyptian, North African, or Spanish Jewish community. The intellectual value of books for Jews of the period has been embodied in the ethical will that Judah ibn Tibbon, "the father of translators," left to his son:

> Go over your Hebrew books every month, the Arabic ones once in two months, and the bound volumes once in three months. Arrange everything in good order so that you need not go to the trouble of searching for a book when you need it.[3]

Love of books went hand in hand with love and encouragement of the written word. Book collecting would continue as an active tradition until the 1492 expulsion, when refugee scholars would describe the loss of their libraries as the most bitter consequence of exile. In more than one case involving a famous scholar, moreover, books were somehow salvaged from destruction only to come in handy as ransom money for the ill-fated owner.

Most of the poets of the Golden Age worked in a variety of literary disciplines. Gabirol, for example, produced excellent works of philosophy, grammar, and ethics as well as a prolific outpouring of poetry. He claims that at age sixteen he composed a 400-verse poem setting forth the rules of Hebrew grammar. Nagrela, as we have seen, was a substantial Talmudist and polemicist; he was also a versatile and prolific poet and grammarian, who wrote several treatises in philology. Perhaps surprisingly, his political prowess as vizier and military leader seems to have enhanced rather than diminished his poetic skills. Judah Halevi (1075–1141) was equally at home in religious and secular poetry, philosophy and medicine. Hasdai ibn Shaprut's grandson, who mastered music in both theory and practice, also excelled in speculative philosophy and politics, rising to the position of vizier to the king of Saragossa in 1066. He was proficient in arithmetic, geometry, physics, logic, and Arabic. Abraham ibn Ezra (1089–1164), a biblical exegete of extraordinary erudition, was also accomplished as poet, grammarian, storyteller, astrologer, and mathematician. Much to the delight of contemporary and future audiences, he composed many linguistic riddles. Towering above all of these writers, however, was Moses Maimonides (1135–1204), a giant in almost every field of learning but poetry. These literary figures worked with Arabic as the foundation stone of the poetic revolution, just as the language had been the key to politics for their predecessors. Widely diffused among all the peoples in Muslim lands by the tenth century, Arabic was the medium of science, administration, and the marketplace. The scientific and philosophical works composed by the Sephardic Jews were usually written in the Arabic language but in Hebrew script, thereby further synthesizing the Islamic heritage with their own. By contrast, their poetry was in Hebrew, precisely because they wanted to show off the beauty of their language and of the Bible. The combinations of the two languages, so akin in so many ways, led Jews to devise new modes of Hebrew verse as adaptation of Hebrew to Arabic took place. Like their Arab contemporaries, the Jewish poets were preoccupied with the theory of poetry, and one of them, Moses ibn Ezra, wrote an ars poetica, *Shirat Yisrael*.

As the careers of the courtier-rabbis show so clearly, the use of elegant Arabic was highly prized in Muslim society, but it was never the sole language used in Spain. Hebrew and Romance were also considered instruments of subtle expression and were developed specifically for poetic purposes; on occasion, Jewish poets used all three languages within a single poem. Halevi, for example, wrote Hebrew love poems with final stanzas or poetic refrains in Romance, thus gifting later generations with some of the oldest examples of this medieval Spanish language. In some cases, a Sephardic poet would transcribe the final Spanish lyrics of a love poem in Hebrew. Nagrela wrote poetry in Aramaic, although the language had been primarily confined to Jewish legal literature. Further, the exploration of various languages took place in an atmosphere of curiosity about language in general. Early in the poetic renaissance, dictionaries and manuals of poetry were compiled, and Hasdai supported the scholars Menahem ibn Saruq and Dunash ben Labrat in their studies of comparative linguistics. Gabirol's long poem on Hebrew grammar was part of this activity.

These and other linguists were heirs to a tradition of philological studies that had originated in Baghdad or North Africa and been transported to Spain by immigrant scholars. By studying the grammatical foundations of Hebrew, it was possible to enrich the language by coining words not found in the Bible. This was particularly important because, unlike Arabic, Hebrew had not been a spoken language for centuries and therefore had a somewhat limited vocabulary. Much like Arabic, however, it is a language in which minute changes in vocalization can produce major changes in meaning; therefore, the work of the philologists was crucial in defining the rationale for linguistic expansion.

Far from being simply an intellectual exercise, however, the new experiments with Hebrew were motivated by profound ideological aims. The Muslim claims that the Koran represented the perfect expression of God's will and speech had a marked effect upon the Jews, who were encouraged to delve into the text of the Bible in order to discover and exalt the special beauties of their own tradition. Another stimulus to biblical studies was the challenge from the Karaites, a Jewish sect that emerged in Baghdad in the eighth century and spread to Egypt, Palestine, North Africa, and Spain, becoming a force to reckon with in Iberia by the tenth and eleventh centuries. They were outspokenly opposed to using the Talmud and rabbinic tradition as authoritative sources, arguing that they were manmade rather than divinely revealed. The Karaites studied the Bible and the Hebrew language intensively in order to derive traditional justifications for their innovations in Jewish practice. In response to this challenge, the rabbinic leadership also intensified its study of the scriptures.

As the medieval poets learned more about their tradition, drinking deeply of biblical Hebrew, scriptural influence grew more pervasive, whether as direct quotation, arcane allusion, or indirect reference. Nagrela wrote a poem addressed to his son describing his successful relief of the siege of Lorca that contains no less than seventeen recognizable biblical allusions in its thirty-one lines. Occasionally, a poem might be memorable only because of its allusiveness or deft alternation of a biblical text.

Yet the use of religious themes and linguistic innovations ran parallel with a revolution in poetic content, for the new poetry was intended for new purposes: entertainment, amusement, and self-expression, as well as for displaying virtuosity. The standard bearers of the Golden Age approached both life and art with *joie de vivre*; laughter and playfulness went hand in hand with lyrical expressions of religious sentiments. This blend of secularity and piety mirrored the Muslim conviction that the pleasures of this world are insignificant compared to the rewards of the next. Yet it was common for the same individual to celebrate both worlds with equal verve. A poem would most likely be introduced to guests after a leisurely meal, recited by the poet, while a charming youth, male or female, served goblets of wine throughout the evening's entertainment, which would normally include professional dancers and musicians. The resulting mixture of alcohol, perfume, soft music, dozing, and verse sometimes glistens through the lines of a sensual courtly poem.[4] The scintillating conversation focused on politics and literature. These elegant salons and drinking parties—exclusive convivial events for a select group of Jewish men who considered them the best setting for the recitation of poetry—brought together communal leaders, religious thinkers, and other members of the most prominent social class.

For such gatherings, whether Jewish or Islamic, there were set themes for improvisation, which was a highly valued skill. Poets vied in cleverness, composing works that could be recited both backwards and forward, or using only words that started with the same consonant, or writing a lengthy poem without ever using a particular letter. Sometimes, such ingenuity was carried to the extreme, as when the thirteenth-century writer Judah al-Harizi composed a 200-word letter in rhymed prose and also a ten-verse poem in which every word contained the letter *resh,* along with a similar letter and poem in which that letter was entirely absent.

Wine was a favorite topic for improvisation among Arabs, despite Islamic injunctions against consumption of alcohol. So, too, the Jews picked up the theme and embellished it. The poet would bring his talents to bear upon the bouquet, color, and bubbles of the wine, or even upon the beauties of the crystal goblet in which it was served. Some poets composed entire collections of wine poems. One by Nagrela, written at the Granada court, reveals how the themes and spirit of Hebrew poetry were deeply connected with the general cultural milieu of the eleventh century:

Friend, lead me through the vineyards, give me wine
And to the very brim shall joy be mine;
Perchance the love you pledge me with each cup
May rout the troops around my care's ensign

And if in love for me, eight toasts you drink
Fourscore the toasts in love for you I link;
And should I pre-decease you, friend, select
Some spot where vineyards twist, my grave to sink.

In grape-juice have my body laved, and take
With divers spices, grape-pips—These shall make
All my embalming. Mourn me not, guitar
And pipe with music's sound shall cheer my wake.

And on the place that shall conceal my mold
Let not the earth be heaped and rocks be rolled
To raise a monument: to mark the spot
Rather a pile of wine-jars, new and old.[5]

In another poem, Nagrela celebrates a night of drinking as a source of literary inspiration:

My friend, tell me,
When shall I pour you my wine?
The cry of the cock woke me.
And sleep has deserted my eyes.

Come out and see the morning light
Like a scarlet thread in the East.
Make haste, give me a cup,
Before the dawn starts to rise.

Of spiced pomegranate juice,
From the perfumed hand of a girl,
Who will sing songs. My soul
Revives and then dies.[6]

Even Gabirol, best remembered for his religious poetry, composed at least ten poems on the subject of wine.

But almost any object might become the focus of a poem in this tradition. The thirteenth-century poet Judah al-Harizi, for example, enumerated the exploits of a flea in rhyme, and Halevi could not resist composing an ode upon the discovery of his first gray hair:

When a gray hair appeared all on its own
Upon my head, I cut it down.
"You are the victor now," it said,
"But what will you do, once my banners are spread?"[7]

Even on inconsequential subjects, Halevi exhibits the skills of a master craftsman:

The night the girl gazelle displayed to me
  Her cheek—the sun—beneath its veil of hair
Red as a ruby, and beneath, a brow
  Of moistened marble (color wondrous fair!)
I fancied her the sun, which rising reddens
  Clouds of morning with its crimson.[8]

And Abraham ibn Ezra was able to transform his reflections upon an old, tattered cloak into a work of art:

I have a cloak that is like a sieve to sift
wheat or barley. I spread it out like a
tent in the dark of the night, and the stars
shine through it: through it I see the moon and the
Pleiades, and Orion,
flashing his light. I am afraid of counting
all its holes, which are shaped like the
teeth of a saw. No thread can hope to mend
its gaps with warp and woof. If a
fly landed on it with its full weight, it
would quickly regret its foolishness.
O God, give me a robe of glory in
exchange—This would be properly
tailored![9]

Yet for all of this lightheartedness, melancholy meditations upon death and the ephemeral nature of life were never very far removed from the imagination of the typical court poet, sometimes even breaking through in moments of merriment and carousing. Rather than conclude that one must seize the day, however, thoughts of the imminence of death provoked profound religious expressions of God's eternity. A flood of refreshingly new devotional poems composed to fill specific spots in the religious calendar were transformed by the poet's inclusion of his own religious feelings. This new liturgical poet might address his own soul or interject musings upon philosophical and scientific ideas. Gabirol enriched the standard poetic praise of the marvels of the universe as proof of the wonders of the Creator with descriptions based upon the new findings in astronomy and cosmology. Similarly, Isaac ibn Ghiyyat (1038–89) used scientific data in his religious poetry for Yom Kippur, another example of a medieval thinker interweaving nature with the Divine in order to extol the majesty of God. Gabirol's philosophic ruminations on the kingship of God in his *Keter Malchut* enlarged the religious self-expression of the Jewish people for their most solemn High Holidays. At the same time, every stanza of this extended poem closes with a biblical quotation, to the undoubted delight of his discerning audience.

Far from being rare, this remarkable facility for moving between the secular and religious was typical of the Golden Age poets. Most of the liturgical poets also introduced themes from secular Arabic love poetry into their verse as well as reworking familiar themes from *The Song of Songs* in refreshingly new ways. Gabirol composed a series of thirteen poems in which God and Israel address each other on the subject of redemption. As Israel, the lover, demands union either with God or his annointed Messiah, erotic allusions are interlaced with themes from *The Song of Songs:*

> *Come to me at dawn, love,*
> *Carry me away: For in my heart I'm thirsting*
> *To see my folk today.*
>
> *For you, love, mats of gold*
> *Within my halls I'll spread.*
> *I'll set my table for you,*
> *I'll serve you my own bread.*
>
> *A drink from my own vineyards*
> *I'll pour to fill your cup—*
> *Heartily you'll drink, love,*
> *Heartily you'll sup.*
>
> *I'll take my pleasure with you*
> *As once I had such joy*
> *With Jesse's son, my people's prince,*
> *That Bethlehem boy.* [10]

Gabirol may have been the first to use such secular love themes to describe the love between God and Israel, but the idea of frustrated love became a favorite for other Jewish liturgical poets, who felt that it mirrored the plight of the nation. Also, the biblical image of God's desert romance with his chosen people was not far removed from the romantic desert ballads that were standard fare in pre-Islamic poetry.

The intrinsic appeal of natural beauty was not ignored by the Hebrew poets of this period. In a complex poem that wedded biblical allusion with religious symbolism, Moses ibn Ezra celebrated the loveliness of a rose in the garden along with the pleasures of drink. For ibn Nagrela, a rose in full bloom, scented with myrrh, is both a summons to revelry and a reminder of mortality. The poem Gabirol composed in honor of his murdered patron draws its solemnity from the juxtaposition of natural beauty with the fact of death:

> *Behold the sun at evening, red*
> *As if she wore vermilion robes.*
> *Slipping the wraps from north to south*
> *She covers in purple the western side.*
> *The earth—she leaves it cold and bare*
> *To huddle in shadows all night long.*
> *At once the sky is dark; you'd think*
> *Sackcloth it wore for Yequtiel.*[11]

But perhaps the most novel of all medieval Jewish poems are Nagrela's works about his experiences and accomplishments in warfare. Anything but conventional, as we have seen, and convinced that he was the noble descendant of ancient Israelite kings, he compared his deeds with those of antiquity. At the same time, even when most caught up in the frenzy of battle, he would pause to reflect upon the meagerness of his power in contrast with the countless legions of faceless warriors who had succumbed on the battlefield throughout the ages: "Where are the folk who long ago inhabited this place?/Where are the men who built and those who wrecked?" Nagrela would claim that some of his battle poems were no more than a pedagogical tool, dictated to his young sons in order to introduce them to the fine arts of calligraphy and prosody. Even if that is true, the work stands alone, for no other poet writing in Hebrew shared his knowledge of military action. In his poem

about the Battle of Alfuente, luridly authentic descriptions evoke the
great victory of August 1038:

Then Av—the mouth of ancient woe—
departed, and Elul arrived, speeding good fortune.
Ibn Abbas pitched his tents on the mountainside,
and we pitched ours in the pass, taking no heed
of his army, as though it were a passing caravan.
Then he drew near and, with many words, tried
to incite my men against me. But when my adversary
saw that my company spoke with my voice, as one man, he
uncovered spears, swords, and lances, and prepared
his weapons for battle.

My enemy rose—and the Rock rose against him.
How can any creature rise up against his Creator?
Now my troops and the enemy's drew up their ranks
opposite each other. On such a day of anger, jealousy,
and rage, men deem the Prince of Death a princely prize:
and each man seeks to win renown, though he must lose
his life for it. The earth's foundations, overthrown
like Gomorrah, reeled to and fro. Every face turned
red, or black as the bottom of a pot. It was a day of
darkness and thick fog. The sun was as black as my
heart. The tumult was like that of a cloudburst,
like the roar of breakers when the sea is swept by a
storm.

As the sun came out, the earth rocked on its pillars as
if it were drunk. The horses lunged back and forth like
vipers darting out of their nests. The hurled spears
were like bolts of lightning, filling the air with
light. Arrows pelted us like raindrops, as if our
shields were sieves. Their strung bows were like
serpents, each serpent spewing froth a stinging bee.
Their swords above their heads were like glowing torches
which darken as they fall. The blood of men flowed upon
the ground like the blood of the rams on the corners of
the altar.

*Still, my gallant men scorned their lives, preferring
death. These young lions welcomed each raw wound upon
their heads as though it were a garland. To die—they
believed—was to keep the faith; to live—they thought—
was forbidden . . .*[12]

Like medieval Jews everywhere, the Andalusian writers mostly concentrated on a somewhat different struggle, their tenuous position between the warring worlds of Islam and Christianity. As Halevi expressed
it, "When they are locked in battle, we fall as they go down." Similarly,
themes of exile and redemption were central to Jewish poetry, reaching
new heights of poetic expression in the works of the Golden Age.
Often, the poet laments the lost glory of the Jews or expresses the hope
of future redemption, asking how long God can continue "to cast off
the remnants of Joseph." Halevi, confident that God was still attached
both to his people and to their traditional land, wrote a marvelous
collection of odes to Zion in his mature years, as he began to think of
emigrating to Israel. One of them is perhaps the most famous of all
medieval poems:

*My heart is in the East and I am at the
edge of the West. Then how can I taste
what I eat, how can I enjoy it? How
can I fulfill my vows and pledges?
while Zion is in the domain of Edom,
and I am in the bonds of Arabia? It
would be easy for me to leave behind
all the good things of Spain; it would
be glorious to see the dust of the
ruined shrine.*[13]

As we have seen, the poetry of the convivial Golden Age was enmeshed in a materialistic, hedonistic way of life that allowed for the
coexistence of worldly and religious impulses. While this tension lay at
the heart of their literature, it is not at all clear how successfully the
Sephardic intellectuals balanced these seemingly irreconcilable poles in
their daily lives and careers. We do, however, have some hints here and
there. In introspective passages, Halevi expressed misgivings about the
indiscretions of his youth, and the drinking songs he composed early in

his career stand in stark contrast to his mature ballads and odes. In some works, ibn Ezra championed a life of pleasure and abandon, but he also composed complex penitential liturgy. Ibn Gabirol certainly participated in court life but expressed loathing for the excesses and superficialities he encountered there. But how lax in behavior were the courtier-rabbis, when all is said and done? It is hard to say. True, there was rabbinic dispensation for some behavior that must have appeared to many to be a breach of Jewish conduct. For example, in the eleventh century, one of the greatest medieval rabbinic leaders, Hai Gaon of Baghdad, condoned (or at least weakly rationalized) the frivolity of winefests in the following *responsum:*

> As to your question as to one in our time who drinks [wine] to the accompaniment of music, especially among non-Jews: he is culpable and to be excommunicated, unless he is a courtier and works for the protection of the Jews and trusts himself not to lapse into licentiousness, and unless it is known that at the time (of drinking and listening to music) he is concentrating on the destruction of the Temple, and he is forcing his heart to be sad and not enjoying himself. And when he listens (to the music) only out of deference to the king in order to benefit Israel. For the last hundred years and more there have been in Iraq men in the king's service whom the rabbis permitted such things.[14]

Medieval Andalusia marked the high point of Jewish assimilation of Muslim cultural trends, but there were dangers inherent in this process. Assimilation sometimes took the form of social breakdown or intellectual floundering, and voluntary conversions from Judaism were hardly unheard of. As we shall see, some Jews were frankly confused by the novel philosophical arguments and rational discussions they heard in the exclusive salons of Islamic society. It would take their greatest leaders in the East and West, Saadiah Gaon in the tenth century and Moses Maimonides in the twelfth, to meet this intellectual challenge.

Jewish philosophy was almost as radically influenced by the encounter with Islamic culture as Hebrew poetry. The Muslim conquests had been followed by an official program of translating Greek classics into Arabic; consequently, for the first time, Jews were exposed fully to the conceptual world of classical antiquity as they adopted the Arabic language. In this way, Arabization introduced them to an entire philo-

sophical literature, originally written in Greek and Syriac, and to a new
theological language capable of expressing new concepts. By the tenth
century, the Muslims were seriously engaged in the task of trying to
reconcile their own revealed religion with the philosophies of ancient
Greece, particularly Aristotle's. It was because of this tradition of seeking the wisdom of ancient Greece that ibn Shaprut was commissioned
to translate the Greek text given his caliph by the emperor of Byzantium, who was apparently confident that such a gift would not offend
the Muslim ruler.

Like Islam, Jewish civilization was predicated upon respect for both
theological and philosophical wisdom; neither, in contrast with the ancient Greeks, had developed these ideas through a rationalistic approach.
Hence, it could be assumed that no conflicts would arise between the two
modes of learning. In medieval Spain, however, Muslims and Jews both
began to contemplate religious questions in a new way, thanks to the
Arabic translations of Greek thought. As Jews reread the Bible in light
of unfamiliar rationalistic philosophic formulations, they began to question its textual contradictions as well as its numerous anthropomorphic
references to God, even as they tried to reconcile apparent conflicts between reason and revelation. In the Bible, and in the Koran as well, God
is depicted as a person when he is acting as creator, judge, ruler. The
philosophically trained were disturbed by the scriptural metaphors that
refer to God in bodily terms—his outstretched hand, his feet—and by the
passages that attribute to him such emotions as anger.

By the ninth and tenth centuries, in fact, a large and elite class of
Jewish thinkers became engaged with Greek ideas. First in Baghdad,
then in Spain, this new Jewish philosophy permeated the thinking and
teachings of communal and religious leaders, then filtered down to
educated laypeople. Greek literature wasn't confined to scholars. Included in the Cairo Geniza is the inventory of a physicians' library
placed at auction; it contained thirty-seven volumes of Galen's writings
translated into Arabic.

As ideas flowed freely among the different faith communities of the
Iberian peninsula, Jews had to learn to hold their own, for religious
polemic had attained a new level of sophistication. Following the Muslim lead in regard to the Greeks, but puzzled by the challenges of the
classic authors, Jews with advanced training in the rabbinic tradition
and a growing familiarity with science and philosophy slowly began to
develop a distinctive new philosophical literature.

On the other hand, not only did Jewish and Muslim thinkers (*Mu-*

takallimun) share a common vocabulary and common intellectual concerns, they also found that they would arrive at similar answers to theological issues. For example, both believed that the existence of God is proved by the fact that a created world implies a creator, and both agreed that the attributes applied to God were not the same as his essence, for he is transcendent and unknowable. In fact, the philosophical interchange among the various faiths in Spain was so close that not until the nineteenth century—and then only by accident—was it discovered that Avicebron (or Avicebrol), the unknown author of the medieval philosophical work called the *Fons Vita,* was actually Gabirol. Until his Hebrew original, *Mekor Hayyim,* was discovered in a rare manuscript collection at the Bibliothèque Nationale, scholars through the ages had assumed Avicebron to be Muslim or Christian.

Gabirol was only the first of a series of important Spanish Jewish philosophers: Bahya ibn Pakuda, Abraham bar Hiyya, Judah Halevi, Joseph ibn Zaddik of Córdoba, Abraham ibn Daud of Toledo, and Moses ben Maimon, who was also known as Maimonides or the Rambam. Halevi and Maimonides are of particular interest.

Judah Halevi, like Gabirol, was an innovator in poetry as well as philosophy, though in his maturity he would renounce verse with a stern warning: "Let not the wisdom of the Greeks beguile thee; it has flowers and no fruit." His intellectual journey from consummate Spanish poet and courtier to pilgrim and wanderer is mirrored in the conversations of the pagan king and rabbi in his most famous work, the *Kuzari.* Composed in the 1130s, it is his most important personal statement on the nature of Jewish history and the Jewish people, and would appear in no less than twenty Hebrew editions between 1506 and 1887. The plot is centered upon the dramatic conversion of a pagan Khazar king to Judaism, a story popularized among Spanish Jews by correspondence between Hasdai ibn Shaprut and a later Khazar ruler, King Joseph, in 960, as discussed in chapter 2.

According to King Joseph's account to ibn Shaprut, one of his predecessors, King Bulan, had a series of dreams in which an angel appeared and promised him might and glory. Thus encouraged, Bulan was indeed victorious in many battles. Taking note, both the Byzantine emperor and the Muslim caliph sent him envoys with presents and also missionaries, hoping to induce him to adopt their respective religions. The king decided to engage the Muslim and Christian emissaries in an examination of their faiths and asked a rabbi to participate as well. Questioning each of the three separately, Bulan discovered that, while each believed his religion to be best, both the Muslim and the Christian respected Judaism as a repository of religious truths. Therefore, he decided to convert to Judaism, a decision that was in effect a declaration of neutrality, as well as being an adroit political move for a kingdom located at such a vulnerable crossroads.

Borrowing this historical event, Halevi fictionalizes a series of wide-ranging dialogues between king and rabbi in which the latter defends Judaism against the dominant faiths. Using both characters as his mouthpiece, Halevi airs some of his major preoccupations, including the perfection of the Hebrew language, the relationship between God and Israel, the reasons for the survival of the Jewish people, and the deceptions of the other monotheistic faiths and philosophy. Questions of power and powerlessness, however, were uppermost in the author's mind, for no medieval Jew could ignore the taunts of the other faiths that the lack of Jewish sovereignty—their continuing subjugation to other nations—was a sign of divine rejection. But for Halevi, the real source of truth was in history, not in philosophical speculation or contemporary signs of power. Metaphysical truths, unlike those of logic, cannot be gleaned from philosophers, for "the God of Abraham is different from the God of Aristotle" just as the history of the Jews is unlike the history of all other nations. The Jews possessed the word of God, for they had all stood at Sinai. Moreover, prophecy had not only been bestowed upon them then but would once again be granted them when they returned to Israel, a land peculiarly suited to prophetic revelations and communion with God. In addition, the Hebrew language is the sole medium for true prophetic communication.[15]

At the end of his enlightening, persuasive exchange with the rabbi, Halevi's king asks why, if the land of Israel is superior to all others, the rabbi himself doesn't go there. The question had been troubling Halevi for at least a decade. His arguments for the primacy of Hebrew had been framed as a repudiation of an Arab chauvinist movement, *al-arabiyya*. His odes to Zion were written at this time. Not too long before his announcement that he was emigrating, he had declared, "Greece and its wisdom have drowned me in mucky grease, Islam and its language have painted me dark, and Christendom has dissected and destroyed me."[16] Plainly reflecting his creator's personal decision, the rabbi in the *Kuzari* replies to the king, "Jerusalem can only be rebuilt when Israel yearns for it to such an extent that they embrace her stones and dust," a reference to Psalms 102:14–15. Indeed, it was soon after completing the *Kuzari* that Halevi announced that he was becoming a pilgrim to Palestine.

Yet his inner contradictions were not so easily resolved. Despite his impassioned denunciation of poetry, he continued to compose poems until his last days and would immortalize his voyage to the East in 1140 in an unusual sequence of poems about the sea in the beautiful Andalusian style:

> *This wind of yours, O West, is all perfume—*
> *it has the scent of spikenard and apple in*
> *its wings. Wind, you come from the store-*
> *house of spice merchants, and not from the*
> *common storehouse of winds. You lift up the*
> *swallow's wings, you set me free, you are*
> *like the purest perfumes, fresh from a bunch*
> *of myrrh. Everyone here longs for you; by*
> *your good graces, they ride over the sea*
> *upon a mere plank. Oh, do not abandon the*
> *ship, when the day draws to its end or when*
> *it begins. Smooth out the ocean, break a*
> *path through the sea until you reach the*
> *holy mountains, and there subside. Rebuke*
> *the east wind that whips up the sea and*
> *turns it into a boiling cauldron.*
> *But how can the wind help, for it is a*
> *prisoner of the Rock—sometimes held back*
> *and sometimes let loose? Only God can grant*
> *my deepest wish: for He is maker of high*
> *mountains and the creator of winds!*[17]

During the hazardous journey, the poet burst forth in song:

> *Has a flood come and laid the world waste?*
> *For dry land is nowhere to be seen. There*
> *is neither man, nor beast, nor bird. Have they*
> *all perished, all lain down in torment*
> *and died? If only I could see a hill or*

valley, I would be comforted; even a desert
would delight me. I look in every
direction, and there is nothing but sea and
sky and ship and leviathan churning
the deep, until it seems that the abyss is
white with age! Deceitfully, the sea covers
the ship, as though it had taken it by
theft. The sea is in turmoil, but my soul
is full of joy, for she is drawing near to
the temple of her God. [18]

Contrary to popular legend, Halevi did not travel directly from Spain to the Western Wall of Jerusalem, only to die violently before reaching it. New information from the Cairo Geniza describes a chapter of Halevi's life that was previously completely unknown: he served as court poet in Egypt and tarried for almost a year in Cairo and Alexandria, spending time with his business associate and confidant, the enterprising merchant-scholar Halfon ben Netan'el Halevi. Drawn back into the world of courtiers, he composed panegyrics, became once again involved in communal intrigues, and even professed his fascination with the veiled women of Egypt in a poem confiding, "The heart is enchanted and forgets its age." Still, having traversed half the known world to weep in Zion, Halevi did board a ship for the East. Reliable history leaves him there in the harbor, impatiently awaiting the west winds and continuing to compose in Andalusian meters.

Moses Maimonides towers over his contemporaries as the greatest son of Sepharad, the outstanding representative of Jewish rationalism for all time. Living at the end of the Golden Age, a time of renewed persecution and uncertainty for Jews, Maimonides attained wide recognition and enormous influence as a jurist and philosopher, community leader and physician. His enormous intellectual and literary output constitutes one of the era's greatest individual achievements. His prodigious legal writings mark a high point in the history of Jewish legal thought. Soon after his death in 1204, his most famous philosophical work, *Guide for the Perplexed,* sparked widespread and furious controversy, and for generations his supporters and detractors would argue about this work. So great was his impact that Jewish admirers in later generations would rank him near Moses, the legal giant and founder of Judaism, saying, "From Moses to Moses, there was no one like Moses." Christian medieval scholars would pore over his works for centuries, and his Muslim contemporaries mourned his death with official public ceremonies in Egypt. At his request, he was buried in Tiberias in Palestine. The original epitaph (later removed) on his gravestone read: "Here lies a man, and yet not a man; If thou wert a man, then heavenly creatures created thee."[19]

Because he was a prolific writer of letters and legal opinions to Jewish communities far and wide, we know a great deal about his life. He was born in Córdoba in 1135, son of Maimon, a judge (*dayyan*) in the local rabbinical court. Maimonides' father was descended from a long line of judges and had studied with the greatest legal scholar of Spain, Rabbi Joseph ibn Megash (who was also Halevi's teacher). In keeping with the accepted practice among educated Jewish families of the time, the father served as tutor to his son, introducing Maimonides to the broad curriculum of sciences and law, languages and philosophy, so popular among Sephardim. Maimonides' mother died in childbirth, and the young Moses was reared by his father's second wife in the company of a younger brother, David. Some accounts also mention a sister, but the sibling relationship between the two brothers was especially close. Maimonides later recalled, "He was my brother and my pupil; my only joy was to see him." The family took its roots quite seriously; Maimonides was told that his lineage went back to Rabbi Yehudah ha-Nasi, the great second-century editor of the classic Jewish legal compendium known as the *Mishnah,* and even farther back to King David.

In 1147 a fanatical fundamentalist Muslim dynasty known as the Almohades swept into Spain from Morocco. North Africa had already provided Spain with a series of warriors of the faith, the Almoravids, to engage with the Christian troops of the Spanish reconquest. Although the Almohades were Berber tribesmen like their Almoravid predecessors, unlike them they were consumed by a puritanical spirit. Railing against the religious laxity and sumptuous courts of the Almoravids, they demanded the conversion of all Jews and Christians. Their lightning push out of the Sahara, through Morocco, and into Spain left a trail of Jewish martyrs and forced converts. The Maimon family, like tens of thousands of other Jews in Spain, began to wander.

Most Jewish refugees from the Almohades fled northward to the

Christian realm, but the Maimons fled to Almería, wandering for several years through Muslim Spain, witnesses to devastation everywhere. Despite the continuous upheaval of these years and Maimonides' youth, he nonetheless managed to write his first two books, an introduction to the terminology of logic and a work on the rules of the calendar. The former revealed how basic Aristotle was to his training, temperament, and life's work; both sprang from a youthful interest in logic and science that would continue throughout his life. Like all of his writing except his great Hebrew work, the *Mishneh Torah,* these books were composed in Arabic.

In 1159 and 1160 the family settled in Fez, a choice of asylum that continues to puzzle historians. Since Morocco was the heartland of the Almohades and no practicing Jew was tolerated, scholars are divided over the question of how the Maimons managed to survive there without converting. Persecutions did wax and wane; it is possible, but not at all certain, that the Maimons entered the country during a lull and were not forced to convert. Thousands of Moroccan Jews had been martyred in the first wave of persecutions, and thousands more had accepted Islam in order to save their lives. Probably, most of the Jews who endured the fury of the 1140s continued to practice a subterranean form of their faith, observing whatever they could in their homes while paying lip service to Islam. Maimonides later alluded to these years in the introduction to his *Mishneh:* "Since we went into exile, the persecutions have not stopped. I have known affliction since childhood, since the womb."

Jewish leaders urged their fellow believers to stand firm against forced conversion, even if the result was martyrdom. In his *Epistle on Martyrdom,* however, Maimonides suggested that the persecuted Jew should publicly adopt Islam while maintaining crypto-Judaism and not seek martyrdom unless forced to transgress Jewish commandments in public. He also excoriated one writer who advocated martyrdom for "long-winded foolish babbling and nonsense" and for misleading and hurting the Jews. In a sweeping view of the Jewish past, Maimonides marshals examples of heretics and sinners from the Bible to show that even oppressors of Israel were rewarded by God for a single act of piety or respect. How much greater then, he argues, will be the reward of the Jews "who despite the exigencies of forced conversion perform commandments secretly." His response to calls for martyrdom is logical as well as humane, for he divides Jewish precepts into those which must always be obeyed (e.g., the prohibition against murder) and those which may be violated if necessary. In his opinion, concessions *were* possible without compromising Judaism, and Maimonides therefore counseled temporary conversion followed by departure from the lands of persecution:

> A victim of this persecution should follow this counsel: Let him set it as his objective to observe as much of the Law as he can. . . . He must not think that what he has already violated is far more grievous than what he observes, let him be as careful about observance as possible. . . . What I counsel myself, and what I should like to suggest to all my friends and everyone that consults me, is to leave these places and go to where he can practice religion and fulfill the law without compulsion or fear. . . . Moreover, when two Jewish cities are at one's elbow, one superior to the other in its actions and behavior, more observant and more concerned with the precepts, the God-fearing individual is obliged to depart from the town where the actions are not at their best, and move to the better township. . . . But if the place is gentile, the Jew who resides there must by all means leave it and go to a more suitable location. . . . If he is compelled to violate even one precept, it is forbidden to stay there. He must leave everything he has, travel day and night until he can find a spot where he can practice his religion.[20]

According to Maimonides, since the Almohades were aware that Jewish professions of faith in Islam were insincere, Jews were in effect being asked to make a false utterance, not to become martyrs. His response served to counteract the wave of despair among the Jews of Morocco.

Maimonides remained with his family in Morocco for at least five years. In light of his advice to depart rather than profane Judaism, it seems that he did not face religious coercion. Apparently, most Jews in North Africa, for at least a generation, weathered the Almohade onslaught by following Maimonides' advice. So widespread in fact was crypto-Judaism that the Almohade ruler Abu Yusuf Ya'qub al-Mansur (1184–99) supposedly remarked, "If I knew for certain that they became faithful Muslims, I would allow them to mix and intermarry with Muslims; if I knew for certain that they were infidels, I would kill the men and hand their children and property over to Muslims. However, neither fact is certain."

In 1165, when a new wave of persecution began, the Maimons abruptly fled to Palestine. Jewish life was scarcely tenable in a Holy Land under the domination of the Crusaders, however; after a brief sojourn, the family departed for Egypt. When their father died there, the two brothers pooled their inheritance to start a gem business. David managed the firm while Moses, the silent partner, pursued his scholarship. While the one would ply the Indian Ocean, the other would compose his major works in Old Cairo. Several letters that somehow found their way into the Geniza illuminate the deep affection shared by the two brothers.

In 1173 David's boat capsized in the Indian Ocean and he was drowned, a tragic personal loss that Maimonides would repeatedly lament for the rest of his life. His brother's death also meant that his material security evaporated, forcing him to draw upon his knowledge of medicine to support himself. Soon, his fame as a physician brought him to the attention of the ruler Saladin and his vizier, al-Afdal. This courtier was a lover of rare books, a skilled military and financial administrator, a writer, and also, according to some accounts, a hypochondriac. In 1187, when al-Afdal fell seriously ill, he had Maimonides brought into the official council of doctors. Thereafter the skilled new physicians' fame began to spread. Ever the scholar, he composed many important medical tracts on nutrition, drugs, poisons and antidotes (that favorite topic of Muslim potentates), sex, hermorrhoids, and asthma. These papers were characterized by the principle of moderation in diet, in sleep, and in one's overall approach to life: man should lead a life pleasing to God through a proper balance of food, drink, and rest. He should do nothing to harm his health, eat less than required to surfeit himself, and exercise caution in his choices: "Eat what is easily digested, fowl rather than oxmeat, and beef rather than bull meat. These are harmful foods which should be avoided—large salted fish, old fermented cheese—nor would I recommend milk more than a day old." He also recommended a small amount of wine on a daily basis.

Maimonides' tracts would be required reading in European medical schools for centuries, until the entire curriculum of most schools changed in accordance with the teachings of the Renaissance. The medical oath attibuted to Maimonides, however, is still used in some schools for its stirring idealism:

> *Thy eternal providence has appointed me to*
> *watch over the life and health of Thy*
> *creatures. May the love for my art actuate*
> *me at all times, may neither avarice nor*
> *miserliness, nor thirst for glory, or for a*

great reputation engage my mind; for the
enemies of truth and philanthropy could
easily deceive me and make me forgetful of
my lofty aim of doing good for Thy
children. May I never see in the patient
anything but a fellow creature in pain.
Grant me strength, time, and opportunity
always to correct what I have acquired,
always to extend its domain; for knowledge
is immense and the spirit of man can extend
infinitely to enrich itself daily with new
requirements. Today he can discover his
errors of yesterday and tomorrow he may
obtain a new light on what he thinks
himself sure of today.
Oh God. Thou has appointed me to watch over
the life and death of thy creatures; here am
I ready for my vocation, and now I turn unto
my calling. [21]

In addition to his medical works, Maimonides wrote several treatises on astronomy, a choice of subject that, along with his use of Arab
and ancient authors for reference, was typical of the broad, enlightened
background of Jewish medical practitioners trained in the Golden Age.

Service in the palace and the harem, which would have been considered a distinct honor for most people, was to Maimonides a painful
distraction from his scholarly and communal responsibilities. By the
1180s he had probably become the official head of the Jewish community. Even so, he somehow found time to answer hundreds of questions
on Jewish law addressed to him from all over and to produce major
works of law and philosophy. We get a vivid glimpse of his daily
routine from Maimonides himself, in a letter he sent to his translator
Samuel ibn Tibbon:

I dwell in Misr (Fustat) and the Sultan resides in Cairo; these two
places are two Sabbath days' journey distant from each other. My
duties to the Sultan are very heavy. I am obliged to visit him every day,
early in the morning; and when he or any of his children, or any of the
inmates of his harem, are indisposed, I dare not quit Cairo, but must
stay during the greater part of the day in the palace. It also frequently
happens that one or two of the royal officers fall sick, and I must

attend to their healing. Hence, as a rule, I repair to Cairo very early in the day and even if nothing unusual happens, I do not return to Fustat until the afternoon. Then I am almost dying of hunger. . . . I find the antechambers filled with people, both Jews and Gentiles, nobles and common people, judges and bailiffs, friends and foes—a mixed multitude who await the time of my return.

I dismount from my animal, wash my hands, go forth to my patients, and entreat them to bear with me while I partake of some slight refreshment, the only meal I take in the twenty-four hours. Then I go forth to my patients, write prescriptions and directions for their several ailments. Patients go in and out until nightfall, and sometimes even, I assure you, until two hours and more during the night. I converse with and prescribe for them while lying down from sheer fatigue; and when night falls, I am so exhausted that I can scarcely speak.

In consequence of this, no Israelite can have any private interview with me, except on the Sabbath. On that day, the whole congregation, or at least, the majority of the members, come unto me after the morning service, when I instruct them as to their proceedings during the whole week; we study a little together until noon, when they depart. Some of them return, and read with me after the afternoon service until the evening prayers. In this manner, I spend that day.[22]

In 1165, the Jews of Yemen were subjected to persecution and forced conversion. As often happened in such times, a messianic pretender arose among them, promising redemption if they converted. When the despairing Yemenite Jews turned to him for advice, Maimonides recognized that he faced a twofold challenge. On the one hand, he must reaffirm the community's belief in Judaism, which had been weakened by taunts that Islam had triumphed, and do so in such a fashion that Islam would be unequivocally repudiated. On the other, it was necessary to neutralize the pretensions of the false messiah while affirming the integrity and validity of the Jewish belief that the future redemption promised in biblical prophecies would one day come. Moreover, beyond these immediate and urgent questions, Maimonides faced the implicit issues of the significance of the Yemen community's suffering, the need for an effective way of responding to Islam's claims, and the possibility of predicting the date of the Messiah's coming.

His *Epistle to Yemen,* composed in 1172, shares the despair of the persecuted community and renounces Islamic assertions in no uncertain terms. Using biblical prooftexts, he demolishes Islam's arguments of religious supremacy. In addition, while maintaining that the precise date of redemption could not be ascertained, he nevertheless revealed that an ancient tradition passed down in his family through the generations held that the Messiah would appear in 1216. By offering such a distant date, he could calm the messianic fever but also console the suffering Jews.

Yet neither his medical treatises nor works of religious philosophy best exemplified the man's originality and brilliance; his most enduring influence derives from his encyclopedic writing in the field of Jewish law. His earliest legal study, a *Commentary* on the Mishnah, formulated the "Thirteen principles of the Jewish faith," which were later incorporated into the Jewish prayerbook. This alone established the pioneering work as a classic of Judaism, but it has also been deemed important for its argument that the interpretation of Oral Law is a rational enterprise subject to specific rules.

Maimonides' greatest legal study is the *Mishneh Torah,* completed in 1178, and to this day its fourteen books are regarded as one of the most important Jewish works ever written. In contrast to his other writings, which are often highly technical and even esoteric, this monumental attempt to organize all of Jewish law in a single code is written in a clear Hebrew, undoubtedly intended to be read and understood by the entire Jewish world. In addition, it is systematically organized so that the reader can immediately find what Jewish law says about a specific issue. (Systematization of Jewish tradition had begun in Iraq in the ninth century under the influence of Arab legal traditions.) Moreover, unlike the Talmud, the *Mishneh Torah* does not set down the many different points of view derived from centuries of legal disputes among rabbinic scholars about intricate points. Rather than try for such comprehensiveness (with the attendant confusing diversity of opinion and disputed decisions), Maimonides aimed to facilitate comprehension of the law and illustrate the logical connections between subjects covered in the Talmud. Finally, he did not resist adding daring explanations of law that marked a deviation from the accepted Talmudic mode of discourse, and he included discussions of philosophical issues. Although such melding of Jewish legal tradition with broader philosophic currents was pervasive in Sephardic intellectual circles, it was still quite novel for a text of Hebraic law.

But it was Maimonides' last major work, the *Moreh Nebukhim* or *Guide for the Perplexed,* that is his richest symbiosis of the classical philosophical and ancient Jewish traditions. Completed in 1190, it posed special challenges to his contemporaries as well as to succeeding generations, in part because it was not written for the average reader. In fact, the very title indicates the intended audience, those select contemporaries learned in classical science and philosophy as well as rabbinic scholarship who might be floundering in the apparent inconsistencies between the two traditions. Maimonides' formal introduction to *Guide for the Perplexed* makes its aim clear:

> The first purpose of this treatise is to explain the meanings of certain terms occurring in books of prophecy. . . . it is not the purpose of this treatise to make its totality understandable to the vulgar or to beginners in speculation, nor to teach those who have not engaged in any study other than the science of the Law. . . . Its purpose is to give indications to a religious man for whom the validity of our Law has become established in his soul and has become actual in his belief—such a man being perfect in his religion and his character, and having studied the sciences of the philosophers and come to know what they signify. The human intellect having drawn him on and led him to dwell within its province, he must have felt distressed by the externals of the Law. . . . He would remain in a state of perplexity and confusion as to whether to follow his intellect.[23]

For this reader, troubled by an Aristotelian rationality that seemed to conflict with revelation, Maimonides could explore the sophisticated, perhaps confusing notions that biblical material could be allegorical and that Aristotelianism could provide proof of the existence of God. In his view, divine revelation had been purposely couched in a fashion that could meet the needs of both the masses and the elite, enabling the former to live properly while offering the latter a key to the secrets of the universe. In other words, he felt that Judaism and its traditions could be presented as a rational system, even if, on the surface, some of its modes of presentation seemed to conflict with reason.

Yet Maimonides was equally convinced that the perplexity of the elite believer could not be resolved by reason alone. In the first place, he thought that conflicts between faith and reason were more apparent than real; thus he believed that every instance of an expresssion in Hebraic literature that repelled reason was in fact a figure of speech that could be translated into the language of reason. Secondly, what ultimately mattered was man's knowledge of God, which could be exquisitely attained by the performance of Mitzvot as well as by an understanding of created things. Occasionally, intellectual insight into religious truth was granted to the most profound of prophets, like

Moses. Yet even this highest form of knowledge was not attained by arbitrary divine intervention but because prophets were the most intellectually refined and rationally prepared of men.

Like Halevi, Maimonides sensed the ironies of his age. He had found refuge from Spain on the doorstep of Palestine in Egypt, the ultimate symbol of exile. Despite his power and honors in the Jewish community, his fame throughout the Mediterranean, and his mastery of so many fields of knowledge, he understood and was concerned by the continuing decline of Jews in Muslim lands. Suspecting that the weight of Jewish history was turning from the world of Islam toward Christendom, he reveled in the intellectual brilliance of the correspondence he received from his brethren in France, as is evident in a letter he wrote in 1202 to scholars in Lunel:

> My friends and colleagues, be strong and of courageous hearts. In this difficult period, you and those who live in your vicinity are the only ones who carry high the banner of Moses. You study the Talmud and cultivate the other sciences as well. But here in the East the men of wisdom are decreasing and dying out. Palestine still has three or four places where intellectual life prevails. In all of Syria there is only Aleppo, where a tiny few cultivate the study of Torah, but they are not very ardent about it. In Babylon there are two or three places of learning; in Yemen and the other Arabic countries there is little study of Talmud, and there is no interest whatsoever in theoretical research. . . . In Maghreb, as we know, a heavy doom weighs upon the Jews. Thus salvation can reach us only from you. Be strong and courageous and stand by the law. You cannot rely on my labors. I can no longer come and go. I am old and weary, not with the burden of years, but because of my suffering body.[24]

Even as he wrote so profoundly of ancient and continuing tradition, however, Maimonides in forced Egyptian exile was a symbol of the decay and dispersion of the Golden Age, as was Halevi, who had chosen to leave Spain. Other great talents who were scattered around the Mediterranean by the persecutions of the Almohades included the Kimhis and the ibn Tibbons, and Abraham ibn Ezra, all products of the special Andalusian environment that fell apart in the twelfth and thirteenth centuries. Understandably, Jews today often look back at the culture-rich 200 years or so of the Golden Age as emblematic of all Spanish history. In the glow of shared memory, the combination of striking cultural artifacts, political ease, and economic integration into the dominant culture outshines the Almohade destruction that followed. Jews in Muslim Spain had fashioned a rich culture without sacrificing many of their traditional values. Integration of Muslim interests in literature, philosophy, and science with ancient Jewish norms was the result.

For a while, the Sephardim were able to sustain their new forms of creativity in the Christian north. Removed from the special atmosphere and human alchemy of al-Andalus, however, the unique symbiosis of Jewish and Muslim culture did not survive long, and a new era in Sephardic life began to unfold in Christian Spain. There, the intellectual heirs of the Golden Age, whether philosophers or translators in southern France, or poets, mathematicians, and scientists in Castile and Aragon, were forced to contend with unfamiliar forces of reaction and repression. No longer would their heritage of synthesizing secular and religious learning be considered appropriate or acceptable.

4

The *Reconquista*
Jews and the New Realities of Christian Spain

On our side, Christ, God and man. On the Moors', the faithless and damned apostate, Muhammad. What more is there to say?

—*Chronique latine des rois de Castille*, 43

The advent of the fierce Almohades postponed but could not long prevent the relentless fall of one Muslim city after another to reinvigorated Christian forces. A decisive battle at La Navas de Tolosa in 1212 and the capitulation of Seville to Ferdinand III in 1248 virtually completed the long centuries of Catholic reconquest, the *Reconquista*. Only the small enclave of Muslims in Granada, as we have seen, was able to hold out until 1492. In the course of the prolonged crusade for hegemony on the peninsula, the two societies, Christian and Muslim, stood side by side, each restructured with a new and more militant perception of self. But Spain was not a unique or isolated country; she was part of Europe and the Mediterranean world, and her Jews were increasingly subject to forces changing the landscape of both.

During the long campaign of reconquest from the eleventh through the thirteen centuries, Spain's Jews had found themselves constantly on the move. Muslims, ever more fervent in their religiosity as they endured increasingly prolonged and fierce encounters with the Christian enemy, adhered more strictly to Islamic precepts, including the enforcement of restrictions against non-Muslims. The Berber forces who came from North Africa to stem the Christian tide of reconquest affirmed and strengthened this trend. Jews found themselves enticed into Christian Spain, moving from an area of active intolerance into one of past and future animosity. At the same time, Christian warriors believed themselves launched upon a great crusade. The ideal of reconquest was partially religious—to launch a massive offensive against Islamic foes—and partly ethnic—to oust the Muslim usurpers of the old Visigothic state. A special spirit of piety was forged on the battlefield that would yield trouble for the Jews later on. The burgeoning Catholic religious orders—primarily Franciscans and Dominicans but also Cistercians and Benedictines—grew in influence, as did a peculiar and obsessive notion of honor (*honra*), noble birth, and Christian valor in the new military orders of Calatrava, Alcantara, and Santiago organized in response to the Almohade invasions. In these new orders, knights were ordained in a quasi-religious ceremony and imbued with a spirit of chivalry and warfare in the service of the Christian community. Close internal and family ties united the orders fraternally with the ecclesiastical hierarchy. As in the other crusading movements of Europe, deep religious passions were aroused, capable of seriously undermining the increasingly fragile position of the Jew. Moreover, Spain's crusade against Islam had a special edge. The warriors of the faith did not have to go east to fight the"infidel"; the battle was fought almost entirely on Iberian soil.[1]

At first, the Sephardim found themselves in a favorable position as the five Christian kingdoms of Spain sought to colonize the newly recaptured towns and territories. In some places—Toledo, Saragossa, and Tortosa—Jews were offered special inducements to replace the fleeing Muslim population: land grants, elective privileges, and tax exemptions. Occasionally, as in Valencia and Catalonia, the Jewish community (*aljama*) was even exempted from internal customs duties for several years. These incentives were spelled out in charters called *fueros* also affirming that Jews were to be tolerated under the protection of the king. As a result, the autonomy of the *aljama* was strengthened as old Jewish quarters were augmented or resettled and new ones established. Jews rented stalls in the bazaar, used grants given them to farm the land, and leased houses from nobles, princes, and monasteries. Abandoned agricultural properties were distributed to them as individuals or as groups. Favorable laws made clear that their lives and property were to be secure. Not only Jews, however, but also the Christians (the so-called *mozarabs*) and even Muslims (termed *mudejar* in the recaptured lands) were induced and cajoled to remain in the reconquered areas as artisans and tillers of the soil.

By and large, a mutually beneficial arrangement seemed to be evolving: while the Christians pursued the business of war, it was left to the Jews to cultivate a great variety of the arts of peace, including the building and reorganization of commerce and industry.[2] In addition, they were often settled in fortresses to serve as a garrison or assigned other military responsibilities. Some were given charge of the finances of Catholic religious orders, such as the order of Santiago, and others were entrusted with collecting the tribute from Granada. (Though remaining an independent Muslim state, the Nasrid kingdom of Granada was required to pay a heavy tribute to the Christians.)

Periodically, the anomalous situation arose of Jews being placed in a position of authority over Muslims, who remained a majority of the population in the newly conquered Christian kingdoms, as when James I of Aragon conquered Valencia in 1238 and appointed the Jews as *bailes* to administer the town, rewarding them for their efforts with houses and estates. Such visible exercise of power by Jews was not only offensive to Muslims but also ran counter to Church doctrine, as well as popular conceptions of the "proper" place of Jews. As early as 1081, Pope Gregory VII had admonished Alfonso VI on this very subject: "Do not in your kingdom permit Jews in any way to be lords of the Christians or to have any authority over them." By the thirteenth century, this doctrine was so widely accepted that King Alfonso X incorporated its restrictive spirit in his famous code of law, *Siete Partidas:* "No Jew may ever hold an esteemed position or public office so as to be able to oppress any Christian in any way whatsoever" (7:24.3).[3] Yet, even as new legislation was repeatedly enacted to reinforce this concept, Jews continued to hold conspicuous administrative and political offices until 1492.

In fact, in comparison with the rest of Europe, reconquered Spain remained a country of wide opportunity for Jews. And as monarchs exploited the know-how of their Sephardic subjects and installed them in positions of prominence, other Jews were attracted to settle in the community, even from abroad. The case of Toledo, the capital of Castile, is typical. When Alfonso VI reconquered the kingdom in 1085, the local Sephardim were permitted to remain. Soon, encouraged in part by the rescue activities of the local Jewish courtier Joseph ha-Nasi Ferrizuel (also known as Cidellus), more Jews joined them. Ferrizuel, the king's personal physician, served in several important capacities, including tax collector and bailiff, and enjoyed wide political and economic power in Castile for a generation. Acknowledged by the authorities as the local *nasi,* he worked to consolidate the reconstructed Jewish community. During the reconquest of Saragossa in 1118, a Jew named Elazar served the king, later entering the service of Ramon Berenguer, count of Barcelona.

In sum, Jewish service facilitated a smooth transition from Muslim to Christian rule. Internally, the transition was also less dramatic than might appear, since the structure of the *aljama,* the location of the Jewish quarter, and the actual status of the Jews did not change drastically. Indeed, their participation in commerce as well as in the all-important textile industry grew significantly, and it looked, on the surface at least, as if they might retrieve their former prestige and power during the economic recovery of the *Reconquista.* Nonthreatening because they were politically neutral, they were generally trusted by their Christian monarchs to handle heavy responsibilities, despite any objections from Church authorities. Unlike the nobility, after all, the politically weak Jews were in no position to revolt against a king.

But the situation challenged the very core of canon law and the ecclesiastical worldview. Gregory VII was only one in a succession of popes who chastised Spanish kings on this point, but their warnings generally proved fruitless, even as the protests did not prevent Ferrizuel from continuing to serve Alfonso VI and several of his heirs. In fact, a sustained tug of war over the status of Jews was waged between royal and ecclesiastical authorities in Europe, partly as a feudal struggle over turf and partly as a question of principle. To take another example, Pope Honorius III became irate when Ferdinand III (1217–52), conqueror of Seville and Córdoba, did not require Jews to wear a special badge and clothing, as decreed by the papacy at the Fourth Lateran Council in 1215. When he demanded an explanation, the king replied that Castilian Jews would flee to Muslim Granada if the humiliating restrictions were enforced. Such an exodus, he claimed, would be disastrous for the revenues of his kingdom. In this instance, the pope relented.

On the other hand, the local laws and customs (*fueros*) were more typical of favorable royal attitudes toward the Jews as a whole. For example, the *fuero* of Teruel in 1176 states, "The Jews are the slaves of the crown and belong exclusively to the royal treasury." Therefore, anyone who injured or murdered a Jew had to pay a special fine or *wergild* (the amount subject to negotiation) not to the family of the victim but to the king. The terms of royal protection of Jews were also spelled out in a royal proclamation when James I, the king of Aragon, conquered Majorca in 1247. In consolidating his kingdom, he granted many privileges specifically to Jews and offered financial inducements for them to settle there. It should be noted that the economic considerations behind such a policy were not slight: an estimated thirty-five to sixty percent of the income in every one of the Iberian kingdoms was provided by Jews.

It logically followed that royalty's assumption of jurisdiction over the economically productive and politically skilled Jews would become an issue in relations between kings and their municipalities, whose town charters gave them the right to regulate their own finances, conduct elections, and administer justice. Why, then, should the monarch be allowed to control the Jews who lived within their precincts? As municipal institutions matured during the Middle Ages, they grew strong enough to clash with royalty, especially on this issue. Consequently, the *fueros* often drafted to entice Jews into newly reconquered areas were a reflection of competing forces in Spanish society: crown, Church, nobility, and municipality. The *Book of Customs of Castile* asserts that Jews, even when living on lands owned by the nobility or the religious orders, are "the property of the King, and live under his protection and for his service." The *fuero* in Ledesma places Jews under joint custody of king and city, while the charter of Salamanca makes a different distinction: Jews may indeed have no lord but the king, yet they are under the protection of the city and must pay their taxes to its officers. In all of these cases, however, the concept of "protection" was

amorphous at best, even when articulated in a legal deed. These laws
and charters were no guarantee of permanent security to the Jews:
moreover, they were never intended to offer political and economic
equality.

Ultimately, conflicts between the various social forces would place
the Jews in a precarious position as the balance of power shifted back
and forth. There were inherent dangers in being a recipient of royal
protection, for the Jewish official gradually became associated in the
popular imagination with royalty and its privileges, even as municipalities, the knights, and the burghers began to articulate a separate collective identity in opposition to the kings. Royal domains increased,
and crown revenues swelled, but so, too, did the expenses of the never-
ending spiral of accelerating warfare, a burden imposed only by royalty
but often collected by Jews in their service. Especially when a king was
absent or politically vulnerable, anti-monarchic sentiment, from whatever quarter, could spill over to engulf the Jews who were in highly
visible positions of power.

Parenthetically, the historical stereotype that Jews were the sole, or
even the principal, group of state financiers in this period is belied by
the facts. Most finance officials, tax farmers, and moneylenders were
Christian, and the Jews who assumed these roles were being assimilated
into, rather than differentiated from, this mainstream endeavor. The
role of the Sephardim in state finances has been erroneously exaggerated in the written record because, unlike their Christian counterparts,
they were subject to special regulation and their activities were specifically reported. In addition, their own brethren deeply resented the
advantages of the powerful few and repeatedly opposed the favored tax
status that could be granted or sold to Jewish fiscal agents down until
the reign of Ferdinand and Isabella. Tax exemption was especially bur-
densome to the minority community since these royal officials were
often its richest members. They and their families, emerging as a divisive class of "privileged" Jews, were considered to be an assimilating
and otherwise negative presence. Communal regulations repeatedly
placed the recipients of royal favors under a ban.

For a deceptively long while, *reconquista* Spain retained many of the
cultural features of Andalusia and would change only gradually. For

centuries, in fact, the Castilian state remained a curious blend of three traditions: the Arab princely courts, European agrarian feudalism, and the unique strain of Christian piety peculiar to Spain. The contact between Muslim and Christian cultures and the "osmosis of manners" were pervasive in all spheres of life, most notably in agricultural techniques and technology, as well as language and literature.[4]

As the former structures of the vanquished Muslim states were dismantled, Jews reemerged as a cultural bridge between the two. As far as their own cultural development was concerned, Jewish religious and cultural life remained rich and varied. The former seats of Jewish learning—Córdoba, Lucena, Granada—now lay in ruins, but Sephardic scholarship continued and indeed thrived in Toledo and in the Catalan port city of Barcelona. Iberian Jewry held a central place in the Jewish world during the centuries of reconquest, absorbing cultural influences from the more pietistic Ashkenazic Jews of the North and serving as a major force in the cultural life of Jews in Europe. Poets continued to write in the Andalusian mode at the same time that Kabbalistic cultural strains were strengthening.

As we have seen, the Jews who earlier fled Muslim Spain had scattered in all directions, carrying Andalusian traditions with them. In addition to the prominent Maimon and ibn Aqnin families, who fled to Morocco, others sought asylum in Europe. In Provence, for example, the emigrés Joseph Kimhi and Judah ibn Tibbon would produce translations of Judeo-Arabic classics (going from Arabic to Hebrew to Latin or the vernacular) that would influence Northern European Christians as well as Jews. Many Andalusian luminaries, however, relocated within reconquered Catholic Spain, often encouraged by rescue committees set up at the frontiers by courtiers like Judah ibn Ezra. They would return to prominence, but the transition was not always smooth; in fact, many found adjustment to the less sophisticated ambiance of *reconquista* Spain distinctly painful. The distinguished scholar Abraham ibn Daud, or Avendauth, nostalgic for the "good old days" of Córdoba, reconstructed a history of the Jews intended to validate the former way of life of the courtier-rabbi class. The eleventh-century poet Moses ibn Ezra, virtually alone in Granada after his friends and colleagues fled, bemoaned the "desert of savages" among whom he lived:

> Throughout my life I have known success. . . . But now the tears flow from my eyes as I seek to overcome my grief at my loneliness in my native land, without a companion at my side . . . and I see no man

about me of my family and kin. I remain in Granada, a city of declining bustle and splendor, like a stranger in the land . . .[5]

Less dramatically, most of the other Andalusian intellectuals tried to hold onto their unique heritage, seeking patrons who appreciated this culture and would encourage them to perpetuate it. But the aging courtier-rabbis were estranged from both Jewish laymen and Christian courtiers. They were increasingly out of step with the changing times, which had no place for the former ideal cultural model that blended secular sciences with Hebraic traditions. The supremacy of philosophy was soon to be challenged by more conservative Jewish voices.

Meanwhile, Arabic would for some time remain the spoken language of the region, particularly around Valenica. Consequently, many Jews found a niche in the new Christian society by virtue of their mastery of the language and Islamic culture. Because these intellectuals were also at home in Latin as well as all of the Spanish regional vernaculars—Castilian, Catalan, Navarrese—they could provide very specialized services to their monarchs. The courtier Sheshet Perfet, for instance, reportedly attained a high position "only through the writing of Arabic." When James I conquered Majorca, there was no one capable of writing out the treaty of capitulation except two Jewish courtier-interpreters from Saragossa, Bahya and Solomon Alconstantini.

As in Andalusia, successful interpreters frequently moved on to become diplomats for the Christian kings, serving as ambassadors to the various Muslim kingdoms in North Africa. Other former courtier families re-emerged to vie with upstarts among their brethren. The venerable Andalusian families of ibn Ezra, ibn Shushan, Alfakhar, Halevi, Abulafia, and ibn Zadok returned to public service as tax farmers, administrators, physicians, and courtiers in Toledo. In Barcelona and Saragossa, the Sheshet, Benveniste, and Eleazar families continued their close relationship to the court, becoming advisors to kings, bailiffs, and property owners. As in former times, these prominent families combined political power with patronage of arts, usually married among themselves, and fought fiercely for favors from rival contenders for power. There was a distinguishing and dispiriting new factor, however. In Muslim Spain the rank and file of the Jewish population had shared the values of the courtier-rabbis and tended to emulate their tastes and habits; but now there was a widening gulf between courtier and *aljama,* exacerbated by a gradual decline in the social position of the Jews as a whole. As time passed, the privileged classes no longer read the same books or even necessarily shared the same interests as their humbler brethren. Not all courtiers continued to regard themselves as defenders of the community, and some became cynical and self-serving.

The transformation of Spain to Christian rule was accompanied by a new mixing of cultures, for coexistence of Muslim and Christian peoples ranged along a continuum from active warfare or tense stalemate to mere proximity, from absence of conflict to mutual borrowing. Within this perspective of changing relationships and *convivencia,* Jews again found a niche as cultural intermediaries as they had in Umayyad Spain. In reconquered Toledo, for example, where Christians, Muslims, and Jews rubbed shoulders in a daily exchange of goods and ideas, the Sephardic courtiers became the vital link in the process of cultural transmission of ancient and Islamic classics to Christian Europe. After all, an entire center of Muslim culture, including scholars, scientists, and artists, along with their libraries, had entered the heart of Spanish Christendom intact. When Toledo's Archbishop Raimundo (1126–52) formed an interdenominational, international group of scholars to translate Arabic classics into Latin, he invited several Jews and Jewish converts to participate. The work of translation in medieval times was not a largely objective act, accurately reproducing a work from one language in another. Scientists would create as they translated, in the process forming new syntheses of knowledge. Alfonso X (1252–84) concentrated the translation activities that had been scattered about Spain in one location and subdivided and organized the labors of his translators. Being multilingual, Jews could easily render the Arabic text into a Castilian or Catalan version that a Christian scholar would translate into Latin. This project was truly cooperative in practice as well as spirit, for scholars worked by reading aloud to each other. At precisely the same time, scholars were swarming into the city from other parts of Europe, making Toledo the continent's entryway for the knowledge that had come from the East in mathematics, philosophy, medicine, botany, astronomy, and practical geometry and was being translated from the Arabic by the former residents of Andalusia.[6]

Gerard of Cremona, Domingo Gonzálvez, Johannes Hispanus (probably a convert known as John of Seville), and Avendahut (probably the Jewish scholar Abraham ibn Daud) collaborated on several important translations of Arab and ancient Greek classics. Another convert, Pedro Alfonso of Huesca (d. 1110), compiled up-to-date astronomical tables from the Arabic as well as moral tales and fables that would later be used by Boccaccio. During the reign of Alfonso X, the reader in the synagogue of Toledo, Isaac ibn Sid, edited the famous astronomical tables that became known as the Alfonsine Tablets, while three of the king's physicians, Judah Kohen and Samuel and Abraham Levi, translated Arabic astronomical and astrological works into Castilian. Another Toledan Jew, Maestro Pedro, translated the entire Koran into Latin in a single year, 1143. It was as a result of this extraordinary outpouring of translation, too, that the philosophies of Maimonides, Gabirol, Averroes, and al-Ghazzali, the giants of Andalusian Judaism and Islam, reached a European audience and eventually influenced the great medieval Christian scholars Albertus Magnus and Thomas Aquinas. These activities would reach their peak under Alfonso, who was known as "the Wise" because of his penchant for learning, and summoned Jews to his court specifically to translate works from Hebrew as well as Arabic. The translators had to create a Castilian language that could accommodate the new philosophy and science, for neither the Spanish vernacular nor the Latin of the day had the appropriate vocabulary for such concepts. With their return to Christian Spain, Hebrew became the main vehicle of Jewish cultural expression.

Castilian was of particular interest to Ferdinand III, who patronized scholars and promoted the use of the language after he reconquered Seville. He encouraged Jews to contribute their talents to this and other enterprises of the state. As noted earlier, the multilingual inscription on his tomb in the chapel of the cathedral of Seville—Arabic, Hebrew, Castilian—symbolized his vision of his kingdom as the home of all three faiths. Similar cultural exchange occurred elsewhere on the Iberian peninsula, as large populations migrated and commercial relations with the rest of Europe were expanded. As we have seen, even poets writing in Muslim Spain, like Judah Halevi, would include entire strophes written in contemporary Castilian, or Romance. Even as late as the fifteenth century, when the condition of the Jews had sharply deteriorated, they were still engaged in cultural interaction and transmission. The exceptional Bible translation of Rabbi Moses Arragel, for example, the Alba Bible, was executed in collaboration with a Dominican friar and Christian illuminators while persecution of his people raged throughout Spain.

Even earlier, however, the intermingling among the three groups

Jewish life in Spain can be traced as far back as the ancient Roman province of Hispamia. Evidence of Jewish cultural integration alongside the practice of Judaism is seen in ancient Jewish tombstones like the one above, containing Latin inscriptions. Remnants of a *mikveh* or ritual bath (*right*) in Besalú attest to the continuous presence of organized Jewish communities with well-defined religious institutions throughout the Middle Ages. (*ASAP/Mike Ganor*)

The city of Toledo (*above*), the center of Christian political and cultural life in Spain until 1516, also housed a vibrant Jewish quarter (*judería*), visible at right. (*Frédéric Brenner*) The Muslim conquest of Spain in 711 inaugurated an era of Jewish cultural flowering. One of this period's greatest Hebrew poets and philosophers was Solomon ibn Gabirol, whose statue (*below left*) commemorates his career in the Muslim kingdom of Malaga. (*ASAP/Mike Ganor*) When the Almohade dynasty conquered Spain in the 12th century, Moses Maimonides (*below right*), the greatest Jewish philosopher and jurist of the Middle Ages, was among those who fled the ensuing fundamentalist persecution. (*Beth Hatefutsoth*)

רבנו משה ברבי מימון זל
יד רמ״ה תתצ״ה - כ׳ טבת תתקס״ח

Jews served in the courts of the Muslim Kingdom of Granada until its fall in 1492. The Lion's Court of the Alhambra (*below left*) is thought to have been modelled on the home of Jewish courtier Samuel ibn Nagrela. After the Christian reconquest of Seville in 1248, Jews presented the symbolic keys above to Ferdinand III with the inscription (in Hebrew, Latin, and Castilian) "God will open, then the king will enter." (*ASAP/Mike Ganor*) Ferdinand's tomb in Seville with its similar trilingual inscriptions (*below right*) bears further testimony to the multicultural character of medieval Spain. (*Photo MAS*)

Alfonso X (called the Wise) patronized all kinds of learning at his court, and the "Book of Chess" (*above*) which he commissioned depicts the shared intellectual and social life of Christians, Muslims, and Jews during his reign. At the same time, his repressive legal codes betray the spread of anti-Jewish attitudes in Spain, and his famous "Cantigas de Santa Maria" (*below*) portray a demonized image of Jews. (*Photo MAS*)

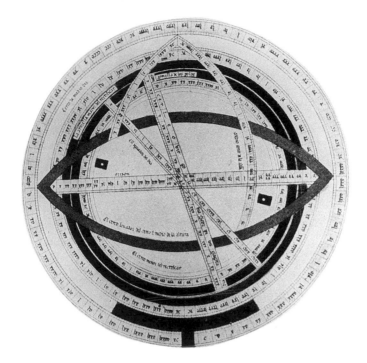

Despite increasing persecutions, Jews were central to the explosion of scientific and technical learning that launched the great age of discovery. The armillary sphere above was constructed around 1200 by a Jewish astronomer for Alfonso X. (*Beth Hatefutsoth*) The famed Catalan Atlas, showing the world and its navigational routes in six panels, was drawn by the Jewish cartographers Abraham and Judah Cresques in Majorca around 1375 and presented to Charles V of France. (*Bibliothèque Nationale*)

Two surviving synagogues in Toledo are monuments to the continuity of Jewish communal strength in Christian Spain. The synagogue built in 1203 by Joseph ben Shushan, who was financier to Alfonso VIII of Castile, was converted to a church in 1411 and became known as Santa Maria la Blanca. It is an elegant example of mudéjar architectural style. (*Above, ASAP/Mike Ganor; right, Frédéric Brenner*)

The synagogue known as El Transito (*below left*) was built in 1357 by Samuel Halevi Abulafia, the treasurer of Peter I. Abulafia was eventually executed by this king, called Peter the Cruel; but the street that leads to the synagogue (*below*) still bears his name. Noted for its decorative friezes and inscriptions, the synagogue was converted to a church in 1494. At left is a view of the women's gallery. (*ASAP /Mike Ganor*)

In 1480, as Ferdinand and Isabella prepared to launch their final war against the Muslim stronghold of Granada, the Inquisition was established to root out false converts (*conversos*) who engaged in secret Jewish practices. Sentencing and punishment were carried out in dramatic public gatherings, like the one above in the Plaza Mayor of Madrid, known as *autos da fé*. These persecutions continued to intensify until, in March of 1492, shortly after the fall of Granada and the reestablishment of Christian hegemony, the king and queen issued a writ (*below*) that decreed the expulsion of all Jews from Spain. (*Photo MAS: Auto de Fé on Plaza Mayor de Madrid. Painting by Francisco Rizzi. Musco del Prado, Madrid*)

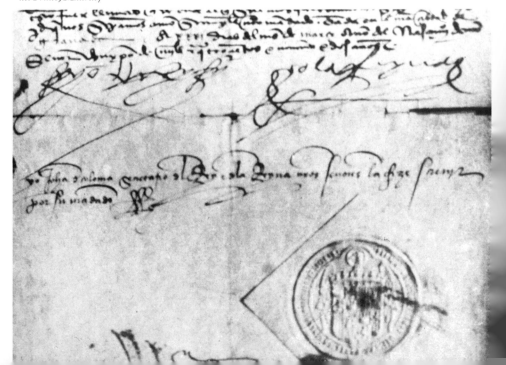

symbolized on Ferdinand III's burial monument was never as joyous and productive in reconquered Christian Spain as in Andalusia. Each time the king met with the Cortes, he had to listen to harangues and petitions from malcontent nobles who wanted to restrict the rights of Jews. As the thirteenth century wore on, still other anti-Jewish currents flowed into Spain from many different directions. From northern Europe appeared French, Italian, and German settlers and adventurers who sought their fortune in the still sparsely occupied regions of recaptured Spain, transporting anti-Jewish traditions flourishing in northern Europe. Also moving southward were crusaders, including pious pilgrims on the way to Spain's national shrine at Santiago de Compostela, along with migrating followers of the Cluniac and Cistercian monasteries. By the middle of the thirteenth century, these extremely negative influences combined with the settling down of society as the *Reconquista* neared its successful conclusion. The time was ripe for traditional negative attitudes toward Jews to reassert themselves. Spain's porous borders were breached as she began to share Europe's deeply rooted anti-Jewish patrimony.

In the summer of 1263, Rabbi Moses ben Naḥman of Gerona (also known as Nahmanides), the great biblical and Talmudic scholar and rabbi, was ordered by James I to appear at the royal palace in Barcelona. At the instigation of a zealous apostate, the Dominican friar Pablo Christiani, the king was staging a religious debate; Nahmanides was to serve as the Jewish disputant for a subject fraught with danger and laden with centuries of controversy. Had the messianic mission been fulfilled with Jesus? Did the Talmud itself offer proof that Jesus was in fact the Messiah, and was the Messiah divine or human? Pablo hoped to hasten the conversion of the Spanish Jews by convincing his opponent that the Messiah had indeed come in the person of Jesus and that the Jews' most Jewish of texts proved it. (According to some modern commentators, the debate was actually part of a Dominican plan to convert all Jews in Europe.)[7]

Nahmanides, then in his sixties, was probably not surprised by the royal summons, for he had already played an active role in other heated ideological controversies, such as the debate convulsing the Jews of France as well as Spain over the proper place of rationalism in Jewish life. As one of the greatest rabbinical figures of the thirteenth century, Nahmanides showed consummate skill in amalgamating the several intellectual trends then emerging among the Jews in Spain. His legal writings bear the influence of the Jewish Talmudic scholars of France (the *Tosafists*) and the mystics or kabbalists of Provence. A personally modest man, he had earned a reputation for being able to mediate disputes, even as he had seen the climate of opinion shifting in his lifetime from free inquiry to fear of dissent. He had already been called upon to defend Judaism, probably even engaging, albeit reluctantly, in contentious religious dialogues with some of the actively conversionist friars. In this instance, however, he could hope that his good personal relationship with the king would protect him and his brethren from any negative reactions to his presentation. James had specifically promised the rabbi that he could speak freely and that public decorum would be maintained. In any event, the royal command could not be refused.

The summons was unusual but not inexplicable, for thirteenth-century Europe was a continent obsessed with questions of dogma and faith, conformity and nonconformity. Fear of heresy was rampant, and Spain lay at the very border of southern France, the territory that was considered the seat of heresy in the twelfth and thirteenth centuries. In addition, as we have seen, the papacy had long been pressing vigorously for greater restrictions on the Jews. In pursuit of these related aims, control of orthodox thinking and control of the Jews, the popes turned their gaze toward Spain, which was fully entering the orbit of European politics at last.

To counter the threat of heresy—which included any supposed blasphemy against the saints, rituals, and credos of the Church—Rome created special preaching orders of Dominicans and Franciscans, empowering the former order in particular to combat all hints of religious nonconformity. Thus, the special mechanism of inquiry known as the Inquisition was established so that the Dominicans could more effectively ferret out and extirpate all heretics.

The life-and-death struggle waged by the new mendicant orders against heresy and "the forces of darkness" introduced a new weapon, the so-called "dialogue of controversy," specifically designed to spread the faith and preserve orthodoxy.[8] Now, armies of learned Christians would actively pursue the conversion of Muslims and Jews as a high priority, preaching the mysteries of the faith in order to persuade the uninitiated. This ideal, fervently held in the highest ecclesiastical circles, was deeply shared throughout European culture. Marco Polo gives a long account of the "secret conversion" of the caliph of Baghdad in the opening chapter of his famous journal, for example. Undoubtedly, his readers were moved by this tale although it was no more than wishful thinking. Closer to home, Franciscans were courting martyrdom to bring the message of the Gospels to Tunis, the heartland of Islam.

The mendicant friars who formed the vanguard of this proselytizing movement had been carefully trained in special schools where instruction in Hebrew and Arabic language and philosophy formed the core of the curriculum. As early as 1235, the Dominican master-general wrote from Milan to all Dominicans, enjoining them to "be prepared to learn Arabic, Hebrew, Greek, or some other outlandish language." At least five Dominican language schools focusing on conversation were set up in the kingdom of Valencia alone in the thirteenth century. Perhaps the most effective teachers were the many zealous converts from Judaism or Islam, who were eager to prove their orthodoxy and were sensitive to the psyche of their former co-religionists as well as being adept in their mode of arguing. During the heated exchanges of the debate in Barcelona, Nahmanides turned to Christiani and asked, "Are you the one who asked the king to assemble the Jewish scholars that they might debate with you?" The question suggests that he understood the apostate's role in persuading James I to stage the event.

Barcelona was a major base for these missionizing activities. Its leading spirit from 1238 to 1240 was Raymond de Peñaforte, the driving force behind the mission schools and master-general of the Dominicans. He aimed his program simultaneously at Muslims and Jews. His presence beside the king in the royal court during the disputation in 1263 was consistent with his activist stance toward missionizing. It was de Peñaforte who opened and closed the proceedings at Barcelona, concluding with a lengthy disquisition upon the doctrine of the Trinity.

The movement had its luminaries, whose efforts underscore the fervor of its aims. Ramon Lull, for example, a Franciscan troubador-turned-mystic, was as unswerving in energy as indomitable in faith. Two massive handbooks were produced especially for the preaching friars: the *Pugio Fidei adversus Mauros et Iudaeos* by Raymond Martini (present at Barcelona as a silent witness and perhaps also as coach) and the *Summa contra Gentiles* by Thomas Aquinas.

Coincidentally, the kings reigning in the thirteenth century were the most vigorous and learned in Spanish history, and they vied with each other in supporting the conversionary movement. James I, busily engaged in proselytizing efforts in Aragon, chastised Alfonso the Wise for spending more time on scholarship than on converting Muslims. Alfonso had indeed founded his Arabic and Latin language schools in Seville in 1253 in order to explore Islamic culture, not "save souls." Still, his legal corpus *Siete Partidas* not only endorsed the missionary outreach to Jews but also offered economic incentives for conversion. At the same time, following canon law, he decreed that Christians who converted to Judaism would be executed. Royal spouses, too, became involved in the movement. Queen Blanca of Aragon, wife of James II, provided in her will for a scholarship fund for "the Dominican friars at Jativa, studying in Hebrew and Arabic."

But aside from the conversionary movement, the battle for Christian supremacy in Iberia assumed several other forms. For one thing, the Church sought to exercise control over the minds of the faithful by banning the use of Bibles written in the vernacular. For another, in response to concerns about heresy among practicing Christians rather than Jews or Muslims, bloody crusades were launched in southern France against the groups known as Albigensians and Waldensians. By extension, threats to orthodoxy could include the "proper faith" of Jews as well, since their internal disagreements might spill over into the Christian community. Once it was decided that heretics could not be tolerated in the Church, the question of the continued toleration of the presence of Jews in Europe was inevitably raised.

For the moment, however, the advocates of toleration prevailed, for pope and king were in agreement that the continuation of the benighted Jewish community performed a positive function. As Alfonso X phrased it, "Their 'captivity' serves as perpetual reminder of descent from those who crucified Jesus."⁹

On the other hand, toleration did not mean renouncing the conversionist dream. Beginning in southern France and Italy, the proselytizing movement began to gain wide acceptance, and the centuries-old opposition to forced conversion began to weaken. It is no accident that this latter trend emerged when anti-Jewish sentiment was on the rise.

The pernicious role of converts to Christianity looms large in the breakdown of the Jewish community in Spain. Their number seemed to increase in response to the growing legal restrictions upon the community, and ecclesiastical authorities did not fail to notice this obvious cause-and-effect relationship. But they argued that the introduction of humiliating measures against the Jews, such as the wearing of special clothes and distinguishing badges, did not constitute forced conversions; rather, they were inducements to "voluntary" conversion. In Spain, discriminatory clothing legislation provided the kings not only with a weapon of intimidation but with a new source of revenue as well, because exemptions to the restrictions were sold. In some cases, wealthy courtiers, physicians, and other influential people were able to keep buying exemptions practically until the eve of the expulsion.

Another approach to persuasion, related to the staged religious disputation, was the introduction of compulsory Christian sermons into the synagogues. They were delivered in the vernacular and had a particularly demoralizing impact on the Jews. In 1242, Aragon's James I issued a typical decree:

> Whenever the archbishops, bishops, Dominicans or Franciscan monks, visit towns or localities inhabited by Saracens or Jews and wish to espouse the word of God to those Jews or Saracens, the latter shall foregather at such calls and patiently listen to these persons. Should they refuse to come voluntarily, our officials shall compel them to do so without subterfuge.[10]

Three years later, the imposition of such sermons was incorporated in a papal bull. In the event, James would soften his original decree somewhat. At first, he allowed the monks into the synagogues en masse, but in response to Jewish pressure, he relented slightly in 1263, declaring that no more than ten monks and their attendants could "invade" a synagogue at one time. This restraint calmed the Jews to some extent, since it eliminated the hostile crowds who often accompanied the impassioned preachers and caused riots and injury.

Meanwhile, the Dominican order's goal of intruding itself into the Jewish community as policeman of Jewish thought was furthered by the inner tensions and internal disputes raging among the Jews of Spain and southern France over the philosophical writings of Maimonides. Perhaps it was inevitable that Jews should begin to echo the narrowing intellectual horizons of their surrounding environment as Christian Europe turned from rationalism toward pietism and mysticism. But more than ideas was at stake in the Jewish debate, which reflected deepening social as well as intellectual cleavages that became explosively charged by the 1230s. Especially in Provence, quarrels raged amidst bans and counterbans, as two ideological camps arose in battle between "faith" and "reason." This tragic controversy within the Jewish community enabled the Dominicans to gain a foothold.

In 1232, some Jews in southern France, unable to resolve their inner divisions about philosophy and free thought, invited the Dominicans to intervene in the so-called "Maimonidean controversy." (Nahmanides had tried to intervene but failed.) Of course, the friars were only too happy to oblige, for such spiritual crisis and disequilibrium could only advance their designs for greater control over the minority community. Thus a dangerous precedent for interference in internal Jewish life was set. In this case, the Dominicans acted with alacrity. In 1233, Maimonides *Guide for the Perplexed* was burned as a heretical work. In 1242, an apostate in France, Nicholas Donin, charged that the Talmud was a heretical work and persuaded the pope to have it publicly burned at Montpellier.

Meanwhile, some Church authorities realized that it would be preferable to use the Talmud for missionary purposes rather than consign it to the flames. A foremost proponent of this approach was the apostate Pablo Christiani. It was upon his appearance in public life at the Disputation of Barcelona that zealous converts, some of whom showed special malevolence, began to emerge as the bane of Jewish life in Spain. Christiani, for example, was knowledgeable in Jewish sources and adept in the writing of polemics; he devoted his life to attacking the Jewish people and rabbinical literature. He may have been pursuing a personal vendetta, for during his long career he took several initiatives to undermine the strength and self-confidence of his former co-religionists. While he represented the new trend in ecclesiastical circles toward missionizing as opposed to crusading, he also felt that it was imperative to approach the infidel on his own terms in a multipronged attack.

Even after the passage of more than seven centuries, the proud, solitary figure of Moses Nahmanides in the royal palace, courageously confronting the combined forces of church and state in the persons of the king, the leading Dominicans and Franciscans, and hostile elements of the general population, evokes awe and sadness. Not only did the occasion pit him against experienced foes and the new scholarship of the friars, it also sharpened conversionary pressure on his brethren. In addition, he was compelled, for tactical reasons, to question the authoritative nature of parts of the Talmud, thereby opening up a Pandora's box in the long, steady decline in self-confidence of the Jews of Spain.

The Jews were most reluctant to engage in any religious debates with either Muslims or Christians. Such debates were fraught with peril, a no-win situation for the Jewish participant. If he spoke freely, he might arouse the ire of his powerful opponents; but if he was too submissive, he could demoralize his brethren. Therefore, as defender of the faith, Nahmanides had to satisfy two audiences simultaneously. He had to counter Christiani's missionizing arguments by proving that his opponent did not truly understand Judaism, but he also had to justify the belief of Jews in the classical sources of their religion.

The Christian participant was also not unaware of the palpable dangers of religious debate. Should he fail, he might engender doubts among Christian believers, or even subject himself to mockery from his Jewish opponent. On the other hand, if he succeeded, he might inspire a wave of Jewish apostasy or (less desirable from the official perspective) an upsurge in persecution of the Jews. The stakes were extremely high.

Two versions of the Disputation of Barcelona have survived, Nahmanides' own record in Hebrew and a Latin account penned by his foes. Despite the varying points of view, both agree that the rabbi succeeded in speaking openly during the four or five sessions held during the week of July 20. Obviously, Nahmanides had prepared himself very well. From prior encounters, he was familiar with Christiani's technique, daring and innovative for its time, of reading the Talmud Christologically. In other words, just as Christian apologists had for centuries used the Old Testament to prove the "truth of Christianity," the friar tried to use the Talmud as a prooftext. He could certainly achieve a major victory if he could convincingly demonstrate that this quintessential Jewish source showed Jesus to be the Messiah, thus nullifying the continued relevance of the ceremonial and legal traditions being practiced by the Jews.

As Nahmanides expected, Christiani brought up an obscure text he had found by scouring through the vast Talmudic corpus; it declared that the Messiah was born on the day of the destruction of the Temple. In dealing with this text, the rabbi faced a serious dilemma. If he denied the authenticity and binding authority of a rabbinic text, he would be placed in an unfavorable light with the Jews and might even call the cherished messianic tradition into question, which would be troubling and even traumatic for his brethren in the audience. On the other hand, he could not accept Christiani's reading of the text. Nahmanides' solution was to dismiss the importance of the passage. Specifically, he argued spiritedly that only the legal part of the Talmud, known as the *halakhah,* was authoritative to Jews. The text cited by Christiani was in the sermonic and homiletic body of Talmudic material, the *aggadah.* Furthermore, the rabbi argued, even if the text had been in the *halakhah,* it would prove nothing about the messiahship of Jesus: he was long dead when the Temple was destroyed. But in drawing distinctions between different layers of tradition in the Talmud, Nahmanides was using an argument unknown outside limited circles of learned Jews. The suggestion that any part of the Talmud was not an authoritative guide to Jewish life could prove in the long run to be confusing at best or deeply demoralizing.[11]

The king took an active part in the debate, interjecting a question now and then to bolster his friar's arguments or to clarify a moot point. Despite his efforts and the fervent arguments of Christiani, however, Nahmanides was so impressive that the Franciscans asked that the debates be discontinued, and the crowd in attendance became unruly. James I ended the disputation, but he supposedly remarked to Nahmanides, "Never have I seen anyone who was in the wrong argue so well as you have." He is also reported to have provided the rabbi with some monetary compensation, presumably for the mastery of his performance.

After the disputation, Nahmanides lingered in Barcelona in order to rebut some charges raised by de Peñaforte in a compulsory sermon in the synagogue the following Sabbath. Thereafter, he returned to Gerona and composed his account, apparently giving a copy to the bishop of the city. In this fashion it may have fallen into the hands of Dominicans, who in any event charged the rabbi with writing blasphemy. The self-assured tone of his writing so enraged the Order that he was forced into exile in 1267, leaving his family behind and settling alone in Palestine. Meanwhile, James I acceded to Christiani's request to be allowed to missionize among the Jews of Aragon; he also set up a commission to purge all Jewish books of "blasphemy" within three months. Thus was the main thrust of Raymond de Peñaforte's program against the Jews fulfilled and the victory of Nahmanides, if victory it was, nullified.

The Disputation of Barcelona is one of those historical turning points whose full importance becomes clear only with hindsight. We can see now that the personality and interests of Nahmanides reflect a new intellectual reality in Spain, for the traditions of northern European Jewry were gaining wider currency as Christian Spain became increasingly detached from the Islamic world. Talmudic scholarship had become a new focal point of learning among the Sephardic elite, challenging the former unique blend of science and philosophy with rabbinics.

In fact, by the thirteenth century many Spanish Jewish leaders not only shared the intellectual orientation of their brethren to the north; they were also developing a new and profound interest in the spreading notions of pietism and mysticism known as *kabbalah*. It has been suggested that the rapid acceptance of this new movement was a definitive rejection of the dazzling, sophisticated Andalusian culture. Indeed, nothing was further from the intellectual kabbalists than the previous attempts at harmonizing Judaism with foreign cultures. Opportunities for interreligious communication were dwindling in any event, and Jewish creativity turned inward, exploring new and more irrational realms of Jewish religious experience. The scholars working at a vibrant kabbalistic center established in Gerona included Nahmanides. A Sephardic scholar, Moses de Léon, produced a classic of kabbalist thought, the *Sefer ha-Zohar* (*Book of Splendor*), between 1280 and 1286.

In Castile the mystics formed a partial alliance with the anti-rationalists who were involved in the continuing Maimonidean controversy. Finally, the great Barcelona rabbi and communal leader Solomon ibn Adret (1235–1310) issued a sweeping ban in 1305 on the study of philosophy (called "Greek thought") and science, except medicine, by people under the age of twenty-five:

> *Woe to mankind because of the insult to the*
> *   Torah!*
> *For they have strayed far from it.*
> *Its diadem have they taken away;*
> *Its crown have they removed.*
>
> *Every man with his censer in his hand offers*
> *incense*
> *Before the Greeks and the Arabs.*
> *Therefore have we decreed for our community*
> *that for the next fifty years, under threat*
> *of the ban, no man under twenty-five shall*
> *study the books which the Greeks have*

written on religious philosophy and the
natural sciences. Nor shall any member of
the community teach any Jew under twenty-
five any of these sciences lest they drag
him away from the superior law of Israel.
How can a human being not be afraid to judge
between the wisdom of man and that of the
Supreme Being. . . . Medicine, though one of
the natural sciences, has not been included
in our general prohibition because the Torah
permits the physician to heal. [12]

As is clear from the above, ibn Adret could not entirely condemn "Greek thought," not did he unqualifiedly support a turn to mysticism. Like many Sephardic intellectuals of this changing time, he counseled a moderate path between the extremes of rationalism and mysticism.

In addition to mysticism and anti-rationalism, the Jewish leaders' response to the declining position of their community and growing pressures from the outside also took a collective political form. The rabbis tried to strengthen communal discipline by promulgating sweeping regulations to strengthen the *aljama* and create an advisory council of representatives of the larger Jewish communities. Although efforts to establish a centralized supracommunal organization never lasted, in times of crisis assemblies of communal representatives did meet to take a united stance on critical issues of security. In Aragon in 1354, such an assembly met to confront the persecutions of Jews sparked by the Black Death (see below). Similarly, the Jews of Castile convened in 1432 in Valladolid to cope with the rapidly declining conditions and passed broad regulations regarding internal discipline. Additionally, communal authorities were invested with broad powers to maintain discipline and punish transgressors of Jewish law.

These abortive attempts at unified political action in the face of persecution had little hope of countering the most alarming new factor that began to impinge upon Jewish life in Spain. Not from the highest levels of church and state but from the common people and their pastors arose an unprecedented popular image of the Jew as an odious, even diabolical figure. Spreading everywhere—in art and architectural ornament, in music and religious pageant, in weekly sermons and rumors spread by priests—this harmful depiction was reinforced, with cruel irony, by the increasing isolation and segregation of the Jewish community. Drawing ultimately upon early pagan and Christian sources, the popular imagination conjured up images of Jews as destroyers of Christianity, purveyors of evil, desecrators of hallowed Christian relics, sorcerers, enemies of mankind—indeed, veritable incarnations of the Devil, or at least traffickers with him in evil. The Devil was a real presence in the mind of medieval man, and through a long process beginning with the equation of the synagogue with the Devil in the Gospels, the Jew and the Devil were linked. Theologically, one belonged either to the kingdom of Christ or the kingdom of the Devil. The medieval world also inherited the ancient calumny that Jews were sorcerers who used Hebrew as the medium of their magic. The identification of Jews as poisoners had already appeared in Alfonso X's *Siete Partidas,* which decreed that a Christian could take medicine from a Jew only if a Christian physician was acquainted with the contents.[13]

By the early fourteenth century popular belief in the Jew as poisoner, intent upon the destruction of Christianity, began to spread in Europe. Sometimes the Jew was accused of alliance with lepers in this plot. The results were devastating. In town after town, and by 1321 throughout the whole of France, the Jews were temporarily expelled. Nor was there any limit to the crimes that the gullible population of Europe attributed to the Jews. The more fantastic the charge, the more plausible it seemed. It was believed that Jews needed Christian blood, together with lizards, spiders, frogs, sacred hosts, and human flesh, to concoct a brew that would disguise their distinctive signs and odors![14]

Among the catalogue of alleged atrocities was the kidnapping and murder of Christian children for the purpose of obtaining their blood for ritual use. Although papal authorities repeatedly repudiated and condemned this calumny, it cropped up everywhere in Europe after it first appeared in the twelfth century, becoming a ready source of income for the establishment of local shrines dedicated to the martyred "victims" of the Jews. Most of these accusations, usually linked with Easter, were instigated by the clergy, but even the liberal, broad-minded Alfonso X was not above lending credence to the myth. In his *Siete Partidas,* he declared, "We have heard it said that in certain places on Good Friday the Jews steal children and set them on the cross in a mocking manner."

In such an atmosphere, it is not surprising that Jews were even assigned the blame for cataclysmic natural disasters. In 1348, the dreaded Black Death swept mysteriously through Europe, erupting virtually overnight without warning and carrying off almost twenty percent of the continent's entire population. The inconceivable, apparently inexplicable horror led to hysterical popular outbursts against the diabolical Jews, who were accused of spreading the disease by poisoning wells. Rumors of well-poisoning raced through France, Spain, and Germany, gaining immediate credence, for no one doubted that Jews were associated with sorcery. In truth, Jews suffered equally from the plague; so great was the number of their victims that new cemeteries had to be acquired. But neither logic nor royal calls for restraint could silence the vile accusations. In response to this crisis, the Jews of Aragon formed a regional association that would not only seek the king's support but also send representatives to Rome to ask the pope to condemn the calumnies. They also agreed to come to the joint defense of any community that was attacked and to send "envoys from all the communities" to the sessions of the Cortes in order to "watch over the interests of the communities." This practical program reveals that the community in Aragon, at least, was sensitive to the needs of the hour. In the event, their representative body would not outlive the crisis of the plague, but they did obtain a papal bull denouncing the accusations of well-poisoning.

Unfortunately, the persistent and growing anti-Jewish sentiment across the land could not similarly succeed in melding the Jews of Iberia into one strong communal organization. On the one hand, democratizing tendencies were undermining the traditional privileges of the oligarchy of select families, and several attempts were made to bring about such unification. On the other, social and regional divisions remained too persistent, too profound, for the reform attempts to endure. Even so, the communal regulations from the thirteenth and fourteenth centuries show that the separate Jewish communities joined together in a large network of welfare institutions. They also shared a willingness to accept communal discipline and a deep concern for the communal good, as if the divisions seen in the internal ideological battles had not really riven the community. Similarly, it seems that the weakening of self-confidence produced by anti-Semitic legislation was offset by a feeling of continuing cohesion. Nonetheless, the hate, destruction, and killing caused by the superstitious barbarism of 1348 was not an isolated or anomalous incident. With dismal regularity, the ludicrous but potentially lethal rumors surfaced again and again, particularly the charge that Jews made a habit of desecrating the host.

In this atmosphere of heightened tension a prelate in Seville, Ferrant Martinez, launched an anti-Jewish campaign in 1378, haranguing his townspeople about the "iniquity" of the Jews. His proposals to alleviate the "Jewish problem" were drastic: destruction of every one of the city's twenty-three synagogues, confinement of all Jews to a ghetto, cessation of all contact between them and Christians, and the removal of Jews from all positions of influence. His activities became more bellicose and ominous after the deaths of the archbishop and king of Castile in 1390. No one opposed his poisoned diatribes, and the Jews of Seville were attacked on June 4, 1391. A contemporary record notes succinctly that the rioters, after setting fire to the gates of the Jewish quarter, "killed many of its people, but most changed their religion . . . and many died to sanctify the Lord's name and many violated the holy convenant [by converting]."[15]

Obviously, the soil was fertile for Martinez's attacks. As the pogroms spread quickly from city to city throughout Iberia and the Balearic Islands, Jews were everywhere given the same choice: conversion or death. In Castile in particular, the mobs felt that they could rampage with impunity because of the void at the center of power, and few communities were spared. Estimates of the total Jewish population in 1391 range widely, but it is generally believed that, when order was finally restored after about a year of riot, perhaps 100,000 Jews converted, another 100,000 had been murdered, and yet another 100,000 somehow survived by going into hiding or fleeing to Muslim lands.

The religious fervor propelling the persecutors was unmistakable; converts were spared without exception. The rioters marched upon the Jewish neighborhoods as if embarked on a crusade, and the disorders ceased after the Jews converted and their synagogues were transformed into churches. The "crusaders" themselves came from all walks of life. In Valencia, the holy war was instigated by the heads of the municipalities, but in other areas the impetus came from the common folk. (The mobs, in particular, were also motivated by economic envy of the size, wealth, and prominence of the medieval Jewish community, and it is no accident that the first objects destroyed were the records of loans owed to Jewish moneylenders.)

In some instances, Jews were able to avoid conversion for a time by paying generous sums to nobles who agreed to hide them in local fortresses, but they were ultimately handed over to the tenacious mobs and converted. There was slightly less pressure in Aragon, thanks to feeble attempts by the king and queen to control the rioters. But it was only the frantic intercession of Rabbi Hasdai Crescas, the leader of the kingdom's Jewish community, that rescued the Jews of Saragossa from certain destruction. Elsewhere, the work of conversion was not impeded, and it should be stressed that not just the simple folk or the highly assimilated chose to convert rather than be killed. In Córdoba, "great and small did not remain who had not changed their religion." On Majorca, the governor evacuated the Jews to a fortress in Palma, but there, too, the mob broke through and presented the standard ultimatum. Among the island's forced converts were Yehuda Cresques, a famous cartographer, and Isaac Nifoci, a noted astronomer. In the obliteration of the Barcelona community, which would not be reestablished until modern times, even its renowned rabbi, Isaac bar Sheshet Perfet, may have been among the converts.

Although the year-long orgy of anti-Jewish destruction was unusual even by the standards of medieval anti-Semitism, much more unusual was the Jewish response. Until 1391, conversion in the face of persecution had been literally unthinkable in Christian lands. When Jews faced the fury of the mobs in the Rhineland during the First and Second Crusades in 1096–1147, they unhesitatingly chose martyrdom, becoming an example that echoed in Jewish liturgy and shared memory. Before taking their own lives, these Ashkenazic Jews had recited a blessing: "Blessed be thou the Lord our God, King of the Universe, who has commanded us to sanctify His name in public." Their martyrdom, or *kiddush ha-Shem* (sanctification of the name of God), was considered the norm. Given the context of long-standing Judaic tradition, then, the collective conversion in 1391 of nearly 100,000 Jews, whatever their individual motives, is evidence of an enormous erosion of faith. The presence of these new converts, known as *conversos,* would be a source of prolonged anguish for the Jews and of mounting antagonism from the Christian population. As Christians they would no longer be subject to discriminatory legislation and would rapidly rise to prominence. Many, however, forced against their will to convert, would have great difficulty adjusting to their new identity. Ultimately, the issue of the *conversos* would lead directly to the drastic remedy of expulsion. Thus, the year 1391 set the stage for the last chapter of the Sephardic exile in Iberia.

5

Path to Expulsion

The Decline and Destruction of Spanish Jewry

And what will it profit our lord and king to pour holy water on the Jews calling them our names, "Pedro," or "Pablo," while they keep their faith like Akiba or Tarfon. . . . Know, Sire, that Judaism is one of the incurable diseases.

—ibn Verga, *Shebet Yehudah*

Among the riches and pleasures of joyous Asia I find myself a poor and wearied traveler, amidst the abundance of gold and fatness of the burning land of Africa, a wretched, famished and thirsty exile. Now Europe, O Europe, my hell on earth, what shall I say of you . . . ?

—Samuel Usque, *Consolation for the Tribulations of Israel*

After the devastation of 1391, the Jews attempted to reintegrate the fragments of their surviving communities under the leadership of Rabbi Hasdai Crescas of Aragon. Homeless refugees had to be resettled, the *aljamas* rebuilt, and normality reestablished. But more than physical rehabilitation was needed in the ruined *juderías* (Jewish quarters), for the survivors were traumatized and anguished. It was not easy to restore their self-confidence or to find an explanation for the complete destruction of their former glories. Jewish leaders counseled repentance, taking the traditional view that persecution had been divine punishment for sin.

Still more troubling was the phenomenon of the unprecedented mass conversions. On a practical level, the survivors had to deal with the most intractable question of all: how to relate to the growing body of *conversos* who were, after all, their own relatives. On a spiritual level, they had to come to grips with understanding the meaning of the wave of conversions. Obviously, some of the forced baptisms were the instinctive responses of frightened victims who assumed that they could return to Judaism once the storm died down, while others were motivated by pragmatic self-interest as much as fear. In addition, some *conversos* may have been considering the option even before the riots but had hesitated because of the social stigma. But these and other explanations did not address the central fact: the overall scope of the conversions was mind-boggling.

Not surprisingly, several contemporary commentators thought the *converso* phenomenon was symptomatic of a major spiritual crisis unique to Spanish Jewry. In *Iggeret Musar* (*Epistle of Ethical Admonition*), Solomon Alami, an eyewitness to the rampages, argued that the conversions stemmed from a breakdown within the Jewish community. Offering the traditional explanation of divine punishment for Jewish "sins," Alami singled out the prideful, decadent, and flamboyant behavior of community leaders in Spain:

> If we ask ourselves why all this happened to us, then we have to accept the truth: we ourselves are at fault. . . . We and our iniquities caused this evil to happen. Our sages were jealous of each other and disrespectful . . . there was much quarreling among the wise men. . . . Then there were those scholars who attempted to interpret the Scriptures in the Greek manner and clothe it in Greek dress. They believed that Plato and Aristotle had brought us more light than Moses our master. . . . Now, if a man should not be able to "live by his faith," why should he suffer death for it and endure the joke and the shame

of dispersion among the nations? It serves no good purpose to quote Scriptures as support for philosophical opinions: the way of reason and the way of faith are too far apart and will never meet. . . . Those who read a few columns in a book of Greek philosophy will soon tear to shreds the scroll of the Torah. . . . The next in line of decadence were the leaders of the communities and those favored and trusted by the kings. Their riches and their high position made them forsake humility. . . . They acquired costly wagons and horses, dressed in precious garments. . . . They gave up study and industry and cultivated idleness, vainglory, and inordinate ambition. . . . Everyone chased after coveted positions; envy estranged a man from his fellow and they didn't mind denouncing one another before the Court. . . . The burden of taxation they shifted to the poorer classes. In the end, the Court itself found them despicable and removed them from their power. . . .

There is no communal spirit among us. People quarrel over trifles; they hold banquets, listen to music, imitate the gentiles in their clothes and hairdress.[1]

If we are to credit Alami's sweeping indictment, power and access to the court had corrupted the Jewish leaders, while their own law courts were weakened by ignorance and indifference. Materialism and vanity had become rampant as assimilation destroyed the moral fiber of the community. Of course, he singled out the study of philosophy for special condemnation, for his point seems to be that the Sephardim stumbled precisely as a result of those qualities that had made them unique—their ability to imbibe secular culture, their ease of association with kings and courtiers, their esthetic appreciation and understanding of ancient science and philosophy. The very hallmark of their distinction and creativity had been their undoing. For Alami, in short, the breakdown of Spanish Jewry was a breakdown of spirit.

Yet his analysis, if indeed it reliably sheds light on the motivations of the upper-class *conversos*, does not explain the conversions of thousands of simpler folk, who were not reading Aristotle or perfuming themselves for appearances at court. Nor does it explain why the conversions continued voluntarily after the cessation of the pogroms of 1391. Throughout the next century, in fact, still further demoralization would become apparent. In that vein, as many as 50,000 more Jews joined the Christian fold by 1415.

At the same time, and perhaps also demoralizing for those left behind, many of the potential victims of the riots managed by one means or another to emigrate, marking the beginning of a significant new demographic trend. For example, several famous scholars converted and set off soon afterward to find a more congenial place to revert. Profiat Duran, a grammarian and philosopher, may have professed Christianity but secretly practiced Judaism in Perpignan for several years, writing polemical works and defenses of his traditional faith while in exile there. Barcelona's Sheshet Perfet reached Algeria after a period of wandering in Tunisia. Armed with an extensive library salvaged from the upheaval, he was duly acknowledged as rabbi and judge of the Algerian community, despite his earlier conversion. Also, scholars and their coteries from Valencia and Majorca departed for North Africa, including Zemah Duran and his son Simon ben Zemah, who had not converted. The tribulations experienced by most, if not all, of the emigrants to North Africa are echoed in the following report:

> One day, a ship arrived here from Majorca with forty-five forced *conversos* from Majorca, Valencia, and Barcelona. The governor wanted to admit them to the city for reasons of self-interest, for he would collect from them one doubloon per head, an arrangement prompted by a certain person. They were originally admitted free of charge, and the *qadi* rebuked some Arabs who came and asked him not to let them land because of the rise in prices. . . . But that person called upon the people to urge the governor not to let them land, in order that they might return to Majorca and none of them come here.[2]

Despite the difficulties, however, the refugees succeeded in establishing emigré communities on North African soil, in some cases consciously imitating the ordinances and precedents of Toledo. Ironically, as their brethren dealt with persecution and weakened communities in Iberia, they would encounter or provoke friction with indigenous Jews in their new homes. Jewish customs have always differed from place to place, with local customs prevailing provided they do not run counter to Judaic law. The Sephardim angered North African communities by their attempts to introduce their own customs in certain areas of personal law (i.e., marriage and inheritance) as well as in *kashrut*, or dietary practices. In addition, the indigenous Jews were annoyed by the attitude of the newcomers that their ways were superior. Finally, the many conversions among them raised a host of vexing social problems. Soon, an important body of rabbinic literature was created in an attempt to resolve these issues.[3]

A statistically significant emigration of *conversos* to the eastern Mediterranean began after 1391, gaining momentum throughout the fifteenth century. Recoil from the persecutions in Spain impelled some to emigrate; others were motivated by a fervent conviction that the messianic era was near. Entire family groups banded together and rented ships to make their way to Palestine since they were barred from Christian vessels. This movement contrasted sharply with the previous migration, which involved primarily the scholarly and the elderly who sought burial in the Holy Land. Soon, the Sephardic settlement in Jerusalem increased noticeably, and by the mid-century the community had become so heterogeneous that Hebrew, the only language shared by all, became its spoken language. Sephardic colonies also grew in Constantinople, Valona (Albania), Crete, and the Venetian islands in the Dodecanese. After 1440, renewed messianic expectations were inspired by biblical prophecies, astrological indications, and stellar configurations, as well as the feeling that the fall of Constantinople in 1453 was a sign of imminent redemption. Meanwhile, in all the lands of their dispersion, intracommunal rivalries between Jews enlivened their daily exchanges.

The frictions in the Muslim countries closest to Spain foreshadow similar problems that would recur for at least a generation after the expulsion of 1492. In most cases, refugees would cling stubbornly to their Iberian customs and would also reassume, with apparent spontaneity, their roles as diplomats, financiers, courtiers, and translators in service to the North African kings and princes. Of course, the nuclei of Sephardic settlements from 1391 would ease the adjustment and integration of the much larger influx of the expulsion; in fact, these later refugees probably followed routes into exile carved out by relatives a century before. A principal difference between the two events, however, is the veritable resuscitation of sleepy communities in North Africa by the migrations at the end of the fourteenth century. For the first time in several centuries, scholars and physicians, mathematicians and astronomers, reappeared in person and actively, vibrantly carried on their work in the midst of these communities.

Meanwhile, as the dust was settling in Spain, the Jews were deeply divided into three separate groups: those who openly continued to practice Judaism, those who had become *conversos* and remained so, and those who privately renounced their forced baptisms secretly maintaining their adherence to Judaism. Somehow, either through hiding or flight, the faithful Jews had remained a recognizable community, even though they were impoverished, defeated, and severely traumatized. Even after the year of riots, bands of marauders and flagellants continued to wander through the Spanish countryside, subjecting com-

munities to forced conversionist sermons and converting surviving synagogues into churches. Often at the head of these mobs was Vincent
Ferrer, a fiery preacher and zealous advocate of forced conversion who
would lead mobs into the Jewish quarters of Spain and forthwith convert the synagogues. His dreaded arrival in a *judería*, accompanied by
bands of frenzied believers whipping themselves with chains, usually
ended in mass conversions of frightened Jews. Ferrer was instrumental
in winning over to the cross some of the most articulate and prominent
converts, such as Solomon Halevi of Burgos. Christened Pablo de Santa
Maria, he rose to the position of chancellor of the kingdom of Castile
and soon emerged as one of its most inflammatory anti-Jewish leaders
and the guiding spirit behind a body of far-reaching anti-Jewish legislation enacted in 1412. These Laws of Valladolid restricted Jewish residential rights, increased limitations on Jewish occupations, and
drastically circumscribed relations with Christians.

In such an environment, the surviving Jews were torn between
summoning the will to rebuild and succumbing to grief. Their homes,
synagogues, and workshops were destroyed, their careers in ruins, and
the tax-paying base of the community severely depleted. Most scholars
had been martyred, and no qualified judges remained to man the courts
of Jewish law. Worse, no family had been spared death or conversion.
Poignant testimony to such tragic dissolution is available in surviving
wills in which a Jewish woman leaves her property to both her Jewish
and her Christian children, the latter now known by their baptismal
names. Yet the communities did manage to endure. Convening immediately after the disaster to strengthen and rebuild, despite the progressive narrowing of the Jewish economic base, they placed special
emphasis on replenishing the ranks of scholars by supporting Hebrew
education. They also strengthened internal discipline, spelling out penalties to curb the influence and activities of Jewish informers. These
informers would denounce their brethren to the secular authorities,
thereby endangering the safety of the community as well as its judicial
autonomy. Sometimes, they sought to gain favors at court in return for
their betrayals.[4]

The second group, the perhaps 100,000 *conversos* or New Christians, were referred to by practicing Jews as the *anusim*, "the forced
ones." Whatever the label used, the communities did not turn their
backs on these converts, who were still their children, siblings, and even
spouses. In return, some *conversos*, as we have seen, assumed their new
identity with gusto, even to the point of becoming zealous Jew-baiters;

but most tried to merge inconspicuously into the general population. At first, the majority were an ill-defined group, no longer Jewish in name but not yet Christian in deed. Some, probably only a very few, became nonbelieving Catholics who could follow the outward forms of the dominant faith with few qualms because of their general religious skepticism. Their study of philosophy and free thought had convinced them that no religion held the "truth" and they had already ceased to be believing Jews. For all *conversos*, whether struggling spiritually or not, the lifting of the economic restrictions that formerly applied to them as Jews meant that their material lot improved overnight. Their pent-up talents now released, they were able to rise to some of the highest positions in areas that were previously off limits—the nobility, the municipal offices, and even the military and religious orders.

The third group, Jews who had converted only under extreme pressure and secretly returned to Judaism when the wave of persecution ceased, now faced hostility from the majority population, who derisively called them *marranos* (swine), or turncoats. They of course preferred to regard themselves as *anusim*. They may have constituted a significant if pathetic minority within the *converso* category, but their actual number is still the subject of controversy. Crypto-Judaism, by its nature, eludes the eye of the historian and escapes all written records. True, later Inquisition reports projecting the memory of victims back to the 1430s and 1440s describe various secret Jewish practices among the *conversos* at the time. On the other hand, such evidence, usually extracted under torture, must be interpreted with caution. It is known that *marrano* networks of family and business ties were strong. *Marranos* from various localities would help each other, and they were careful to contract marriages only among themselves.

According to later Inquisition trials, *marranos* would continue to make especially valiant attempts to adhere to fundamental Jewish precepts, even though their notions of what constituted Jewish practice would, of necessity, become blurred with the passage of time. With utmost secrecy, they avoided forbidden foods, fasted meticulously, prepared their homes for the Sabbath, and kindled Sabbath candles. People would feign illness to avoid working on the Sabbath and might prepare two separate dinners on Friday evenings, the meat dinner that was considered appropriate for the Sabbath and also a fish dinner, in case an outsider happened by. Ritual slaughter of animals had to be performed only within inner courtyards, of course. Some family festivals, like the Passover Seder, could be performed at home; the participants paid careful attention to detail and stressed the underlying message of freedom for the nation. In order to avoid detection, other festivals would be observed in the countryside. Purim, which commemorates the miraculous deliverance of the Jews of Persia through the efforts of Queen Esther, became the archetypical *marrano* festival. She was, after all, a *marrano*-like figure, circulating incognito in the court of the enemy. With time, she would become even more celebrated and revered as Saint Esther in the separate Judaism of these *conversos*.[5]

Significantly, these secret Jews often found it necessary to enlist the active cooperation of Jewish authorities in the observance of such customs as circumcision, bar mitzvah, and other life-cycle events. Rabbis would officiate at a *marrano* couple's wedding or at a burial after the "public" church rites had been performed. Naturally, even though the Jewish ceremonies were clandestine, rumors about secret *marrano* observances circulated widely.

Bound by ties of history and family, the three groups—observing Jews, *conversos*, and *marranos*—remained in touch with each other, initially living side by side in the same neighborhoods. Boundaries were fluid. According to Jewish law, after all, forced conversions had no validity because a man can be held responsible only for those actions he takes of his own free will. In other words, the *conversos* were still Jews, albeit Jews who had "sinned." In response to the Rhineland massacres of 1096 mentioned earlier, in fact, medieval rabbinic traditions tended to regard converts with special consideration, especially if they did not publicly transgress Jewish law and attempted to observe at least some Judaic precepts. Certainly, the door was open for the convert to return. Practicing Jews were at first quite compassionate and sympathetic to the converts, therefore, while communal solidarity and tradition required that assistance be given to any co-religionist who sought aid in continuing to practice Judaism. This harmonious ideal became complicated, however, by the question of what relationship would be appropriate for the community to maintain with the sons and daughters of converts. Steeped in the Christian way of life, this generation became increasingly detached from the beliefs and traditions of their parents as the fifteenth century progressed.

The question of the "Jewishness" of the *conversos* population is complex. Like any group, the New Christians included people with a variety of motives, beliefs, and approaches to life. The convert lived in a kind of "interim" society, his identity perhaps in flux for decades. At any one point, he might well find himself playing more than one role—as a practicing Christian trying to integrate himself into the majority culture socially and economically, and as a loving relative still in intimate contact with his Jewish family members. If he met total rejection from the Christian world, he might become more passionately committed to his heritage; conversely, he could counter the difficulties inherent in his new identity by becoming a Jew-baiter.

Were most of the *conversos* reluctant Christians, but Christians nonetheless, quite prepared to assimilate if they were not constantly reminded of their origins by an anti-Semitic population? Or were most really Jews? At what point did a *converso* stop thinking of himself as a Jew? An added obstacle to evaluating the religious quality of the convert's life, which would be virtually impossible in any case, is that no special provisions were made for teaching him the ways of his new faith. Besides, even a sincere convert might continue practicing Jewish mores as a matter of habit. Cultural and ethnic aspects of Jewish identity would not be obliterated by forced baptism. What we lack are the tools for discerning inner attitudes.

At first, Church authorities were not troubled by this problem. Assuming that the converts would become sincere Christians over the course of time, they tended not to distinguish between New and Old Christians. Unfortunately, the masses did not share this attitude of acceptance. Unprepared for the massive influx of new converts, unsettled by their rapid and highly visible economic ascent, many Spaniards regarded them as hypocrites who only wanted to push themselves into the choicest places in society. In short, the common people totally rejected their new fellow communicants, and the nobility were at best ambivalent, even though *conversos* gained entrée into society and their children did intermarry with the upper classes. To the surprise of the clergy, the people began to demand that the converts be separated from other believers.

The Church was prevented from making any such distinction, however, on doctrinal grounds. A conversion, even if forced, was deemed irrevocable. Baptism was indelible, regardless of the personal motivations of the convert. (Consequently, converts could not be allowed to revert, no matter how severe their inner doubts or feelings of remorse, and any manifestation of Judaism would earn the death penalty for heresy.) Doctrinally, ecclesiastical authorities simply could not draw the racial or ethnic distinctions that seemed so obvious to the general population.

Of course, the position of the clergy opened avenues of advancement for many sincere *conversos* within the hierarchy of the Church and its religious orders. One of the most famous was Solomon Halevi, whom we have met before. This former rabbi of Burgos, who became bishop of the city under his baptismal name of Pablo de Santa Maria, became best known, unfortunately, for his anti-*converso* attitudes and programs. Even more prominent were Bartolomeo Carranza, who became archbishop of Toledo and then primate of all Spain, and Hernando de Talavera, who became archbishop of Granada. St. Ignatius Loyola's successor as head of the Society of Jesus was the *converso* Diego Lainex. There is an even more astonishing example of devout conversion: the patron saint of Spain, Theresa of Avila, was of *converso* descent. At lower levels of the Church, monasteries and convents proved to be good places of refuge for the New Christians, for few questions about one's past would be asked there and it was possible to train for a distinguished career in one of the religious orders.

It was also possible, it turns out, for such retreats to become islands of crypto-Judaism. Certainly, this was the suspicion of the general population, who believed that virtually all of the converts were guilty of Judaizing. Reinforcing this suspicion, of course, was the continuing existence of the Jewish communities. Observing Jews could be the source of information about Hebraic tradition for *conversos*, giving them the assistance that would enable them to become *marranos*.

For this reason, the clergy became even more zealous in attempting to convert the remaining Jews, but they were not supported by royalty, who tended to assist practicing Jews in strengthening their communities. For one thing, the kings of Spain were typically interested in preserving the self-serving relationship with the Sephardim from which they had derived so much benefit for centuries. For another, royalty quite sensibly distrusted public disorder, and they feared that the *converso* question might take on an anti-Establishment coloration. Finally, the high literacy rate and wide array of talents found among the converts made them a particularly attractive group of civil servants. Despite all of these motives, however, the kings of the fifteenth century were able to do little to keep anti-*converso* hostilities in check. Most were so weak they could barely hold onto their thrones.

Even in light of all of the obstacles and growing hostility, the waves of conversion did not cease. The Jews had scarcely recovered from 1391 when they were ordered to send delegates to Tortosa "to be lectured on the truth of Christianity" in a public disputation, the longest ever staged, from February 1413, through November 1414. This time, however, there was no Nahmanides, or in fact any other towering intellectual leader, to speak self-confidently with a voice of authority. In fact, several of the Jewish participants probably harbored doubts about their faith even before they were summoned, because several of them, including key members of the prominent houses of Caballeria, Bonifos, and Don Vidal (Benveniste), converted and entered the royal service while the debates were still in progress.

"Debate" is hardly the word for the actual event, which was more like a pageant, held in the intimidating presence of Pope Benedict XIII in a large auditorium draped in ecclesiastical purple. According to Jewish accounts at the time, "there were seventy chairs for the cardinals, archbishops, and bishops, all dressed in gold vestments. There also were other grandees of the Roman Church as well as burghers and nobles, approximately one thousand persons. . . . This was true throughout the disputation. Our hearts melted and turned to water." At times, the audience was as large as 2,000.

Presiding as the chief spokesman for Christianity, depressingly enough, was the *converso* Gerónimo de Santa Fé (Joshua ha-Lorqui before Ferrer converted him during the 1412 campaign), who was a particularly learned and aggressive opponent of Judaism. He never allowed his hapless opponents to see the texts used against them or to coordinate their rebuttals; indeed, they presented a sorry spectacle as they disagreed with each other. Of course, not even the most polished and convincing of performances would have made much difference to the outcome of the Disputation in the particular circumstances of Tortosa. The truth of Christianity was never considered to be in question, as the pope made clear in his opening statement:

> You, the Jewish sages, ought to bear in mind that I am not here, nor have I sent for you to come to this place, in order to discuss which of the two religions is true. For I know that my faith is the only true one;

yours had once been true but it has since been superseded. You have come here only on account of Gerónimo who has promised to prove, through the very Talmud of your masters who are wiser than yourselves, that the Messiah has already come. You shall debate before me this topic exclusively.[6]

In effect, the Jewish delegates were subjected to one long conversionist sermon regarding the indisputable truth of Christianity. Spurious sources were produced in order to confuse them; mockery and disrespect were flagrant. Even before the proceedings were brought to a close, rumors flew throughout Spain that the Jewish delegates had been soundly "defeated" and had all converted. This hearsay precipitated a mass rush of disheartened Jews to the baptismal font, further swelling the ranks of the problematic *conversos*. Consequently, throughout the second decade of the fifteenth century, the defections of Jews were publicly and widely trumpeted by the gleeful clergy. Many Jewish communities entirely disappeared, and the demoralization of the Sephardim throughout the land increased.

Perhaps the most telling evidence of Jewish fear during these troubled years can be found in a series of laws promulgated in 1432 by representatives of several active communities of Castile at the initiative of Rabbi Abraham Benveniste, treasurer to King Juan II and *rab de la corte*, or chief rabbi. Convening in Valladolid (where earlier anti-Jewish laws were enacted in 1412), the representatives produced a series of ordinances (*Takkanot*) designed to introduce regional cooperation to meet the challenges they faced at the local level. The wide range of issues included the upkeep of synagogues and schools and agreement on the methods of electing judges and the extent of their judicial powers. More reflective of the threatening atmosphere, however, were several ordinances that touched specifically on Jewish-Christian relations. For example, Jews were prohibited from summoning a co-religionist before secular or ecclesiastical courts. Additionally, measures were adopted to prohibit individuals from obtaining tax exemptions, a subject of increasing bitterness within the community. Special legislation, known as sumptuary legislation, was introduced to prevent Jews from displaying any luxury or extravagance.[7] We know that such sumptuary laws were generally introduced in medieval France, Germany, or Italy when Jewish relations with their neighbors were especially troubled. Rabbi Benveniste set a personal example of modesty for the community, reportedly wearing nothing but black on his visits to the court.

Eventually, it became clear that the *converso* issue in Spain transcended lines of class, ideology, or religious faith. Even by the middle of the fifteenth century, there was simply no easy answer to the question of who was a Jew or a Christian. But for most of the population, the conviction began to spread that Jewish ancestry or "race," not professed religious belief, defined who was a Jew. Therefore, as *conversos* continued to rise in prominence in every walk of life, calls for restrictions and discrimination against them mounted. Thousands of them had only the dimmest memories of their prior religion by this time, yet in the eyes of so-called Old Christians they bore the stigma of their origins. The hostility toward Jewish converts climaxed in Toledo in 1449 in a pogrom aimed exclusively at the *conversos*. In its aftermath, the municipal council introduced statutes that differentiated between "Old" and "New" Christians in religious and governmental employment, strictly limiting the activities of the converts. The resentment of the Christian populace was clearly evident in the preamble to these "purity of blood" (*limpieza de sangre*) ordinances:

> We declare the so-called *conversos*, offspring of perverse Jewish ancestors, must be held by law to be infamous and ignominious, unfit, and unworthy to hold any public office or any benefice within the city of Toledo, or land within its jurisdiction, or to be commissioners for oaths or notaries, or to have any authority over the true Christians of the Holy Catholic Church.[8]

By this act, the very purpose of the pogroms of 1391 and subsequent conversionary movements—i.e., to convert the Jews and bring them completely and permanently into the Christian fold—was thwarted. The *conversos* were now isolated as a new class, neither Jewish nor Christian, that was unassimilable and could not be redeemed. Paradoxically, the restrictive laws became increasingly complex as the actual Jewishness of the *conversos* became more remote, even mythical.

The Toledo statutes were swiftly overruled by Pope Nicholas V because they violated the precept that, as he declared, "all Catholics are one in body according to the teaching of our faith." Although he thus decreed that racial origin did not determine whether or not one was a Catholic, the kings nevertheless approved the racial laws in 1451. "Blood purity" statutes would not only prevail but increasingly cast an ever-wider net throughout Spain and Portugal in the sixteenth century. By 1555, *limpieza de sangre* was an official requirement for entry to public office; thereafter, all descendants of Jews were barred from holding positions of authority in the army, the university, the Church, and the municipality. In order to discredit Spaniards of questionable or ambiguous ancestry, elaborate books of genealogy were compiled. For the next several generations, until the odious statutes were wiped off the books in the eighteenth century, Catholic descendants of medieval converts were stigmatized unless they were able to devise or purchase false genealogies. In the sixteenth and seventeenth centuries, for example, the safest claim was ancestry from peasant stock, for urban origins, evidence of literacy, or any connection with the liberal professions, particularly medicine, immediately tainted one. In that vein, merchants and men of affairs were automatically considered to be descended from *conversos*.

It is little wonder that a sixteenth-century Spanish cleric, Padre Pedro, was bewildered and exasperated by the attitudes of his people:

> We Spaniards have succeeded in creating a nation of madmen. We still distinguish between New Christians and Old Christians. . . . We search for Jewish blood which hardly exists, almost one hundred years after the expulsion of the Jews. With such an attitude, it can only bring dishonor on us.[9]

The marriage of Ferdinand and Isabella in 1469 seemed to augur the possibility of stability after a prolonged period of political chaos and civil war. From the Jewish perspective, the union of the two greatest Iberian kingdoms of Aragon and Castile through matrimony would have a stabilizing effect. From their tragic past experience as a small, vulnerable minority in medieval Europe, they had learned that their best hope for security lay with a strong central power that could keep order. Also, it was privately believed among Jews that Ferdinand was himself descended from Jews and would therefore oppose further persecutions. Abraham Seneor, the chief tax farmer of Seville, along with other prominent Jews and *conversos* of the court, pressed the king's candidacy for Isabella's hand, engineered a clandestine meeting between the two, and even, according to Hebrew accounts, provided the betrothal gifts that Ferdinand needed to seal the match. Jewish chroniclers recorded the community's hopeful attitude toward the wedding:

> And in every province and city, word that the king of Aragon was now also the king of Castile was greeted with joy and exhilaration by the

Jews, because they said to one another: "He is our brother and flesh, with Jewish blood in him. You have blessed the work of his hands, and his substance is increased in the land." (Job I:10)[10]

At first, their expectations appeared to be fulfilled, for the united crown was shared by two very energetic leaders who were quite capable of gradually restoring order to Spain. Also, Jews were immediately appointed to prominent positions in the royal administration, reassuring the frightened community. In addition to Abraham Seneor and Isaac Abrabanel, there were the *converso* statesmen Luis de Santangel, Gabriel Sanchez, Alfonso de la Caballeria, Sancho de Paternoy, and Felipe Climent. Within the royal household, Isabella was able to conceive Prince John because of the medical treatment of her Jewish physician, Lorenzo Badoc.

The king and queen, attempting to curb the excesses of the nobles and city councils, made clear by example that Jews should not be harmed. On several occasions, they intervened personally to stop anti-Jewish disorders and punished those who fomented the violence. When she defended the Jews of Trujillo in 1477, Isabella declared, "All the Jews of my kingdoms are mine and are under my shelter and protection, and it is up to me to defend and protect them and to maintain their rights."[11] Moreover, when the municipalities defaulted on their debts to Jews, the royal couple supported the creditors. Or when a town like Bilbao barred Jews from spending the night within its walls, they were defended by the monarchs. Ferdinand and Isabella also protected the *aljamas* from abuse by the city councils by establishing orderly means of collecting the Jewish tribute; in some cases, as in Cáceres, they chose to intervene to lighten the community's tax load.

In short, a wealth of evidence reveals that, until the very eve of the expulsion, the rulers of Aragon and Castile regarded the Jews as lawful subjects deserving protection. In fact, even as plans for the expulsion were being laid, they continued to uphold this royal policy. Jewish confidence in their support was indeed not, as some scholars have claimed, based on lack of sophistication or wishful thinking.

What lay behind Ferdinand and Isabella's long-standing support and defense of the Jews? On one level, they were concerned to uphold the supremacy of the state by maintaining both the public order and the sound condition of the treasury. But they also took their religious responsibilities seriously and were apparently alarmed by the reports they constantly received about alleged Judaizing activities by the *con-*

versos. It was not exclusively for political reasons that they received the title of "the Catholic monarchs" (*los Reyes Catolicos*) from Pope Alexander VI in 1494.*

Isabella, in particular, was said to have been deeply impressed by the rumors. Alonso de Hojéda, a Dominican prior of Seville, warned her that *conversos* were meeting secretly to practice their ancient rites and argued that this threat could be countered adequately only by an Inquisition under royal control. He explained that it would conveniently serve a dual function: on the one hand, it would strengthen the monarchs' political hand; on the other, it would ferret out and destroy the country's Judaizing heresy.

Therefore, in 1478, the royal couple asked for and received permission from Rome to act upon the prior's advice. The Spanish Inquisition began operating three years later in Seville with a dramatic *auto-da-fé*, in which dozens of members of some of the most prominent *converso* families were burned at the stake. In the following decade, the Inquisition branched out to cover most of the country and caught tens of thousands of secret Jews in its net. It is estimated that 700 people were burned in Seville alone during this period. By the end of the century, perhaps as many as 30,000 *conversos* were destroyed throughout the land.

The officers of the Inquisition seemed to harbor a special animus toward converts who held positions of influence as courtiers and financial agents of the crown, although converts from all strata were victimized. Members of the family of Christopher Columbus's chief sponsor, Luis de Santangel, were among the first to fall—some burned alive, others burned in effigy, with Santangel's son and namesake Luis forced to appear in a public processional on July 17, 1491, in a *sambenito* (sacred sack), a distinctive hooded cloak which was the special garb of a penitent accused of Judaizing.

From the outset, the Spanish Inquisition moved with thoroughness and brutality, its use of secret confessions extorted under torture considered the ideal way to ensnare the maximum number of Jews. During a period of grace, people were invited to come forth to confess and inform upon one another; those who informed would later share in the

---

* Ostensibly granting this title in recognition of Ferdinand and Isabella's services to Christianity in the conquest of Granada, the pope also hoped to gain their support against the territorial ambitions of the French king Charles VIII, who intended to conquer Italy. The title "*le roi catholique*" had been bestowed upon the French monarchy in the fourteenth century.

confiscated property of the accused. Because accusations were made in secret and hearsay was acceptable, the circle of intimidation widened swiftly, as did the practice of blackmail. The accused never met his accuser. Practically overnight, the Holy Office was flooded with hundreds, then thousands, of files packed with detailed testimonies about secret Jewish activities. Those who did not confess during the official grace period but were later implicated in Judaizing faced extreme punishment after long and painful interrogation. The Inquisition became infamous for its diabolical use of water tortures and ropehanging, later depicted so movingly by Goya. In theory, the purpose of the torture was to extract a confession in order to save the soul of the accused.

Partly to spread the word that Judaizing was an extremely grave crime, elaborate public celebrations and processionals were spectacularly staged in public squares like Madrid's Plaza Mayor. Here the sentences and punishments of the "criminals" were jubilantly pronounced before an enormous crowd of spectators, including thousands of peasants who would throng in from the countryside to witness the proceedings in a fiesta-like atmosphere. Following the Inquisitors and the clergy in a solemn processional, the guilty paraded through the square carrying tapers and clad in *sambenitos*. These yellow garments were decorated with the Cross of St. Andrew or with representations of devils being thrust into the flames of Hell. The prisoners also wore tall mitres with similar decorations. The solemn, macabre processionals culminated at stages or scaffoldings specially erected in the square. Thereupon, as a cross was held up, the populace took a common oath to defend the faith. Next, a distinguished clergyman would deliver a long sermon bristling with insults about the accused and their accursed practices. Afterward, the penitents were paraded individually before the pulpit to receive their sentences, a formality that would sometimes take the entire day. The most heinous crimes, including Judaizing, were punished with burning at the stake. The "honor" of lighting the pyre was generally given to some distinguished guest, such as visiting royalty. Sometimes, if the prisoner confessed, he would be "reconciled" to the Church and forced to do penance or receive severe punishment. But in the worst cases, prisoners were burned even after their confessions, some professing to the last their undying belief in the God of Israel. For lesser offenses, some prisoners were condemned to wear the *sambenito* for a lifetime; after death, the garment would be displayed on the wall of the cathedral for generations, subjecting the wearer and his descendants to enduring humiliation and obloquy. Indeed, descendants of all

of the condemned were excluded from any public dignity so long as the
Holy Office held sway in Spain.

The mode of operation of the Inquisition remained virtually un-
changed until its abolition in the nineteenth century, spreading terror
among hundreds of thousands of innocents. It should be stressed that
the public executions were not frequent occurrences; nonetheless, the
shadow of their flames illuminated the memories of Spain's victims for
centuries.

Ironically, the horror of this first decade of the Inquisition caused a
recoil in the *converso* population that sent many of them back to their
Jewish roots. The religion and tradition that was painted as a crime by
the Christians became again a source of honor and pride to the
Sephardim. In fact, Jews became increasingly willing to risk even the
pyre of the *auto-da-fé* in order to remain faithful to the God of Israel.

A policy of partial expulsion, aimed explicitly at separating practicing
Jews from their *converso* brethren, was introduced by the Inquisition in
Andalusia at the end of 1482. Jews were expelled from the dioceses of
Seville, Córdoba, and Cádiz in 1484, and soon thereafter from selective
settlements such as Saragossa and Teruel. Some towns initiated and
carried out expulsions on their own, even in defiance of protests from
the crown. In retrospect, it appears that several experiments in the
treatment of Jews were proceeding simultaneously, not only expulsion
but also confiscation, expropriation, and temporary spoliation. As the
Inquisition uncovered nests of crypto-Judaism, it no longer seemed
sufficient to strive to isolate *conversos* from Jews and both from the Old
Christians. Inexorably, the climate was becoming favorable for the drastic move of expulsion of Jews on a national scale.

In 1478 the battle with the kingdom of Granada was renewed, and
for the ensuing decade Castile relentlessly pursued the offensive against
the last Muslim outpost in Spain. The resources of the Christian state,
reorganized through the acumen of Ferdinand's Jewish and *converso*
advisors, oiled the machinery to continue the battle. The Muslim ruling
house, deeply divided within, was unable to withstand the mounting
zeal of the enemy forces. At the end of 1491, King Muhammed XII,
known to the Christians as Boabdil, agreed to surrender, thereby hoping to spare himself and ensure religious freedom for his subjects. In-

deed, the Muslims were temporarily allowed to retain their mosques or emigrate freely, if they chose. According to legend, Boabdil sighed aloud as he left Granada, while his mother railed that he had not been man enough to defend the city.

The fall of Granada was greeted with jubilation throughout Europe but especially in Spain, where the monarchs could now turn their energies to the unresolved question of the *conversos* and the Jews. In fact, as the final campaign against Granada was reaching its climax, anti-Jewish tracts were being circulated in order to gain even more popular support for a national expulsion.

In 1490–91, a hideous blood libel accusation known as the case of El Niño de la Guardia was trumped up, and lurid confessions of atrocities were extracted from Jews after particularly vicious tortures. Thus began the last trial of the Jews in Spain. In the small town of La Guardia in the province of Toledo a *converso*, Benito Garcia, was hailed before the Inquisition and charged with taking part in the crucifixion of a Christian child on the eve of Passover. Under torture, he named several *conversos* and Jews involved in an alleged plot to overthrow Christianity. Even though there was no missing child in La Guardia, nor the slightest foundation to the pathological charge of ritual murder, the Jews of Spain once again became the victims of this medieval calumny. Grand Inquisitor Torquemada appointed a special investigative commission that predictably found the accused guilty, and a public execution followed in Avila. The townspeople became so agitated by anti-Jewish passion that Jews there had to seek special protection from the king. The sixteenth-century Inquisitor Luis de Páramo later stated that the La Guardia affair was one of the factors that moved Ferdinand and especially Isabella to sign the expulsion decree.[12]

The proceedings of the La Guardia trial reveal that the blood libel charge of 1490 was not solely an action against Benito Garcia or any other unfortunate innocents but rather against the entire Jewish and *converso* population, carefully prepared and orchestrated by the Inquisition with total disregard for even the vaguest concepts of legality. Apparently, Torquemada was preparing the nation for the expulsion decree, which would be made public only three months after the verdict. The decree's anti-Semitic poison would thus fall on receptive ears.

On January 2, 1492, the Spanish standard was raised over the tower of the Alhambra, the palace fortress in Granada that symbolized the former glory of the Islamic kingdom of al-Andalus. Christians throughout victorious Spain exulted, for the struggle against the Muslims had exhausted the energies of the nation for more than a decade. Moreover, the fall of the kingdom of Granada's last stronghold terminated a crusade of reconquest that had been waged off and on for centuries. Yet the Jews had rejoiced along with their neighbors, hopeful that stability and tranquillity could now return to the country.

Soon after the fall of Granada, however, rumors began to circulate in the inner circles of the court that an expulsion decree to expel all unconverted Jews would soon be pronounced. The specific dates for the formulation, promulgation, and public announcement of the decree remain in dispute, but it was probably signed at the end of January and promulgated at the end of March. It was during this interim that Abrabanel and Seneor tried to influence the authorities to revoke the decree. In his introduction to his commentary on the former prophets, Abrabanel recalls that he met three times with the king, ceaselessly but vainly pleading for his people. Although he also enlisted the support of powerful courtiers, Ferdinand stood firm as Isabella goaded him to stick to his resolve to remove the Jews from Spain. Abrabanel is quite succinct in his own description of the dramatic encounter with the royal couple, but Capsali and chroniclers who based their accounts upon his fill in several dramatic details of the last defense of the Sephardim by their noblest leader:

> On that day, Don Isaac Abravanel was given permission to speak and to defend his people. There he stood, like a lion in wisdom and strength, and in the most eloquent language he addressed the king and queen. Don Abram Seneor, too, addressed the monarchs, but eventually all agreed not to pursue the matter any more. . . . Then the two sages decided to write their words down and to send them to Queen Isabella, for they thought that maybe by this means the queen might consent to their plea. . . . Thus Don Isaac Abravanel sent a letter to Queen Isabella, in which he chastised her mercilessly and showed no respect for her rank. . . . He then arranged to have the letter delivered to the queen while he fled for his life.[13]

Another account of a meeting between the courtiers and the royal couple adds a bitter touch of human interest. According to Inquisitor de Páramo, leading Jewish petitioners offered Ferdinand a bribe of unspecified size to induce him to rescind the expulsion. As he hesitated, Torquemada came raging into the room, fearing that the king would relent.

He loved greatly the glory of God and what was good for the Catholic Church, and therefore he gave a clear sign of his love. He went to the palace, hiding a crucifix under his cloak, and he addressed the king with great and holy frankness: "I know about the King's business. See here the crucifix of our Savior, whom the wretched Judas sold for thirty pieces of silver to his enemies and betrayed to their persecutors. If you applaud this action, sell him for a higher price. I, for my part, resign from all power. I will not take any blame; you will be respon sible to God for this business deal." Having said this, he put down his crucifix in front of them and left.[14]

Scholars continue to disagree on the precise motivation and degree of culpability of the various key actors in the formulation of the drastic expulsion measure. Some contend that the decree was the result of a national conversionary wave, part and parcel of the spreading conviction that Spain should be purged of all "infidels" once the Muslim stronghold was vanquished. They buttress this point of view by pointing to the crown's readiness to readmit Jewish exiles who agreed to convert and to the provisions of the decree that expressly enabled Jews who converted to remain in the country. Indeed, the decree appears to be an open invitation to conversion, and those who converted did retain their positions and their fortunes.

Some contemporaries, however, believed that Ferdinand, a wily and avaricious ruler who was the model for Machiavelli's ideal "Prince," was interested only in exploiting the Jews behind a mask of Christian piety. If so, he was extremely clever at hiding his ruthlessness, temporarily protecting his Sephardic subjects during the 1470s and 1480s while apparently planning their elimination. Following this line of reasoning, they cite his borrowing large sums from Abrabanel and his brethren to pay for the conquest of Granada, then expelling them before the debt could be repaid, at the same time confiscating their enormous accumulated assets.

On the other hand, there are many who argue that Ferdinand and Isabella never themselves intended to oust the Jews but were intimidated into making the decision by the queen's confessor, Torquemada. These observers cite the various protective decrees and renewals of Jewish privileges that the monarchs continued to issue as late as 1492.[15] But these protective measures could have been ruses to dull suspicion until every last ducat and maravedi had been drained from the Sephardim before they were expelled. Isabella, in particular, is often seen as religiously zealous enough to engage in such deception, and her fervor for religious crusade and Christian unification was well known. Some of the Hebrew chroniclers closest to the events adopted the view that she was the motivating force behind the expulsion, even if encouraged by Torquemada, likening her to the wicked biblical queen Jezebel.

Eliyahu Capsali's sixteenth-century account, which is the classic Jewish explanation of the expulsion, suggests that she played the decisive role:

> As we mentioned, when Queen Isabella had seen how the city of Granada refused to surrender, she had made a vow. Now that Granada had indeed fallen to Spain, she decided to keep that vow in full. Actually, Isabella had always hated the Jews, and had been involved in an ongoing argument with her husband Ferdinand, for ever since her marriage she had been asking him to exile the Jews of Spain. In this she was spurred on by the priests. . . . When, however, she saw that the king was reluctant to take such a step, she told him: "You no doubt love the Jews, and the reason is that you are of their flesh and blood. In fact, the reason the Jews arranged for you to marry me is so that you would act as their protector." When the King heard this terrible thing, he took his shoe off and threw it at the Queen, hitting her. She then fled the room and the hatred between them continued for a long period of time.[16]

Yet another explanation is found in the surviving fragment of a fascinating Hebrew chronicle of the de la Cabelleria family written immediately after the expulsion. It suggests that court intrigue involving some malevolent *conversos* in the family may have helped foster the decree. They were *conversos* "accustomed to the evil of sinning, starting with the days of Fra Vicente [Ferrer]," who "thought evil of God's nation" and "conspired to destroy the name of Israel from the land." Whether in their eagerness to disassociate themselves from the Jews, or out of fear for their own positions, some *converso* counselors of the king had become the worst enemies of their people.[17]

Some exiles, like Solomon ibn Verga (c. 1450–1520), saw clearly the hand of Torquemada behind all of the traumatic events:

> In Spain there was a priest who had tremendous hatred for the Jews, and the rule is that whoever afflicts the Jews becomes a leader by doing so. He was the confessor to the queen, and he instigated the queen to force the Jews to convert. If they would not, they were to be put to the sword. The queen pleaded to the king and begged him to do this.
> Some time later the king gave in and decreed, at the advice of his

wife, that all the Jews had to convert, and those that did not had to leave his kingdom. This was issued as a royal decree.[18]

In the final analysis, the expulsion is best understood as the culmination of a comprehensive policy of Christian unification that had been emerging in Spanish society even before the conquest of Granada. Other explanations do not hold up. For example, economic jealousy was not central, for the Jewish community was no longer especially wealthy by 1492; the few rich men were greatly outnumbered by a population of modest artisans. Nor had popular antagonism reached an intolerable threshold. Anti-Semitism was unpredicatable and could always be fanned by fanatics, but actual agitation was probably less powerful a factor than in 1449, the time of the Toledo pogrom and its aftermath. In addition, the aristocracy, though perhaps threatened by the rise of a rich *converso* class, was not especially hostile toward Jews. Evidently, some aristocrats resented finding themselves dependent upon them for loans and political backing, but Jewish chroniclers of the sixteenth century make clear that deep cultural affinities and ties had developed between the *conversos* and the nobles who drew their power from inherited status and landed wealth.

The best explanation for the expulsion can be derived from the decree itself. It was necessary, according to the text, to remove the pernicious presence of the Jews and their living Judaism because they were having a corrupting influence on "bad Christians." No other remedy would solve the problem of the *conversos*:

> Thus the great damage caused to Christians by their participation, connection and conversation with the Jews has been discovered. Since it is clearly demonstrated that they always try by all means at their disposal, to destroy and draw away the Christian believers from our Holy Catholic Faith, to separate them from it, to bring them near to their faith . . . by initiating Christians into their rituals and religious customs, by organizing assemblies in which they read to them and teach them and their children, providing them with books from which they could recite their prayers and announce their fast-days, gathering together to read and study the stories of their Bible, announcing to them the festivals before their celebration, informing them what they have to observe and do, giving them from their houses the unleavened bread and ritually slaughtered meat. . . .
>
> Therefore . . . we have agreed to order the expulsion of all Jews and Jewesses in our kingdom. Never should any of them return and come back. . . . And if they are found living in our kingdoms and domains they should be put to death.[19]

The decree of expulsion was greeted by the Jews with despair and disbelief. They were given four months to wind up their affairs and were not permitted to take any gold, silver, or precious metal with them. Recognizing that they could not avoid a forced journey into the unknown, they sought frantically to divest themselves of their property, but the task was virtually hopeless in the time allotted. The accumulated communal treasures of generations included exquisite synagogues and ancient cemeteries, ritual baths and halls. As for private buildings, how could they sell quickly so many villas and vineyards, orchards and grain-fields? The market was flooded still more by workshops and ateliers, thousands of homes, and unremitted debts. The contemporary priest Andrés Bernáldez describes how most possessions went for a pittance: a vineyard for the price of a handkerchief, a house for a donkey, a workshop for a piece of linen or a loaf of bread. Some people buried their valuables in the hope that they would return later. Agonized scholars dispersed family libraries that had been preserved for genera-tions, even as they tried to commit some of this treasured wisdom to memory.

Abrabanel's description is still moving:

> The people heard this evil decree and they mourned. Wherever word of the decree reached, there was great mourning among the Jews. There was great trembling and sorrow the likes of which had not been experienced since the days of the exile of the Jews from their land to the land of foreigners. The Jews encouraged each other: Let us strengthen ourselves on behalf of our faith, on behalf of the Torah of our God . . . if [our enemies] let us live, we will live; and if they kill us, we will die. But we will not profane our covenant, and our hearts will not retrogress; we will walk forward in the name of the Lord our God.[20]

The author of their distress, Ferdinand, coldly calculated how much he could reap from the decree. For one thing, he cynically ordered Jewish communities to pay the communal taxes due for the next several years so that he would not lose revenue by their departure. Debts outstanding to Jews were deferred or transferred to the crown.

To ensure that their children would have extra protectors during the upcoming ordeal, many families hurriedly married them off. The major problem, however, was finding a country of asylum. England and France had banished their Jewish communities in the thirteenth and fourteenth centuries. After the Black Death of 1348, which wiped out almost a fifth of Europe's population, many German towns had expelled Jews or destroyed their communities, accusing them of causing the deaths by poisoning wells. Almost all of Italy had refused to admit the Spanish refugees, while the few existing Jewish communities there could not handle much immigration in the face of restrictions placed upon them. North Africa was a possibility, but the hapless Sephardim had to bribe ruthless ship captains and rely upon unsafe vessels; in the event, many refugees wound up adrift on the Mediterranean.

The exodus began in the first week of July. The majority of the Jews from Castile, numbering about 120,000, set off for neighboring Portugal, where, for a hefty fee, King John II granted them a temporary entrance permit good for eight months. Those unable to pay for the permit were forthwith sold into slavery. At the end of the period of asylum, 600 families of affluent Jews would be permitted to remain, at a cost of 100 cruzados per household, along with a certain number of skilled craftsmen and artisans. The king at first agreed to provide ships to take the rest of the community elsewhere. Much more promising, in the short run, was the reaction of the independent kingdom of Navarre, which refused to be persuaded by the enemies of the Jews to bar their immigration. Several thousand Sephardim sought sanctuary there and set up their own communities of "foreigners" (*foranos*) and "newcomers" (*nuevamente venidos*) alongside the original Jewish inhabitants (*aljama de los judíos nativos*). Unfortunately, the expelled Jews would not long find peace in either Portugal or Navarre, for in both kingdoms they would be forcibly converted to Christianity within a few years.

Perhaps as many as 20,000 Andalusian Jews flocked to the port of Cádiz en route to North Africa, but there is no way of knowing how many actually succeeded in crossing the Mediterranean safely. This route was especially hazardous, according to testimonies from North African communities, because of the piracy endemic to the area. Further risks included a new outbreak of the plague, along with the closing of Muslim coastal cities to the infected wanderers.

Other contemporary accounts give us faint but poignant echoes of the fates of refugees sailing farther eastward. On August 24, nine plague-ridden caravels entered the Bay of Naples after drifting from port to port that had refused them entry. According to a Genoese historian who saw the passengers, "one might have taken them for spectres, so emaciated were they, so cadaverous in their aspect, and with eyes so sunken: they differed in nothing from the dead, except in the power of motion, which indeed they scarcely retained."[21]

Later in the same month, another convoy reached Marseilles, where the small Jewish community was hard pressed to ransom 118 Sephardim from Aragon held hostage by a captain threatening to sell them on the slave market in the Levant. According to the fragmentary Hebrew report of this incident, the local Jews borrowed 1,500 écus from a Christian moneylender, promising repayment within four months, even for those hostages who might convert to Christianity. The refugees were freed, clothed, and resettled, and the debt was paid off the following February, albeit late.

Throughout the final weeks, the steadfastness of the Sephardim was so remarkable that even the generally unsympathetic observer and chronicler Andrés Bernáldez was moved to write with admiration:

> In the first week of July they took the route for quitting their native land, great and small, young and old, on foot or horses, in carts each continuing his journey to his destined port. They experienced great trouble and suffered indescribable misfortunes on the road, some falling, others rising, some dying, others being born, some fainting, others being attacked by illness. There was not a Christian but that pitied them and pleaded with them to be baptized. Some from misery were converted, but they were the few. The rabbis encouraged them and made the young people and women sing and play on pipes and tambours to enliven them and keep up their spirits and thus they left Castile and arrived at the ports where some embarked for Portugal.[22]

Many called out aloud to the Lord for succor on their journey and wept bitterly upon reaching the shores of the Mediterranean. But this was not the entire story. Although something like 175,000 Jews left Spain in the spring and summer of 1492, another 100,000 chose to convert during those final months of panic, swelling the ranks of the already large group of *conversos*. And after experiencing harsh receptions elsewhere, many of those expelled would return and convert, and their property would be restored to them.

As we have seen, among those who chose conversion was none other than the leading Jewish courtier Abraham Seneor, although his case is ambiguous. For one thing, the prospect of exile for an octogenarian is no small matter. For another, sources close to the period suggest that Isabella threatened dire consequences to his brethren if Seneor did not convert. She apparently thought that the entire community would be inspired to follow the example of their leader. On the contrary, his name has been preserved in Hebrew sources as Abraham

Sone Or (i.e., the Hater of Light). He remained as chief counselor and financier to the crown, gaining even greater honors in his new persona as Fernando Nuñez Coronel. Indeed, at least half of all of the Jews could not find the strength to leave Spain and accepted conversion.

As we have seen, many Jews who refused to convert decided to take advantage of the expensive eight-month-long reprieve offered in Portugal by John II, who permitted 600 families of affluent Jews to stay. At the end of the reprieve period, however, the king changed his mind about giving the rest passage elsewhere, accused them of reneging on their part of the bargain, and gave them the choice of conversion or being handed over as slaves to his Christian subjects.

In an act of unaccountable cruelty, the king ordered that many Jewish children be forcibly wrested from parents who refused to convert and sent to the virtually uninhabited Portuguese island of São Tomé, off the coast of West Africa. The Portuguese Jewish chronicler Samuel Usque recalled the incident in his tormented memoirs:

> The island of São Tomé had recently been discovered. It was inhabited by lizards, snakes, and other venomous reptiles, and was devoid of rational beings. Here the king exiled condemned criminals, and he decided to include among them the innocent children of these Jews. Their parents had seemingly been condemned by God's sentence.
>
> When the luckless hour arrived for this barbarity to be inflicted, mothers scratched their faces in grief as their babes, less than three years old, were taken from their arms. Honored elders tore their beards when the fruit of their bodies was snatched before their eyes. The fated children raised their piercing cries to heaven as they were mercilessly torn from their beloved parents. . . .
>
> Several women threw themselves at the king's feet, begging for permission to accompany their children; but not even this moved the king's pity. One mother, distraught by this horrible unexplained cruelty, lifted her baby in her arms, and paying no heed to its cries, threw herself from the ship into the heaving sea, and drowned embracing her only child.
>
> Finally, when those innocent children arrived at the wilderness of São Tomé, which was to be their grave, they were thrown ashore and were mercilessly left there. Almost all were swallowed up by the huge lizards on the island and the remainder, who escaped these reptiles, wasted away from hunger and abandonment.[23]

Temporary relief from conversionist pressure came in 1495, when John died and his successor, Manuel I, ordered that all enslaved Jews be released. The respite was brief. The new monarch was ambitious to ally himself with the throne of Spain by marrying Ferdinand and Isabella's daughter. They would agree to the match only on the condition that he expel the Jews from Portugal. His decree of expulsion, promulgated on December 5, 1496, gave them until the end of 1497 to depart.

In fact, Manuel did not want to encourage the Jews to leave, for a very practical reason. Unlike Spain, his kingdom did not have a *converso* population that could remain behind to serve as the nation's middle class after the expulsion. He wanted, therefore, to eliminate Judaism while retaining the Jews. His solution was to try to force all Portuguese Jews to convert. On March 19, 1497, during the Passover holiday, orders went out that all Jewish children between the ages of four and fourteen by seized and converted; in addition, they were to remain permanently separated from parents who refused to convert. At the same time, Jews who had decided to leave the country were told that they could depart only from Lisbon. When they arrived, coming from all over the country, they were shocked to find that their children, too, were taken away. Moreover, no boats had been readied in port to transport them into exile, and an army of priests awaited them on the palace grounds. After they had been dragged to this site, they were baptized *en masse*. The decree of expulsion did not have to be carried out, because all the Jews of Portugal were now Christians.

The ironies of the situation are as clear as they are poignant, in terms of understanding the *converso* problem. Spain had expelled her Jews in order to eliminate their influence on *conversos*, but the expulsion had only succeeded in swelling the ranks of the *conversos* within her borders. Next door, the forced conversions of Manuel entrapped the stalwarts who had fled from Spain, thereby adding scores of thousands of unwilling converts to the total *converso* community. The combined effects of these two events, therefore, added vast numbers of *conversos* to the body politic of Spain and Portugal.

In the special circumstances of the latter, Manuel accepted the arguments of the forced converts that, given the sudden and violent nature of their conversion, they needed time to adjust to their new identities. He agreed to make no inquiries into their religious practices for the next twenty years and further decreed that no distinctions would be made between New and Old Christians, in the hope that the converts "would lose their accustomed habits and be confirmed in our holy faith."

But the king's assumptions proved to be unrealistic. As in Spain, the distinctive mass of forced converts could not possibly change their religious identity overnight. Stalwarts of Judaism by definition, since they had escaped to Portugal in the first place to avoid conversion, they remained an entire Jewish community—rabbis, scholars, beggars, businessmen—even though they had been forcibly baptized. Immediately, therefore, the populace began to make invidious comparisons between themselves and these New Christians, who quickly began rising to positions of prominence in the country that refused to let them leave. In 1506, a mob led by two Dominican friars staged a massive pogrom in Lisbon, killing at least 2,000 New Christians. The survivors implored the king to let them leave; when he consented, several thousand emigrated, most of them destined for the Ottoman Empire. Their brethren continued to pour out of the country by the boatload until 1521, when the ban on emigration was restored.

Most converts, however, remained in Portugal. By dispatching organized delegations to Rome, they managed to ward off the introduction of the Inquisition to Portugal. Since this effort required the payment of substantial bribes, it seems clear that the New Christian community was a cohesive group able to pool its resources for concerted action. In other words, their sense of group identity continued to be strong. Ultimately, however, they failed at keeping out the Inquisition, which was instituted in Portugal in 1536. The delay seems only to have intensified the fervor of the Inquisitors, for their behavior was even more drastic and sweeping than in Spain, their methods more vicious, and the results more terrifying. Also, the special circumstances of the *conversos* played a role; since they had to face the full impact of Inquisitorial zeal with no practicing Jewish community from which to draw sustenance as fear pervaded their households, their crypto-Judaic practices grew even more subterranean, their Judaism more fervent. For the next several hundred years, in fact, the fading remnants of Judaism were secretly cultivated in Portugal, even as normative Judaism faded. As in Spain, blood purity statutes kept alive the distinction between the converts and Old Christians, consolidating a brotherhood of believers in a conspiracy of suffering.

Over time, a new religion, neither wholly Jewish nor wholly Catholic, evolved among the secret Jews of Portugal. It was a belief that combined secrecy with fear, partial memory with substantial loss. Its observances included much fasting, abbreviated prayers in which only one Hebrew word ("Adonai," or God) was retained, shortened festivals that could be covertly observed at home, and a special set of rituals reserved primarily for women. The forced converts would remain courageously loyal to this new faith even *in extremis*, as is evident from literally tens of thousands of Inquisition dossiers. The echoes of their fortitude would reach across the Atlantic into the New World.

In addition to Portugal, the small kingdom of Navarre had seemed an immediately convenient refuge in 1492. A tiny enclave of Jews gathered there directly from the south of Spain, feverishly threw themselves into rebuilding their lives, and worked on strengthening their *aljama*. By the beginning of 1498, however, the influence of Ferdinand and Isabella had prevailed over the opposition of the local dynasty and these refugees, too, had to face the choice between exile and conversion. Geography played a significant part, in this instance, because Navarre was a land-locked kingdom; France to the north and Castile and Aragon to the south were closed to the Jews. Thus the last forced conversion of Iberia took place, and the story of the Sephardim of Spain as a legally constituted and recognized body came to an end. Their history thenceforward would be of a doubly exiled community scattered to virtually all corners of the earth.

6
Return to the Islamic World
The Sephardic Diaspora in Muslim Lands

Brothers and teachers, friends and acquaintances: I, Isaac Zarfat . . . proclaim to you that Turkey is a land wherein nothing is lacking, and where, if you will, all shall yet be well with you. The way to the Holy Land lies open to you through Turkey. . . . Here every man may dwell at peace under his own vine and fig-tree.[1]

—Isaac Zarfati

Resh Lakish has said: The Holy One, Blessed be He, does not smite Israel unless He has created for them a healing beforehand.

—Babylonian Talmud *Megillah* 13b

The expulsions from Spain and Portugal were echoed in Sicily and many Italian states during the sixteenth century, as Jews were driven out to drift like flotsam from one Mediterranean port to the next, briefly finding refuge only to be pushed out again, always toward the East. Sicily's Jews, under the crown of the kingdom of Aragon, suffered expulsion in the summer and autumn of 1492. The Jews in Sardinia faced the same fate, and a number of them, like a substantial group from Spain, sought refuge in the kingdom of Naples. Naples in turn expelled her Jews in 1497; Apulia and Calabria expelled theirs in 1510. Refugees from the Italian and Spanish expulsions who found asylum on the Dalmatian coast in Ragusa (present-day Dubrovnik) were ousted in 1515. In 1569 the Jews of the Papal States, with the exception of Rome and Ancona, were expelled. In short, 1492 marked the beginning of decades of upheaval. Consequently, global Jewish settlement patterns were drastically altered within a generation: the Muslim world once again became home to hundreds of new or revitalized centers of Jewish life. In this complex diaspora of the Sephardim, two separate branches began to form. Throughout the lands of the Eastern Mediterranean and in the Balkans, there was a large and heterogeneous diaspora of migration of Ladino- and Arabic-speaking Jews. In western Europe, the smaller branch of the Sephardic family was primarily crypto-Jewish and Portuguese-speaking.

As the former group wended their way toward the Holy Land, they tended to be introspective and melancholy, for the world they knew had literally collapsed and no relief seemed in sight. An unprecedented flood of history books flowed from the pens of refugees as survivors sought hints of redemption in the tragedies around them. Samuel Usque's *Consolation for the Tribulations of Israel* painfully assembled a panorama of Jewish disasters, suggesting how each marked the fulfillment of biblical prophecy. Joseph ha-Kohen's *The Vale of Tears* mournfully chronicled the litany of Jewish disasters, seeking signs of comfort. Traditional acceptance of suffering—indeed, transformation of the suffering itself into a privilege of service to God—alternated with fury and inner religious doubts. For Yehudah Zarco, a Hebrew poet from Rhodes, the trauma of Jewish history caused a temporary loss of faith. Elegies written after the expulsion defiantly question the ways of the Divine: "Alas, our Father, is this the recompense we have sought?" "Is this the way a father treats his children?" Rabbi Solomon Alkabetz, the great poet of Safed, wrote that the Jews had already suffered too much, calling upon God to take notice and save them.

Every step of resettlement was strewn with obstacles. Once the hurdles of departure from their native lands were overcome, the expelled Sephardim still had to find modes of transportation and secure places of asylum. In Spain, for example, boats from Italy and North Africa crowded into the country's ports as word began to circulate that tens of thousands of Jews needed passage elsewhere. Unfortunately, all too many ship captains, whether Genoese, Ragusan, Neapolitan, Venetian, Spanish, or Arab, were venal enough to try to sell their passengers and seize their belongings. In addition, the nearest refuge, just across the straits in North Africa, was barred to Jews: the Spanish occupied the ports of Algeria and Tunisia, the Portuguese occupied northern Morocco. Furthermore, the independent sheikhs of the coastal regions refused to grant the refugees access to the interior, even if they were successful in making port. The few exiles who were so determined to make their way to the safety of Fez that they succeeded in moving inland in Morocco were despoiled en route.

A glimpse of the hardships is found in the chronicle of Eliyahu Capsali, who was involved in refugee resettlement in Candia, Crete, and undoubtedly heard the following from eyewitnesses:

> Those communities that lived near the sea boarded boats from Biscay, Catalonia and Castile, some large and some small, for when news of the decree was announced, these boats came from as far away as Genoa and Venice. Some set sail for the Muslim lands, such as Oran, Alcasar, and Bougie, which are far from the coast of Cartagena. Thousands and tens of thousands of people came to the port of Oran. The inhabitants of the country, on seeing the great number of ships, complained and said: Lo, they are making the country narrow for us; and they are coming as enemies, to destroy us and take us as slaves and bondswomen. . . . Assemble yourselves and let us go to the fortified cities and fight for ourselves and our children. And so they did: they shot at the ships with cannon and other instruments and destroyed part of the Jews. But in the end, when they heard of the expulsion, the king received them kindly, for an intercessor stood up for them at the palace in the person of R. Abraham. . . . Once the Jews finally landed on dry land, they sought for themselves places to settle, but the city was too small to absorb them. The king then built them wooden housing outside the city walls . . . [2]

Capsali goes on to report that a bakehouse in one of the wooden huts caught fire and the refugees of Oran lost everything that they had been able to salvage from Spain.

Frequently, ships loaded with exiles were abandoned by their captains at sea and left to float adrift. If the passengers did not die on the
water, they might well suffer the fate described by the Portuguese
Jewish chronicler Samuel Usque:

> They were cast, like victims of contagion, upon a barren beach, far
> from human help. Babies begged for water and mothers raised their
> eyes to heaven for help, while others, reduced to despair by hunger
> and abandonment, dug their own graves.[3]

A similar account by Solomon ibn Verga, (c. 1450–c. 1520) one of
the most important and eloquent chroniclers of the generation of expulsions, provides more details of the special agony of those trying
times:

> I heard pass from the lips of the old, departed from Spain, of a boat,
> and the fatal blow it was dealt. The skipper cast all ashore in a place
> uninhabited, and there most of them died of hunger; those struggled
> to stay on their feet until they could find a place of settlement. And
> one Jew among them, he, his wife and their two sons strove to go on;
> the woman, rather than let her feet stray, fainted and died. The man
> bore his sons, and he also fainted, as did the sons, from the hunger cast
> over them. When the man overcame his weakness he found his sons
> dead. In a frenzy, he rose to his feet and exclaimed, "Master of the
> universe! You hasten to make me abandon you. Know, my Faith,
> against the will of those residing in heaven, I am a Jew and a Jew I
> shall remain; and all that you have caused me to bear and will further
> bring upon me shall not hinder me from worshipping you." And he
> gathered dirt and weeds and covered the two children and went in
> search of a settlement.[4]

It is not surprising that the Jews in exile felt that all the biblical
predictions of catastrophe were reaching fruition.

But there was more. Not long after 12,000 Jews arrived safely in
Tlemcen, a strategic outpost on the border between Algeria and Morocco, almost 3,000 of them would succumb to the plague. Many of the
survivors, unable to withstand the rigors of life in North Africa, re-
treated to Spain, as would exiles from many other Islamic ports. For
one thing, they found themselves caught in the continuing battles between Spaniards, Ottoman Turks, and the local Berber forces. For
another, the Muslim populations were reluctant to receive the large
numbers of wandering refugees. In many cases, however, the local

Jewish communities were able to intercede and bring about the admission of their brethren, albeit at great cost. To take one example recalled by the astronomer and historian Abraham Zacuto, Columbus's famous supporter, in 1499 the Algerian Jewish community generously redeemed fifty Jews who had been imprisoned for two years in Seville.

In the long run, however, the Sephardim who reached Morocco were the most fortunate of the exiles to North Africa. The king of Fez, Mulai Muhammed esh-Sheikh, had agreed to let them settle outside the city walls. Not only the reported "kindness of the King" but also the city's reputation as a center of learning soon attracted as many as 20,000 refugees. Most were suffering from cholera, a circumstance that might explain why they were not allowed to join the Jewish community inside the city. But as they arrived, the local Jews emerged to welcome them, pay their ransoms, and supply them with food and clothing.

Yet readjustment even in this relatively peaceful atmosphere was nonetheless extraordinarily difficult. The introductions to books composed in the Maghreb during these traumatic years are filled with laments over lost libraries, disease, insecurity, and continuing harassment. The recollections of one refugee intellectual, Judah Hayyat, are especially harrowing:

> One Ishmaelite from Spain, from the same locality as I, arrived there [Morocco] and told slanderous stories about me, and people believed him as if there had been three witnesses. They smote me, they wounded me, they took away my veil from me and threw me into a deep pit with snakes and scorpions in it. They presently sentenced me to be stoned to death, but promised that if I changed my religion they would make me captain over them. . . . But the God in whom I trust frustrated their design. When I had been there for almost forty days in darkness and in gloom, with scanty bread and water by measure, my belly cleaving to the ground, in hunger and in thirst and in nakedness and in want of all things, God stirred up the spirit of the Jews in Chechaouen, and they came thither to redeem me, and I rewarded them for my redemption by giving them nearly two hundred books which I had.[5]

In fact, local conditions were so harsh that many refugees decided, if reluctantly, to take up the wanderer's staff anew. Ibn Hayyat, for example, remained only briefly in Fez before moving on to Naples and from there to Venice. He finally settled down in Mantua, where he was able to resume his scholarly career. This odyssey was typical for the exiled Sephardic sages, who characteristically moved from place to place until they finally reached the Ottoman Empire. Some, like Jacob Berab, continued to wander even within the empire; he moved around North Africa for years before settling at last in Palestine. Stability was the exception, mobility the rule, during the first century of exile.

Fragmentary tales of misfortune that have survived show that the suffering was by no means confined to the North African coast. Sephardim forced to flee from Naples in 1540 were robbed by their Ragusan captain and abandoned in Marseilles. Only because the French king Francis I took pity on them were they able to make their way to the Levant. In 1558, a boatload of refugees fleeing Pesaro was barred from Ragusa and sold into slavery in Apulia by the ship's crew. Still more tragic was the fate of fifty-two passengers on a Greek ship in 1583; all were murdered at sea. Frequently, Jews became pawns in the imperial contests of Europe. For example, when Spain's Charles V captured Tunis in 1535, all of the Jews there were sold into captivity. Nor could the assurances of the clergy be trusted. Twenty-four Jewish merchants, formerly *marranos*, were burned at the stake in Ancona in 1553 by order of the Papal Inquisition, even though all had expressly been granted permission to revert to Judaism under charters of protection.

In the fifteenth and sixteenth centuries, therefore, it was the Ottoman Empire, then at the zenith of her power, that alone afforded exiles a place where "their weary feet could find rest." The Ottomans initially established a bridgehead in Anatolia around 1300, then expanded relentlessly from there through southeastern Europe all the way to the Danube. They had bypassed Constantinople but under Mehmet II finally conquered the Byzantine capital in 1453, continuing their campaigns under Selim I with the capture of Syria and Egypt. The last of the conquering sultans, Suleiman the Magnificent (1520–66), captured Hungary in 1526, besieging Vienna in 1529. In the East he took Iraq and most of the Caucasus in 1535, while also extending Ottoman control over most of North Africa. At its peak of expansion, the Empire encompassed approximately 250,000 Jews.

Her sultans—Bayezid II, Mehmet II, Suleiman the Magnificent—were dynamic, farsighted rulers who were delighted to receive the talented, skilled Jewish outcasts of Europe. The artisans and craftsmen among them were recognized as a vital force for an expanding empire. The merchants were seen as a valuable supplement to the existing warrior and agrarian classes, for they were a people capable of taking risks, knowledgeable about prices and economic conditions in far-off places, and eager to retain or renew their contacts all over Europe. In addition, these former Europeans were not at all interested in advancing the military designs of their erstwhile rulers. Bayezid II, responding to the expulsion from Spain, reportedly exclaimed, "You call Ferdinand a wise king, he who impoverishes his country and enriches our own!" He not only welcomed the Sephardic exiles but ordered his provincial governors to assist the wanderers by opening the borders. Indeed, the refugees would find the Ottoman state to be powerful, generous, and tolerant.

Jews have traditionally viewed the events of history, perhaps especially the actions of nations, as part of a larger divine scheme. In this vein, the Ottoman policies, weighed against the vicissitudes of the day by the unusual cluster of historians who emerged among the exiles, were seen to convey hidden messages about God's intentions. Capsali, in particular, discerned special redemptive portents in this unprecedented Islamic largesse and compared the Turkish leaders to the ancient Persian Cyrus, who had invited the Jewish exiles in Babylon to return to the land of Israel. He confidently described the working of God's will in the decisions made by Islamic rulers:

> In the first year of the Sultan Mehmet, King of Turkey . . . the Lord aroused the spirit of the king, Sultan Mehmet, King of Turkey, and his voice passed through his kingdom and also by proclamation saying: This is the word of Mehmet king of Turkey, the Lord God gave me a kingdom in the land and he commanded me to number his people the seed of Abraham his servant, the sons of Jacob his chosen ones, and to give them sustenance in the land and to provide a safe haven for them. Let each one with his God come to Constantinople the seat of my kingdom and sit under his vine and under his fig tree with his gold and silver, property and cattle, settle in the land and trade and become part of it.[6]

Moreover, as did others of his generation, Capsali believed that the open-door policy was part of a divine strategy to bring the Jews nearer the land of Israel in preparation for their redemption.

> Following the establishment of Sultan Selim's rule in Egypt all false gods will be eliminated and banished, and this will be a time of redemption. And our righteous Messiah will come . . . because ever since the expulsion from Spain, God has started to gather the exiled from Israel and Judea in the lands of the dispersion and he is assembling them from the four corners of the earth.[7]

The Empire's policy not only welcomed Jews but also sought to increase their number in specific sites. Initially, this aim was accomplished with a harsh system known as *sürgün*, the forced movement of entire population groups. After his conquest of Constantinople in 1453, for example, Sultan Mehmet decided to make the capital of Byzantium his own, renaming it Istanbul, and sent an order transferring "his own people and many of the Hebrews" to the city. Untold suffering must have attended the transfer of Jews from Thrace, Anatolia, and Rumelia, while those still under Christian control on the nearby islands of Crete and Rhodes composed lamentations in fear of later enduring a similar fate.

The policy was continued or renewed for generations. In 1516, when Selim II conquered Egypt, he brought Jewish craftsmen and merchants from Alexandria and Cairo in order to augment the middle class in the imperial capital. Similarly, when Suleiman the Magnificent captured Rhodes in 1523, he ordered 150 wealthy Jews transferred there from Salonika. When he vanquished Cyprus in 1571, he commanded that 1,000 Jewish families of artisans and merchants be forcibly moved there from Safed, Palestine. In this instance, Jewish delegations repeatedly petitioned him to reduce the number of deportees, warning that Safed's textile industry would otherwise be ruined. The Sultan replied, "In the interests of the said island, my noble command has been written," and ensured that the coerced migrants would be granted tax exemptions for twenty years as well as free housing. Such incentives were obviously not entirely successful, for in 1579 the governor of the island tried to detain 100 Jews from Salonika when their ship bound for Palestine anchored in the Cypriot port of Famagusta.

In the long run, however, the dreaded deportations made it possible for Jews to prosper in the new centers of commerce. Indeed, the *sürgüns* were largely forgotten in historical retrospectives; more important were the major peaceful migrations and the subsequent renaissance of Jewish life throughout the Ottoman lands. The continuing expansion of the Empire, combined with its continuing attractiveness as a haven, contributed to the increase in the Jewish population all through the sixteenth century. As we have seen, the Lisbon massacre of 1506 stimulated the migration of thousands of Portuguese *conversos*. What they encountered, and helped build, was the establishment of Jewish communities along all of the important trade routes from the West to Turkey. Both Ragusa's (Dubrovnik's) "Jew Street," a commercial way station on the route from Venice, and Sarajevo's Jewish quarter date from this period.

Selim II's conquest made it possible for Cairo's ancient Jewish community to accept exiles and assist them in resettlement. On the other hand, many cities saw the establishment of Jewish communities for the first time in centuries. In Vienna, for instance, the refugees from Iberia were granted a foothold despite a general prohibition against Jewish settlement.

Demographically, the sheer numbers of the Spanish exiles, along with their abundant talents and leadership skills, would culturally overwhelm the Arabic-speaking Jewish communities already established in the Levant, although these indigenous Jews, known as the *musta'ariba*, would be able to retain their language. In this fertile intermingling, such communities as Edirne (Adrianople), Izmir (Smyrna), and Bursa enjoyed a new lease on life. The Sephardic influence also led to the creation of several entirely new Jewish centers of great significance at the very heart of the Empire. Above them all, Salonika and Istanbul towered as representative of this new era in Jewish civilization. Salonika especially, soon to be known as the "Jerusalem of the Balkans," dwarfed all other Ottoman cities in terms of its concentration of Sephardic population, number and variety of congregations, diversity of talent and abundance of intellectual leaders, and the presence of influential Jewish diplomats. According to one authority, in 1430 2,509 Jewish households (17,563 people) were registered in the city. By 1519, there were more than 4,000 households, divided into twenty-four congregations, and by mid-century, the total number of congregations had increased to forty-four. In 1553, a German traveler, Hans Dernschwam, presumably using information from the rolls of male taxpayers, estimated that there were 20,000 Jewish males in the city. Jews would thus constitute the majority of the population, outnumbering the combined total of Greeks and Turks living there. Visitors remarked with surprise that the entire commercial life of the city ground to a halt on the Sabbath. During the same general period, Turkish census reports reveal that Istanbul's Jewish population in 1477 was 1,647 households (perhaps 11,529 people), or about 11 percent of the city's total population, but rose by 1535 to 8,070 households (56,490 people). Dernschwam's 1553 estimate found 15,000 Jewish males there. In 1638, the Turkish traveler Evliya Celebi visited the capital and reported that the 11,000 Jewish families (77,000 people) numbered twice the local Greek population.

But census figures alone can hardly convey the diverse cultural richness and cosmopolitanism of the Ottoman Jewish communities. In the first place, the original Greek-speaking Jewish population in Istanbul, the *Romaniots*, retained indigenous traditions that had developed over the course of centuries in Christian Byzantium. In addition, successive waves of immigration from Germany, Hungary, Provence, and Bohemia throughout the fifteenth and sixteenth centuries not only reinforced the *Romaniot* community but also introduced separate houses of worship and ritual practices. The mix became even more complex and diversified, of course, when the post-1492 migrants arrived with their own customs, Spanish language, characteristic life-style, and a new sense of Sephardic pride and assertiveness. It was not long before Ladino triumphed over Greek, Provençal, Italian, and Yiddish in the marketplaces, workshops, and several of the synagogues—a living remnant of the lost "homeland" of Spain.

Coincidentally, the strong desire of the immigrants to retain their distinctive languages and modes of organization was compatible with the decentralized structure of the Empire. Each Ottoman town was autonomous; within its walls, every religious and national group was organized in a separate congregation. From the perspective of their new rulers therefore, it was quite natural for the Jews to preserve and cultivate a welter of suborganizations and subdivisions. Ottoman authorities cared only for the continued maintenance of public order and the timely remittance of taxes by a humble *dhimmi* (Jewish and Christian) population. The sixteenth-century Salonika rabbi Joseph ibn Leb explained how this worked:

> In Salonika, every [Jewish] man speaks his own native tongue. When the exiles arrived, each vernacular group founded an independent congregation, there being mobility from congregation to congregation. Each congregation maintains its poor; each congregation is entirely separate in the Crown register. Thus each congregation appears to be an independent city.[8]

Indeed, not since ancient Alexandria had Jews been so well organized in so many groupings. These independent congregations based on language and common origin elected their own officers, with the wealthier taxpayers generally exercising a controlling influence. Each congregation strove to meet all the needs of its members, setting up separate schools, charity chests, burial grounds, law courts, and, of course, houses of worship. At the same time, all congregations within a city were loosely joined together in a representative body of delegates elected to handle such general questions as taxation, upkeep of the Yeshiva (the school of higher Talmudic learning), and urgent community matters. In Istanbul, the various congregations followed the will of the majority in the representative delegate body, but in Salonika, each congregation had almost total freedom.

In such large cities, dozens of congregations retained a flavor of the "old country," bearing such names as "the congregation of" Lisbon, Evora, Catalonia, *Gerush Sepharad* (Spanish exile), Sicily, Apulia, Calabria, Otranto, the Maghreb, Provence, Saragossa, Corfu, Toledo, Aragon, Andalusia, and Córdoba. The size of a congregation ranged from several dozen to almost 300 members. Splits and schisms were not uncommon, apparently unconnected to size or the passage of time. Although such fragmentation could lead to friction, it could also result in increased opportunities for leadership and self-expression. Perhaps it would seem natural for new groups to coalesce once the first immigrant generation died out, but in fact splits continued to occur and the number of congregations multiplied faster than warranted solely by the new waves of immigration. For example, the Old Catalan and New Catalan congregations may well have been formed as a result of divisions between those who arrived earlier and those who came later, but dates of arrival cannot account for many other congregational breakoffs. Legislation prohibiting splits was adopted, but it was ineffective. The *Gerush Sepharad*, Lisbon, and Catalan congregations each succeeded only temporarily in holding its membership together. One group left the Lisbon congregation to form Evora, then the remaining members of Lisbon split into Old Lisbon and New Lisbon. Individual personal differences were only partially a factor in the schisms and splits. Perhaps the continuing stream of ex-*conversos* into the Lisbon congregation sparked special controversy, because these emigrés tended to keep to themselves, maintaining social ties established long ago in Iberia. In any event, the impression one receives of sixteenth-century Salonika and Istanbul is of large, heterogeneous communities humming with a great variety of activities, crisscrossed by dozens of organizations and multiple identities. Despite these internal tensions and divisions, the community as a whole would band together to assist *marranos*. When, for example, Venice decided to expel its New Christian population in 1550, Salonika's leaders graciously invited the forty families facing homelessness. "Come here on a trial basis," they wrote, "if you will be pleased to stay with us and you find that your affairs will succeed here, you may remain. Otherwise, you may depart without owing us any taxes for the entire period of your experimentation."[9]

Over time, the original regional differences between the Jews began to blur because of at least three factors: intermarriage between the various Jewish groups, mergers of congregations, and the development of new social and commercial ties. The organizational structure that remained kept a strong Spanish coloration in language, dress, customs, and manners. In addition to the passage of time, another factor muting the differences between the Sephardim and other Jews was the introduction of a widely accepted, leveling code of law. The *Shulhan Aruch*, created by Rabbi Joseph Caro in 1564, embodied and codified Sephardic legal usage. Finally, linguistic diversity began to diminish with the triumph of Ladino (Judeo-Spanish), an admixture of Turkish, Hebrew, and Spanish that became the *lingua franca* of the community, gradually helping to meld a more homogeneous culture.

It is still not clear precisely why the original fragmentation was quite so persistent and long-lived. Was it a result of Ottoman policies that tended to divide foreign groups in order to supervise them more effectively? Or had the Jews hoped to ease their adjustment to new lands by preserving some aspects of the Spanish heritage of which they were almost arrogantly proud? Perhaps the answer lies in the conviction of rabbis that diversity would encourage greater religious observance. That is the suggestion of one of Egypt's great Sephardic leaders, Rabbi David ibn Abi Zimra:

> With the breaking away of groups from their fellow-townsmen and their common language, there is also a corresponding breaking up of devout hearts; nor are their prayers of praise to God united. But if they are of one city of origin and of one language, then will peace dwell among them, for each will feel at home and know his status.[10]

In Salonika, newcomers were at first assigned to a particular congregation by lot, in part so that the burden of integrating the refugees would be shared and in part so that no one congregation would expand at the expense of the others. As time passed, however, and exiles arrived whose background was checkered with many false starts elsewhere, it became clear that it would be best to determine which congregational affiliation would be most appropriate for them. To that end, the community worked out an agreement that "anyone immigrating to the city being of second generation Italian birth, even though the grandfather had originated in Portugal or Castile or Aragon or another kingdom, shall go to the Italian synagogue. However, if his father was born in one of the above-mentioned kingdoms, then he shall join the congregation of his native tongue."[11] Even this compromise caused problems with the Aragonese congregation, however, who felt their growth would be inhibited because no one of Jewish origin now remained in Spain except the *marranos*, and they seemed to be settling into a crypto-Jewish existence of increasing assimilation.

Such diversity masked but did not entirely conceal acrimony over many issues. For example, there was much lively discussion of the competing claims of rich and poor in sharing community decision-making. Rabbi Samuel de Medina, Salonika's greatest community leader, came out strongly in favor of the "financial majority" (i.e., those who paid taxes) against the "majority of souls," because it was the wealthy who paid for community services, supported the indigent, and met the government's levies. But even more hotly contested were the legal questions raised by the *converso* past of many of the newcomers. Just as the rabbis of Algeria after 1391 had been sorely pressed to make just decisions when humanitarian concerns conflicted with Jewish law, so too the rabbinical authorities of Turkey, Egypt, and North Africa found themselves wrestling constantly with the problems raised by the forced conversions of Iberia. For many of these new emigrés who had lived as Christians for years in Portugal, Antwerp, or Italy but were now returning to Judaism, only the Jewish law courts of the Ottoman Empire could solve many complex issues of marriage and divorce.

Yet some of the most difficult cases facing Turkey's rabbis, for example, revolved around matters of custom, not law. Both Sephardic and indigenous Jews manifested pride in the customs hallowed by the usages of parents and grandparents and were convinced of the correctness and antiquity of their respective habits and practices. Each group tended to be particularly tenacious where food was concerned. The Sephardim, reacting to the many restrictive laws imposed upon them during the last century of Jewish life in Spain, were more lenient than indigenous Jews in their interpretations of what constituted kosher meat. Debates over this matter erupted throughout the Empire. Occasionally, the two contending communities resorted to Muslim authorities to resolve their essentially irreconcilable differences.

Another source of tension was the wide social gap that resulted as, for the first time, large numbers of European Jews lived among the Jews of the Islamic world. The indigenous Ashkenazim were astonished at the worldliness of the Sephardim, who in their turn were openly disdainful of their less sophisticated neighbors. Previously tranquil communities became embroiled in controversies that sometimes endured for decades. From the bitterness of these squabbles, one gets the impression that much more than halakhic issues were at stake as Sephardim insisted on proclaiming their noble lineage and the sanctity of their divergent customs. For their part, the Ashkenazim condemned the newcomers for their imperious demeanor, fractious temperament, and fierce loyalty to those questionable habits.

Ultimately, however, the superior numbers, erudition, and self-confidence of the Sephardim won out in most places and their customs prevailed, obliterating the centuries-old traditions of the North African, Greek, and Middle Eastern Jews. But perhaps their greatest cultural innovation was the art of Hebrew printing. Soon after printing was introduced in Rome in 1470, the open-minded Jews of Iberia took to this new technique with delight. By the 1480s, Hebrew printing presses functioned in Spain at Guadalajara and Hijar, in Portugal at Lisbon, Leiria, and Faro. At the time of the expulsion printers carried their type with them into exile, setting up presses in Fez, in Italy, and in Turkey. David and Samuel ibn Nahmias, refugee brothers from Spain, set up a press in Istanbul in 1493 and began printing almost immediately. By 1510, a press was functioning in Salonika. Later, it would become famous as the enterprise of the Soncinos, a family of printers who migrated from Italy. Between 1530 and 1547, they published over forty volumes in Hebrew. Printing would continue to flourish in Salonika even after a fire devastated much of the Jewish quarter in 1620. Still later, refugees from Poland set up printing shops in Istanbul and Salonika, and presses sprouted in Smyrna in 1657, in Safed, and in Egypt. The conservative Turkish authorities were wary of this new invention, however, and permitted the Jews to print only in Hebrew or Latin type, never Arabic letters. (When Turkish Muslims finally decided in the eighteenth century to begin their own printing enterprises, they had to turn to Jews for advice and assistance.)

A glance at the works printed in Ottoman lands offers fascinating insight into the world of the literate Jew of that place and time. At one level, it seems that most congregations produced and printed their own prayerbooks (undoubtedly a factor in preserving communal subdivisions). In addition, the early printings included many manuscripts penned by the last generation of rabbis in Spain, probably saving these works from certain extinction. Perhaps most importantly, however, a voluminous literature of rabbinic *responsa* flooded from the presses of Salonika and Istanbul, testifying to the enormous productivity of the rabbis of the first generations of resettlement. Their work helped their troubled brethren cope with the change and adaptation they had to face daily. The literature of Ottoman Jewry also included poetry and scientific works, and from the press in Safed the new kabbalistic writings poured forth to reach all corners of the Jewish world.

One of the most creative figures in the new scholarship was Rabbi Joseph Caro, mentioned earlier as the author of the *Shulhan Aruch*. Born in Spain in 1488, he was brought by his family to Portugal during the expulsion. After the forced conversions of 1497, they moved on to the Balkans, where young Caro would begin the monumental task of compiling all of the Jewish laws in use in his day. This compendium, which he called the *Beit Yosef* and worked on for decades, was a commentary on the earlier Sephardic legal code, the *Arba'ah Turim* written by Jacob ben Asher. For a generation virtually on the point of disintegration, Caro tried to determine and explain the "correct" legal rulings that should be followed by the Sephardim in exile. Their confusion, which was monumental, was caused not only by the expulsion but also by the plethora of *responsa* being produced by the many rabbis in Turkey. Caro based his assessments upon the giants of Sephardic jurisprudence: Maimonides, Alfasi, and Asher ben Yehiel. After he completed the complex and ambitious *Beit Yosef*, he wrote the previously mentioned *Shulhan Aruch*, essentially a digest of Jewish law without commentary or source citations. As we have seen, this clear and concise work not only became the definitive code of Jewish law among Sephardim. With Ashkenazic glosses added, it emerged as the handy legal manual for all of world Jewry, serving as a unifying force throughout the deeply divided Sephardic diaspora. Practically useful as it was, it owed its popularity at least in part to the rapid dissemination made possible by the Hebrew printing presses of the Empire. One would never suspect from this crisp, detached legal compilation that Caro had deep mystical leanings and would settle among a sympathetic group of like-minded exiles in Safed.

Even more ambitious than printing and distributing Caro's *Beit Yosef* was the Salonika presses' publication of the Talmud, a project so enormous few generations have succeeded in carrying it out. The type was brought from Portugal by the printer Don Yehuda Gedalia, and the first tractates appeared between 1519 and 1523. Proudly regarding the expensive undertaking as a communal responsibility, the city's Jews drew up a detailed appeal for financing, including the floating of a loan that would be repaid from the proceeds of selling the work. The surplus was earmarked for the poor of the Holy Land. After the Talmud was publicly burned in Italy in 1552, a second edition was printed on the Salonika presses.

Gedalia's influence extended to secular literature as well. In his house he founded a literary society that would continue to hold meetings for fifty years. The salon's talented members included Saadiah Longo, a famed poet who wrote in the Andalusian tradition, and poets all over the Empire sent their works to be recited there. Gedalia also acted as a patron to scores of needy refugee intellectuals, including the Portuguese physician Amatus Lusitanus (né Juan Rodrigo de Castel-Branco), who had led an extraordinary life as a *marrano* before arriving in Salonika and reverting. After medical training at the University of Salamanca, he had fled Portugal and enjoyed an illustrious medical career in Antwerp, France, and Ancona and Pesaro in Italy. At one point, he gave a series of anatomy lectures to scholars in Ferrara that was considered shocking, in part because at one session he dissected twelve cadavers in front of his audience in order to demonstrate the function of valves in the circulatory system. He was appointed as a physician to the pope, but his position did not spare him the anguish of the *auto-da-fé* in Ancona. He fled to Salonika, wrote about medicine under Gedalia's aegis, and was honored as the glory of the medical world of the day until he fell ill while tending victims of the plague in the city and died in 1568.

In his career and others, we see again and again that the Sephardic exiles were intent upon transporting their multifaceted culture and renewing it on Ottoman shores. Indeed, if one mark of a great civilization is the ability to export itself and establish a thriving culture in distant places, then surely the evidence from Turkey proves the greatness of the Sephardic tradition. Consciously working to this end, in 1547 Sephardic printers produced the Constantinople Pentateuch, a trilingual literal translation of the Bible with the Hebrew, Castilian, and Judeo-Greek texts printed in three parallel columns. Similarly, they had produced a Ladino translation of the Book of Psalms in 1540. In addition to preserving texts, however, the Ottoman presses also sustained links to the living Hispanic culture. It is especially noteworthy that the contemporary bestseller in Spain, the *converso* author de Rojas's *La Celestina*, was published in Salonika in Hebrew translation. The exiles would in fact keep abreast of Iberian literary trends for centuries; in the seventeenth century, Spanish travelers were deeply moved to hear the latest Spanish poems recited in the Jewish quarter of Aleppo, Syria. Even after such links were finally broken, the Ladino presses would remain active, producing an encyclopedic classic of biblical and folk lore, the *Me'am Loez*, in the early eighteenth century and numerous translations from Western literature, especially French, in the nineteenth. When Jewish culture began to decline in Turkey in the eighteenth century as a corollary of Ottoman decline, Ladino presses were founded in Belgrade, the new center of Sephardic civilization, although publishing continued in Salonika and Istanbul. (The preservation of the Spanish language was reflected in oral traditions as well. The Turkish Jews handed down medieval Spanish ballads, proverbs, popular songs, and rhymed couplets well into the twentieth century, with much of the material dating back to preexpulsion times.)

It is impossible to overestimate the role that printing played in keeping the Spanish component of Sephardic culture alive. The presses disseminated Ladino works to Jewish populations, like the Romaniots, who had never known Spanish language or literature. Ultimately, it was this language beloved by the Sephardic exiles that prevented them from blending into the local Jewish communities in the Balkans, Turkey, and elsewhere. The anomaly persisted of a persecuted people—very Jewish, but also very Spanish—who preserved an archaic form of a language, the tongue of their preexpulsion past, that became enriched with new elements from Turkish, Greek, and Slavic sources. In short, the Jewishness of the Mediterranean Sephardi was preserved and transmitted in an archaic Spanish garb that not only prevented total assimilation but also enabled him to "conquer" his Jewish neighbors culturally.

Even back in the sixteenth century, however, not all parts of the Sephardic diaspora were as successful in preserving Hispanic traditions as the Jews in Turkey. Except for the northernmost section of Morocco, where a local dialectical variant (*hekatiya*) was spoken among Jews until this century, Ladino practically died out in that country. The principal cause may be that Hebrew printing was short-lived there because the Inquisition cut off the supply of paper to North Africa in the 1520s. The printers of Fez were forced to seek their livelihood elsewhere, and scholars followed them to Italy, Turkey, and Palestine. Censorship presented overwhelming obstacles to the Sephardic press in Italy in the sixteenth century, causing many printers to move their type, paper, production techniques, and themselves to Turkey or Holland.

As a natural consequence of being a minority population within other cultures, Jews tended to be influenced by the dominant culture wherever they settled. Especially in North Africa, they were deeply influenced by Muslim religious trends, even while they strictly adhered to the Judaic rituals they had transported from Spain. For example, the traditional respect for learning remained a criterion for communal leadership, but the quality of "saintliness" assumed a new importance. This was especially true in those North African regions where Muslim "saints" played a prominent role in the social and religious life of the people. In much the same way, Jewish life began to be shaped to an increasing degree by pious men known for their good works, curative powers, and knowledge of the emerging body of mystical lore (*kabbalah*). Special memorial celebrations (*hilloulot*) at the tomb of a venerated saintly personality generated new forms of religious expression that have persisted among Jews from the area down to the present.

Along with this new influence, however, the Iberian model of rabbinic leadership, the scholar adept in both Hebraic and secular learning, became the Ottoman ideal as well. The traditional Sephardic pattern of lay leaders—merchants, physicians, diplomats—dominating community affairs also continued, for refugees soon gravitated toward the seats of political power, offering their services as courtiers to Muslim rulers in North Africa and Turkey. These two elements of community leadership, the rabbis and the lay leaders, were frequently allied by marriage throughout the Sephardic diaspora. For generations, marital as well as business connections would meticulously preserve the family trees that attested both to the interconnectedness of the emigré community's elite and to their illustrious descent from a great Spanish city or a noted line of courtier families. In other words, the helm of leadership in the newly formed emigré settlements remained in the hands of the Toledanos, Benvenistes, ibn Yahyas, Abrabanels, ibn Adrets, and dozens of other former Iberian "grandees." Nothing like this had ever occurred among migrating Ashkenazim.

In sharp contrast to the structure of Christian religious communities in the Empire, the Jews had no religious hierarchy. Although each congregation was headed by a rabbi, the *marbitz Torah*, who was paid for his services, the sages of the community commanded respect in proportion to their stature as scholars. There was a kind of chief rabbinate in Istanbul during the early part of the sixteenth century, but it soon gave way to the localized rabbinates. The office of chief rabbi, *haham bashi*, was not established until the nineteenth century.

Unfortunately, the remarkable role assumed by the Sephardim in Ottoman diplomacy has never been thoroughly researched. The first openings for governmental service, as in the Muslim conquest of Spain, were in translating and diplomatic negotiating, two roles that were virtually indistinguishable. The Sephardim, given their practiced facility in languages, knowledge of Europe, and evident desire to retain their ties with *marranos* there, apparently sought opportunities to return to Iberia as representatives of Islamic merchants and rulers. On such business trips and diplomatic missions, they could not only keep in touch with relatives but could also help them in secretly observing Jewish rites or in removing their assets abroad in preparation for flight. For example, entire groups of *conversos* who wanted to revert to the faith of their fathers might be circumcised by a visitor from Turkey or Holland. (Reversion was often accompanied by circumcision, a particularly audacious act given the vigilance of the Inquisition.) There was also a kind of underground railroad clandestinely maintained by Sephardic refugees for the crypto-Jews left behind in Iberia. Inquisition records shed occasional but only partial light on these activities, which were by their very nature rarely recorded to reach the eyes of later generations.

The diplomatic role played by the Sephardic emigrés was scarcely less complex. To the delight of their Muslim employers, they frequently harbored a deep and abiding resentment toward Spain, one of the chief enemies of the Ottoman Empire. At the same time, they could accomplish delicate feats of diplomacy at the highest level of government but out of the public eye. For a Moroccan monarch, say, to deal openly with Christian Europe could excite the entire religious establishment and fan the flames of anti-dynastic revolt. In any case, Muslim diplomats were loathe to go to the "lands of the infidel," and the notion of enduring the politesse and rituals of negotiating with "infidels" was anathema. In all ways, it was better public policy to leave such disagreeable assignments in the hands of the *dhimmi*, under the pretense that they were mere commercial agents and translators. Consequently, Jews negotiated treaties between the king of Fez and Portugal, between the Ottomans and France. In all these and similar cases, the ironies always lay close to the surface. For example, as perquisites owing to their high position, both the Jewish ambassador from Fez to Holland, a certain Samuel Pallache, and the Jewish diplomat or resident merchant from Morocco to London were given extraterritorial rights to worship, even while Jewish residents in both places could not. And as the Sephardic diplomatic activities ranged beyond Iberia into France or England, the emigrés were also able to expand their efforts to contact relatives and strengthen their interlocking commercial enterprises.

Yet the allegiance of these diplomats to their Muslim rulers was beyond suspicion. The unforgettable cruelties they had endured had not ended with the extinction of Judaism in Iberia. Periodic eruptions of Inquisitorial zeal sent shockwaves through the Sephardic diaspora as boatloads of emigrés brought harrowing stories of new persecutions. Special memorial services would be held in the new Sephardic communities for the victims of the latest *auto-da-fé* back in Europe. Special prayers calling upon God to avenge the martyrs were composed and inserted in the prayerbooks:

> May the great, mighty, and terrible God avenge the vengeance of His holy servant . . . who was burned alive for the sanctified unity of His name. May he seek his blood from his enemies by his mighty arm and repay his foes according to their deserts. May the King, in His mercy remember unto us His merit, as it is written: "Rejoice, O ye nations, His people, for He will avenge the blood of His servants, and will render vengeance to His adversaries, and will absolve the land and His people."[12]

Clearly, there was no danger that the Sephardic representatives of the Ottoman Empire would waver in their loyalties to the rulers who had protected them from such persecution and allowed their new communities to thrive.

Success in international diplomacy was only the beginning of the Sephardic contribution to the developing Empire. From the Ottoman point of view, the Jews were carriers of Europe's latest technological secrets, whether in medicine, artisanry, or trade. Many of them had studied in the advanced universities of Portugal or Italy before finding refuge in Muslim lands or Holland. To the horror of some European observers, refugees were able to bring their knowledge of how to make gunpowder and munitions to the arsenals of Istanbul, Fez, Marrakech, and Cairo. In 1551, a European visitor to Turkey described the Sephardim there as "not long since banished and driven from Spain and Portugal, who, to the great detriment and damage of Christendom, have taught the Turk several inventions, artifices and machines of war,

The majority of the Sephardic exiles of 1492 gravitated east to the Ottoman Empire where they established important new centers of Jewish life. Observers noted the prominence of Jews in commerce, crafts, and even positions of confidence in the Turkish court. Jewish craftsmen and merchants like the one portrayed above at left (etched in 1714 after a drawing by Jean Baptiste Vanmour) plied their trades throughout the growing empire. At right, a Jewish woman brings her merchandise for sale to the ladies of the harem, who were not permitted to go out. (*Israel Museum*)

Gracia Nasi, also known as Doña Gracia Mendes (*above left*), a *marrano* refugee from Portugal, became a wealthy and prominent cultural patron as well as a political force in 16th century Ottoman affairs. She helped to build new synagogues and other institutions in Salonika, Izmir, and most notably, the Mayor Synagogue (*below*) in Bursa. (*Bronze medal, 1553, by Pastorino de Pastorini: Jewish National and University Library, Schwadron Collection*) Ottoman Jewish life began to decline in the 17th century, however, and the worldwide Jewish furor over the false messiah Sabbetai Sevi (*above right*) was partly responsible for its ultimate loss of vitality. (*Engraving from Thomas Coenen's Book, Arnst, 1669. Jewish National and University Library*)

Sephardic refugees also established important new communities in Italy. Sixteenth-century Venice housed two Sephardic congregations, one of Jews from Portugal and Spain, the other of Sephardic merchants from Ottoman lands. At left, a detail of the latter synagogue, known as the Scola Levantina. (*Beth Hatefutsoth*) Livorno and Ferrara were also centers of Jewish life and commerce. Below, the Great Synagogue of Livorno (Leghorn), which was destroyed in World War II. (*U. Nahon Museum, Jerusalem*)

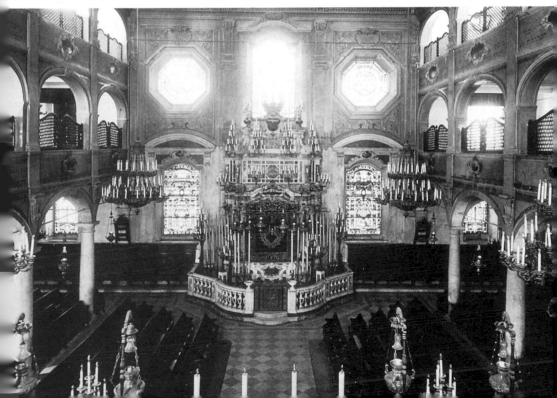

Cultural links with Iberia persisted among Jews, like Don Francisco Lopes Suasso (*right*), who nurtured their aristocratic Portuguese heritage. The Suassos were typical of the great mercantile *marrano* families who engaged in the far-flung commerce and finances of 17th-century Amsterdam. They had served the King of Spain and were loyal supporters of the House of Orange. (*Jewish Historical Museum, Amsterdam, on loan from Amsterdam Historical Museum*)

The most brilliant Jewish community of the 17th century was that of Amsterdam, where Sephardim built rich synagogues, sheltered Jewish refugees, and played an active civic role. Scholar and printer Menasseh ben Israel (*at right*) was also a rabbi and served as a teacher to Baruch Spinoza. Moreover, he went as an ambassador to England to discuss the readmission of Jews with Oliver Cromwell. (*Jewish Historical Museum, Amsterdam: J. van Velzen Collection*)

Rembrandt van Rijn had his house in Amsterdam's Jewish quarter and sketched and painted many Jews, including the Algerian-born Rabbi Jacob Sasportas (*left*), best known for his courageous opposition to the Sabbatean heresy. Below, at left, a view of the Portuguese Synagogue or "Ioden Kerken" in Amsterdam, consecrated in 1675; the most famous synagogue of Europe, its architecture inspired other synagogues in London and the Caribbean. (*Jewish Historical Museum, Amsterdam, on loan from Bibliotheca Rosenthaliuna, Amsterdam*)

The scene below depicts a 17th-century Jewish wedding in Amsterdam. (*Collection of the Centre of the Jews from Holland, Jerusalem*)

Above, a funeral at the Portuguese Jewish cemetery in Ouderkerk a.d. Amstel. The etching by Romegn de Hooghe was made around 1680. (*Jewish Historical Museum, Amsterdam*)

Baruch Spinoza, the greatest modern Jewish rationalist philosopher, was born in Amsterdam in 1632 of *marrano* parentage. For daring to question the fundamental tenets of Judaism, he was excommunicated by the Portuguese community of Amsterdam in July 1656. (*Leo Baeck Institute, New York*)

such as how to make artillery, arquebuses, gunpowder, cannonballs and other weapons."[13] A Spanish visitor remarked ruefully, "Here at Constantinople are many Jews, descendants of those whom the Catholic King Ferdinand ordered to be driven forth from Spain, and would that it had pleased God that they had drowned in the sea in coming hither! For they taught our enemies the most of what they know of the villanies of war, such as the use of brass ordnance and firelocks."[14] Similar complaints were voiced by Spanish diplomats in Morocco.

At the same time, medical knowledge became a pathway to prominence for many Sephardic physicians, as it had in Andalusia so many generations before. Eagerly courted by sultans and pashas, they were given pensions to serve as permanent "official doctors." And, as we can see in the career of Moses Hamon, for example, these royal physicians could be very effective in defending the Jewish community. The Hamon family, which had originated in Granada in the 1450s, emigrated to Turkey after the expulsion. Moses' father, Joseph, became physician first to Sultan Bayezid II and later to Selim I. Moses would serve as official doctor to Selim I, also, and then to Suleiman the Magnificent, becoming one of the most powerful Jews in Turkey. In the 1530s, when several communities were hit with a wave of persecution after Armenians charged that they were using Christian blood for ritual purposes, he obtained an imperial decree (*ferman*) repudiating the blood libel and promising imperial protection against all such accusations in the future.

In his community leadership role, Hamon patronized several of the Jewish schools in Istanbul and Salonika and sponsored the publication of a number of important rabbinical books by the scholars of his day. But he also produced many writings of his own in the fields of medicine and pharmacology and actively participated in Sephardic cultural circles, where Hebrew poets like Saadiah Longo recited and disseminated their work. On the local political level, when some paralyzing squabbles threatened to get out of hand in the Salonika community, he intervened, and several disruptive communal officers were brought to trial.

In the larger sphere of diplomacy, he arranged a peace in 1540 between Istanbul and Venice. In 1588 he negotiated the renewal of the agreement on residential rights and tax for the Jewish community in Salonika. Despite these and other illustrious achievements in both diplomacy and medicine, he ultimately fell from favor, the victim of court intrigues, and bequeathed his privileged status to his sons. The tradition of having physicians serve in official and unofficial capacities in Turkey would continue for more than a century after the expulsion. In

1618, for example, forty Ottoman Jewish physicians were appointed to the sultan's court, in addition to the foreign Jewish physicians employed there.

Even Hamon's remarkable career pales beside the exploits of his contemporaries Dona Gracia Mendes and her nephew Don Joseph Nasi, who were to become the most important Jewish personalities in the Ottoman Empire. Dona Gracia was born Beatrice de Luna in Portugal in 1510, a child of the first generation of forced Portuguese *conversos*. While married to the *marrano* banker Francisco Mendes, she apparently became adept both in banking and the gem trade. When her husband died in 1537, she left Portugal and expanded his business, moving with her family from one European commercial center to the next. It is probably no coincidence that she left her homeland one year after the introduction of the Inquisition; her sojourn in Europe was marked by close shaves with the Holy Office in Antwerp and Italy. In Ferrara she finally discarded all pretense of Christian identity and began openly practicing Judaism. As she continued her complicated business activities, the clients to whom she extended loans included the Hapsburg emperor Charles V and Francis I of France. She was also engaged in helping *marranos* escape from Portugal. In 1553, perhaps because of her former crypto-Judaism, she was forced herself to flee precipitately to Istanbul. Moses Hamon and Sultan Suleiman helped her transfer her capital there. Chroniclers of the day record with awe her majestic arrival in the Ottoman capital, where she settled in a sumptuous villa in an exclusive neighborhood.

Dona Gracia's achievements in Istanbul became legendary, typifying the style and quite possibly the flaws of Sephardic leadership in general. She organized a consortium of Jews and Muslims that traded on a grand scale in wheat, pepper, and raw wool in exchange for European goods. Her commercial agents could be found in all the major Ottoman cities and European ports. She used her extraordinary wealth to publish important books, fund schools and hospitals, and subsidize dozens of students. She also founded houses of worship, including the synagogue of *La Seniora* or *ha-Giveret*, which was named in her honor and still stands in the city today.

Despite all of these activities, however, history remembers Dona

Gracia principally for her extraordinary diplomacy in defense of *marranos*. When the twenty-four merchants were burned in Ancona, as mentioned earlier, she responded in 1556 by trying to organize all Jews in the Ottoman Empire in a boycott of the Italian port. In this effort can be seen three important, interconnected factors in the life of the time: the continuing sense of cohesiveness of the *marrano* community, the clash between the great powers of Istanbul and Rome, and the limits under which even the most adroit Jewish politician was forced to operate.

As noted previously, the *marranos* in Ancona had been allowed to settle there with the express promise that they would not be prosecuted for the "crime" of reverting. Pope Julius III, understanding full well that the conversions in Portugal had been forced, reaffirmed this permission as recently as 1553. But his successor, Paul IV, was a zealous opponent of the Reformation who did not feel bound by the charters granted to Jews so that they could trade in the Papal States. Thus the practicing Jewish merchants in Ancona, including two of Dona Gracia's business agents, were summarily seized, tortured, and condemned to the stake. As soon as she heard of the death sentence, Dona Gracia took decisive steps to save them, recruiting the aid of Suleiman and even dictating the firm letter he dispatched to the pope. At the same time, she roused rabbis throughout the Empire, urging them to join in solidarity with the condemned Jews of Ancona. The surviving *marranos* there fled to the neighboring city of Pesaro, if they could, and sought access from the duke of Urbino, promising to organize a boycott of Ancona to the benefit of this much more modest port. Dona Gracia determined to spread this effort throughout the Empire.

The story of the boycott has been frequently retold through the eyes of twentieth-century political activism.[15] What should be emphasized here is the unusual sense of Sephardic solidarity revealed by the attempt, for the plight of the *marranos* of Ancona was portrayed and perceived as the potential fate of all *marranos*, an outrage to exiles all across the Mediterranean. Equally important is the special assertiveness of Dona Gracia as a political player whose sex, incidentally, seems to have posed no obstacle in rallying forces behind her. Finally, it should be noted that the Sephardic merchants as a group had the ability to shape the policies of a figure as towering as Suleiman the Magnificent.

Initially, most Ottoman Jews indeed followed Dona Gracia's urgings to divert all trade from the Adriatic to Pesaro. In Turkey, she flexed her considerable muscle without apology, going so far as to threaten loss of funds to those rabbis who did not stand firm with her. Even so, Turkish Jews were divided from the start. Some felt that rerouting to Pesaro would cause too great a commercial loss, while others worried that the boycott would endanger the Jews remaining in Ancona and unnecessarily expose Jews in all of the Papal States to retaliation. Still others argued that the *marranos* were responsible for their own fates, having threatened all Jews by settling in the Papal States and reverting to Judaism. If they had only come to the Ottoman Empire in the first place, ran the argument, they would never have faced such persecution.

In the event, despite the enthusiasm of many Ottoman Jews, it proved impossible to achieve united action to sustain the boycott. Several interesting factors help explain why. On the one hand, Dona Gracia's behavior, which can perhaps best be described as determined and self-righteous single-mindedness, was itself controversial. She may have seen herself as the legitimate protector of her fellow *marranos*, but her use of financial clout to get her way with those who opposed her was widely disliked. One can even infer personal distaste for her methods from hints dropped in the anti-boycott rabbinic decision of Istanbul's Rabbi Joshua Soncino. Opposition also reflected divisions within the Sephardic community itself, for the Portuguese ex-*marranos* seem to have been a self-isolating group that provoked jealousies and outright animosity. This factor, too, is implied in the decision by Soncino, who was of Italian descent. Ironically, Dona Gracia gained the support of the Ashkenazic and Romaniot rabbis but could not overcome the congregational and class divisions among Istanbul's Sephardim. (Her failure should not surprise anyone familiar with the inability of Jews in modern times to organize a boycott in the face of the Third Reich. Again, internal communal divisions would prove to be the decisive factor in militating against a united political stand, even as some argued against using this particular economic weapon to protect Jewish security.)

Even though Dona Gracia was not able to implement her cherished boycott, this first businesswoman of Europe had an impressive career from many other standpoints. To this day, she is the subject of legend among the Jews of Turkey. After her death in 1566, her place in Ottoman diplomatic circles was filled by her nephew and son-in-law, Don Joseph Nasi. A favorite of Selim II, he at once carried on the continuing expansion of his aunt's commercial empire and also, to all intents and purposes, acted as the Empire's foreign minister. He negotiated an

Ottoman treaty with Poland, for example, and arranged for assistance to a revolt in the Netherlands against the Spanish Hapsburgs. Meanwhile, like his famous aunt, he worked to rescue *marranos* from Europe. For his keen diplomatic advice that led to the Ottoman conquest of Cyprus, he was rewarded with a dukedom on the island of Naxos and concessions to develop the city of Tiberias in Palestine. Calling upon the Jews of Italy to return to this ancient site in the land of Israel, he rebuilt the city walls and started a silk industry there. Meanwhile, from his palatial Istanbul residence overlooking the Bosphorus, Don Joseph endowed schools and scholars in the manner of Italian Renaissance princes and set up a printing press on his estate. When he died in 1579, his widow, Reyna, took over his philanthropic activities.

Considering the traumas that the refugees had undergone and their continuing sense of dejection, it is testimony to their resiliency as well as their talents that, only one generation after the expulsion, a Golden Age of Jewish culture emerged in Turkey. Scarcely had the first exiles settled down when a remarkable burst of creativity manifested itself early in the sixteenth century, even as more emigrés were still pouring in. Dozens of major intellectual figures began writing important legal decisions and new rabbinic commentaries, publishing them in the emerging Hebrew presses and thus spreading their influence and perspectives beyond their local congregations. Because many refugee rabbis had studied under the last rabbis of Castile, they brought the methods of the Spanish sages to the congregational schools they instituted now in the synagogues of Salonika. Castilian decrees were also introduced as guidelines for community affairs by Sephardim who assumed the mantle of leadership in Egypt, Palestine, and throughout North Africa.

New schools of higher Jewish learning soon dotted the Ottoman map. The most famous, the Yeshiva in Salonika known simply as the *Talmud Torah*, was founded in 1520 by Sephardic exiles and would function for four centuries. The pride of the entire community, the school was noted for a cosmopolitan student body drawn from all over the Empire and Italy, and for a broad curriculum that included Talmudic and Hebraic studies, Greek and Latin, medicine, astronomy, and the natural sciences.

Printing and munitions-making, medicine and diplomacy, did not by any means exhaust the special skills brought to Turkey by the Sephardic diaspora. Jews became especially prominent in gold- and silversmithing, the import-export trade, and textile manufacturing. Salonika developed a reputation as an industrial center largely because of the Sephardic production of superior-quality wool that was comparable to the long-haired Spanish merino wool the Jews had seen manufactured in Spain. The emigrés worked in all facets of textile manufacture, including spinning, weaving, and dyeing, both in factories and in home workshops. The main streets of Salonika, as well as the Jewish quarters of Istanbul, were lined with shops dealing in textile goods. Guilds of Jewish textile workers organized their own welfare and social institutions, generating special legislation to control the production, storage, pricing, and marketing of textile goods, while community authorities periodically issued regulations to control the flow of raw materials, regulate competition, and protect poor artisans in the trade. The agents of the Salonika textile merchants were widely visible throughout the Balkans and Italy, and their wool was so highly prized that the Ottomans opted to collect the Jewish community head tax in the form of bolts of cloth to be used for the uniforms of the *janissaries*, the sultan's elite military force. Unfortunately, some of the more ambitious textile merchants even sent their agents back to Spain, where they were occasionally picked up by the Inquisition and tried as backsliding Christians.

Outside Turkey the diversity of Sephardic occupations was equally impressive. In Bulgaria, Jewish tanners shared control of the leather industry with Muslims. In Morocco, the refugees became synonymous with the gold- and silversmithing monopoly. In Palestine, the Sephardim transformed tiny Safed into a center of silk production for the markets of Syria and Egypt. In every area of the diaspora, in addition, Sephardic merchants were typically the leaders in international commerce, their trade links strengthened by family ties throughout the far-flung provinces of the Ottoman Empire.

Intellectually and spiritually, the Sephardim were a restless lot, torn by doubts about themselves and filled with an anxious sense of urgency to understand the cause of what they called "the enormous wrath" that had descended upon them. As we have seen, the traditional Jewish belief that suffering is a punishment for sin was considered by many to explain the expulsion. More specifically, Rabbi Yosef Yaavetz argued that Jewish scholars who had flirted with rationalism and Greek and Arabic philosophy were responsible for the disaster. At the same time, he believed that expulsion was a sign of God's special concern for the children of Israel, not His rejection of them, because their moral stamina and religious faith were being tested. This tradition-based interpretation was echoed by Rabbi Abraham Gabison in Algeria and Rabbi Moses Almosnino in Salonika.

But theirs was not the only interpretation to be heard as a chorus of voices arose after the expulsion that was unlike anything heard since Jewish antiquity. For the first time in centuries, Jews were writing history not only in order to record the events of their age but also to counsel and console their readers. In addition, throughout Europe there were messianic stirrings in the air. Undoubtedly, one reason was the approach of the half-millennium, but the expulsion experience itself was also a factor. For example, the historian Joseph ha-Kohen explained that he was writing so "that the children of Israel may know . . . for behold, the days approach." Such messages of hope and anticipation fell on extraordinarily receptive ears everywhere, from the depths of *marrano* communities in the villages of Castile to the highest court circles in Italy where Don Isaac Abrabanel made his messianic computations. Paradoxically, this expectation of messianic redemption took hold and strengthened just as the Sephardim were striking new roots in remote places—the Atlas mountains, the Sahara desert, the steppes of Central Asia—while clinging to their Iberian language and customs. Just beneath the surface of the network of new communities, therefore, were submerged the tensions between waiting and rebuilding, hope and despair, that were ready to ignite when the spark of messianism was struck.

With their world in upheaval, it is not surprising that so many Jews turned to radical formulations and possible solutions to the question of the meaning of their history. Seemingly small incidents, like the career of the little-known David Reubeni, reveal the depth of this need. This messianic pretender appeared in Italy and Portugal in the 1520s, proclaiming himself to be a commander-in-chief from the lost Israelite tribes of Reuben, Gad, and Menasseh sent to announce the coming redemption. Countless *marranos* in Portugal were convinced by his message and prepared themselves for wondrous events of liberation.

Among them was a *converso* courtier, Diego Perez, who went so far as to have himself circumcised and change his name to Solomon Molcho. He also went to Salonika to study the *kabbalah*, then followed Reubeni to Italy as the latter tried to engage Pope Clement VII in some fanciful schemes to liberate the Holy Land with the use of *marrano* troops. The pope was intrigued, but Emperor Charles V was alarmed by the stirrings among the *marranos* and handed Molcho over to the Inquisition. He was burned at the stake in 1532, but his novel career made a profound impact upon the Ottoman Jews of his day. Reubeni met a violent end in 1538. Even the most unrealistic schemes were eagerly sought to relieve the suffering of the *marranos*, either through "abnormal" means like military campaigns or more traditional modes of "pushing God's hand to act." Like Molcho, many intellectuals turned increasingly to the study of the *Zohar* and the *kabbalah* in order to understand the significance of their exile.

The most important center for such mystical reflection was the small town of Safed in the Galilean hills of Israel. Not only its silk production but also its remarkable concentration of rabbis, mystics, and spiritual personalities turned this obscure provincial town into a prominent place of refuge in the sixteenth century. Between 1500 and 1600, its Jewish population grew to over 10,000 while twenty-one synagogues and eighteen Talmudic colleges were established. A special school for poor children, supported by the affluent Jewish community in Istanbul, had 400 students.

Drawn from a brilliant gathering of first-generation exiles, the mystics of Safed engaged in study, contemplation, and meditation, while attracting many disciples. Fasting frequently and engaging in mystical meditation, they would take long walks to the tombs of ancient teachers buried in the Galilee and hold special vigils of an ascetic nature. The revered leaders among them—Joseph Caro, Solomon Alkabetz, Moses Cordovero, Hayyim Vital—totally revolutionized the way their contemporaries thought about the relationship of God to Jewish history and the Jewish people.

Their mentor was Isaac Luria, founder of the Safed school of mysticism that would come to bear his name. Born in 1534 in Jerusalem to an Ashkenazic father and Sephardic mother, he was reared by an uncle in Egypt and studied the *kabbalah* there. In 1569 he moved to Safed and introduced an entirely new structure of Jewish mysticism, infused with messianic meaning. In what became known as the Lurianic *kabbalah*, which aptly suited the conditions and aspirations of his generation,

Luria daringly suggested that the exile of the Jews was not divine punishment at all. Rather, it mirrored the divine state and had a cosmic purpose of the highest order. Divine sparks, he explained, had been scattered everywhere during the initial act of creation and still needed to be reconstituted. The exiled Jews were now in a unique position to do just that. In other words, their suffering served a purpose: by means of exile and proper fulfillment of the commandments, combined with mystical preparation and implementation, Jews could gather the divine sparks dispersed among the nations and become partners with God, as it were, in liberating the universe. Moreover, Luria assured his disciples, the process of restoring cosmic wholeness was so near completion that the role of Jews was critical in bringing about the final imminent fulfillment of history. Soon after his death in 1572, his faithful students took his message to the major centers of Jewish life in Ottoman lands and Italy. Even though Lurianic *kabbalah* was an esoteric movement restricted to a select group of followers, its doctrines could be reshaped under the right circumstances to appeal to a much wider audience. If someone charismatic should appear, capable of linking these mystical doctrines to the populace longing for Redemption, the Jewish people were ready to respond.

Even as Luria's ideas began to spread, Ottoman Jewry experienced an extraordinary upheaval that united the many trends in the air—messianism, hopelessness, kabbalism, marranism. The catalyst was Sabbetai Zevi, a man very much the product of his time who was able to stir the messianic hopes of the Jewish world. As a youth, he studied *kabbalah* in Izmir, imbibing the messianism and mysticism around him. Meanwhile, Jews waited expectantly for the year 1648, which fit into the numerological lore of messianism. Jewish mysticism possessed a long tradition of trying to discern the date of the Messiah's advent through a careful reading of biblical and sacred texts. Kabbalists believed that the numerical equivalents of crucial Hebrew words in key passages contained the necessary clues. After the expulsion from Spain, the idea gained wide currency that a time of disaster could turn into a messianic moment. According to one reading of the classic, the *Zohar*, the year 1648 provided a propitious date. In addition, since terrible sufferings would accompany the advent of the Messiah, the pogroms in Poland that year could be construed as the "messianic woes" and "birth pangs" of the messianic tradition. Hordes of Ashkenazic refugees from Cossack massacres perpetrated by Bogdan Chmielnitski flooded into Istanbul.

Suddenly, as if in response to the disappointed expectations, Zevi began to make "messianic" gestures, overturning traditional Jewish law and pronouncing the ineffable name of God. Under the tutelage of a certain Nathan of Gaza, he became ever more convinced of his messiahship and announced reforms that violated many of the norms of Judaism. He publicly proclaimed his messiahship in May 1665. Soon, word of the "Messiah's" bizarre activities spread from Palestine to the diaspora. The populace in several Turkish cities became so wildly agitated by the reports that the bazaars were immobilized and trade came to a standstill.

In 1666, the Muslim authorities arrested Zevi and imprisoned him at Gallipoli, where he held court as Jews flocked to see the "Messiah," composed hymns in his honor, and went forth to spread word of his remarkable feats. In September, determined to squelch the movement, the Turks offered Zevi a choice of conversion to Islam or death. He converted. Many Turkish Jews followed suit, although most, confused, simply awaited the next turn of events. Meanwhile, the resourceful Nathan of Gaza, cleverly using elements of the Lurianic *kabbalah*, explained that Zevi's apostasy was in fact a part of his messianic role. That is to say, by choosing to descend into the abyss of apostasy, Zevi was actually hastening the redemption of the world. Conversion, the symbol and core of Sephardic anguish, thus ceased to be an act of shame, for Zevi had taken on himself the evil of all the *conversos*. In the event, this self-proclaimed Messiah remained an apostate, but even after he died in exile in 1676, the movement in his name continued to agitate the Sephardic diaspora as Nathan of Gaza kept elaborating upon the meaning of Zevi's career. As a result, Jews in Amsterdam and Italy, Germany and the Near East, were joined together in a wave of expectation that offered temporary consolation. Eventually, of course, the true implications of the whole affair became apparent, and deep depression descended upon Ottoman Jewry.[16]

Subsequently, the Sephardic diaspora of the East entered an era of stagnation, even as the conditions in Muslim lands began to deteriorate. Beginning late in the reign of Suleiman the Magnificent in the sixteenth century, the Empire began a slow process of decline that spread to all layers of society. Europe was sufficiently distracted that it was unaware of this pervasive deterioration until in 1683 the Ottomans failed for the second time to capture Vienna. Soon thereafter, the choicest Ottoman conquests in Europe, including Hungary, Serbia, Wallachia, and Dalmatia, were ceded to European rule. With the Treaty of Karlowitz in 1699, the Ottoman forces withdrew from almost all of Hungary, portions of Slovenia and Croatia, the Polish territories, and recognized Venice's claims in the Morea and Dalmatia. This inglorious treaty signaled the beginnings of a long period of unremitting decline.

Meanwhile, the Ottoman Jews were torn by conflicts between believers and nonbelievers in Sabbetai Zevi as records were altered or hidden, almost as if the Jews wanted to extirpate the very memory of this communal disaster. As the seventeenth century drew to a close, the intellectual élan of Ottoman Jewry seemed to be spent. The focus of Sephardic destiny shifted to Europe and beyond, where Portuguese refugees were inventing new approaches to Jewish life as they knocked on the doors of the West.

7

The Westward Journey

Europe and the New World

Therefore (if it please your highness), it follows that the Jewish nation, though scattered through the whole world, are not therefore a despicable people but a plant worthy of being planted in the whole world and received into populous cities.

—Menasseh ben Israel, *Humble Address* to Oliver Cromwell, 1655

The government of the United States . . . gives to bigotry no sanction, to persecution no assistance. . . . May the children of the Stock of Abraham who dwell in this land continue to merit and enjoy the good will of the other inhabitants, while every one shall sit in safety under his own vine and fig tree and there shall be none to make him afraid.

—George Washington to the Jews of Newport, Rhode Island, in 1790

Throughout the sixteenth and seventeenth centuries, a steady stream of New Christians embarked upon two parallel journeys: a physical trek northward to freedom, and a spiritual voyage back to the practice of Judaism. Almost all of these Sephardim were crypto-Jews, born several generations after the expulsion and so with no personal experience of life in a Jewish community. What united them instead was a sense of shared oppression, the collective identity of belonging to the so-called Portuguese *nacion,* and their close family links to Jews in the diaspora. This background, so different from that of the Sephardim who migrated to Ottoman lands immediately after the expulsion, produced an equally different evolution and history. Within decades of the expulsion, small groups or individual *marrano* refugees appeared in western Europe. To outsiders there, they were considered to be Portuguese merchants, but they began taking their first tentative steps toward more open forms of Jewish expression. In relatively intolerant France and Flanders, they did so hesitantly and furtively; in a growing number of cities in Italy, they could observe their religion openly. Wherever they went in western Europe, their status was ambiguous but infinitely more secure than in Iberia.

The newcomers entered a Europe in transition, a continent rocked by religious wars that would destroy its equilibrium for decades. In the North, the Protestant Reformation would inaugurate unanticipated vistas of religious toleration as countries like Holland, smarting under the Spanish yoke, began to consider the advantages of religious freedom. In England, where anti-Catholic feeling also ran high, Protestants regarded Jews with new interest as they deliberated the benefits of Jewish immigration. Mercantilist arguments could be heard alongside Protestant millenarian fantasies about the "approaching end of days and conversion of the Jews." Yet even as the Sephardim began to negotiate a new presence in Protestant Europe, in Italy the Counter-Reformation provoked reaction against the Renaissance and its humanism, instituting repressive measures against Jews. The very communities that had found a new lease on life there after 1492 experienced new hardships in the sixteenth century as fresh expulsions caused a wave of homelessness in the Papal States and the kingdom of Naples.

Still more dramatic was the disruptive impact of the Thirty Years' War, the continuous conflict in the seventeenth century that devastated entire regions. As a result, some absolute monarchs became receptive to admitting groups of Jews to help rebuild their territories. As long as such groups were small enough, they were received with a modicum of tolerance in Germany. But in 1648 a crisis in Poland and Lithuania forced the largest concentrations of Jews in the world from their homes. Over the following six years, perhaps 100,000 Polish Jews were slaughtered and tens of thousands forced to flee in the wake of the Cossack persecutions led by Bogdan Chmielnitski during the Muscovite-Swedish invasion of Poland. These Ashkenazic refugees pushed westward, flooding the small Sephardic communities of Hamburg, Amsterdam, London, and elsewhere.

Thereafter, indeed throughout most of the seventeenth and eighteenth centuries, these wanderers, who were officially called *Betteljuden* or *Schnorrjuden* (beggar Jews) in the West, were a great source of anxiety to their established brethren, for they were extremely poor, traditional in observance, and conspicuously differentiated in dress and demeanor.[1] It was of course essential to find asylum for them, but the prospect of the continuing influx of tens of thousands of such refugees raised the spectre of anti-Semitism among the newly emancipated Sephardim. Indeed, this unequal meeting of impoverished Ashkenazim and aristocratic Sephardim would place unusual strains on ancient Jewish traditions of solidarity and mutual assistance. Moreover, the demographic future of western European Jewry as predominantly Ashkenazic became indisputable by the end of this period, as a result of Ashkenazic fecundity and Sephardic assimilation.

Sephardim would remain vastly outnumbered by their brethren in every Western settlement, rapidly assimilating as they moved up in society. By 1790, the Sephardim in Holland numbered only about 3,500 souls against 25,000 Ashkenazim. Similar situations held true in England and France and would soon be reflected in America as well. In Europe, each group kept its own (if frequently parallel) set of communal institutions—synagogues, charities, and even cemeteries. But over the course of time they grew increasingly distant socially, religiously, and economically. In 1812, for example, the marriage of Moses Montefiore, the future Sephardic leader of all of British Jewry, to Ashkenazic Judith Cohen was frowned upon by his family.

At the same time that Sephardim were on the move everywhere in Europe, many New Christians departed incognito from Spain and Portugal for the New World. Since they were officially barred from settlement in Spain's colonies, utmost secrecy was essential. Frequently, they signed on as ship captains or crew, which they were permitted to do, then illegally transported other co-religionists or jumped ship in South America themselves. It was generally acknowledged that Jewish captains knew all of the secret coves where illegal passengers and goods could be landed in the New World. All of South America, along with Central America and Mexico, was part of the Spanish colonial Empire from 1492 until the 1820s, with the exception of Brazil, which fell to the Portuguese (after brief Dutch rule), and the northeastern coastal region of the continent, which was also briefly held by the Dutch. Secret Jews in relatively large numbers immigrated to the Spanish dominions, playing an important role in the commerce of the Empire. They were propelled by a spirit of adventure and commercial enterprise, combined with the hope that with distance from Iberia they could discard their stigmatized identities and leave their *sambenitos* behind. They would be disappointed in this hope. The Inquisition aggressively pursued them into the New World after its establishment there in 1569, reaching a height of persecution in Mexico in 1596. Another great roundup of secret Jews led to a spectacular *auto-da-fé* in Lima in 1639. Jewish settlements were therefore forced to remain underground, shadowy collectivities of former fellow countrymen and family groups. One of the most prominent of these secret Jews, Luis de Carvajal, rose to the governorship of New Spain in 1579, but after he reverted to Judaism in Mexico he was caught and burned at the stake along with several members of his family.

The secret Jews received some assistance from the legal Jewish presence in the Caribbean islands and from Jews as far away as Venice, Pisa, and Provence. But they led haunted lives, nonetheless, holding secret prayer meetings (sometimes in warehouses) and often communicating among themselves in code in order to avoid detection. Hundreds were eventually caught and prosecuted as Judaizers. Many died as martyrs at the stake; many others were condemned to serve in the galleys that plied the sea between Mexico and the Philippines. Yet despite the vigorous activity of the Inquisition, groups of secret Jews continued to arrive in South America from Iberia and other parts of Europe and persisted in practicing their Judaism. They comprised approximately 10 percent of the non-Indian population. Many escaped into the vast interior of the continent to avoid detection, leaving faint traces of former crypto-Jewish practices still discernible today among Indian groups in Mexico and Brazil.

As suggested earlier, the crypto-Jews of Latin America maintained ongoing spiritual and commercial contacts with the open Jewish settlements that dotted the Caribbean islands administered by the Dutch, French, and English. Whatever disabilities Jews may have faced in the European mother countries were substantially reduced in these islands because the colonial powers were quite interested in promoting trade in the Caribbean. Thus, by the seventeenth and eighteenth centuries, thriving Jewish communities could be found on St. Thomas, Curaçao, Jamaica, Barbados, St. Eustache, Martinique, and in Surinam. Soon thereafter, as we shall see, five small but historically significant Sephardic communities began to flourish in North America. It would have been difficult to predict from their modest beginnings—fugitives from the Spanish and Portuguese or rejected paupers dispatched by London's Bevis Marks synagogue—that these small groups of shopkeepers and merchants would establish the foundations of what would eventually become the most populous Jewish community in history, the Jews of the United States.

During the seventeenth century, the nascent Sephardic communities of western Europe gradually won the right to worship and residence with relatively few restrictions. The Amsterdam community became the mother to the rest, outstripping them in culture, affluence, and Jewish learning. It played the critical role, for example, in reeducating the Sephardim in France and in defending the introduction of legal Jewish residence in England. A satellite community in Hamburg was given essential spiritual and moral support by their Amsterdam brethren. Significantly, it was from Dutch Brazil that Jews were first able to make their way to North America, and it was the Dutch West India Company that successfully pressured Governor Peter Stuyvesant of New Amsterdam to allow them to enter.

In sum, the period of Sephardic ascendancy in western Europe coincided with and was partially dependent upon Holland's vitality in the seventeenth century. A century later, when shifting patterns of European trade spelled the end of Dutch supremacy, transforming Holland into a second-rate power, the aristocratic Sephardic merchant families of Amsterdam also declined, as did the interconnected communities of Bordeaux, Hamburg, Venice, and London. The Sephardim were thus consigned to an increasingly marginal role. At their height, however, they earned a permanent place in Jewish history by nurturing, sheltering, and re-Judaizing the exiles from Spain as well as opening the gates for legal recognition of the right of Jews to live in Europe as practicing Jews. These were not inconsiderable achievements for a group that never numbered more than several thousand, often having to take the greatest of risks and invent ruses and subterfuges to keep their religion alive.

In 1492, approximately 10,000 Jews departed directly for Italy with their leader Abrabanel. Italy was not unified into a single country at the time, and these immigrants lived scattered in several communities enjoying various degrees of sufferance. Although most cities barred them from entering, some more enlightened rulers, deeply immersed in the Renaissance, took a personal interest in the Jews. Before long, the Sephardic impact could be felt in Naples, Ferrara, Venice, and Livorno. After the practicing Jews of 1492 came the *conversos* in the early 1500s. For some Renaissance princes like the duke of Urbino or the Medicis, the Jewish presence represented a commercial asset as well as an intellectual curiosity. The Sephardim in their turn, being temperamentally and historically attuned to the surrounding culture, shared in the general artistic revolution of the Renaissance. Social barriers between Jews and Christians began to break down. Christians could be found attending Jewish plays in the Jewish quarter, and Jews taught Christians about Hebrew printing and language. Renaissance luminaries like Pico della Mirandola would commission Latin translations of Hebrew classics from Elijah del Medigo, a Jewish scholar who had arrived in Venice from Crete. The Jewish poet and playwright Solomon Usque, a Portuguese refugee, translated the poetry of Petrarch into Spanish. In general, Sephardic Jews had a smoother adjustment to Jewish life in Italy than in Muslim lands. The Italian communities were already quite heterogeneous, being composed of indigenous Jews who had been in Italy for over a millennium as well as refugees who had arrived from Germany and France during the course of the fourteenth century. In addition, Sephardic Jews shared many cultural affinities with indigenous Italian Jews, not least of which was a receptivity to the secular culture of their environment. Only in Rome did local Jews object to the arrival of the Sephardim, fearful that the influx would precipitate an outbreak of anti-Semitism. But their opposition did not prevail, and a small Sephardic community established itself in the capital of Christendom.

At the other extreme of hospitality was the city of Ferrara and its ruler from the enlightened house of Este, Duke Ercole I, who permitted the Spanish exiles to settle in 1492. Este policy was to offer refuge to Jews whom they deemed to be "useful" and grant them autonomy, tax reductions, and permission to engage in trade or practice medicine. In 1553 Ercole II went one step further than his father, giving Ferrara's *conversos* the right to settle and to revert. The city now housed ten synagogues and had become one of Europe's most important centers of Hebrew printing, thanks to a press founded by the poet Usque. It was in this same year that the Ferrara Bible was printed. But the enlightened situation changed dramatically almost overnight, in spite of the tolerant local nobility. Only a year later, in 1554, Pope Paul IV introduced several repressive measures. Censorship of Hebrew printing led to the closing of Ferrara's press in 1556. Rome's influence caused the town to require the wearing of a Jewish badge. Before long, the number of synagogues was reduced to three. Finally, the ghetto was introduced in 1624, and the community went into rapid decline.

During Ferrara's heyday, however, several illustrious Sephardic women found a haven there. Jewish women in general shared a brilliant chapter in the artistic life and communal politics of sixteenth-century Renaissance Italy. Whether in medicine, business, poetry, or communal leadership, they engaged in public life to an unusual degree. Benvenida Abrabanel, wife of Samuel, the head of the Naples community, and niece of Don Isaac, was a woman of many talents. Well educated, she served as tutor to Leonora, the daughter of Spanish viceroy Pedro de Toledo and later grand duchess of Tuscany. Benvenida, though described by a contemporary as "one of the most noble and highly spirited women who have existed in Israel since the time of our dispersion," was not unusual among Sephardic women of the time for her involvement in culture and politics, or for her level of education. We hear, for example, of a Talmud Torah for girls in late fifteenth-century Rome. Some women emerged as poets and literati, their salons providing a cultivated setting for artistic soirees.

When the expulsion of the Jews from Naples was decreed in the 1530s, Benvenida, following in the footsteps of her distinguished uncle, tried to have the order rescinded. With the support of her royal charges, she petitioned the emperor but was unsuccessful. She left with her community for Ferrara, where she resumed her business activities with her banker husband. After his death, she continued to engage in business, but her fame rested primarily on her piety. She is remembered for her largesse and for her efforts in ransoming hundreds of Jews from pirates. Her Jewish loyalty and activist approach to life recall her most famous contemporary, Dona Gracia Mendes (who, incidentally, returned openly to Judaism in Ferrara before moving on to Turkey).

Like Sephardic Jews everywhere, Benvenida yearned for signs that Jewish redemption was near. While still in Naples, she was caught up in messianic stirrings sparked in the 1520s by the appearance of the messianic pretender David Reubeni discussed earlier. He announced that he had been dispatched by his king to request a meeting with the pope and asked the Jews of Venice to arrange a papal audience. In 1523 Reubeni entered Rome on a white horse in accordance with one of the many Jewish traditions about the Messiah; during this impressive entry, a banner was unfurled that had the Ten Commandments embroidered on it by Benvenida. Reubeni made a proposition to Clement VII that was audacious and fantastic but also quite in keeping with the spirit of the age: the Jews would join forces with Christendom in a Crusade to oust the Turks from the Holy Land.

Reubeni progressed from Rome to Portugal, where he caused a furor among the crypto-Jews. Eagerly hoping for release from their captivity, many of them recognized him as the long-awaited Messiah. Reubeni's impact on Diego Perez (Solomon Molcho) has already been described. The dramatic careers of these two men reveal how avidly the Sephardic diaspora sought a redeemer, even in enlightened Renaissance Italy. The link between this yearning and activist political schemes to liberate the secret Jews is characteristic of the culture of post-expulsion Sephardim everywhere.

Venice was even more culturally vibrant than Ferrara, for it housed a large, heterogeneous Jewish community that included several different Sephardic elements. Some had come directly from Iberia in the 1490s, others had arrived a little later as *conversos* and socialized somewhat separately, and still others were Sephardic merchants from Turkey and the Levant. Each group formed a separate congregation, supported its own synagogue, and perpetuated its own ritual and subculture.

Venice offered a curious mixture of tolerance and intolerance, reflecting the general tides of fortune of Italy's Jews. As early as 1492, the city forced its Jews to wear distinguishing hats (yellow until 1500, then red). Its ghetto was established in 1516 on the site of an iron foundry, from which the word "ghetto" derives, and would eventually become one of the most crowded in Europe, enduring until 1797. Yet its denizens were profoundly Italianized and highly prized the city's flourishing secular culture. We know that Jewish dance masters and musicians delighted the community, while rabbis were vexed by the prevalence of cardplaying on the Sabbath and by the frequency of amorous liaisons between Christians and Jews. Hebrew printing began in 1515 upon the arrival of Daniel Bomberg, a Christian printer from Antwerp. Several printing houses thrived, attracting Sephardic scholars from all over Europe and North Africa.[2]

But in Venice too, as in the other Italian cities, the Catholic Counter-Reformation had a crippling economic and cultural impact upon the Jews. In 1550, *conversos* who had reverted were expelled from the city's ghetto. In 1571, Jews were barred from working in printing and paralyzed by prior censorship which had not been enforced earlier; the famed Venetian printing industry rapidly declined. Nevertheless, as long as Venice remained a significant emporium with a thriving Eastern trade, her Sephardim continued to prosper, playing a special role in that commerce as a result of their family and business connections in the Ottoman Empire.

The only place in Italy where the Catholic reaction did not prevail was Livorno (Leghorn). No ghetto was introduced there, nor was distinctive Jewish clothing required. In an enlightened charter issued in 1593, the grand duke of Tuscany, Ferdinand I de Medici, assured the Jews to whom he was granting settlement rights that "none shall be able to make any inquisition, inquiry, examination or accusal, against you or your families, although living in the past outside our Dominion in the guise of Christians."[3] This declaration was tantamount to an invitation to *conversos* to settle and return to Judaism.

By the seventeenth century, Livorno had become a fascinating center of Sephardic life and also a great Mediterranean port, having replaced Pisa in importance because of the silting of the River Arno. In 1675 the town was declared a free port, and international commerce took a leap forward. By 1689 more than 3,000 Jews could be counted in

Livorno, and Portuguese and Spanish served as the major languages of commerce (and of all communal business until the nineteenth century). Of the 150 commercial houses in the 1700s, fifty were owned by Jews engaged in trade with Egypt, North Africa, and Turkey. Livorno's Jews formed their own diaspora of commercial colonies in the Levant and also set up a separate "nation" in Tunis, where they lived in a separate quarter. Known as the *Grana,* a term derived from the Arabic for Livorno, they were sometimes in conflict with the local Jewish population, the Tuansa, who resented both their separatism and their special commercial relationships with the authorities. Meanwhile, Livorno, unlike the other Jewish communities in Italy that began to languish in the seventeenth century, remained a very cosmopolitan center into the eighteenth century. Later sons of the community who achieved fame outside included Moses Montefiore, the painter Modigliani, and Sabato Morais, the founder of Conservative Judaism in America.

In sum, then, the Sephardic community in Italy enjoyed the fruits of the Renaissance in their first generation of expulsion from Spain, but in most places that freedom was cut short by the zealous Counter-Reformation. Censorship, ghettoization, the decline of printing, and the zeal of the Italian Inquisition in pursuing former *conversos,* as at Ancona, ended what began as a new diaspora of great promise. Moreover, even as tolerance flourished briefly in the North, Jews were being evicted from the South. In a myriad of different forms, from the music of Salomone de Rossi with its echoes of Monteverdi to the spell-binding sermons of Leone de Modena in the Venetian ghetto, from the enduring illuminated Hebrew manuscripts to the achievements of multitalented rabbis, Italy's Sephardic refugees enjoyed an exceptional, if brief, flowering in the sixteenth and early seventeenth centuries. Their decline set in gradually, subject as always to vagaries, whims, and prejudices of the regnant authorities. As reaction hardened, Sephardim sought more favorable places to settle, using Italy as a stepping-stone to either Holland or Turkey.[4] Their continuing propensity to wander during the centuries after the expulsion is nothing short of extraordinary.

The fate of Jews who moved northward was quite different from their reception in Italy. In general, they had to enter countries surreptitiously, usually as "Portuguese merchants," although the truth behind this disguise was no secret. Their numbers are difficult to estimate because many never joined the clandestine Jewish enclaves that began to congregate in Bordeaux, Antwerp, Hamburg, and Amsterdam in the sixteenth century. Nor can we say with certainty why some chose to leave Spain and Portugal and others did not. At times, the motivating factor was a brush with the Inquisition, as when a *marrano*'s name was extracted from a torture victim.[5] Sometimes, a sense of revulsion against Christianity might sweep over the New Christian forced to watch an *auto-da-fé*, reawakening an appreciation of his Jewish heritage. Most often, though, the new emigré was impelled by his sense of frustration at the social and professional restrictions caused by the laws of blood purity.

In many cases—how many, we shall never know for sure—the New Christian who decided to become a secret Jew was following in the footsteps of family members who had insisted on passing down Jewish traditions, ever dimming though they were, from one generation to the next. Also, a random encounter with a Jew visiting from abroad could inspire the Iberian *converso* to reconsider his identity. Even the negative assessment of Old Christians suggests how deep the longing must have been; they claimed that every New Christian lived with *esperanza,* the hope that he would someday rejoin the Jewish people. It is remarkable, considering the nearly insurmountable obstacles standing in the way, how many of the New Christians eventually acted upon those desires.

The number of these new emigrés varied from decade to decade, but the exodus never entirely ceased. As we have seen, emigration was banned in Spain and Portugal after the expulsion. It was hoped that the New Christian would adjust to his new identity once he accepted the fact that no exit was possible. On the eve of Passover in 1506, however, a bitter massacre of the New Christians occurred in Lisbon. As a result, they succeeded in convincing King Manuel to lift the ban on emigration temporarily.[6] A fresh wave of panic emigration followed immediately upon the introduction of the Inquisition into Portugal in 1536. Each new *auto-da-fé* would send shudders through the New Christian community, propelling a new wave of emigrés beyond its borders.

Ironically, the first choice of refuge became Spain, which joined in a political union with Portugal in 1580 that would last until 1640. During that period, countless New Christians made their way back to Spain, encouraged by the ruling that they could not be tried there for "crimes" of Judaizing committed in Portugal. The separate Holy Offices in the two countries did indeed exchange information on suspected crypto-Jews, but Spain decided not to extradite fugitives from her jurisdiction. The unexpected result was that she once again faced a *marrano* problem that had become nonexistent within her borders by this time. The Portuguese immigrants, suspected of crypto-Judaism by definition, were regarded as a separate group of Christians—the *portugueses de la nación hebrea* or simply *portugueses de la nación* or *homens da nação*. Even among themselves, the *conversos* in Lisbon, Madrid, or Seville referred to each other as "Portuguese" or "Men of the Nation," and the term "Portuguese" became synonymous with "Jew" or "Judaizer" not only in Spain but wherever these Portuguese New Christians went in western Europe.

What distinguished the *conversos* who went north, regardless of their motives for flight, was the fact that they knew precious little about their heritage. Even those who fervently sought to embrace Judaism immediately and in full did not know precisely what rabbinic Judaism was or what membership in an openly constituted Jewish community actually entailed. Consequently, their re-Judaization was not always smooth. The Amsterdam community would be forced to engage in a constant struggle to reintegrate these Jews. Another factor was that, in contrast with the Sephardim who were welcomed by indigenous communities in the Muslim world, they found no open Jewish communities in Europe to buttress them from culture shock. Everything had to be created from scratch; in the beginning, their communities had to be formed in secret.

Many myths about the unusual piety and steadfast loyalty of these *marranos* have survived, but the more sober reality is that, like most people, these pioneering Jewish settlers who returned to their faith in Europe had human frailties. Courageous they were, but they were also not above pettiness and snobbery, insecurity and self-consciousness, as they set out to gain acceptance in a Europe that was not yet sure that it would tolerate them. With tenacity, they would convince the gentile authorities to accept their presence, they would provide the impetus for opening many new lands to the renewal of Jewish life, and they would contribute to their new homes commercial élan and entrepreneurial skills. Even more remarkably, they would produce scholars and rabbis, dignified leaders and enthusiastic followers, create a vibrant Jewish literature in Spanish and Portuguese, and establish vital communities in lands that had either never seen a Jew (i.e., Brazil) or not permitted Jewish life for centuries (i.e., England). During the seventeenth century, the Portuguese Jewish diaspora stretched rapidly from the Ottoman Empire to Goa on the Indian subcontinent, from Denmark and northern Germany all the way to Brazil and the islands of the Caribbean. Though so widely scattered, its members retained their identity as Portuguese Jews, seeing themselves as citizens of a nation with a uniquely heroic and tragic past.

The life of Balthazar de Orobio offers a fairly typical example of the special difficulties of this journey.[7] Born in the Portuguese town of Braganza around 1617, he belonged to a community that had produced generations of New Christian martyrs. At the *auto-da-fé* of 1593–1602 in Coimbra, more than 800 of them had been tried and punished, including de Orobio's maternal and paternal grandparents. Not long after his birth, his family, like so many other Portuguese New Christians, fled to Spain to avoid the Inquisition. Even though conditions were only slightly less ominous there, they were able to teach the boy the practices of Judaism. He also learned the terrors of discovery when his uncle was caught and imprisoned by the Portuguese Inquisition.

Like many others of his background, de Orobio chose to go into medicine, one of the few professions not barred by the "blood purity" regulations. From 1633 through 1635, he combined his medical studies with Christian theology. This academic program was not at all uncommon among the New Christians, as would become evident later. In some cases, for example, the result would be skepticism toward both Judaism and Christianity when emigrés moved to the relative freedom of the North. In fact, there were many intellectuals who went so far as to deny the central Jewish doctrine of the unique election of Israel and indeed to reject all religious particularism. For many New Christians, study of Christianity was useful later on in interfaith discussions with dissident Christians in Holland. In the long process of returning to Judaism, in other words, they could draw upon their arsenal of theological knowledge in order to understand better the divergences between the two faiths.

But de Orobio's career was suddenly interrupted when he went into hiding in 1640. It seems that his family had been betrayed at last to the Holy Office, their valiant maintenance of crypto-Jewish practices laid bare in minute detail, and they were forced to escape to Bayonne. Eventually de Orobio, turned in by a servant, was arrested, tortured, imprisoned, and then penanced in an *auto-da-fé* in 1656. Thereafter, he was sentenced to a kind of house arrest in Seville. The writing on the wall was clearly legible, however, and he himself fled to Bayonne not long before his family was burned in effigy at a great *auto-da-fé* in Seville in 1660. By 1662, when he migrated to Amsterdam, he was finally ready to throw off the cloak of being New Christian. Joining the Jewish community there, he changed his name to Isaac, and his wife Isabel became Esther. He explained this transition with unapologetic frankness:

> In Spain, I presented a Christian appearance, since life is sweet; but I was never very good at it, and so it came out that I was in fact a Jew. If, then, whilst I was there, confronted with the risk of [loss of my] freedom, status, property, and indeed life itself, I was in reality a Jew and a Christian merely in outward appearance, common sense shows that in a domicile where Providence from above affords me a life of freedom, a true Jew is what I shall be.[8]

After instruction with Moses Raphael d'Aguilar of Amsterdam, de Orobio became one of the leading intellectuals and apologists of the community, composing major defenses of Judaism in Spanish. Such stellar accomplishments were indeed unusual for someone cut off from Jewish life for so many decades, but in its overall contours, de Orobio's biography was a familiar story of the day: flight from the Inquisition, study of medicine and theology, temporary asylum in France, wholehearted embrace of Judaism in Holland. As can be expected, he also had the characteristic Sephardic affection for all things Spanish.

As de Orobio's career suggests, France was important as an underground railroad to freedom, even though no Jews were legally allowed there after the expulsion in 1394. The case of the Bordeaux region, however, was somewhat ambiguous, since it had been occupied by the English at that time; i.e., it had not technically been a part of France. In the event, New Christians began drifting into the country almost immediately after the Spanish expulsion, but they were forced to live as Catholics and settle primarily in a few places near the Spanish border, most commonly in the border town of St.-Jean-de-Luz, Bayonne, and Bordeaux. It was better to seek asylum further away, using France only as a stepping-stone to Amsterdam or to Flanders, which was frequently the portal to Italy or the Ottoman East.

At first, New Christians who chose to stay in France remained for all intents and purposes a *marrano* community, secretly practicing Judaism. Soon after the establishment of the Inquisition in Portugal, however, they began to seek regularization of their precarious existence and some degree of protection from prosecution by petitioning the French government for letters of naturalization. Perhaps the move was taken at that time because of pressure caused by the increased flow of emigration from Portugal. In any event, the French government did respond in 1550 with "Letters of Naturalization and Dispensation" (more commonly known as *Lettres Patentes*) that granted the "Portuguese merchants" the right to settle and trade in the territories of the Bordeaux Parliament. The language is telling:

> Among the said Portuguese, known as New Christians, there has arisen a great desire, which grows day by day, to take up residence in this our Kingdom and to bring their wives and families, bearing with money and chattels, in the manner that has been set forth to us by those whom they have sent hither.[9]

In other words, the word "Jew" is not used here or anywhere else in the letters, although it is made clear that no inquiries will be made into their private lives. These instruments of recognition and protection were considered so important by the Jews that they paid dearly for their renewal in 1574, 1656, 1723, and 1776, even though the documents did not grant them equality, freedom to settle anywhere they chose, or the right to engage in any occupation other than trade. By the renewal of 1723, language caught up with reality. The "Portuguese merchants" were called "Jews," and from then on, they would openly deal with the government as practicing Jews in an organized Jewish community.

It would be wrong to infer, however, that life for the French community immediately became settled and secure. For one thing, from its emergence in the sixteenth century it remained quite small, leaning heavily on the great Jewish center of Amsterdam for both material aid and, more importantly, the spiritual support needed for re-Judaizing refugees. Business ties also linked the two communities, but most refugees stayed only temporarily in France before going on to the "Dutch Jerusalem." For another, Jewish life itself remained precarious. In 1619, for example, Catherine de Fernandes, a sixty-year-old *marrano* newly arrived in St.-Jean-de-Luz, was caught feigning communion by a Portuguese priest who saw her remove the consecrated wafer from her mouth. She was immediately imprisoned, but an angry crowd removed her from her cell, dragged her through the streets, and burned her alive. All New Christians were immediately expelled from the tiny border town.[10]

Even in Bordeaux after the promulgation of the *Lettres Patentes,* the New Christians practiced Judaism secretly, continuing to have their

children baptized and registered in the parish registries, which referred
to the fathers as "Portuguese merchants." Throughout the sixteenth
and seventeenth centuries, in fact, most Sephardim of "the Nation"
bore two names, the Christian name of their baptism and their Jewish
name. Although they were tacitly recognized by the surrounding population as Jewish, they were also well integrated into mainstream life,
able to trade and circulate in Catholic society with relative ease. This
economic result of the *Lettres Patentes* was their greatest benefit. Nonetheless, the stereotype that all of the New Christians of Bordeaux were
rich, successful merchants is unfounded; although several wealthy families did indeed dominate communal life there for generations, the majority of the emigrés remained poor. Only some of the New Christians
ever became openly active in the Jewish community, which gradually
strengthened and became more cohesive. Eventually, the elders in their
executive council, or *Mahamad,* could exercise great control over members of the congregation, even expelling those deemed to be "undesir-
ables." Other New Christians, however, preferred to remain secret Jews
or "unaffiliated," feeling sufficiently insecure about openly proclaiming
themselves to be Jewish. As late as 1734, perhaps confirming their fears,
the government closed the Bordeaux synagogue.

Bayonne, the other major settlement on French soil, developed
along much the same lines as Bordeaux, commencing as an inconspicuous enclave of *marranos* and emerging as an open community only in
the seventeenth century. According to Inquisition records, it also served
as a center for re-Judaization of Iberian emigrés and also provided
ongoing spiritual assistance to crypto-Jews who remained behind in
Iberia. A series of dates is revealing: in 1654, the community obtained
land for a cemetery; in 1670, it hired a rabbi; by 1679, the synagogue no
longer had to be concealed.

In both of these communities, as elsewhere, the Sephardim continued to feel fiercely proud of their aristocratic roots. When in the eighteenth century Voltaire hurled his verbal attacks at Jews in general, the
French Sephardim defended themselves by emphasizing their separateness from their lesser (as well as more traditional and less well-off)
Ashkenazic brethren and the superiority of their moral qualities. In
revolutionary France, to the abiding disapproval of many other Jews
(and of historians), they petitioned the Malesherbes Commission for
the emancipation, not of all Jews, but only of "the Nation." They got
their wish in 1790, a year before the Ashkenazim, who were the majority
of the Jews in the country. (When the latter were emancipated, the

separate status of the Sephardim as "the Nation" disappeared.) The arrogance of some Sephardim was not confined only to more traditional Jewry, however; members of the two French communities complained frequently throughout the eighteenth century about the high-handed rule of the privileged elders. Not until the French Revolution would this oligarchy agree to relinquish control.

Thus, in looking back at Sephardic life in France, we see an uneven development. Their elitism, whether toward Ashkenazim or less fortunate Sephardim, is not attractive but may in part have reflected the hostility they encountered in their new country. Having worked so long to establish their social integration as secret Jews, they felt their safety and economic well-being threatened by association with the much more conspicuous, differentiated Ashkenazic Jews of eastern France. The mentality of the elite Sephardim in France is frequently revealed in the nature of their appeals for toleration from the larger society. They vaunt their economic usefulness as well as the enlightenment of their ways. In Bordeaux, for example, the small community numbered about 1,000 in the eighteenth century. Their enterprises included large-scale banking and, because they had several firms that could outfit ships for oceangoing commerce, significant trade with the French colonies across the Atlantic. At the same time, they did not turn away brethren who were in need, although help was usually a matter of assisting poor *marranos* in moving along elsewhere, to French colonies like Canada or to Amsterdam.

In the final analysis, any evaluation of the place of the Sephardim in French history must remain tentative, for there is no authoritative history of the community during its formative years. Offering a convenient transit route and source of Judaization at the very gates of Spain, the community was also pivotal in introducing the concept of legal recognition for open, visible Jewish settlements and in wringing emancipation for the Jewish people as a whole. In fact, its achievements became the standard against which revolution and emancipation elsewhere could be measured.

New Christian settlement in the Netherlands reflected the tumultuous religious wars of the sixteenth century. Catholic Spain's dominion over Catholic Flanders and Brabant and Protestant Holland created an uneasy union. Although Jews from Iberia were attracted to the Spanish Netherlands, and Antwerp in particular, because of its central role in European commerce, their identities had to remain subterranean. Emperor Charles V permitted New Christians to move to Antwerp provided they did not revert to Judaism. Indeed, many New Christians who went to France and the Netherlands were not *marranos*. They simply wanted to take advantage of the greater commercial opportunities and more relaxed atmosphere the Netherlands offered in contrast to Spain or Portugal. Many, however, were secret practitioners of Judaism who correctly assumed that the local Inquisitions would not molest them. Among Antwerp's most prominent secret Jewish residents were Diego Mendes and his sister-in-law Dona Gracia, new arrivals from Portugal in 1537. By the 1570s a secret Jewish community in the city numbered between 400 and 500 souls. Philip II complained bitterly in 1564 that they assembled in their synagogues, followed their rites in secret, and made a mockery of the Catholic faith. When Holland revolted and won her independence from Spain in 1579, Antwerp remained under Spanish rule. During the revolt and subsequent occupation by Spanish troops, the city was subjected to especially harsh treatment that led to the ouster and departure of thousands of Protestant and New Christian merchants in 1585. Most of these victims of religious warfare made their way to Holland.

The bloodletting of the Flemish population continued in the protracted hostilities of the Wars of the Spanish Succession. When warfare between Spain and the Dutch finally ended in 1648 after eighty years of conflict, the Low Countries were split. The Protestant North emerged as an independent, religiously tolerant Holland, while the Catholic South, the Spanish Netherlands of Flanders and Brabant, continued to bar legal Jewish settlement. Not until the occupation of this area by French revolutionary forces in 1792 were Jews there able to discard their crypto-Jewish masks.

Dutch principles of religious toleration were born out of the exigencies of warfare and the need to establish peace among her religiously heterogeneous population. New Christian skills and contacts were welcomed during the protracted warfare with Spain. Article XIII of the Treaty of Utrecht, which ratified the union of the northern provinces, declared that no one was to be prosecuted for his religious beliefs. Although this clause was intended to benefit the Protestants and keep peace among Christians, it provided the legal basis upon which Jews immediately began to take up residence and seek recognition in Holland. There the Sephardim would find the ideal conditions to create a New Jerusalem.

The Dutch capital was the emporium of seventeenth-century Europe, her harbor teeming with ships brimful of goods from the Americas and the Far East. Her people eagerly invented themselves as a new nation; beguiled by commerce and its possibilities, they were nonetheless characterized by sobriety of behavior and a distaste for both superstition and any pretension of nobility. The city's great wealth was based on three factors: her fleet, her thriving trade, and a policy of tolerance that attracted some of the most enterprising and ambitious souls on the Continent. Indeed, it was clearly recognized that tolerance of religious diversity was sound policy:

> Next to the freedom to worship God comes freedom to make one's living for all inhabitants. Here [in Amsterdam] it is very necessary to attract foreigners. And although this is of disadvantage to some old residents who would like to keep the best solely for themselves and pretend that a citizen should have preferences above a stranger, the truth of the matter is that a state which is not self-sufficient must constantly draw new inhabitants to it or it will perish.[11]

In this newfound mercantilism, *marranos* became especially prominent. In 1604 a certain Manuel Rodrigues de Vega petitioned the city's burgomasters to be allowed to establish silk mills there along with two other Portuguese Jews. In short order, the Sephardim would develop not only the domestic silk industry but also the silk trade, much of the tobacco trade, and commerce in sugar, corals, and diamonds. Eventually, Sephardic poets, dramatists, calligraphers, and copper-etchers would also be found alongside the customary merchants, bankers, and physicians.

Now that it seemed the Jews could finally cease their wanderings, they began to pour into Holland from Spain, Italy, Portugal, Germany, and Antwerp. At first, religious services were held inconspicuously in private homes as well as at the residence of Samuel Pallache, a Sephardic Jew who was Morocco's ambassador to the Netherlands from 1612 to 1616. To a certain extent, the position of the Jews was regularized in 1597 when burghers' rights were granted to members of the "Portuguese nation" in Amsterdam. It is not until 1606 that one finds the first official reference to *Joodsche Gemeente* (the Jewish Congregation), but by 1609 the Sephardic community numbered 200 souls and supported two synagogues. A decade later, a third house of worship would be founded. In

1614, the cemetery of Ouderkerk was purchased and would remain the community's hallowed burial ground for generations.

This growth of a distinctive community, combined with lively religious discussions between Christians and *marranos,* induced the city government in 1615 to confront squarely the question of how to handle the Jews. Should they be officially permitted to settle? If so, should they be granted religious freedom? The municipality addressed these questions to two leading citizens. One of them, Hugo Grotius (1583–1645), rendered a landmark opinion in the battle for toleration of the Jews in Europe. Grotius was only thirty-two years old when he was approached on the question of the admission of the Jews to Holland, but he was already a distinguished Hebraist, prominent theologian, and a recognized dramatist. He would later be considered the father of international law for his classic work on the law of war and peace. He was a friend of Amsterdam's eminent rabbi and scholar Menasseh ben Israel (born Manuel Dias Soeiro as a New Christian), a charismatic personality of whom we will hear more later. In *Remonstantie,* his tract on the Jewish question, Grotius provided a barometer of the emerging attitudes of toleration of the Jews in a fascinating blend of medieval prejudices and more enlightened ideas.

Although he duly catalogued the alleged "crimes" committed by Jews through the ages, Grotius advocated admitting them to Holland, explaining that their anti-Christian behavior was caused by the persecutions they had suffered for their religion. He fervently hoped for their ultimate conversion but felt it impossible as long as they associated solely with Catholics. In other words, it was essential to welcome Jews into the country because only members of the Dutch Reformed Church could lead them eventually to the baptismal font.

In addition, Grotius argued, the presence of Jews could be beneficial in more ways than one. Associating with them could help non-Jews improve their knowledge of Hebrew (an argument commonly made by seventeenth-century Protestants). Moreover, in true medieval fashion he explained that the continuing existence of the Jews as a separate people "serves as an example and as evidence of the truth of the Holy Scriptures of the Old Testament." To forestall the objections of those who feared that their religion might somehow be imposed upon the country, Grotius wrote that Judaism, being most foreign, was the least likely religion to constitute a danger to "true belief."[12]

But after conceding the Jews the right to practice their faith, he proceeded to set down forty-nine articles for regulating their status in

Holland. They were to demonstrate their faith in monotheism and not spread heretical beliefs among Christians. Their total numbers could be limited, he felt, but he also proposed the revolutionary idea that they not be restricted in occupation or place of residence. They should be allowed to observe their own Sabbath and to operate their own printing presses. On the other hand, they should be prohibited from holding public office, proselytizing, intermarrying with Christians, or bearing arms. Despite the blend of tolerance and bigotry, Grotius's approach came out on the liberal side. The concrete result was that the community in Holland was legally recognized by the municipality in 1615 and was never burdened with the medieval restrictions of having to wear badges and live in ghettos.

Once the decision was made, Amsterdam became an even more powerful magnet for oppressed Jews from other parts of Europe. The atmosphere of toleration was made more attractive by the growth of dozens of organizations and welfare institutions in the community, for the city's Jews were living openly as Jews. In 1615, a boatload of emigrés arrived from Nantes; in 1617, seventy-three Sephardim expelled from St.-Jean-de-Luz appeared.

Ironically, it became better to be known in Amsterdam as a Jew than as a "Portuguese merchant," thanks to anti-Iberian sentiment after the breakaway from Spain. Many Dutch intellectuals became fascinated with the somewhat exotic inhabitants of the Jewish quarter and sought them out for conversation. At the outset of his career Rembrandt, young and unknown, sketched many of his Portuguese neighbors, including Menasseh ben Israel. Conversely, the Sephardim reaped the benefits of the lively intellectual life created by Amsterdam's savants, who eagerly cultivated theology, philosophy, jurisprudence, mathematics, and oriental languages.

In 1617, two years after Grotius's affirmation of their right to do so, the heads of the Jewish school voted to establish a printing press. Within the decade, several private Hebrew presses were also set up, including that operated by the renowned intellectual Menasseh ben Israel. During its first twenty years, his multilingual press produced more than sixty titles, including Bibles, prayerbooks, and his own original works. Well known among the philosophers, scientists, and theologians of Amsterdam, he gave sermons that attracted flocks of Christians as well as Jews, and would even represent his enterprise at the Frankfurt Book Fair in 1634. By this time, since Hebrew printing had decayed in Venice, Amsterdam was effectively the Judaic printing capital of Europe. One especially successful printer was Joseph Athias, who founded his press in 1658 and was admitted to the booksellers' guild three years later. The scope of his operation can be inferred from his remark that "For several years I myself printed more than a million Bibles for England and Scotland."[13] At some point, he gained the exclusive right to print the Bible in Yiddish; in 1670 he was granted a fifteen-year monopoly on the sale as well as the printing of English-language Bibles.

Meanwhile, in contrast with the Sephardim in the Ottoman Empire, the Portuguese Jews of Amsterdam remained deeply immersed in Spanish and Lusitanian high culture as it evolved in the sixteenth and seventeenth centuries. While the Ottoman Sephardi distinguished himself by continuing to use medieval Spanish in everyday speech, writing this Ladino in Hebrew characters and incorporating Hebrew and other words and expressions, the Amsterdam Sephardi used the living Spanish or Portuguese of his day, constantly changing linguistically and written with Roman characters. In fact, the culture of the Portuguese Jewish emigrés bore so few traces of the traditional Hebriac spirit that most of its members knew no Hebrew at all when they arrived in Amsterdam. They had to be laboriously schooled as adults by the community's tutors and rabbis. As surviving lists of private book collections show, they continued their interest in Iberian literature, which was a major source of their shared community pride. They created something of a miniature Lisbon or Madrid on the banks of the Amstel, on Jodenbreestraat, populated by poets and dramatists writing in Spanish and Portuguese as well as men resembling Jewish *hidalgos* (Spanish noblemen of lower rank) who preserved the manners of the nobility and retained their solidarity with other Iberian Jews.

In this latter regard, they were of course sharply attuned to the fate of the *marranos* being hounded on the peninsula. Who was not, for example, profoundly moved by the fate of the twenty-four-year-old Isaac de Castro Tartos, a Brazilian Jew who dared to visit Portugal in 1647? When he was denounced by spies and hailed before the Inquisition in Lisbon, he refused to renounce his faith and was burned at the stake on December 15. When news of his death reached Amsterdam, Rabbi Saul Morteira (1596–1660) delivered a poignant elegy in the Amsterdam synagogue.[14]

For all their sophistication and pride in their secular heritage, however, most continued to harbor well-founded fears of the Inquisition. Even in Amsterdam Sephardic Jews used aliases in business, if only to protect relatives and business associates who had remained behind in Iberia. Some people even assumed several pseudonyms. Their fears were not paranoid. In 1655, the Spanish consul to Holland, helped by spies, collected the actual and assumed names of Amsterdam Jews who traded with Spain, along with the names of their correspondents there, the assumption being that relatives of Dutch Jews must be crypto-Jews. These lists were turned over to the Inquisition. New Christian merchants in Spain, in turn, would often keep their records in a coded shorthand in case they were caught by the Inquisition or had to flee in haste.

Yet, further testifying to the intellectual ferment and spiritual complexity of life in Amsterdam's Jewish community, it is often clear that some of its members had returned to Judaism with split identities. In this context, the life of the great seventeenth-century poet and dramatist Daniel Levi (Miguel) de Barrios (1630–54) is especially revealing. Born in the Andalusian town of Montilla into a New Christian family, he became a devotee of Spanish culture, even serving as a captain in the national army. But when his family moved to Italy in 1660, he reverted to Judaism under the influence of an aunt and was circumcised in Livorno. After an ill-fated trip to America, de Barrios settled in Amsterdam in 1662 and five years later founded a theatrical company there. Even a decade later, he could write with pride of his Iberian roots:

> *Hail to thee, Montilla, my progenitor,*
> *Hail to thee, O Spain,*
> *For the lion snatches me away from thee by*
> *   force.*[15]

Far from being simple nostalgia for the "old country," this was a cultural devotion that extended back to Seneca and the Stoics of antiquity as well as to such Spanish Renaissance figures as the poet Luis de Gongora. This stance aroused so much criticism from the community establishment in his new home that de Barrios was forced to retreat to Brussels, where he befriended the local and Spanish aristocracy while continuing to write Spanish poetry and express his love for things Iberian.

But the community's ethnic or quasi-racial definition as Spanish or Portuguese was nonetheless indisputable, as can be seen clearly in the example of the dowry society known as the *Santa companhia de dotar Orfans e Donzelas pobres*. This charitable organization, established in 1615 by the community exclusively for the benefit of young girls of Portuguese origin, had grown to 400 members by 1683. Its bylaws reveal an unusual tension between ethnic attitudes and rabbinic norms, for the definition of potential loan recipients actually contradicts Jewish law, which is matrilineal. The illegitimate daughter of a "Portuguese" man and a non-Jewish woman was eligible to receive a dowry, but not the illegitimate daughter of a "Portuguese" woman and a gentile father. In other words, lineage was passed down through the father, in contradiction to Jewish law.[16]

Amsterdam's Jews have been called a "brand plucked from the fire."[17] The enormous challenge facing their rabbinical leaders throughout the sixteenth and seventeenth centuries was how to help immigrating *marranos* adjust to the texture of Jewish customs and the formalities of an organized community. They well understood that a Jew who had learned about his heritage from a Christian text was going to be a different kind of believer from one who had grown up within a community and would need help in reintegrating. He would need primers to teach him from scratch and might balk at the strictures of Judaism. Amsterdam's spiritual leaders were less concerned with what Jewish returnees believed privately than with what they said publicly, fully aware that there would be lingering after-effects from the experience of an only partially transmitted crypto-Judaism. At the same time, many *marranos* returned to the faith of their fathers with great zeal and high expectations. Naturally, some were more strongly interested in theology than in ritual, and some would grapple for years with split identities.

Amsterdam's Jewish leadership was invested with the authority to control the conduct of its members, including religious behavior. Their weapons included fines and an awesome ban of excommunication. Nevertheless, because of the relatively free and open atmosphere of the Dutch metropolis, it soon became apparent that some returnees to Judaism felt compelled to express their religious doubts regardless of the social consequences.

In the intellectual ferment that excited Amsterdam's Jews in the seventeenth century, three dissenters tried to assert their religious independence within the Sephardic community. Although by no means the sole dissenting voices, Baruch (Benedict) Spinoza (1632–77), Uriel da Costa, and Dr. Juan de Prado were the most famous skeptics. Each in his individual fashion rejected some of the fundamental principles of Jewish faith and set the elders of the community on edge. De Prado and da Costa were New Christians born in Iberia who had returned to Judaism, while Spinoza was born of *marrano* parents in Amsterdam and educated within the Jewish community there. They would all be banned. Da Costa, humiliated by his excommunication, committed suicide, declaring himself neither Jew nor Christian but a deist who believed only in reason and the law of nature. De Prado, by contrast, responded to excommunication by publicly recanting his unorthodox views but continuing to espouse them privately, while Spinoza withdrew entirely from the community.

Their intellectual problem was complex. For Spinoza especially, one of the most brilliant minds to emerge in Amsterdam's Portuguese Jewish community and a founder of modern secularism, many traditional Jewish tenets appeared to be in conflict with reason and the laws of nature. He found the notion of miracles uncomfortable, the descriptions of God in the Torah unacceptable to his reason, and the laws of the Torah arbitrary. His attacks on the Bible as a man-made document and his doubts about the unique nature of the Jews as God's chosen people led to his excommunication on July 27, 1656, when he was only twenty-four:

> The gentlemen of the Ma'amad [the ruling council] make known to you, that having for some time known the evil opinions and works of Baruch de Espinoza, they had endeavored by various ways and promises to drawn him back from his evil ways: and not being able to remedy him, but on the contrary, receiving every day more news about the horrible heresies he practices and taught to others, and the awful deeds he performed . . . resolved that the said Espinoza be put in *herem* [ban] and banished from the nation of Israel. . . . We warn that none may contact him orally or in writing, nor do him any favor, nor stay under the same roof with him, nor read any paper he made or wrote.[18]

The *herem* was not uncommon in Spinoza's day. A person could be excommunicated by the stolid Dutch Calvinists or the aristocratic Sephardim for any number of minor offenses, such as speaking too loudly during prayer services or associating with people who didn't pay their taxes. What distinguished Spinoza's case was his choice to remain outside the community after excommunication, a lonely man in a world where the unattached and unaffiliated were not yet a common phenomenon. He did not become a social outcast or pauper, however, but continued to associate with theologians while earning a modest living as a lens grinder and optician and receiving an allowance from friends and admirers. His scholarship was daunting as he attempted to strike out on an independent intellectual path. When Spinoza died in February 1677, he had not returned to the community but had hammered out new and revolutionary notions about individual reason and the definition of God. Even today, his lonely course has gained him recognition as a founder of modernity but has barred him from being fully accepted as a son of the Sephardic community of Amsterdam.

On the very day that Spinoza was excommunicated, his famous teacher, Menasseh ben Israel, was in London. A familiar figure in the lively thoroughfares and literary salons of the seventeenth-century Dutch emporium of Amsterdam, he was known for scintillating sermons to which both Jews and Christians would flock. From his printing press, which set new standards of excellence in Europe, poured forth his own plays and treatises in several languages. His house was a gathering place for scientists. But his enduring fame would be gained on this trip to London to petition Oliver Cromwell for the readmission of the Jews, even though he would feel that he failed dismally.

When ben Israel arrived in 1655, the illegal Jewish presence in England was already several centuries old. Legally, Jews had been barred since their expulsion in 1290, but, as elsewhere on the Continent, Portuguese New Christian merchants had established a small, secretly organized presence in the 1500s. One of their most famous members was Dr. Rodrigo Lopez, physician to Queen Elizabeth. By the late 1580s, when anti-Spanish hysteria was rampant in England, New Christians even gained a measure of acceptance and were able to supply useful information to the English through their relatives and informers in Spain and Portugal. The Flanders relatives of a Dr. Hector Nuñez conveyed important information about the Spanish Armada to him in London. He and Alvardo Mendes of Constantinople proposed forming an Anglo-Turkish alliance against Spain, the common foe—only one of various anti-Spanish schemes being bandied about at the time. Still, most popular appraisals of the Jew were decidedly negative, combining medieval religious and economic stereotypes. Shakespeare and Marlowe, writing in the 1580s and 1590s, were familiar with the general anti-Jewish sentiments of their day. In addition, it has been suggested that Shylock in *The Merchant of Venice* was inspired by the trial of Dr. Lopez in London in 1594 on charges that he had tried to poison his royal patient. In 1609, for reasons that are still unclear, all Portuguese New Christians were expelled from London. Despite this incident, however, a new philo-Semitism was emerging in England, born of the Puritan religious revolution.[19]

For one thing, the Protestant familiarity with the Old Testament and the Hebrew language, in particular, rendered the Jew an object of positive curiosity. It was suggested that Hebrew was the original language of humanity or *lingua humana*. In fact, several theologians hoped to recover the secrets of the ancient biblical prophets through a better understanding of Hebrew learning; this aim led them to closer scrutiny of both the ancient Hebrews and contemporary Jews. On an entirely different level were the expectations of the millenarians who were cropping up in England and wanted to hasten the "end of the days." By 1650, they had won broad support, and although they had not devised any precise program for readmitting Jews, the millenarians had reminded the common folk that these biblical people still existed and had portrayed them in a positive light. Moreover, the multiplicity of sectarian groups in England struggling for recognition made the idea of religious pluralism increasingly acceptable if not inevitable. By 1650 the climate for toleration had been established "not excepting Turkes, nor Papists, nor Jewes."[20]

Menasseh ben Israel could also capitalize on another stream in English thought: many English Protestants were familiar with conditions in Holland, where they had come into contact with Jews and had also seen at close quarters the economic benefits of religious toleration. Practical arguments regarding such economic advantage would not fall on deaf ears. From ben Israel's personal perspective, his uppermost concerns were undoubtedly the new spectre of tens of thousands of Ashkenazic refugees streaming westward from Poland, straining to find refuge, newly created Dutch refugees from Brazil returning to Europe in search of asylum, and the constant litany of stories of martyrdom coming from Iberia. Only recently, new *autos-da-fé* had been staged in Lisbon, Evora, and Coimbra. The fact that England had overthrown its royalist government and was under Cromwell's eccentric republic seemed to augur well for a reversal of the ban on Jews.

Ben Israel's mission in the autumn of 1655 was swift, his stay in England brief. Traditional scholarly accounts claim that his plea for readmission played upon Puritan religious sentiments, arguing that

England alone, by barring Jews, was holding up the Second Coming. Indeed, he had in 1650 drafted a pamphlet, *The Hope of Israel,* in which he consoled the Sephardim with the hope that redemption was imminent, but he did not use this argument with Cromwell. Instead, in a pamphlet titled *The Humble Addresses,* he tried to cajole the leader into considering the economic advantages of readmission and requested that Jews be granted equality, freedom of worship, a cemetery, and synagogues.

Cromwell in turn submitted ben Israel's petition to a Whitehall conference of prelates, lawyers, and merchants. The records of the proceedings have been destroyed, but it is clear that the assembled group could not agree beyond conceding that there was no legal objection to readmission. Aware that the argument of political expediency and the Jew's economic usefulness would not prevail against the merchants of London, Cromwell played upon the religious sentiments of the participants, invoking the dream of converting the Jews. Apparently, he did not succeed. It was agreed only that "there is no law which forbade the Jews' return into England," on the assumption that the expulsion had been a matter of royal prerogative and therefore affected only the people immediately concerned at the time. No law was passed to readmit the Jews to England.[21]

Soon after, in March, Menasseh ben Israel joined with several *conversos* to petition Cromwell once again. This time, however, they asked simply to be allowed to worship privately without being molested and to bury their dead. Without fanfare, they were permitted late in 1656 to lease a house to be used as a synagogue and to acquire a burial plot in 1657. This proved to be the sum and substance of the great "debate for readmission of the Jews to England." On the positive side, however, since no declaration for readmission was made, none could be stricken from the statute books when Cromwell was overthrown, the monarchy restored, and his enactments annulled.

A crestfallen ben Israel left England in 1656, and he would not live to see the fruits of his labor. A tiny community of forty families in 1660 would grow to 800 souls by 1695, when the Bevis Marks synagogue was established, and would spark the curiosity of the inquisitive Samuel Pepys, who paid a visit. There were no residence limitations or economic restrictions, and English Jewry grew without public deliberations or pronouncements.

The Sephardic community of England was a model of dignity and decorum. Because of greater acceptance of nonconformist religious groups in the late seventeenth century, they were able to feel somewhat more secure. Concentrating on overseas trade and brokering, they enjoyed the fruits of England's economic ascendancy as Holland's fortunes began to decline. They engaged in a diverse range of trades but were particularly active in commodities and the diamond trade with India. Compared to the battles of their brethren on the Continent, their emancipation was anti-climactic. In the long run, any wrenching national debate over their existence was averted by the familiar and practiced Sephardic ability to integrate without requiring major adjustments on the part of the surrounding society. By the second and third generation, many had integrated so completely that they were members of the Church of England and could be found on country estates amusing themselves with such pastimes as hunting and shooting.[22] Indeed, between 1740 and 1800, the number of marriages celebrated at Bevis Marks fell by 43 percent, as radical assimilation undercut the strength of the organized Sephardic community. The most famous product of this process was, of course, the nineteenth-century political giant Benjamin Disraeli, no longer a member of the community but still quite conscious of his noble origins. Of course, it should be mentioned that many loyal members of the Sephardic community continued to have great influence upon British Jewry, probably none more strongly than Sir Moses Montefiore, the nineteenth-century leader who was indefatigable in the defense of beleaguered Jews everywhere.

The story of the establishment of open Jewish life in the New World begins in Brazil. After the Dutch conquered this colony from the Portuguese in 1623, Sephardim from Holland as well as Iberia flocked there. Very quickly, an important Jewish settlement was anchored in Recife, with synagogues, a rabbi, charitable institutions, and a kosher meat slaughterer. During the Dutch occupation, which lasted until 1654, the community grew to 1,000 worshippers. These settlers became actively engaged in the sugar trade, many as plantation owners, and in merchant shipping, but most members of the community eked out their living as petty tradesmen in the town. This basic pattern of occupational distribution remained characteristic of the colonial Sephardic Jew in America, although a few ventured into unconventional trades, like the owner of a gambling hall in Recife. In the early 1650s, as the enterprising community of emigrés thrived under the leadership of Rabbi Isaac Aboab de Fonseca, who crossed the seas from Amsterdam, permanent Jewish settlements arose elsewhere in the region: in the Dutch colonies of Surinam and Curaçao, in the English colonies of Barbados and Jamaica. Intracommunal relations among the few settlements strengthened, but the young colony in Recife would be short-lived. When the Portuguese recaptured Brazil in 1654, the Sephardim fled in all directions, fearful that their reversion to Judaism would make them prime targets of the Inquisition. Some moved on to the Caribbean, others returned to Europe. Not interested in fighting a battle against the Portuguese for religious freedom, these refugees from Brazil instead sought a measure of anonymity so that they could live out their lives safely and productively, avoiding the Inquisition at all costs.

One group of twenty-three refugees floated into the harbor of New Amsterdam in September 1654, after a harrowing several months, having been taken captive by Spanish privateers as they fled Recife. Thanks to Governor Peter Stuyvesant, their first reception on North American soil was a rude one. Unable to pay for their passage at sea, they petitioned the governor for permission to land. Stuyvesant, who had already revealed his antagonism toward Jews in prior encounters in Curaçao, responded by asking the Dutch West India company to ensure that "the deceitful race—such hateful enemies and blasphemers of the name of Christ—be not allowed to further infect and trouble this new colony." Along with his anti-Semitic feelings, he was also convinced that giving the Jews freedom would open the doors to others whom he disliked almost as much: "Giving them liberty, we cannot refuse the Lutherans and the Papists."[23] An autocrat, he believed that the colony should be in strict conformity with the tenets of the Dutch Reformed Church. But the West India Company had other goals. Mindful of the commercial role the Jews were playing so well in Holland, its board ruled that the emigrés be allowed to remain, provided that they not become a public charge.

Within the decade, New Amsterdam fell to the English, and the initial trauma of settlement in North America was probably forgotten. When the colony became New York, its Jews already had a burial ground and were meeting privately in homes for worship. In 1730, the community built its first synagogue, *Shearith Israel,* on Mill Street.

But it is important to recognize that Stuyvesant's reception and religious objections anticipate what was to be a leitmotif in colonial America. Popular conceptions notwithstanding, the colonies were a cauldron of religious intolerance. The degree may have varied widely, with ambivalence toward Jews in some colonies matched by outright exclusion in others, but most were quite restrictive. Paradoxically, colonial religious diversity proved to be very fortunate for the Jews, since the extent of outward difference displayed by Sephardim in Protestant colonies was infinitesimal compared with the varied rites of Shakers, Quakers, Baptists, and Catholics. The Sephardim wanted only to be left to pray quietly and did not seek to establish sweeping principles of how to govern minorities. But the religious diversity was so great and the antagonisms so deep between Protestants and other Protestants, between Protestants and Catholics, that it was eventually realized in America that the only path to survival, much less prosperity, lay with toleration.

Yet even though the Jews of colonial America were practically invisible—only 2,500 out of a population of two and a half million at the time of the American Revolution—they faced occasional dangers. For instance, Jacob Lumbrozo, a Maryland merchant, was charged with blasphemy in the 1650s because he denied the divinity of Jesus.

Initially, only five colonies permitted Jewish settlements: New York, Rhode Island (Newport), Pennsylvania (Philadelphia), Georgia (Savannah), and South Carolina (Charleston). In Georgia, the Sephardic as well as Ashkenazic newcomers, were paupers dispatched from London to be dumped on Governor Oglethorpe. At first, the Savannah settlers, whose charter specifically barred Catholics, did not want to take the Jews either, but the presence of a Dr. Nuñez in the group changed their mind. Yellow fever had recently decimated their miniscule ranks, and the local physician was one of the victims. Soon, Jews emerged as an important commercial element in Georgia, trading in vanilla and indigo and becoming the first vintners in the colony.

Conditions in Rhode Island were also conducive to settlement because the colony's founder, Roger Williams, like the Puritans of England, held Jews in high regard. He welcomed them, seeing them both as potential converts and as repositories of Old Testament wisdom. Jews were attracted (as were Quakers) because Williams did not want to set up an established church in his colony. By the eighteenth century, Newport had become the most important port in New England, and its congregation boasted a beautiful, colonial-style house of worship, now the oldest-standing synagogue in the United States. The ships of the city's Sephardic merchants Aaron Lopez and Jacob Rivera exported colonial products to Jamaica, Barbados, and London. Lopez's bills of lading indicate how extensively a Jewish colonial merchant could engage in all branches of commerce, from fish, cheeses, chocolate, rum, potash, and soap, to kosher meat for the Jamaican market. His fleet totaled thirty ships; like Rivera's, some carried slaves, though Lopez was not himself a slaveowner. Aside from these two men, there is scant evidence of Jewish involvement in the eighteenth-century slave trade, despite the moral context within which slavery flourished. One reason may have been that the British barred Jews from owning slaves, allegedly because it was feared they would encourage slave insurrection. Jewish lack of participation in slaving is particularly surprising in light of the commercial and family ties that linked the Jews of the North American mainland with those in the Caribbean islands. The well-known routing of the slave trade in triangular fashion through those islands meant that much of Caribbean commerce was involved.

The South Carolina colony was especially promising for Jewish settlement. One drafter of its charter was the great English political philosopher John Locke, whose advocacy of religious toleration in his homeland was enshrined therein. It is therefore not surprising that South Carolina would later become the first state to grant Jews the franchise. Moreover, the first Jew recorded as holding political office in the colonies, the English Sephardic Jew Francis Salvador, represented South Carolina at the first and second provincial congresses in the 1770s. He also fought as a volunteer in a Georgia regiment, riding twenty-eight miles to arouse that colony's militia against the British attack on South Carolina in 1776. When he was killed by Indians in July of that year, he perhaps became the first Jew to die in defense of the new United States.

In Pennsylvania, William Penn restricted the rights of Jews, barring them from voting or holding public office. Ironically, the Liberty Bell, which was cast in London, was brought to American shores in 1751 on the *Myrtilla*, a ship owned by the Philadelphia Jewish firm of Levy and Franks. David Franks, a third-generation American, was excluded from voting in the colony because as a Jew he "didn't profess belief in Jesus Christ."

Nevertheless, the first Sephardic synagogue in Philadelphia, *Mikve Israel*, had been founded by 1747. Throughout the colony, as elsewhere, Jews became actively engaged as traders and merchants, taking the amenities of the city to a predominantly agrarian population. The Jewish peddler with a pack on his back was a common sight on the frontiers. He took a great risk in going among the Indians and backwoodsmen, but colonial merchants were apparently an intrepid lot.

After all, the major arena of Sephardic activity in America was in the economic sphere, not in theology or religious discussion. Although it was Sephardim who built the first synagogues in the country, their congregations took scant interest in scholars. Instead, these God-fearing merchants were eager to become part of their new society, to stand guard on the Hudson, to venture into the wilds of the interior, or to fight for the right to bear arms. Their cultural frame of reference was the Sephardic diaspora, especially its Caribbean, London, and Amsterdam poles, but they quickly became Americanized, even as they dutifully continued to keep the minute books of their congregations in Portuguese well into the eighteenth century. This is particularly surprising since Ashkenazim from Germany and Poland already outnumbered Sephardim by the American Revolution. Yet for some time, the Ashkenazim bowed to Sephardic custom and remained within the few Sephardic congregations. None of the acrimony between the two branches of Jewry in Europe spilled over onto American shores. Perhaps on explanation for this harmony lies in the fact that they simply had to get along in order to survive, let alone to find eligible Jewish mates for their children, to assure the continuity of the community.

As friction with England increased in the 1770s, most Sephardim threw in their lot on the side of the Whigs. They saw their future as American and republican and decided to disband their congregations in New York and Newport as the British approached. New York's Gershom Seixas moved his congregation to Philadelphia; the Newport community fled to Connecticut. For the first time, Jews served as commissioned officers on Washington's staff, and a company of South Carolina troops included so many Jews it was dubbed the "Jews' Company." One of Washington's staff, Benjamin Nunes, had begun his military service with General Pulaski before serving in regiments headed by General De Kalb and Lafayette and would lead French troops in the crucial siege of Savannah. It was Nunes who memorably proclaimed, "On religious grounds I am a Republican."

By the end of the eighteenth century, Sephardic Jews were at home in America. The level of integration they had achieved would remain inconceivable in Europe for many more decades. Yet while they considered themselves American, they had also succeeded in transplanting and reestablishing a community much along the lines of what they had known for centuries. Few were very rich, few very poor. If almost none was learned, they appeared to be content with their lot as a merchant community, hoping to be left alone after so many generations of wandering. Perhaps one of American Jewry's most prominent figures, Georgia's Mordecai Sheftall, a patriot condemned by the British as one of the subversive "liberty people," best summed up the American Jewish view in a letter to his son in April 1783:

> Every real wisher to his country must feel himself happy to have lived to see this longe and bloody contest brot to so happy an issue. More especially as we have obtained our independence—An entire new scene will open itself, and we have the world to begin again.[24]

At the time of the American Revolution, Sephardic Jews were living in a society that was still coming to terms with new experiments in religious openness and toleration of diversity. As late as 1787, eleven of the thirteen colonies continued to deny Jews political equality. It would take many years for the new principles of the revolution to prevail. But Sephardic numbers were small and their disabilities minor. Their principle problems of survival and continuity in America would stem not from intolerance but from that very openness and unprecedented acceptance that poses such a challenge to American Jewish survival in our own day. For, given the enormous potential for religious strife, America sensibly resisted the temptation to set up an established church. Consequently, religious acceptance of the Jews evolved within a broader framework of religious toleration. To achieve civic harmony, the American solution was to emphasize the elements that all groups had in common. Naturally, this suited the temperament of the Sephardim, who had become masters in accommodating to the dominant cultures among which they always constituted a small minority. They had also learned to restrict their religious practices to their homes and synagogues, thus compartmentalizing their lives, as it were, in a way that made them inconspicuous.

The Sephardim succeeded in fostering the resettlement of Jews in western Europe and America because of the unique attributes that they had gained from their historical background. In sum, they were crypto-Jewish immigrants schooled in secular learning and also in the survival skills necessary to conceal their true religious identity. At the same time, they had not lived in cultural isolation prior to their arrival in France, Holland, England, or America, and they were unwilling to live in cultural isolation once admitted. Professor Yosef Yerushalmi describes them as the "first considerable group of European Jews to have had an extensive and direct personal experience completely outside the organic Jewish community and the spiritual universe of the normative Jewish tradition."[25] It was this experience that made it relatively easy for them to enter the mainstream of western European countries and the United States. In fact, by the end of the eighteenth century, many families of *marrano* descent had completely cut their ties with the Jewish community and were settled on their country estates in Hertfordshire or Surrey, removed entirely from the Jodenbreestraat in Amsterdam, or living on their own in the Ohio River Valley. They did not resolve the tensions of living undifferentiated lives in an open society while remaining Jews, but that is the dilemma of all minorities, perhaps especially Jews, in the modern world. What they did do, and admirably, is establish pioneering settlements in Western societies, successfully sustaining their encounters with dominant non-Jewish cultures, and in effect lay down the guidelines for the modern Jewish experience.

8

Encounter with Modernity

Ottoman Decline and the Ascendance of the West

I am ill at ease in my own land and I know of no other. My culture is borrowed and I speak my mother tongue haltingly. I have neither religious beliefs nor tradition. . . . To try to explain what I am, I would need an intelligent audience and much time. I am a Tunisian, but of French culture. . . . I am Tunisian but Jewish, which means that I am politically and socially an outcast. I speak the language of the country with a particular accent and emotionally I have nothing in common with Muslims.

—Albert Memmi, *Pillar of Salt*

Napoleon's invasion of Egypt in 1799, brief though it was, marks a dramatic turning point in the history of the Sephardic diaspora in Muslim lands. The sudden encounter with European technology and ideologies initiated a process of change whose consequences can still be felt today. Jews in the East were not only introduced to European ways, however, but also brought in touch ultimately with European Jews in the process of attaining emancipation. Soon after the French conqueror's campaign, in fact, Europeans became protectors and trendsetters for the Eastern Sephardim, and the European powers provided a protective shield behind which reforms of the traditional Muslim societies and their indigenous minority communities were urged. The parallel meetings with European culture and European Jews were separate but interrelated, each leading to profound transformations in the East.

At the beginning of the nineteenth century, Jews could be found throughout the Near East and North Africa. While no reliable census figures exist, it is generally accepted that their numbers were in an advanced state of decline. Not until well into the century would the effects of modernization and Westernization begin to reverse this trend, as well as cause increases in the general population. The number of Ottoman Jews would rise from around 100,000 in 1800 to over 250,000 in 1906. By 1908, according to estimates of the *Alliance Israélite Universelle,* the Empire's Jewish population reached 439,000, but this figure included non-Ottoman Jews who lived there.[1]

They were spread out from Morocco to Iran, with important concentrations in most of the urban centers of the Middle East. By 1914, Istanbul's Jewish population increased from its 1844 total of 24,447 to 52,126, Edirne's total of 12,000 in 1873 rose to 28,000, and Palestine's 1850 total of 30,000 grew to 80,000. When the British occupied Egypt in 1882, there were no more than 10,000 to 15,000 Jews in the country, but by 1897 their numbers had increased to 25,000, by 1917 to approximately 60,000—in other words, between 1880 and 1920, the Jewish population of Egypt increased by 50 percent each decade. In Syria, there were 15,000 to 20,000 Jews at the end of the nineteenth century, but by World War I their numbers had grown to 30,000. Similarly impressive population growth occurred in the North African countries as well. One factor was the immigration of tens of thousands of Jews from the Balkans and Russia because of pogroms and nationalist upheavals, but natural increase was also important. The continuing growth is all the more impressive in light of the accelerated emigration of the Ottoman Empire's Jews during this period to Europe and the Americas. As we will see, the breakup of the Ottoman Empire triggered convulsive nationalism which was frequently accompanied by pogroms.

Meanwhile, the spread of European influence galvanized the economies and societies of the Near East as ports were expanded, canals dug, and roads constructed. Not all change was beneficial. By the 1870s, an entangling web of European loans hastened Ottoman and Egyptian bankruptcy. The introduction of railway lines to Egypt drastically altered the Nile Valley and Delta region. The appearance of cheaply manufactured British textiles in Syria and Anatolia slowly eroded their native industries.

Eventually, this European economic preeminence was reinforced by colonial occupation and imperialist domination, and the Muslim world lost its independence. In 1830, Algeria became the first region to be occupied by France; it was incorporated into metropolitan France a decade later. The French occupied Tunisia in 1871, and almost all of Morocco in 1912. Britain, primarily focusing on the route to her Indian Empire, took Aden in 1839, occupied Egypt in 1882, and brought Iraq and Palestine under her mandates after World War I. Italian cultural and imperial interests spread to Libya by the turn of the century. At the same time, much of Turkey's Central Asian population came under the domination of the Russians, whose traditional encroachments into the country met with increasing success.

For the Ottoman Sephardic population, imperialism brought more direct contact with Europe in all spheres of life. And for the first time, European Jews confronted the depressed condition of their brethren in the East and slowly realized that this state of affairs could impinge upon their own status at home. It was a realization that colored the changing relationships between European Ashkenazim and Ottoman Sephardim, determining the shape that change would take. The newly emancipated Jews of Europe viewed their Eastern kindred, correctly, as a benighted people in need of protection. When they assumed the task of protecting and also transforming the Sephardim into what they considered to be a "modern" Jewry, their thinking was based on European experiences and assumptions. Consequently, their efforts of reform, though zealous and well meaning, were attuned to a different set of realities from the situation in the Ottoman Empire.

After all, the Jews of western Europe had been the first to respond to the opportunities and challenges of political change wrought by the French Revolution, recognizing that they would thereafter be citizens but no longer a collective legal entity. In the process of exchanging group solidarity for civic rights in the modern nation-state, French Jews discarded many of their traditional and distinctive ways. The task of modernization was daunting. No Jewry had ever before been offered entree into the broader society; therefore, there were no precedents for the required changes. The very slogans of emancipation—"Be a Jew at home, a man in the streets" or "To the Jews as individuals everything, to the Jews as a nation nothing"—rang like clarion calls for change but provided little indication of how that change should occur or what it might involve. Inevitably, fierce disagreements erupted in Europe as Jews contemplated the degree of accommodation and transformation required of them and their religion before they would be considered "worthy" and "capable" of becoming citizens.

The attainment of equal rights in the West was slow and uneven. Although Napoleon's conquests in central Europe introduced Jewish emancipation and broke down the physical walls of the ghetto, French occupation was short-lived and these changes were rescinded by the German states in the aftermath of his defeat. Thus in 1815, as the *status quo ante* was restored, Jews not only became painfully aware that emancipation was fragile; they also came to believe that they had to be on their best behavior to prove themselves worthy of it. Perhaps not surprisingly, some of the most radical proposals for changes in Judaism would emerge precisely in those regions of Europe where emancipation had proved most elusive. German Jewry stood at the vanguard of religious reform, stripping Judaism of many national features, including the millennial hope for reconstitution in Palestine and the almost exclusive use of Hebrew in the synagogue.

Jewish intellectuals as well as Christian thinkers and politicians of the eighteenth century began debating the possibility or advisability of granting citizenship to European Jews. The course of their debates clarified one issue: Jews as they then existed were unacceptable to the modern state, which would not tolerate corporate groups or estates with separate jurisdictions and privileges. Both friends and foes of the Jews might argue endlessly whether or not Jews were capable of becoming part of the projected modern nationalist state, but there was no disagreement that dramatic change would be required of traditional Jewry. In the new political reality, citizenship would be extended only to the Jew who would transform himself, relinquishing traits that had "national" overtones. The old, all-embracing community, or *kehillah,* would have to be discarded. Religion would be relegated to the private sphere, and the individual would define his identity rather than having it defined by the community. For many Jews, this shift spelled liberation, but for others it boded the destruction of familiar, hallowed custom. What made the process worthwhile in Europe was the reward of becoming a Frenchman, an Englishman, and so forth. In the Ottoman countries by contrast, as we shall see, the eventual outcome of emancipation would be less clear. In fact, the entire European process of emancipation was not totally relevant to the cultural assumptions of the world of Islam, and even today it is not clear what citizenship for a Jew or Christian means in a Muslim state.

In France, Jews were granted all the rights of Frenchmen as a result of the Revolution; in turn, they renounced their separate corporate status, endorsing the changes in a theatrical Grand Sanhedrin convened by Napoleon in Paris in 1807. They committed themselves to self-reform, vowing that Jewish tradition would not come into conflict with the requirements of their new citizenship. The traditional compulsory *kehillah* was replaced by boards of rabbis and laypersons known as Consistories. These would oversee Jewish life, maintaining synagogues and religious institutions and compelling Jews to make drastic changes in their modes of employment, yet be accountable directly to the government. As the state assumed many of the functions previously provided by the community and its courts, the hold of Jewish law over the individual was radically reduced.

Although Napoleon's regime was crushed in 1812, his reforms regarding the Jews endured in Revolutionary France, which became the beacon for all of Europe and the model for liberals everywhere to follow. French Jewry, as the first emancipated community, assumed the role of vanguard of emancipation in Europe, the first resort in emergency for Jews elsewhere. Yet it should not be assumed that the movement to modernize the Jews of Europe was solely a response to the emancipation and debates sparked by the French Revolution. Jewish intellectuals, known as *maskilim*, had previously discussed the ideology of change and "self-improvement" in their circles of Enlightenment (*haskalah*). Among themselves, they had advocated major occupational restructuring and "productivization" of their brethren. Placing great store in education, they had supported the introduction of secular subjects into Jewish schools as a means of preparing the community for citizenship.

They spoke specifically of the need for sciences, modern languages, and vocational subjects, railing against Talmudic studies. Beginning with Moses Mendelssohn in Germany in the 1780s, the *haskalah* spread to the Austrian Empire, Galicia in particular, by the 1820s and reached Russia in the 1840s. Only faint echoes of the movement penetrated the Middle East, and then not until later in the century. At that time, *haskalah* received an enthusiastic hearing among a small segment of the Jewish population, even in traditional societies like Yemen and Libya. Of course, Middle Eastern Jews did not consider their culture to be inferior or feel the same urgency to abandon old ways as did the modernizing Jews of Europe. By and large, they would remain content to maintain their traditional institutional framework even as individual members became less traditional. The exuberant European receptivity to change, along with the belief in the inevitability and unlimited perfectibility of the Jew and his position in society, was a specifically Western and liberal Jewish phenomenon.

Once the reformers in Europe defined Judaism solely as a religious denomination, Jews were forced to redesign their faith to fit more easily into the modern (i.e., Western and Christian) understanding of the nature of religion. The debate over emancipation had laid bare many of the most deep-seated prejudices against the Jews, forcing them to reconsider their identity in new and revolutionary ways. It was only a matter of time before they would subject their faith to the closest scrutiny and implement major revisions. Some of the earliest reforming intellectuals, such as Mendelssohn, saw no difficulty in adapting traditional Judaism to modern life. Others hoped to improve the image of the Jews by making their services conform to surrounding (German Protestant) religious practices. The resulting Reform Judaism was characterized by a greater emphasis on simplicity and solemnity, the use of the vernacular for prayer, and the introduction of the family pew as well as choral singing, mixed choirs, and organ music. These changes were extremely divisive, causing decades of acrimony as both the reformers and their foes tried to enlist the help of the government in their passionate battles over forms of worship. The reformers regarded traditional prayer, with its informality, as unseemly and cacophonous. They also felt that the traditional messianic dream of reconstitution of the Jewish people in Palestine coexisted uncomfortably with the day's new concepts of citizenship.

By the 1840s, increasingly radical religious reforms were proposed in a series of Reform Rabbinical assemblies in Germany. For example, the Berlin Reform Society advocated a prayer service almost entirely in German, abolition of the head covering, and the easing of Sabbath and dietary restrictions in order to bring Jews closer to their Gentile neighbors. In other words, religion was to be relegated to the private sphere.

Needless to say, the religious innovations so bitterly contested among the Ashkenazim in Europe had no connection with the experiences of the Sephardim in the Middle East and were not intended for them. Yet some notions of modernization were welcomed by the group of Sephardim, popularly known as *francos,* who had come to the Ottoman Empire from Italy, part of an international Italian Jewish commercial class scattered throughout the principal cities of the Mediterranean. *Francos* tended to be under the protection of foreign consuls and were to play a critical role in the introduction of European education among Turkish Jews. They often acted as agents of European Jews interested in investing in the Empire's railroad, banking, and mineral concessions.

The role played by *francos* in the early stages of the modernization of Ottoman Jewry is well illustrated by the achievements and frustrations of Abraham de Camondo, one of their outstanding representatives. He was born in 1785 in Istanbul to an old Spanish-Portuguese family of financiers who had been in Venice for generations. They moved to the Ottoman Empire in the eighteenth century, becoming financiers to the sultans, but also continued to advise Austria and Italy. Typically, Abraham de Camondo was knighted for financial services to Italy while he rose to prominence in the courts of sultans Abdel Mejid (1839–61) and Abdel Aziz (1861–76). His bank financed the Ottoman Empire during the Crimean War. A friend of the Rothschilds and the Bleichroders, de Camondo was widely known as the "Rothschild of the East" and "the Great Official." He befriended Rothschild's agent Albert Cohn (1814–77) when he came to the Empire in the 1850s to dispense Rothschild charity. Indeed, the two men, who saw eye to eye on the need for reforms in Ottoman Jewish education and communal life, together established the community's first modern school on property donated by de Camondo. Almost immediately, a storm of protest broke out because the French director of the school, brought from Paris, quarreled with a staff member who was a local rabbi. The school was excommunicated by conservative forces and condemned as contrary to Judaism for teaching French. Bans and counterbans were hurled back and forth within the Istanbul community, and the government finally intervened after a massive peaceful demonstration of thousands of Jews supporting de Camondo. The reformer was permitted to keep his new school open but was ordered to donate a subsidy to the traditional Talmud Torahs of the city.

In 1862 conflict erupted again, this time over de Camondo's support of a liberal Ladino journal that backed reforms and freemasonry. It was at this point that a new chief rabbi, more attuned to reform than his predecessor, was appointed. Nevertheless, de Camondo was apparently fed up with trying to modernize Jewish education and departed in 1869 for Paris, where he would die four years later. One of his last acts before leaving Turkey was to secure subsidies for the European-style school of the *Alliance Israélite Universelle* in Istanbul. Like most other Jewish reformers of the nineteenth century, he believed in the transformative powers of modern education and held out the hope, shared by many in that optimistic era, that Jewry was progressing toward an ever-brighter future. His campaign in Turkey fought the battle for educational reform there even before the *Alliance Israélite Universelle* was created in France in 1860, thereby smoothing the way for the eventual acceptance of modernization of education among Jews in the Muslim world.

Controversies over the pace of change would punctuate Jewish life everywhere in the nineteenth century, even in the remote Ottoman province of Yemen. But only the most diehard conservatives denied the need to reform an Ottoman system in steep decline and a Jewish mass mired in disease and superstition. Even as the status of Jews in Europe was slowly improving, the Sephardim in the East were languishing. Over the course of centuries since their welcome in Turkey, they had gradually lost contact with the innovations of European technology and culture, which had instead become the preserve of Greeks and Armenians who willingly sent their sons to universities in the West. Also with the passage of time, the initial distinctions between the indigenous communities and the Iberian newcomers had blurred as the more dynamic Sephardim assumed the reins of power in the Jewish quarters of Muslim cities. Even though Middle Eastern Jews and the Sephardim did not share the experience of Iberia of course, their liturgies and legal traditions were similar, and the two groups were slowly melded into one community. Many commentators do question whether it is technically correct to speak of both under the rubric of "Sephardim." To be sure, many of the newcomers maintained their sense of separateness by clinging to their customs and their Ladino, but the various differences among Jews within the Eastern diaspora paled before their common bonds of fate and culture in modern times.

The long, tortured decline of the Ottoman Empire began as early as the final years of the reign of Suleiman the Magnificent, and the fortunes of the Sephardim mirrored this gradual loss of imperial vigor. In the seventeenth and eighteenth centuries, the legendarily dynamic Ottoman sultans were succeeded by one incompetent after another, each catapulted to the sultanate through palace intrigues and schemes of the harem. The balance of power within the Empire that had formerly enabled the administration to rule its heterogeneous constituencies began to crumble. In the military sphere, after centuries of virtual invincibility, the Janissary corps suffered mounting defeats abroad and became the scourge of the countryside at home as they attacked the peasantry, extorted bribes from the urban population, and preyed upon all segments of the population. They even set fires frequently in the overcrowded cities as a pretext for looting. As political and social anarchy spread, the centralized economy also began to collapse, brigandage abounded, and the widespread, intricate communications system began to disintegrate.

Because so many people were forced to flee the growing chaos in the countryside, cities became overcrowded and thus particularly vulnerable to urban disasters. Plague and fires had long been hazards of city life. Between 1606 and 1698 in Istanbul alone, there were twenty-six major fires, and the Jewish quarter was destroyed many times. During the great fire of July 24, 1664, for example, more than 80,000 homes were burned to the ground, including thousands in Jewish neighborhoods. Dona Gracia's Giveret yeshiva was also destroyed. In the eighteenth century, the fires would number in the dozens, repeatedly causing massive losses of Jewish business and communal property that would place heavy burdens of debt upon the entire community. In fact, similar disasters, both natural and man-made, sapped the affluence and strength of all major Jewish communities throughout the East.

Anarchy replaced government everywhere in the Muslim world, beleaguered Jewish communities were pushed even farther into penury, and the increasingly autonomous local governors became more corrupt and extortionary. The depredations of these officials, combined with frequent military revolts, caused a rise in physical insecurity and abuse to all minorities in the Empire, not just the Jews. In response, Christians sought protection from foreign powers under a system called "capitulations." Initiated by France in 1535 as a means of protecting her financial agents (French Catholics living in Ottoman lands), the concept was slowly adopted by other nations determined to protect minorities with whom they shared cultural and historical affinities. The Russians, for example, allied themselves with the Greek Orthodox and Armenian minorities. Under capitulatory arrangements, a foreign nation's protégés would be offered extremely favorable terms of trade as well as religious and political protections, and most of the Empire's Christians were able to benefit. The system provided European countries a pretext for intervening in Ottoman affairs, for they could protest that their clients were being molested or even move in troops as a prelude to occupation. It was through this avenue that European political and commercial hegemony developed and expanded in Muslim lands. In the process, the Europeans also increased the numbers of their protégés by setting up hospitals, hospices, schools, and missions in Turkey and the Near East.

Jews were usually not included in capitulatory arrangements. The exceptions included Jewish merchants (*francos,*) many of whom came from Livorno to seek their fortune in the disintegrating empire, and some few Sephardic aristocratic families whose special connections with a foreign consul enabled them to win the privilege of tax exemption. More frequently, the capitulations, along with the steady decline of imperial power, became a second factor that worked to the detriment of the Jews. Either at the request of the Christian minorities or at their own initiative, the European nations often refused either to deal with the sultan's Jewish translators and intermediaries or to handle the merchandise of Jewish merchants. Consequently, most of the Sephardim were pushed out of international commerce and relegated to petty trade by the eighteenth century.

There was a third important factor in the declining status of the Jews. After the sixteenth century, most Iberian refugees chose to go to Holland or Italy rather than Turkey. Thus, as the Sephardim lost their ties with the latest innovations in Europe, they also lost the linguistic and technical advantage that had enabled them to excell in the Ottoman state. Consequently, they were increasingly replaced in state affairs by young Greek and Armenian Christians who, having studied in Europe, could offer the kinds of services previously associated with Jews. In domestic commerce as well, the Sephardim became progressively more isolated and impoverished as Greeks became the international merchants of the Empire and Armenians gained ascendancy in banking. Inevitably, the tense relations between Jews and Christians were exacerbated by the growing political and economic competition.

But European intervention brought even more adverse effects upon the position of the Jews in Ottoman lands, for the cultural baggage of the West included anti-Semitic motifs previously unknown in the world of Islam. The Blood Libel, for example, was frequently, almost annually, brought forward during the nineteenth century by Greek, Armenian, and Arab Christians, occasionally with the support of a foreign consul or merchant. Beginning in the time of Suleiman, the Jews had managed to obtain occasional *fermans* from sultans denouncing the charge as baseless, but these decrees proved ineffective.

Yet another factor in the decline of the Sephardim in the East was the low estate of the intellect, which was effectively strangled by superstition and ignorance. Having never recovered fully from the disappointment following the debacle of Zevi's messianic movement, the Jews turned increasingly to mysticism. Their spiritual leaders counseled fatalism, humility, and dignity in the face of the cycle of mounting poverty and insult. What little Judeo-Spanish culture still endured was increasingly mired in superstition and belief in "evil spirits," far removed from the advanced philosophic and scientific flair cherished by their ancestors. Pride in past achievements was pitiably fused with fatalistic acceptance of contemporary poverty. The low level of expectations may be summed up by the characteristic phrase mentioned earlier: *Basta mi nombre que es Abrabanel.* Throughout the Muslim world the level of Jewish education was rudimentary if not primitive. Learning by rote, boys gained only the barest essentials of literacy in the *meldars* of Turkey or the *slas* or Morocco, which were one-room Jewish schools in the charge of inadequate and often punitive teachers.

The physical decay of the community led to a decline in the number of Jews living in the Empire. As this decrease combined with mounting fiscal demands, the community fell into very serious debt and had to cut back services and also sell off common property and religious artifacts. Communal dissension grew heated over the ability of the wealthy to avoid their obligations by obtaining tax exemptions through their connections with European merchants and consuls. A vicious cycle set in: as the community's needs grew ever more desperate, the wealthy few gained further exemptions through the system of capitulations, and the majority was further impoverished.

The ramifications of poverty were far-reaching. Schools became seriously overcrowded or were closed, children were apprenticed at an early age, and disease and substandard living conditions became widespread. Those who could afford to do so moved away from the teeming Jewish neighborhoods in Istanbul, Cairo, or Alexandria, as the numbers of beggars multiplied.

The conspicuous misery of the Jews, scarcely relieved by the existence of a few prominent Sephardic merchant families, struck many visitors to Muslim lands in the eighteenth and nineteenth centuries. When the Italian Jewish poet Samuel Romanelli paid an extended visit to Morocco in the late 1700s, he found the Jews there to be "oppressed, miserable creatures, having neither the mouth to answer an Arab, nor the cheek to raise their head." He found the ubiquitous *corvée*, or forced labor, so arbitrary that Jews were even pulled out of their synagogues on the Sabbath. In places like Morocco and Yemen, the situation of the Jews was the most extreme, because they were the sole non-Muslim minority. Yet their lot was not much better when they shared their tribulation with other groups. The Englishman William Lane, who visited Cairo in the 1830s, remarked in his *Manners and Customs of Modern Egyptians* that Jews in Egypt lived under a government less oppressive than in any other country of the Turkish Empire. What he meant by "less oppressive" is grim enough:

> Not long ago, they used to be jostled in the streets of Cairo, and sometimes beaten merely for passing on the right hand of a Muslim. At present, they are less oppressed: but still they scarcely ever dare to utter a word of abuse when reviled or beaten unjustly by the meanest Arab or Turk; for many a Jew has been put to death upon a false and malicious accusation of uttering disrespectful words against the Koran or the Prophet. It is common to hear an Arab abuse his jaded ass, and after applying to him various opprobrious epithets, end by calling the beast a Jew.[2]

There was nothing novel about these verbal and physical assaults; on the contrary, they were common throughout the world of Islam, particularly in North Africa. The large Jewish community in the *mellahs*, or ghettos, of Morocco suffered some of the most extreme degradation. With the exception of a few coastal towns, these Jews were required to go barefoot outside their quarter. The French visitor Mouette noted in 1683, "They rarely go alone into the countryside because the Arabs and Berbers slaughter them for the most part. There is practically never justice for them in these lands."[3] A century later the traveler Lemprière commented, "In every country where they reside, those unfortunate people are treated as another class of beings; but in no part of the world are they so severely and undeservedly oppressed as in Barbary."[4] Jews who went out after dark in Tunis were not permitted to carry a lantern. If they had to pass the *kasbah,* they were required to fall prostrate as a sign of submission and then walk with lowered heads.

An American visitor to Istanbul in 1835 was struck by the depressed and backward state of the Jews:

> I think it will hardly be denied that the Jewish nation in Turkey is in a complete state of indigence, as is sufficiently proved by the mean and vile employments to which individuals devote themselves. . . . There is no appearance of comfort, no appearance of competency among them; everything, where sight and smell are concerned, among them is extremely disgusting, and passing through their quarters, the sounds that assail the ears prove that they are a querulous race . . .[5]

Discriminatory clothing regulations were applied to Jews in most parts of the Muslim world, exposing the Jews to public abuse from all quarters. In the *haras* (ghettos) of Tunisia the burnouses worn by Jews could be only blue or black, their shoes and caps black. In the Mzab (southern Algeria), Jews were required to dress only in black when they appeared in public, and they were forbidden to emigrate. The system of institutionalized contempt encouraged expressions of scorn and abuse everywhere; children would pelt Jews in the street. If a Muslim chose to conjure up the false accusation that a Jew had uttered a disrespectful word against the Prophet, almost no defense was possible. The relative tolerance of the Islamic world in medieval times was replaced in the modern period by profound contempt, as the Muslim civilization declined and was subject to progressive lawlessness and anarchy.

Iran is not technically part of the Sephardic diaspora, but the deplorable situation of the Jews there was not atypical. In the late nineteenth century, a European visitor was moved to set down this heavily ironic account:

> At every public festival, even at the royal salaam before the King's face, the Jews are collected, and a number of them are flung into the *hauz* or tank, that King and mob may be amused by seeing them crawl out half drowned and covered with mud. The same kindly ceremony is witnessed whenever a provincial governor holds high festival: there are fireworks and Jews.[6]

Persecution of Iranian Jews culminated in the forced conversions of the Jews of Meshed in 1839.

Elsewhere, the outrages could be even more extreme. In Yemen, Jewish orphans were snatched to be raised as Muslims, and Jewish adults were required to clean the public latrines. Especially troubling for the pious Jews of Yemen was the decree known as the Crown Decree that required them to go bareheaded. This measure remained in force from its introduction in 1673 until the Turks conquered the country in 1872. At the other end of the Muslim world, the rabbi of Algiers was beheaded in a Muslim revolt against the *dey* (military governor) at the beginning of the nineteenth century. In sum, the Eastern Sephardim entered the modern period in a state of advanced decline and insecurity. Aside from a few outstanding merchants and bankers (*sarrafs*), most Jews were destitute.

Meanwhile, the realization began to dawn upon the powers of Europe during the 1800s that the dreaded Ottoman Empire was in fact a sick institution on the verge of dissolution. Some Western politicians were gleefully eager to hasten its demise in order to share in the spoils; others, like Lord Palmerston and Stratford Canning, realized that collapse would raise a host of new problems and destabilize the balance of power in Europe. In their view, it would be wise to promote reforms in the hope of propping up "the sick man of Europe" (a famous expression that, surprisingly, was not used until late in the century). Among the changes most eagerly advocated by Westerners was an improvement in the status of minorities.

The plight of non-Muslims, especially Christians, had proved to be a constant source of potential European intervention in Ottoman affairs. Russia, ever alert to slights against Greeks, Armenians, or Slavs, often exploited such occasions as a pretext to initiate war against the Empire. For a long time, the truth about Ottoman decline had been masked by the constant wars among Europeans. Once these ceased in the eighteenth century, it became apparent that the Empire was no longer a match militarily for the aggressive appetites of the West. Therefore, it was in the interest of the European powers to deprive any one power of an excuse for intervention by pressing the Turkish authorities to reform themselves.

Encouraged in this direction by the West, Vizier Mustafa Rashid Pasha began a new chapter in Ottoman history in 1839 by inaugurating a reform movement known as the *Tanzimat*. This movement succeeded in restructuring the state and granting equality to the non-Muslim population of the Empire. In a relatively short period of three decades, far-reaching structural changes were introduced that vitally affected the status of the minorities. For the first time, non-Muslims were granted civil equality, the use of derogatory labels for them was prohibited, and their special tax, the *jizya,* was abolished. In practice, this last reform was not quite so remarkable, because a special military exemption tax was immediately imposed. More importantly, however, the principle was established that the life, honor, and property of *all* Ottoman subjects was now guaranteed by the state. A citizenship law passed in 1869 included all Ottomans, regardless of religion. Like the modernizing state in Europe, the Ottoman Empire hoped to annul part of the autonomy of its minorities by introducing civil, commercial, and penal codes applicable to all groups. One result was a contraction of the power of the Jewish community and its rabbinical courts. At the same time, the office of grand rabbi was revived in order to assure more central control over the community. In addition, minority groups were organized into *millets,* or nations. Constitutional changes and legal reforms included the establishment of mixed courts to facilitate litigation between Muslims and non-Muslims. The most severe corporal punishments, like the *bastinado* (whipping the soles of the feet), were abolished. The rationale behind all of the reforms was twofold: to stave off European intervention by improving the lot of the minorities, and to strengthen the arm of the central administration by streamlining the state. Since the entire system depended upon the vitality of the center, one purpose of the *Tanzimat* was to reinvigorate and rationalize the central government along the lines of the modern Western state. Both of the movement's great reform decrees, the *Hatt-i Sherif of Gulhane* of 1839 and the *Hatt-i Hümayun* of 1856, emerged in response to crisis and were intended to rescue an empire teetering dangerously on the edge of disintegration. In addition, the reforming faction hoped that streamlining the bureaucracy and bringing non-Muslims more directly under government control would eliminate some of the independent powers of the minorities and their foreign protectors.

The reaction of the various Ottoman minorities to the reforming legislation is revealing. When the *Hatt-i Hümayun* was promulgated in 1856 promising equality for all Ottomans, Jews were jubilant, but Christians were dismayed, even though both minority groups were equal beneficiaries. Christians, like Muslims, protested being lumped together with the Jews. A high Turkish official, Cevdet Pasha, took note of this shared consternation:

In accordance with this *ferman,* Muslim and non-Muslim subjects were to be made equal in all rights. This had a very adverse effect on the Muslims. . . . Many Muslims began to grumble, "Today we have lost our sacred national rights, won by the blood of our fathers and forefathers. At a time when the Islamic *millet* was the ruling *millet,* it was deprived of this sacred right. This is a day of weeping and mourning for the people of Islam."

As for the non-Muslims, this day when they left the status of *raya* [literally, chattel] and gained equality with the ruling *millet* was a day of rejoicing. But the patriarchs and the other spiritual chiefs were displeased . . . whereas in former times, in the Ottoman state, the communities were ranked, with the Muslims first, then the Greeks, then the Armenians, then the Jews, now all of them are put on the same level. Some Greeks objected to this, saying: "The government has put us together with the Jews. We were content with the supremacy of Islam."[7]

Similarly, a law introduced by the French in Tunisia in 1857 to grant equality to non-Muslims had to be rescinded seven years later because of violent Muslim opposition. If anything, intercommunal tensions among the minorities mounted during the nineteenth century as the tide of nationalism rose. A British traveler made the following observation in the 1870s:

They hate one another. The Sunnites excommunicate the Shiahs and both hate the Druzes; all detest the Ansariyyeh, the Maronites do not love anybody but themselves and are duly abhorred by all; the Greek Orthodox abominate the Greek Catholics and the Latins, all despise the Jews.

In addition to mandating equality of citizenship, the reforming decrees also organized the minority communities internally. Local rabbinical powers were strengthened, and in 1835, a grand rabbi for the entire Empire was appointed to bring more central control over the Jews. The office, which had not been used since the sixteenth century, was in part necessary because the old courtier families who had wielded most influence had been murdered in the previous decade when the Janissaries were destroyed. On the one hand, the grand rabbi was to be his community's official representative to the Ottoman administration, responsible among other things for the remittance of taxes. On the other, as community and religious leader, he would oversee the functioning of all communal institutions and wield power over other rabbis

ephardic Jews were among the earliest European settlers in the New World. Synagogues in
e Caribbean, like the one above in Paramaraibo, Surinam, often had sand-covered floors—
ossibly recalling the settlers' *marrano* past, when footsteps had to be muffled to avoid detec-
on, or perhaps in memory of the desert sojourn of the Israelites. (*Beth Hatefutsoth, M. Arbell
ollection*)

With the Portuguese conquest of Brazil, Jews fled once again. These refugees were the founders of Jewish life in North America. The first synagogue on this continent, Shearith Israel, was founded on Mill Street in New York in 1730. The congregation's spiritual leader, Gershom Mendes Seixas (*above left*), was a patriot of the American Revolution and a trustee of Columbia University. Its move in 1860 to a new site on West 19th Street, near Fifth Avenue, was covered in the New York press (*right*).
(*American Jewish Historical Society, Waltham, Massachusetts*)

The Touro Synagogue in Newport, Rhode Island (*left*), designed by Peter Harrison in the sparse colonial style, was dedicated in 1763 and designated a national monument in 1946. Its notable features include a trapdoor behind the lectern (visible in foreground). (*Frédéric Brenner*) Some claim the tunnel was used to hide runaway slaves; others attribute it to the fears of *marrano* founders like Aaron Lopez, who was one of the most respected merchants and manufacturers in the American colonies. His wife, the daughter of Sephardic merchant Jacob Rivera, was the subject of a rare portrait by Gilbert Stuart (*above*). (*American, 1755–1828; Mrs. Aaron Lopez and Her Son Joshua; 1772/73, oil on canvas; 66 cm h × 55 cm w; copyright © The Detroit Institute of Arts, gift of Dexter M. Ferry, Jr.*)

In the 19th century, Sephardic Jews in the Ottoman Empire fell victim to disease, misrule, and anti-Semitic outbursts like the infamous Damascus Blood Libel. Their greatest defenders in Europe were Sir Moses Montefiore of England (*above left*) and Isaac Adolphe Crémieux of France (*above right*). (*Jewish National and University Library; Bibliothèque Nationale*) In America, Sephardic Jews were vastly outnumbered by Ashkenazic immigrants. Their sufferings in Eastern Europe evoked the sympathy of Sephardic poet Emma Lazarus (*right*), whose poem "The New Colossus" is inscribed on the Statue of Liberty. (*American Jewish Historical Society, Waltham, Massachusetts*)

Modernization and other Western trends began to modify the traditional mores of Jews in Muslim lands during the 19th and early 20th centuries. The adoption of European dress, as in the 1920 photo of the Aboulafia family at left, was one sign of this trend. Still, traditional customs, particularly those that surrounded life-cycle events, continued to prevail among Sephardim in the Balkans and Muslim world until World War II. Below, two Jewish women serve tea in Moroccan dress. (*Israel Museum*)

Sephardic Jews were not spared the devastation wrought by World War II. The great Sephardic community of Salonika was totally annihilated, along with that of Yugoslavia. Almost all of Greece's Jews were deported to Auschwitz. Above, the roundup and roll call of all Jewish males in Salonika between the ages of 18 and 45 on July 11, 1942. Below, the deportation of the Jews of Macedonia in spring 1943. (*Beit Lohamei Haghetaot*)

At the end of World War II, Arab nationalism erupted and engulfed the native Jews. Whole communities prepared to emigrate, and within a few years after the creation of Israel in 1948, almost all had fled the Muslim world. At left, the aliyah of a Tunisian family. (*Courtesy Robert Attal*) Today, Sephardim constitute a majority of Israel's population and have begun to revive ancient customs, blending them with newer ones, as in the Sephardic services below at the Western Wall. (*Etan Dor-Shav*)

Although Israel is the center of the Sephardic world today, a small and fading remnant of Jews or *marranos* can still be found in isolated villages in South America and Portugal, where some have guarded their traditions and secret Jewish rites for almost 500 years. Above, *marranos* prepare for Passover in Belmonte, Portugal, in 1988. (*Frédéric Brenner*)

and the Jewish court system. If he was progressive, he could play an important role in pushing reforms; if conservative, he would have a decisive voice in preventing their implementation. Therefore, the choice of incumbents became a new source of bitter conflict within the community in the nineteenth century. Only toward the end of the Ottoman regime, with the advent of the Young Turks in 1908 did power in the rabbinate pass decisively to the reformers, when the grand rabbinate came under the control of rabbis who had received some of their training in Western-style Jewish schools.

In February 1840, a Capuchin monk known as Father Thomas disappeared in Damascus. Because he was a Sardinian under French protection, the monks of the order immediately turned to the French consul, the comte de Ratti-Menton, and asked him to investigate. Exercising his rights as consular protector, Ratti-Menton rounded up several Jews as suspects and proceeded to interrogate and torture them under the baseless suspicion that the disappearance was part of a Jewish plot of ritual murder. In the first few days of the investigation, dozens of Jewish children were imprisoned along with the leading members of Damascus Jewry. Under torture, some of the prisoners "confessed"; others died or converted to Islam. The blood libel accusation spread like wildfire among the Ottoman Christians to engulf the Jews of Rhodes, Beirut, and Smyrna. Although the accusation was a familiar calumny in the stock and trade of Western anti-Semitism, the results of what has come to be known as the Damascus Affair marked a revolutionary turning point for the Jews of the East. For in the wake of this tragic event, the welfare of Ottoman Jewry emerged as an issue to be placed repeatedly on the international agenda. Western Jewish defense of the Damascene community would forge new ties of solidarity, both sentimental and institutional, between the Ashkenazim of Europe and the Sephardim of Muslim lands.

Immediately after the incarceration of the innocent suspects, a six-month-long campaign to obtain their release began throughout the world. At the time, Damascus was a fanatical city of between 80,0000 and 100,000 inhabitants. Since 1831, Syria had been under the control of the viceroy of Egypt, Mehmet Ali, not the Ottomans. Ali, his son Ibrahim, and son-in-law Sherif Pasha enjoyed close personal relations with France. The majority of the 6,000 Jews in Damascus were quite poor, living in a filthy, disease-infested quarter, but the commerce of the city was in the hands of a few Jewish and Christian families. When the Jewish notables were imprisoned and put to the torture, the community turned immediately to their brethren in Istanbul, London, and Paris. The Jews of Great Britain, who had a central organization known as the Board of Deputies of British Jews, were able to respond at once. The Damascene community quite naturally turned also to France, regarded as a court of appeal by virtue of its revolutionary aura as protector of human rights. French Jews represented the vanguard of emancipation, and their consistory system gave the community the appearance of unity. Because they had been the first to be emancipated, France itself was regarded as a defender of liberty.

In the meantime, Ratti-Menton was not only inexhaustible in trying to extract confessions from his hapless victims. He also ordered an Arabic translation of portions of the Talmud to produce "proofs" that Judaism demanded ritual murder. From the outset, therefore, the Damascus Affair brought together several issues in the minds of the defenders of the Jews. That is to say, the welfare of the Jews of the Ottoman Empire in general (and of Damascus Jews in particular) was linked with the question of whether Judaism in fact enjoins ritual murder. Also at issue was the miscarriage of justice in the Ottoman East.

The international campaign on behalf of the Jews of Damascus provides a fascinating barometer of the degree of self-confidence attained by the newly emancipated Jews of Europe, as well as their willingness to undertake the defense of foreign Jews. It also indicates the direction of future relations between the predominantly Ashkenazic European Jews and the Ottoman Sephardim. From the beginning, British Jewry took the lead, as was natural given both the strong interest taken by Great Britain in all matters concerning the Ottoman Empire and her continuing rivalry with France and Russia in the Near East. British humanitarians, who were pressing for Ottoman reforms, were especially aroused by the use of torture in the affair. The issue dominated much of the correspondence between the diplomats of Britain and France.

The defense of the Damascus Jews was part of a larger campaign by emancipated Jewry, reflecting the feeling in European circles that free Jews were obligated to defend their less fortunate brethren and press for emancipation everywhere. In London, the self-confidence of Jewish reformers was undoubtedly enhanced by the strong support they enjoyed among English liberals. At a meeting called by the lord mayor at Mansion House on July 3, hundreds of distinguished Christian politicians and clergy resoundingly condemned the Blood Libel. In accord with a new sense of political sophistication and recognition of the importance of public opinion, the Board of Deputies launched a carefully orchestrated campaign that included petitions to Parliament, letters in the press, public demonstrations, and even, to prove the absurdity of the libel, the reproduction of much of the Passover Haggadah in the *Times* of London on August 17, 1840. As the paper had editorialized four days before, "The whole Jewish world watches since it is not just the Jews of Damascus but Judaism itself on trial."

Earlier that year, in June, two leading statesmen of European Jewry, Sir Moses Montefiore (1784–1885) of London and Isaac Adolphe Crémieux (1796–1880) of Paris, had set off together to meet with Mehmet Ali in Egypt and the sultan of Turkey, Abdel Mejid, in Istanbul. Montefiore, then fifty-five years old, cut an impressive figure as he traveled through Europe to engage in personal diplomacy, sometimes attired in his uniform as lieutenant of the City of London and accompanied by his wife Judith, his personal secretary, his physician, and his kosher cook. He believed in quiet diplomacy at the top and would undertake countless other missions in defense of Jews everywhere well into his ninth decade. Already a man of great repute when the Damascus Affair erupted, he had served as president of the Bevis Marks synagogue and president of the Board of Deputies. Born in Livorno while his parents were visiting relatives in Italy, Montefiore grew up in London and retired from business at an early age in order to devote himself to philanthropy and diplomacy. His life exemplified the growing conviction among Jews in the West that one could be integrated yet still maintain Jewish loyalties. Traditional but socially integrated, Montefiore moved in the highest social circles in Britain and shared the values and way of life of that class. On the other hand, in the course of a long and vital career, he visited Palestine seven times, establishing new settlements, agricultural projects, hospitals, and schools there. He interceded for the Jews of Russia on two separate visits to St. Petersburg and at various times traveled to Rumania, Morocco, the Vatican, and Turkey to press for the rights of his persecuted brethren. Though not always successful in his missions, he was always persistent. In the Damascus Affair, he and his government were in agreement that the French and their agent Ratti-Menton had to be stopped and that the Ottoman Empire needed to be reformed. In addition, the independent Mehmet

Ali had to be contained, lest he weaken the Empire to the point where Russia would intervene in the East.

In other words, Montefiore's interest in the Damascus Affair dovetailed perfectly with the broader interests of his government. Not surprisingly, the queen rewarded him with a hereditary knighthood upon his successful conclusion of the Damascus diplomacy. The position of his diplomatic partner Crémieux was much more delicate, since the French government was directly implicated on the side of the torturers and the French press stood squarely behind Ratti-Mention. As Crémieux recognized, "La France est contre nous"—hardly an easy or comfortable realization for a nineteenth-century French Jew.

If Montefiore was Orthodox in practice but thoroughly British and liberal in politics, descended from an old Sephardic family and married into circles that included the Rothschilds (his brother-in-law), Isaac Adolphe Crémieux was cut from quite a different cloth. A radical lawyer from Provence, he had in 1817 refused to take the humiliating oath required of all Jews entering the French bar. In contrast with Montefiore's scant education and lifelong religiosity, he was highly educated and secular. Crémieux rose within the ranks of the Marseilles consistory system and was serving as vice president of the Central Consistory in Paris when the Damascus Blood Libel occurred. After he and Montefiore succeeded in their joint diplomatic endeavor, he was seated as a member of the Opposition in the French Chamber of Deputies in 1842 and became president of the Central Consistory in 1845. That very year, however, he felt compelled to retire from leadership in French Jewish life when his wife and children were baptized. Active in the revolution of 1848, the campaign to abolish the death penalty for political crimes, and the abolitionist movement, Crémieux became minister of justice after the fall of Louis-Napoleon's government. He continued his Jewish communal career as president of the newly formed *Alliance Israélite Universelle* in 1864 and as sponsor of the Decree of 1870 (known afterwards as the Crémieux Decree), which granted citizenship status to the Jews of Algeria. Although he was highly assimilated in personal religious practice, he remained involved as the foremost French defender of Jewish rights until his death—an audacious fighter for just causes, no matter how unpopular.

When these two men and their wives departed for the East, they were received by Jews everywhere en route with honors and much fanfare. But they endured weeks of discomfort in the sweltering summer heat of Alexandria awaiting a personal audience with Mehmet Ali, an ordeal further exacerbated by several instances of personal tension between the two couples. Nevertheless, their diplomatic success would be almost total. In September 1840, the Jews of Damascus were released. Montefiore proceeded on to Istanbul, where he obtained a *ferman* from the sultan officially condemning the blood libel. In addition, he pressed for specific mention of the Jews in the Ottoman Reform Decree of 1839. Wined and dined by the British ambassador, Lord Ponsonby, he also engaged in some charitable work on behalf of Istanbul's impoverished Jewish masses.

During their mission Montefiore and Crémieux gained fresh insight into the precarious situation of the Sephardim, an insight they would repeatedly apply during the ensuing decades. In keeping with the new expectations of the nineteenth century, they hoped to expand the rights of Jews abroad, especially those in the East who were in need of "protection" and "regeneration." The experience of the Damascus Affair had given the two foremost emancipated Jewries a taste of Jewish solidarity and interconnectedness. It had also added the question of the rights and civil status of Turkish Jews to the agenda of the West.

The Damascus Affair produced several other important results. Because of the lively press campaign it aroused, the "Eastern Jewish Question" was introduced in Western capitals. As Montefiore explained in a letter to Colonel Hodges, Britain's representative in Alexandria, "To the press of London we are deeply indebted and I fully agree in the propriety of feeding the public mind upon this subject, for, after all, it is London that must act upon the world and through its press leave the imprint of its civilization, its liberal feeling and its humanity in the East."[8]

Although Montefiore could easily have paid for the mission to Egypt himself, he wisely sought the diplomatic and financial backing of Jews everywhere. Contributions arrived from almost every continent, from communities as diverse as Hamburg, Altona, Philadelphia, New York, Curaçao, St. Thomas, Copenhagen, Livorno, Tangiers, and Berlin. The many remarkable manifestations of solidarity included a public fast in Metz, communal prayers in Livorno, and dedications of poems and *megillot* of deliverance throughout Europe. Collectively, these responses served to transform the Jewish question into an international issue and the various national Jewries into a unified body animated by collective concerns. In the same vein, a new recognition of the importance of a Jewish press led to the emergence of fifty-three Jewish newspapers in thirteen different countries between 1840 and 1846. Those who lagged behind in their public response, like the Jews of America, endured much soul-searching later and had to deal with the realization that they needed to organize more responsive collective bodies on behalf of troubled communities abroad.

Finally, the Damascus Blood Libel marked a turning point in the self-perception of Europe's leading Jews and the beginning of their sustained involvement in the affairs of the Jews of the Muslim world. Western Jews had never before thought much about the situation in the East, but the almost daily bulletins from Damascus fostered a new awareness that their brethren were in sorry straits. Paradoxically, this new sense of Jewish solidarity paralleled the rise of a new liberal internationalism in Europe. British reformers, in particular, seized upon certain aspects of the Damascus campaign as yet more proofs of Ottoman backwardness and the need for broader reforms in the East. It is equally paradoxical that the French Consistory, that creation of the Revolution intended to break down the organizational separatism of French Jews and their sense of solidarity, emerged in 1840 as a voice for Jewish interests, recognized near and far as a liberal defender of endangered Jews anywhere in the world.

The new sense of international Jewish solidarity was perhaps most fully expressed in 1840 by the prominent American Jewish leader and Philadelphian, Rabbi Isaac Leeser:

> Around me are those who have assembled for no other purpose than to express, in language not to be misunderstood, that they feel for their brothers who languish under the cruel bondage of oppression; that every cry of anguish uttered by their fellow-believers elsewhere, touches a sympathetic chord in their own hearts. We have no country of our own; we have no longer a united government, under the shadow of which we can live securely; but we have a tie yet holier than a fatherland, a patriotism stronger than the community of one government; our tie is a sincere brotherly love, our patriotism is the affection which unites the Israelite of one land to that of another. As citizens we belong to the country we live in; but as believers in one God, the inheritors of the Law, the Jews of England, Russia and Sweden are no aliens among us, and we hail the Israelite as a brother.[9]

Indeed, from Jamaica and Barbados to Hamburg and Warsaw, the Ashkenazim joined ranks with the imprisoned Jews of Damascus. Never did their attitude appear to be patronizing, nor did the prolific press accounts and many public expressions of solidarity ever suggest that the

Sephardim were a people in any way separate from Western Jewry. If anything, a new sense of common fate was repeatedly expressed. In the words of the flamboyant American Jewish politician Mordechai Manuel Noah, "We are still one people; bound by the same religious ties, worshipping the same God, governed by the same sacred awe, and bound together by the same destiny."[10] Evidently, this feeling of kinship was widely shared, even though the newfound status of citizen granted Jews in America and Europe inevitably exaggerated the differences between Jews of West and East.

In this vein, Montefiore understood from the outset of the Damascus Affair that special protection for Jews going beyond the reforms of the *Tanzimat* would be necessary. As their rescue mission progressed, he and Crémieux voiced shock at the depressed state of the Sephardim they encountered. Each immediately took modest but significant steps to ameliorate the downtrodden economic condition of Ottoman Jewry through charitable contributions. Both men realized that the key to improvement lay in education. Crémieux set up separate modern schools for boys and for girls while he was in Egypt in 1840. The institutions proved to be temporary, but they provide an indication of the thinking and direction that European reformers would take vis-à-vis the Sephardim in the coming decades. When in Istanbul, Montefiore ensured that all of the synagogues of Turkey posted a declaration from the chief rabbi proclaiming that Jewish schools would introduce instruction in the Turkish language. The Turkish foreign minister's comment to the Englishman is also revelatory of new realities:

> If you had done nothing more than this in Constantinople you should consider yourself amply compensated. In advising your brethren to acquire a knowledge of Turkish, you have been instrumental in enabling them to raise themselves to some of the highest offices of the Empire.[11]

The intense involvement of Western Jews in the Damascus Affair was an expression of the hopes of the first generation of Jews to be emancipated, or partially emancipated. From their perspective, the Damascus triumph was only one step in the inevitable progress toward the emancipation of all Jews. At the same time, the whole affair had aroused deep concerns about the possible impact of the blood libel upon their own newfound, still fragile emancipation. In other words, their assumption of the role of protector of the Sephardim was a complex reaction of Ashkenazim who were still insecure about their own well-being. Because the situation in the East could potentially undermine Western gains, they began to formulate a program to "uplift" the Jews in Muslim lands, both for their own and their protégés' sakes.

The Jewish struggle for acceptance in Europe was not won in one campaign. Even in France, the Jews confronted continuous assaults to their emancipation from forces on the political Right as well as the Left. Each blood libel that cropped up in the East—and they appeared endless—was heralded in the right-wing press in Paris. The growing realization that the condition of Jews abroad impinged upon Jewish status at home began to spread. France was particularly sensitive to the issue of Jewish "backwardness," since she had already included a depressed community within her colonial borders by incorporating Algeria. In the 1850s, proposals for the organization of some form of international Jewish defense organization or congress to bring the fruits of emancipation to all corners of the globe began to be floated.

In May 1860, a group of leading French Jews founded the *Alliance Israélite Universelle* for the express purpose of serving as a "center of moral progress, of religious solidarity and of protection for all those who suffer for being Jewish."[12] They took the "Universelle" in the title quite seriously, playing down Jewish particularistic traits in favor of universal canons of liberalism. The group's global call for membership among Jews everywhere clearly predicted the direction of their future programs:

> If you believe that a great number of your coreligionists, overcome by twenty centuries of misery, of insults and prohibitions, can find again their dignity as men, win the dignity of citizens;
>
> If you believe that one should moralize those who have been corrupted, and not condemn them, enlighten those who have been blinded, and not abandon them, raise those who have been exhausted, and not rest with pitying them . . .
>
> If you believe in all these things, Jews of all the world, come hear our appeal . . . [13]

Defense of co-religionists, which would be accomplished through diplomatic intercession and extensive use of the press, was only one of the major themes made explicit at the outset by the *Alliance*. It set for itself no less a task than working for the emancipation and the "regeneration" of the Jews of the East, and also determined to aid all those who suffered simply because they were Jews.

This ambitious agenda was a reflection of the nineteenth-century mode of Jewish thinking that derived from the *haskalah*. In this vein, it was widely held by Jewish reformers like Crémieux and Charles Netter that improvement—indeed, a transformation of the face of the traditional Jew in the West as well as the East—was imperative. In the words of the *Alliance*, the task of uplifting Jews in the East was a "civilizing mission." Their sorry state was caused not only by discrimination but also by their concentration on petty trades. At the heart of change lay education, especially the dissemination of European-style education and instruction in the French language. The optimistic founders of the *Alliance* were convinced that the latter would imbue the student with the emancipatory ideals of the French Revolution. They won the sympathies of the German Jewish financier and railway tycoon Baron Maurice de Hirsch (1831–96), builder of the first Turkish railroad system. In 1873 he donated 1,000,000 francs to the *Alliance* in Paris to support the education of Turkish Jews; half of the sum went to the *Alliance* agricultural school in Palestine. De Hirsch bore most of the expense of the *Alliance* trade schools until his death, a commitment that paralleled his efforts to uplift the Jews of Russia, whose deplorable state was even worse than that of their brethren in the Ottoman Empire.

It was hoped that Jews would acquire new identities, new occupations, and new moral character in the *Alliance* schools. On the practical level, "productivization" would be increased by encouraging them to branch out from their menial occupations and go into agricultural work. *Mikve Israel*, Netter's agricultural school founded by the *Alliance* in Palestine, and de Hirsch's soup kitchens and agricultural colonies for poor Russian emigrés in Argentina, were outgrowths of this line of thinking.

The overall task was clearly defined by the *Alliance:*

What was, what is the aim of the Alliance? . . . In the first place, to cast a ray of the civilization of the Occident into the communities degenerated by centuries of oppression and ignorance; next, to help them find jobs more secure and less disparaged than peddling by providing the children with the rudiments of an elementary and rational instruction; finally, by opening the spirits to Western ideas, to destroy certain outdated prejudices and superstitions which were paralyzing the activities and development of the communities. But in addition, the action of the Alliance [is] principally aimed to give to Jewish youth, and subsequently, to the Jewish population as a whole, a moral education rather than a technical instruction, to create rather than semi-scholars tolerant men, attached to their duties as citizens and as Jews, devoted to the public good, and to their brothers, knowing how to reconcile the needs of the modern world with the respect of ancient traditions.[14]

Not surprisingly, the goals and attitudes of the founders of the *Alliance* have been occasionally condemned as imperialistic, but the charge is unfair. Their views were typical of the paternalistic notions of regeneration held by bourgeois nineteenth-century reformers and were not even primarily Jewish in character. Like many middle-class Europeans, they believed that the child was essentially a *tabula rasa* whose well-being and moral qualities could be molded through education. Reformers looked to education and social engineering to create "a new man" and to "civilize" the lower classes in Europe as well as in the Ottoman lands. The emerging activism of all European Jews, not only the members of the *Alliance,* was based upon a new orientation and new understandings of what constituted an "emancipated" and "modern" Jewry.

The first *Alliance* school was established in Tetouan, Morocco, in 1862. By the turn of the century, a network of over 100 schools stretched from Morocco to Iran. Istanbul, Salonica, and Edirne all had several schools, with a total student population of about 1,000 in each city. Smaller towns like Bursa or Aydin in Turkey had from 200 to 400 students each. Yet despite the popularity of the *Alliance,* many Jewish youth in the Near East continued to study in the traditional Talmud Torahs, and many could be found in the mission schools established by French, English, and Scottish missions. By 1911 the *Alliance* schools could claim 9,764 children in Turkey, or 35 percent of the school-age Jewish population. These schools were the primary tool for the extension of European, and especially French, cultural influence among Jews in the Muslim world. By the end of the nineteenth century, even the traditional Talmud Torahs were turning to them for support and guidance. Using French as the language of instruction, the separate *Alliance* schools for boys and girls emphasized basic reading skills, simple mathematics, instruction in such crafts as needlework, and a small amount of Jewish studies (less for girls than for boys), especially the Hebrew language. The Judaica in the curriculum was taught by local rabbis, but the rest of the faculty was trained at an *Alliance* institution in Paris.

Rather than initiate the founding of schools, the *Alliance* waited for a community's invitation before appearing on the scene. Usually, it was a local reformer or a member of the *franco* population who served as the primary catalyst for the new school as well as its economic mainstay. In 1863, for example, a regional committee of the *Alliance* was established in Istanbul with de Camondo as president. Always, local cooperation was vital to the success of a school. Even following a local initiative, the appearance of the *Alliance* sometimes provoked passionate opposition from conservative leaders in the community. In general, however, parents flocked to enroll their children in the schools, expecting them to learn a skill that would raise them above the family's poverty level. These parents intuitively understood that the acquisition of a European language was the key to competing with Greeks and Armenians for employment. Usually, the *Alliance* schools were imbued with the missionary goals of the organization. Follow-up studies of graduates reveal that the instruction not only served as a vital stepping-stone into the professions but also provided an avant-garde of modernization. Not surprisingly, graduates tended to identify culturally with France as well as with modernization efforts in general.

Another fundamental aim of the *Alliance* was to protect Jews everywhere. To its Paris headquarters came a steady stream of correspondence in the form of reports by its administrators and complaints by aggrieved individuals, all detailing abuses suffered by Jews at the hands of local populations and their officials. In response, the *Alliance* would use its political influence to persuade the European powers to intercede when necessary. But it did not generally regard itself as an arm of the colonial administration, nor did the French government utilize it as a tool or provide any subsidies to it. The question of whether the schools were nonetheless unwittingly a tool of the expansion of French interests is difficult to resolve. By the second half of the nineteenth century, everything that emanated from Europe was assumed to be superior. Also, the *Alliance* created a francophone Jewish middle class as most Jews adopted French as their spoken language; it was forbidden to speak Ladino in *Alliance* schools. It was in fact a hallmark of French imperialism to place great emphasis on French-language schools. A member of the *Alliance* declared in 1891, "the French language gives French habits, French habits lead to the buying of French products. He who knows French becomes a client of France."[15]

At the same time, few of the *Alliance* graduates were exposed to the

Muslim majority culture, and it can be argued that their preoccupation with French increased their alienation from the people among whom they lived. The politics of French schooling loomed large in the Near East, but the French concentrated their efforts and involvement there almost exclusively on missionary schools. In North Africa, however, where there were no Christians (and thus no missionary schools), the home government took a livelier interest in the *Alliance* schools.

Neither actively political nor solely cultural in their aims, *Alliance* members took their role as catalysts for social change quite seriously. For example, in 1903 they wrote the rabbis of Morocco to deplore the community's practice of child marriage, urging them to oppose the custom on moral and hygienic grounds. Inevitably, the schools' focus on educating women to assume economic roles outside the home eroded traditional mores. Similarly, the curriculum's emphasis on practical vocational subjects weaned many youths away from traditional occupations and from traditional villages as well.

By the turn of the century, the *Alliance* had achieved far-reaching influence in the Sephardic Jewish community. Its work had gone beyond the establishment of schools to include cultural and philanthropic concerns such as unemployment funds, cooperative groceries, reading clubs, hiring a full-time physician in some towns, soup kitchens that distributed tens of thousands of free meals, and hospitals. By the 1908 Young Turk Revolution, a cadre of secular Jewish leaders had been created by the *Alliance* schools. Three out of the four Jews seated in the new Ottoman Chamber of Deputies were *Alliance* graduates. But these changes had not come without cost. They had caused divisions within the community as well as alienation and a sense of split identity. There had also been a note of paternalism in the *Alliance* goal of educating the Sephardim out of their bad habits. By echoing contemporary notions that vocational training was necessary to combat poverty and Easterners had to be cured of Oriental "laziness" and "vices," the *Alliance* views bore many parallels to those of Cecil Rhodes, Lord Curzon, or Lord Cromer of Egypt.

In contrast to the situation in Europe, real emancipation was not an option in Muslim lands. Only briefly, during the Ottoman Young Turk period, did Jews appear to be on the verge of possibly obtaining such emancipation. They were unable to gain security from this short-lived regime, however, because conditions in the Empire had been so exacerbated by the struggles of the national minorities for independence. In addition, the Muslim world was suspicious of all reforming movements that suggested the possibility of religious reform. Incentives for radical Jewish transformations were deemed unnecessary since no amount of change would automatically assure Jews political equality with the Muslim majority. Nor could any degree of Westernization transform them into Frenchmen in Beirut, Englishmen in Egypt, or Italians in Libya. Only in Turkey, after Ataturk's secular revolution in 1923, was there a possibility for Jews to become full-fledged members of a predominantly Islamic society.

Sephardic Jews never experienced the radical reforms of Europe, because of the different conditions in the Muslim world, and therefore Sephardic Judaism remained a relatively harmonious blend of devotion to traditional Judaism and respect for bonds between family and ethnoreligious loyalties. Consequently, the crisis of Jewish identity caused by modernization, that further alienated the individual from his surrounding culture without substituting a clearly defined new identity, was quite novel. The forces of modern nationalism further intensified this crisis for the Sephardic Jew. In his autobiographical *Pillar of Salt,* Albert Memmi recalls this dilemma after his emigration from Tunisia to Paris. The identity crisis of many Sephardic intellectuals was barely resolved before they would be confronted yet again by the necessity of assuming new national loyalties in the twentieth century.

During the latter part of the nineteenth century, the colonial powers introduced greater internal security and rapid technological changes that fostered population redistribution within Ottoman lands. Railroads, canals, and new roads made it easier for Jews to leave their small villages for the cities, where they hoped to find greater safety and economic opportunity as employees of the occupying Europeans. This rapid urbanization disrupted the tight familial society of the villages with its traditional rhythms of life and its local shrines and lore. Many Jews consequently felt a sense of loss of essential tradition that anticipated the even greater disruption caused by the eventual emigration of the Sephardim to Israel after 1948.

At the same time, the new economic opportunities served as a magnet for Jewish migration within the Islamic world. Much of the population growth in Cairo and Alexandria, for example, was caused by an influx of Jews from Syria and Turkey as well as from Europe. Such changes, too, challenged traditional family structures, traditional occupations, and Jewish community. One significant sign was the apparently simple matter of changing dress codes: among the Sephardim, the merchants were among the first to discard traditional Middle Eastern clothing for European attire. Also, women began to leave the confines of home, and such new leisure activities as theater and Zionist clubs replaced the timelessness of the past.

In this changing world, one of the most significant demographic developments was the growth of an agricultural and commercial Sephardic community in Palestine. Beginning early in the nineteenth century, Jews from North Africa, Egypt, and Turkey began to migrate there. By the 1880s, they were joined by Jews from Yemen and Bukhara. The growth of the Sephardic presence in Palestine is frequently overlooked or obscured because it overlaps chronologically with the more revolutionary emergence of Zionist immigration from Europe. It should be noted, however, that Sephardim made up the majority of the Jewish population of Palestine until the twentieth century. Recent studies have shown that some of their patterns of settlement were not dissimilar to those of modern Zionists—that is, they did not live off charity from abroad but established themselves as artisans and entrepreneurs. Such families as the Navons, Moyals, Amzalaks, Chelouches, and Eliachars played an active role in building a modern infrastructure of roads, agricultural settlements, and citrus groves and also served as intermediaries between the new settlers from eastern Europe and the landed Arab population.

Despite the substantial advances Jews began to enjoy in many parts of the Empire as a result of the introduction of the *Tanzimat* and the *Alliance* schools, the safety of Ottoman Jewry was not assured. In North Africa the presence of the colonial powers may have enhanced the safety and status of Jews, but in the long run also aroused xenophobic responses among the Muslim populations, leading to the eventual dismemberment of all Jewish communities there. In southeastern Europe, outside interference in Ottoman affairs also provoked ethnic hatred. As the individual peoples of Bulgaria, Serbia, Greece, and Rumania won their independence, they pounced upon their Jewish minorities. Thus, the surge of modern nationalism became the second great force to alter the destiny of Sephardim in the East.

Between 1821 and 1914, the Ottoman Christian minorities fought unremittingly for independence from their Turkish overlords. The long struggle was characterized by violent hostility to other minorities, by Russian and Austrian exploitation of nationalist movements to further imperialist aims, and by the suspicions and reprisals of the Turks. In the cauldron of Balkan politics, Jews discovered that they were a convenient target. The first of the nationalist uprisings in the period, the revolution in Greece, anticipated a century of anti-Semitic turmoil: Jews in the Morea on the Greek mainland were massacred, Jews on the Greek islands were wiped out, and Jewish quarters throughout the country were repeatedly burned by bands of rebels.

A contemporary observer, the Reverend John Hartly, vividly described the pogrom in Tripolizza:

> Thus did Jewish blood, mingled with Turkish blood, flow down the streets of the captured city. The sons of Isaac and the sons of Ishmael, on this occasion as on every occasion during the Greek revolution, met with a common fate. Their corpses were cast out of the city, and, like the ancient sovereign of Judah, they received no burial superior to that of an ass.[16]

Each subsequent nationalist uprising brought another wave of persecution. Apparently, the resurgence of national movements also unleashed long-dormant national anti-Semitic sentiments. In addition, Jews were often associated with the dreaded Turkish overlord in the popular imagination and were forced to bear the brunt of popular anti-government passions. In the 1870s the Rumanians gained their independence with the help of Russian troops, whose intervention was accompanied by the burning and pillaging of Jewish villages. In the Bulgarian uprising in 1876–78, the Russians intervened again and Bulgarian mobs joined with them in murdering Jews. Serbs, too, began persecuting Jews on the eve of independence, and a wave of Jewish refugees streamed into Istanbul, Salonica, and Izmir. Neither the intervention of the Western powers at the Congress of Berlin in 1878 nor the personal intercession of Baron de Hirsch and Sir Moses Montefiore could succeed in alleviating the suffering of the Jews in the Balkans or in gaining protection for all religions in the newly independent states.

On the contrary, the very mention of special protections for Jews and Muslims produced still more outbreaks of destruction.

On the eve of World War I, the ancient Jewish communities of the former Ottoman Empire were in a state of full-fledged panic and flight. During the Balkan Wars of 1912–13, the conquest of Ottoman Thrace and Macedonia by Bulgarians and Greeks had unleashed new waves of persecution. Jews who had fled from Bulgaria to Salonika were forced to flee yet again. The *coup de grâce* to this historic Sephardic center, "the Jerusalem of the Balkans," occurred in the wake of the great fire in 1917, which razed the entire Jewish quarter. In its aftermath, the Greek government decided to Hellenize the city and refused to permit Jews to return to their old neighborhood. Compensation for their losses was set at a rate lower than for Greeks, new laws required markets to be open on Saturdays, and in some cases Jews were literally pushed out of the city. Greek anti-Jewish policies reached such a pitch that the Zionist Federation of Greece, writing in 1931 to the American Jewish Committee, warned, "the Jewish world should know that the Jewish community of Salonica is dying and that it is necessary to come to its aid in order to prevent its complete fall into ruin and oblivion."[17]

Paradoxically, as if oblivious to or defiant of the carnage around them, the Sephardic communities of the Ottoman Empire were experiencing their last great cultural efflorescence. In the latter part of the nineteenth century, there had been a revival of literature in Ladino as well as in French and Hebrew, from popular romances and novels to pamphlet collections of medieval proverbs and ballads. The majority of the authors, publishers, and printers who translated and adapted works into French and Hebrew were merchants who favored modernization. A lively Jewish press flourished in Salonika, Izmir, Istanbul, and Sofia, using French and Ottoman Turkish as well as Ladino. Most publications were aimed at entertainment, but several newspapers, like that of David Fresco (1850–1933), took a strong political stand in favor of reform. Since the regime was suspicious of reform during the declining sultanate of Abdel Hamid II (1876–1909), some of its advocates had to seek asylum in British-occupied Egypt. There, one of the most famous of the era's journalists, Abraham Galante, (1873–1961) took up the cudgels on behalf of modernization in the pages of his newspaper *La Vara* (The Stick). The leading Ladino novelist, Elie Carmona, also published his works in Egypt between 1902 and 1908.

At the turn of the century, many of the major Ottoman Jewish population centers housed literary, theatrical, and humorous journals.

European operas were performed in Jewish communities, several of which had their own choirs, music ensembles, brass bands, and orchestras. A lesser-known aspect of this culture was the new development of Jewish songs, often under the influence of Muslim dervishes. The music of Rabbi Isaac Algazi, the most famous Sephardic musician at the beginning of the twentieth century, drew heavily upon both Sephardic and Turkish musical traditions. Still another sign of the revival of Balkan Jewry can be seen in the new majestic synagogues erected in Sarajevo and Salonika.

Sephardic Jewish intellectual life was sharply divided between reformers and modernizers. By the turn of the century, in response to Balkan nationalism and the spread of Zionism in the wider Jewish world, the Ottoman Sephardim were drawn into the Zionist debate. The impact of the *Alliance* produced an anti-Zionist attitude that was reinforced by the deep Turkish suspicions of Zionism, but the divisions within the community over the nature of Jewish national identity cut across all economic and social lines. The alignment of secular reformers of the *Alliance* with other opponents of Zionism, however, ignored a basic reality: nationalist movements within the Empire were placing Jews in a precarious situation. Now, the nineteenth century's facile optimism in the triumph of progress and assimilation was being belied by the growing persecutions of the twentieth century. In addition, local nationalism among Muslims in, for example, Egypt or Algeria, was assuming an anti-Western coloration. Around the office of the grand rabbinate in Turkey, battle lines for the soul of the Turkish Jewish population were drawn between Zionists, reformers, and Turkish nationalists who sympathized with the Young Turk movement. In a sense, each group nourished a competing vision of how the Jewish future would best be secured. The reformers trained in the *Alliance* establishments were convinced both that Jews would be emancipated wherever they lived and that the culture of France promised to bring the benefits of civilization to the masses. They were willing to work together with the Young Turks within the new constitutional framework set up after the Revolution of 1908. The Zionists, however, projected quite a different vision based upon their reading of the destructive power of the contemporary nationalist movements. With a strong base in Sofia and a growing band of sympathizers in Salonika, they contended that only Jewish settlement in Palestine would provide salvation for the Jewish people. Of course, their program was anathema to Turkish authorities, whether the sultan or the Young Turk reformers, because it threatened to dismember still another province of the Empire in the name of nationalism. Therefore, the government officially banned Zionist settlement in Palestine, deporting most of the province's Jewish community during World War I. Nevertheless, Zionist sympathies grew in the Balkans and North Africa, and the intellectual ferment aroused by the competing visions within the Jewish community persisted until the last days of World War I and the death of the Ottoman Empire.

Just before the collapse of Ottoman rule, the reformers finally achieved power in the Jewish community, a victory embodied in the election of Haim Nahum (1873–1960) as grand rabbi in January 1909. His tumultuous career illustrates both the coexistence and the competition between the various trends and visions within the Eastern Sephardic community.[18] Nahum's education, like his later career, combined tradition with innovation, political networking with Jewish community politics. He was trained in a traditional Yeshiva but studied law at the Ottoman Imperial School of Law in Istanbul. In 1891 he went to Paris on an *Alliance* scholarship to study at the Rabbinical Seminary, a modern rabbinical training institution under *Alliance* influence. He also earned a law degree and enrolled in a program of Oriental languages at the Collège de France. The first rabbinical figure in the Ottoman Empire to be at home in the Turkish language, while in Paris he befriended several Turkish exiles who would later become involved in the revolutionary government of the Young Turks. Upon his return to Istanbul, Nahum began teaching in the *Alliance* schools. His advocacy of moderate reforms along with his opposition to Zionism made him the *Alliance* faction's ideal candidate for the grand rabbinate, for he represented the new generation of Turkish Jews that spoke Turkish and were products of an *Alliance* education. A transitional figure who was first and foremost a politician deeply engaged in the struggles for modernization within the community, Nahum had vigorously pressed his successful candidacy. Even after his election, however, the quarrels between advocates of Zionism and Turkish nationalism, European-style reform and traditional Jewish identity, persisted. Although the anti-Zionist, accomodationist influence of the *Alliance* was overwhelming, events beyond the control of the Jews would soon prove that attempts to accommodate with the modern nation-state were ill-founded. Neither Greece and Yugoslavia in the Balkans nor Tunisia and Libya in North Africa would or could adequately protect their Sephardic communities.

At the conclusion of the world war, the old empires of Europe—the Hapsbugs, the Hohenzollerns, the Ottomans, and the Romanovs—all lay in ruins. U.S. President Woodrow Wilson's prescription that postwar settlements should be "open covenants openly arrived at" ran counter to the guiding principles of the European powers as they scrambled to divide the spoils of war. During the course of the conflict, Great Britain, France, and Tsarist Russia had entered into a series of public and secret negotiations to determine the distribution of the remnants of the Ottoman Empire. In part, these negotiations had been predicated upon the need for allies during the war and also the hope of achieving an Arab revolt in Arabia that would cripple Turkish support of the Axis powers. At the same time, the British engaged in discussions with the Zionists, believing (erroneously) that Americans would thus be encouraged to join the conflict. From this complex mixture of entangled, self-serving calculations, Great Britain embarked upon a succession of contradictory agreements. In the Hussein-McMahon talks of 1914, a secret correspondence with the Arabs, she spoke of dividing the Middle East to satisfy Arab nationalist demands. In an open proclamation to the Zionists, the Balfour Declaration of November 1917, she recognized the principle of the reconstitution of a Jewish homeland in Palestine. Another secret set of arrangements, Sykes-Picot of 1916, divided the Near Eastern territories of the Ottoman Empire between the British and the French (as well as Tsarist Russia, which later repudiated this arrangement). The result of these various commitments was that the victorious imperialist powers of Europe had made several potentially conflicting promises for the disposal of former Ottoman territories. The Treaty of San Remo in 1920 set out the new territorial divisions: the French would occupy Syria and Lebanon, the British would tighten their hold on Iraq and Egypt, and Palestine would become a British mandate, incorporating the commitment of the Balfour Declaration. French forces remained in Morocco and Tunisia, while Algeria formed a part of France proper. Only in Saudi Arabia was an independent Arab kingdom recognized. No sooner had the ink dried on the treaties than Arab nationalists began to contemplate how to undermine these imperialist arrangements. Their violent response to their sense of betrayal was understandable, their attacks on native Jews less so. Soon, the bitter anti-colonialist feelings were brought to bear upon Jews throughout the Arab world, including the community in Palestine.

By the 1930s several developments were discernible. For one thing, the British were ceding their colonial territories in return for treaties that would enable them to retain control of certain strategic sites. Thus, Iraq and Egypt gained independence, but the Suez Canal was still occupied. Secondly, the British commitment to the idea of a Jewish national home in Palestine was whittled down with the separation of Arab Transjordan from the Palestine mandate and the implementation of restrictions upon Jewish immigration and acquisition of land. Finally, an Arab rebellion against the British broke out in 1936, rocking Palestine for the next several years. Its moving spirit was the head of the Muslim Arab community, Hajj Amin el-Husseini, the mufti of Jerusalem. As the Second World War approached, he ignited the Arab masses with his pro-Nazi radio broadcasts. Such anti-Semitic Nazi propaganda as the *Protocols of the Elders of Zion,* a text originating in Tsarist Russia that proclaimed a Jewish conspiracy to dominate the world, was printed and reprinted throughout the Arab world. Arabic-language copies of Hitler's *Mein Kampf* (with the anti-Arab portions deleted) circulated freely as well. Meanwhile, the anti-British agitation was matched by mounting anti-French sentiment in North Africa and the Levant. In light of the pro-fascist convictions demonstrated by Arab nationalists, it was clearly in the interests of the native Jewish populations that the Western powers not weaken their grip in Arab countries. Muslims looking forward eagerly to their coming liberation envisioned new states in which citizenship would be founded upon Arab or Islamic identity. In other words, the passionate nationalist calls for independence gave Jews no cause for celebration. Indeed, they slowly began to realize that when Muslims eventually threw off the imperialist yoke, their own sojourn in the East would at last be over.

The interwar period was also marked by a decline in the Jewish position in the former Ottoman states of Europe as pro-fascist sentiments spread there as well. Hundreds of thousands of Sephardim could be found scattered throughout these territories—in Yugoslavia, Bulgaria, and Greece as well as the new Republic of Turkey—and nationalism in each of these successor states entailed sweeping cultural adjustments for Jews. Among the younger generation, Ladino was replaced by Greek in Salonika, by Bulgarian in Bulgaria. In Yugoslavia, Jews were caught in the middle of a mosaic of interwar nationalisms.

The older generation of Yugoslavia continued to speak and write Ladino, while younger Jews adopted Serbo-Croatian. In both Greece and Yugoslavia, two types of literature existed side by side: Jewish works in Ladino, and works written by Jews in the national language. Yet a third layer of identity also flourished in the Balkan region, a Hebraic identity sponsored by the spreading Zionist movement.

At the same time, the nationalist fervor that was mounting among the Arabs across the Mediterranean was echoed among Bulgars, Croats, Hungarians, Rumanians, Greeks, and Slovaks. Now, the negative historic attitudes developed toward Jews when each of these groups was still a minority under the Ottoman could be expressed openly. Throughout the interwar period, the offices of the *Alliance* were deluged with reports of assaults upon the Jews of southeastern Europe and requests for intercession, but they could do precious little to help.

When World War II broke out, the entire Jewish world faced probable death and certain devastation. In the Nazi scheme of things, no distinctions were drawn between Jews in the West and Jews in the East, between Ashkenazim and Sephardim: all were targeted for murder. The fate of individuals or groups of Jews was determined by geography, the nature of Nazi occupation, the degree of local cooperation with the Nazis, or sheer luck. Wherever the Germans ruled directly, as in Greece or Yugoslavia, the Sephardim suffered almost total annihilation. The 60,000 Jews of Salonika were deported to Auschwitz between March 14 and August 7, 1943, and only a handful survived. The Sephardim of Thrace, Macedonia, and the Ionian islands were totally destroyed. In Croatia and Serbia the German occupiers found local collaborators who eagerly facilitated their task of ridding the area of Jews. Even the Croatian church played a hand in implementing the "Final Solution."

The escape of the Jews of prewar Bulgaria is an exceptional case, a subscript to the tragic annals of the Holocaust.[19] Bulgaria, hesitant to become a full partner in the Axis, was reluctant to take irrevocable measures against the Jews. Throughout the war, in fact, the Bulgarians would regard their Jews as a "strategic commodity" to be traded for political gains. When German fortunes were in the ascendancy, Bulgarian Jews were massacred; when the tides of war turned, the killing stopped. Consequently, 50,000 of Bulgaria's Sephardim survived.

Like their Ashkenazic brethren, Sephardic Jews played a prominent role in the partisan movements of southeastern Europe. In contrast to Poland or the Ukraine, where partisans frequently refused to let Jews fight alongside them in the common battle against the Nazis, in Yugoslavia the Jews played an integral role in Tito's partisan units and found a haven in the regions they liberated. The Jews of Athens were sheltered in the countryside and welcomed into areas liberated by the Greek Resistance (EAM), which included a guerrilla band led by Rabbi Moses Pesah. Italian occupying forces stationed in the Athens area refused to comply with Nazi anti-Semitic policies. Obviously, levels of prewar anti-Semitism were a factor in determining where Jews would be sheltered and where they would be turned over for deportation and execution.

The moment war was declared in September 1939, Maghrebi Jews rallied to the cause of France, frantically volunteering to fight for their adopted fatherland. To their astonishment, the French rejected their help for fear of offending the native Muslims. The Vichy forces began to implement racial laws, confiscation, and ghettoization against Sephardim. The fall of France in June 1940 was greeted with shock and disbelief. Marcel Aboulker, a demobilized officer, described it as "a moral as well as a military disaster" for Jews. In Algeria, one of the most crushing blows to the Jews was the loss of French citizenship when the Crémieux Decree of 1870 was abrogated on October 7. The more than 150,000 Jews there suddenly faced the realization that the betrayal by France was total. In Algeria and also in Tunisia, Jews were conscripted in forced labor columns notorious for harshness, and ghettoization and confiscation of property were instituted.

In general, the Muslim authorities in North Africa had no choice but to go along with the harsh measures introduced by the Vichy French. Yet, even though the sultan of Morocco, Muhammad V, and Tunisia's ruler Munif Bey were not personally sympathetic to these measures, they did not actually attempt to thwart their implementation, as has been claimed in later popular legends and by some researchers. In sum, the Vichy occupation heaped misery on the Jews of the Maghreb for two years.

Following German occupation of Tunisia in November 1942, the condition of that country's 90,000 Jews went from bad to worse. Only the brevity of the occupation and distance from the railway lines of Europe saved them from certain destruction. Indeed, the Nazis were beginning to deport some communal leaders to concentration camps toward the end of the occupation. Further east, in Italian-held Libya, forced labor exacted a high toll in fatalities, and there were some deportations to Europe's death camps although geography, once again, saved the community from wholesale slaughter.

In Algiers on the night of November 7 1942, a daring Resistance operation was executed to prepare the way for the Allied landing. Two hundred Resistance fighters, 85 percent of them Jewish, cut the communications of the city under the leadership of José Aboulker, son of Professor Henri Aboulker, a lay leader of the Algerian Jewish community. The entire operation had been planned in his home.[20] Much to the shock of the Jewish community, the Resistance leaders, including both Aboulkers, were rounded up and kept in prison in central Algeria for months while the anti-Semitic Vichy officials were retained in office under American protection. In November of the previous year, U.S. consul Felix Cole had advised his government against intervening on behalf of the 150,000 Algerian Jews on the grounds that "such a policy would almost entirely alienate the active and passive sympathy now felt by the Algerians of French nationality for the great democratic powers and thus provide an additional obstacle to the anti-German cause."[21] Liberation thus represented a bitter disappointment and realization for the Jews in French North Africa. The hostility of France was unapologetic; American assistance was belated, materializing only after considerable pressure had been exerted by Jews in the United States. Little wonder that the eloquent Memmi would be moved to express the disillusionment of his generation:

> It was the painful and astounding treason . . . of a civilization in which I had placed all my hopes and which I ardently admired. . . . I was all the more hurt in my pride because I had been so uncautious in my complete surrender to my faith in Europe.[22]

The shocking events of the twentieth century shattered the faith in the West that had characterized so much of the modern Jewish experience. The many efforts that had formerly been expended on behalf of French education, religious reformation, community restructuring, and assimilation could not survive the impact of the betrayals and the horror of the Second World War. As the war ended and the terrible toll of destruction of Jews became apparent, isolated stragglers returned to Greece to find that the Sephardic "Jerusalem" in Salonika had been destroyed. Even the most deeply rooted community of the Arab world, the Jews of Iraq, could not overcome the disillusionment and sense of insecurity produced by wartime events. Deeply etched in their memory was the recollection that the pro-Nazi mufti of Jerusalem had been given asylum in Iraq and that the Iraqi government of Rashid Ali had been in close contact with Berlin. Still worse was the shock when a pogrom on June 1, 1941, took the lives of 179 Jews while British troops stood by. It was "simply" an Arab rampage and the British didn't want to get involved and lend their support to the regent. During this incident, known afterward as the *farhud,* women were raped, babies were smashed in front of their parents or thrown into wells, pregnant women were mutilated, and Torahs and synagogues were desecrated.[23]

This had happened in Iraq, not in Nazi-occupied Europe. And now that the colonial powers began to implement their postwar commitments to leave the Muslim world, the simmering anti-Jewish and anti-Zionist feelings exploded. The millennial Sephardic diaspora was coming to a violent and dramatic end.

9
Revival and Return
Sephardic Jews in the Post-War Era

In the cemetery of Bagneaux, département de la Seine, rests my mother. In Old Cairo, in the cemetery of sand, my father. In Milano, in the dead marble city, my sister is buried. In Rome where the dark dug out the ground to receive him, my brother lies. Four graves. Three countries. Does death know borders? One family. Two continents. Four cities. Three flags. One language: of nothingness. One pain. Four glances in one. Four lives.

—Edmond Jabes, *Return to the Book*

The scope of the Holocaust had hardly been assessed, much less comprehended or psychologically absorbed, before the Jewish world was once more confronted with upheaval and massive immigration. Everywhere, the handful of survivors were straining to leave the bloodstained lands of Europe, joining in an irrepressible wave of immigration that pressed against the gates of Palestine, which had been closed by Great Britain.

The massive destruction of the Jewish communities of France, Holland, Italy, and Germany had obliterated the European Sephardic population centers. Approximately 1,600,000 Jews in the Balkans, 10 percent of them Sephardic, came under German control during the war. The fate of thousands more in the region, who were subjected to Italian control, oscillated with the course of the war—between Italian efforts at protection and Germany's zealous prodding to destroy them. Tens of thousands were murdered outright: 7,000 in Sarajevo, 60,000 in Greece, 6,000 to 7,000 in Thrace, and thousands more in Albania, Rumania, and Hungary. Nor did the Jews on the islands of Rhodes (2,200), Crete (300), Corfu (2,000), and Zante (300) escape deportation and annihilation.[1] Only the Jewish community of Old Bulgaria was spared destruction. Together with the 100,000 Jews of neutral Turkey, the 50,000 Bulgarian Jews formed the last remnant of the once far-flung Sephardic diaspora of southeastern Europe.

Stragglers who returned to Greece or Yugoslavia from the death camps or emerged from their hideouts at the end of the war discovered that their communities were gone and—in the case of Greece—their history annihilated. Even their great cemetery wasn't spared total destruction. No remnant of their glorious past was left intact. Especially devastating was the blow to the "Jerusalem of the Balkans," for all the Jews of Salonika had been deported to Auschwitz and Treblinka between March and May of 1943. So horrendous was the thousand-mile cattle-car journey of their deportation that most, unable to pass the initial selections upon entry to the death camps, were murdered upon arrival. The majority had undoubtedly begun the trip in very poor health after being subjected to crippling labor columns and starvation in the Baron de Hirsch barracks in the city during the especially harsh winter of 1941–42. The Greek Jews of Macedonia and Thrace, provinces that had come under Bulgarian sovereignty in 1941 when Greece was divided between Germany, Italy, and Bulgaria, were also destroyed. And the lustrous Serbian community was gone, for the most part asphyxiated in gas vans on Yugoslav soil.

The one million Sephardic Jews of the Islamic world survived the war badly shaken by the years of persecution but still intact, their casualties limited by the turning tide of battle. Within only a few years, however, their ancient communities would be abruptly, totally uprooted. When martial law was eased, anti-Jewish violence exploded, reaching crisis proportions in 1947 when the United Nations voted to partition Palestine into a Jewish state and an Arab state. Even though no Jewish community in the Arab countries had taken part in the restoration of Jewish life in Palestine—indeed, they had frequently been required to issue repudiations of Zionism along with fervent declarations of loyalty to their countries—they became the target of the frustrated Arab mobs. In Libya in 1945, anti-Jewish rioters stormed into the community, crying *jihad fil kuffar* ("holy war against the infidels"), killing 130 Jews in three days. "From a historian's perspective," one researcher has concluded, "the deep and decisive significance of the 1945 pogroms is that a radical change took place not only in Arab-Jewish relations but in the relation of the Jews to Libya itself."[2]

The impact of these riots was similarly assessed by one director of the *Alliance Israélite Universalle:*

> An unprecedented blow has been dealt to the Jews' sense of security and any illusions they had for taking initiatives: there is terror, poverty, disease, and suffering, without a glimmer of hope to brighten the dark future. Should they go away? If so, how? And where?[3]

Both the traditional and the modernized sectors of Libya's 35,000 Jews were irreparably shaken. They saw that British colonial administrators were either unable or unwilling to protect their defenseless communities and went before the UN Security Council to protest that their situation was "unbearable materially, economically, as well as morally."[4] Meanwhile, similar scenarios were being repeated across the Arab world. By and large, colonial administrators merely stood by as Jews were attacked by Arab mobs.

It was already apparent that there would be no place for Jews in the new Arab nationalist states emerging in the post-colonial period. Not surprisingly, therefore, when the British lifted their exit restrictions on Jews in February 1949, approximately 8,000 Jews in Tripoli alone rushed to sign up for visas to Palestine. Similarly, when Iraq temporarily lifted such restrictions in March 1950, registration for emigration was frantic, even though the once-affluent Iraqi Jews were permitted to leave with nothing but the clothes on their backs. Already that year, the community had been terrified by bombings of synagogues and other Jewish sites, show trials and public hangings of prominent leaders in the community, and the dismissal of all Jews from government employment. In a dramatic clandestine escape through Iran, the approximately 125,000 Iraqi Jews emigrated *en masse* to Israel.

In 1960, Algeria's 150,000 Jews chose emigration to France when an incendiary wave of anti-Jewish violence accompanied the colony's independence. As the colonialist chapter of Middle Eastern history came to an end, it was clear that the fate of Jews everywhere in Muslim lands, once the "protective" presence of European troops disappeared, was unpredictable.

Some departures for Palestine were organized, others haphazard. In Yemen, where Britain opposed emigration, a tent city outside Aden became clogged with sick refugees who had walked barefoot hundreds of miles across the desert to escape. This and other pressures on London became so relentless that Israel was allowed to operate an airlift rescue operation (code-named "Operation on Wings of Eagles" in a phrase from Exodus 19:4 but later renamed "Operation Magic Carpet") that transported almost the entire community of 45,000 Jews on 430 flights between June 1949, and September 1950. In Egypt, by contrast, departures ebbed and flowed as each new Arab-Israeli war brought about temporary lifting of restrictions upon emigration. In this cycle, a new conflict would become the catalyst for new attacks upon Jewish property, the taking of Jewish lives, or the imprisonment of thousands of Jewish males. Sustained foreign pressure was necessary to effect the release of such prisoners and gain permission for the emigration of these penniless refugees. Ultimately, the entire Egyptian community numbering approximately 80,000 was dispersed in stages—first in 1948, and again in 1956, 1967, and 1973—scattering to France, Italy, Israel, and North America. The story of the unraveling of each community in former colonial lands varied, depending upon local conditions, but all were eventually caught in the crossfire between colonialism and independence.

Between 1948 and 1951, it seemed as if the entire Sephardic world was on the move toward their ancient homeland, as Israel evacuated community after community by means of emergency flights, clandestine voyages by sea, and secret overland treks. In 1956, after a brief lull, this mass emigration from Muslim lands resumed on the heels of the

Sinai campaign. During the 1960s the large communities of the Maghreb were dismantled. Most of Algeria's 150,000 Jews emigrated to France, Tunisia's Jewish population of 110,000 departed for France or Israel, and Morocco's 286,000 Jews, the last community to depart, left in stages, the majority going to Israel. The fate of a Sephardic community bore no relation to whether it was Zionist, non-Zionist, or anti-Zionist. When Morocco's King Mohammed V and Tunisia's President Habib Bourguiba tried to reassure their loyal Jewish citizens as independence approached in 1956, the Muslim masses had other ideas. Wide-scale looting and arson spoke with a louder voice than either the aging monarch or the nationalist leader.

The Syrian community alone did not succeed in emigrating *in toto*. Most of its members had managed to escape in the aftermath of violence that had erupted against them in the late 1940s, but a remnant of 4,000 to 5,000 was entrapped and held hostage in a ghetto-like setting in Damascus, where they were housed amidst hostile Palestinian neighbors and held accountable for the flight of any of their number. Clandestine escape attempts frequently ended in blackmail or murder at the hands of the smugglers who had agreed to assist. Occasionally, Jews were arrested and executed on charges of helping Israel or accused either of Zionist activity or of engaging in illegal attempts to emigrate. Efforts at intercession by American presidents and French premiers over the decades were unavailing; similarly, pressures from international human rights groups upon the ruling *junta* in Damascus fell on deaf ears. Only after the demise of the Soviet Union, Syria's major patron and arms provider, did President Assad apparently decide to use his entrapped community as a bargaining chip to win rewards from other nations. It appears that this community has now quietly begun to emigrate, joining their brethren who earlier settled in New York.

Today, to all intents and purposes, Jewish life in Muslim lands has ended. The Sephardim of the great diaspora of the East are concentrated in three major areas: approximately one million in Israel, another 300,000 to 400,000 in France (coming from North Africa and Egypt), and perhaps a quarter of a million in North America (approximately 200,000 in the United States, 50,000 in Canada). In addition, smaller numbers have found asylum in Italy. In the East, only remnants survive: perhaps 25,000 in Turkey, and a diminishing community of 15,000 in Morocco. Finally, there is again an organized community in Spain, a symbolic postscript to the long Sephardic journey.

In the centuries following the expulsion, the legend arose that the Jews had placed a solemn ban (*herem*) on ever setting foot in Spain again. Historically unfounded, the legend aptly reflects the bitterness Jews felt about their rejection in Iberia as well as the continuing strict prohibition against Jewish settlement there lasting for centuries, and reiterated by the King as late as 1816. The occasional Jewish merchant or traveler who crossed the borders did so at his own risk and, as we have seen, might pay for his folly at the stake. Virtually all traces of the Hispanic Jewish past were obliterated as cemeteries disappeared and synagogues were converted into churches. As the modern era dawned in the West, Spain had become a backwater to the great events of the day, isolated both from its own past and the rest of contemporary Europe.

As early as the seventeenth century, there were tentative discussions about readmitting the Jews in order to bolster the Iberian economy. The proposal was resoundingly rejected, for Jews were feared as much as Freemasons, Protestants, and freethinkers. Only after the Holy Office of the Inquisition was finally abolished by Royal Decree on July 15, 1834, were proponents of readmission able to be heard. That is not to say that the forces of reaction did not continue to dominate nineteenth-century Spanish life; indeed, as late as 1850, professing Jews were prohibited from traveling through the country. Still, as Jews in other parts of Europe began to call for a reversal of policy, there were organized attempts to bring about readmission.

One of the most eloquent arguments was voiced in a petition in 1854 by Ludwig Philippson, the leader of German Jewry:

> We do not come to demand the estates that were taken from our fathers, to demand restitution for the inestimable goods of which they were robbed, not even to recover the ancient temples which were once our hallowed sanctuaries and whose battlements can still be seen. . . . We come only to blot out our disgrace of banishment, to obtain free entry to those of our faith who may wish it. It will not cost you anything except one word, but a word most dear, for it is a word of love, humanity, justice, civilization.[5]

Rabbi Philippson's appeal inspired comment and thoughtful discussion in Spanish intellectual circles, but the time was not yet ripe for a renunciation of the nation's Catholic unity in favor of religious liberty and tolerance.

In 1868, on the heels of a revolution that toppled the reactionary monarchy of Queen Isabella, a republic was established in Spain. When its first president, Emilio Castelar, denounced religious intolerance, the Sephardim of neighboring Bordeaux and Bayonne felt encouraged to petition him:

> We, the descendants of ancient Jewish families from Spain and Portugal, who fled to France as a result of the persecution [of 1492]. . . . Our chief desire is to pay homage to the generous *élan* which has led you to proclaim the sacred principle of religious liberty. Anticipating that the nation, through its constitutional Cortes, will be able to give this principle solemn and enduring expression, we respectfully address ourselves to the Executive Power which has taken the initiative in revoking all restrictions, and we beseech you to complete your work by repealing the Edict of 1492 which doomed the Jews of Spain to exile.
>
> Our fathers labored during many centuries for the prosperity and glory of Spain. Outlawed, they took to France, England, Holland, the Spanish civilization, language and literature, and it seems fair to say that in these countries their descendants enjoy standing that does honor to the ancient homeland. . . .
>
> Our request is not that of an interested party. We are French citizens, and shall never wish to leave a fatherland to which we have become attached by three centuries of protection. . . .
>
> In addressing ourselves to you, our sole purpose is to discharge a pious duty toward the revered memory of our ancestors.[6]

In response, after an impassioned parliamentary debate on freedom of religion, the Cortes declared in Article XI of the Constitution of 1869 that, while Catholicism was the religion of the state, "No one shall be molested or persecuted on Spanish soil for his political opinions nor for his particular form of worship so long as he keeps within the bounds of Christian morality, but no other ceremonies, and no other public manifestations than those of the religion of the state shall be permitted." The new constitution went still farther: "The nation undertakes to maintain the worship and ministers of the Catholic religion. The exercise in private or public of any other religion is guaranteed to all foreigners resident in Spain without any further limitation than the universal rules of morality and law."[7] (Jews were included in the category of "foreigners.")

In the decades that followed, Jews and other non-Catholic foreigners won the right to obtain naturalization under specific conditions (e.g., through marriage to a Spanish Catholic woman, the rendering of special services to the state, the establishment of an important factory). But Spanish society was deeply divided on the issue of religious freedom. Liberal and moderate monarchists who upheld the principles of toleration and Jewish repatriation vied for influence with powerful opposition forces among the clergy and pro-monarchists who counseled the restoration of religious unity.

As the Spanish political climate of opinion began shifting toward greater liberalism, a trickle of Jews began to filter back into the country, forming an inconspicuous community in Seville. But in 1903, the issue of legal admissibility received an unexpected boost from Dr. Angel Pulido, a respected physician and liberal senator who represented the University of Salamanca in the Cortes. On a cruise down the Danube, he was astonished and profoundly moved by meeting the Sephardim of the Balkans, who told him in Ladino about their far-flung diaspora. Afterward, he eloquently described for others these "Spaniards without a Fatherland" and evoked visions of how the half million Sephardim scattered across the globe could return and resuscitate Spain. To Dr. Pulido, this would be a singular opportunity to "resurrect some of Spain's greatness," now that her Empire in the Pacific and the New World was lost. Spaniards were not excited by this prospect, and neither were the Sephardim, for Theodor Herzl had already issued a call to return to Zion that resounded throughout Europe. While some former friends accused Pulido of being descended from Jews, he continued his campaign into the 1920s, largely ignored and with no appreciable results. Later, his ideas would reach a wider audience. Two works he wrote to buttress his arguments—*Los Israelítas españoles y el idioma castellano* (*Spanish Jews and the Castilian Language*) and *Españoles sin patria y la raza sefardí* (*Spaniards without a Homeland and the Sephardic Race*)—still provide valuable details on the Sephardic dispersion in the 1920s. Even in his day, cultural interest in Judaism as distinct from support for the return of Jews was growing, as indicated in 1915 by the appointment of the noted Jewish orientalist Dr. Abraham Shalom Yahuda, to the newly established professorship of Rabbinic Language and Literature at the University of Madrid. (Opposition at the university was so bitter, however, that he ultimately abandoned the post.)

In 1923, Spain signed a peace treaty with Turkey, and the capitulations treaties, which had enabled the European powers to place Ottoman non-Muslim subjects under their protection, were dissolved. The question now arose about the future of people under Spain's tutelage but lacking Spanish citizenship, such as the Sephardim. In December 1924, Madrid announced that "all individuals of Spanish origin" who were "already enjoying protection by the diplomatic agents of Spain as if they were Spaniards" could acquire full civil and political rights. They need only present their credentials before their nearest Spanish consular representative within the following six years (i.e., by December 31, 1930). Several thousand Sephardim in the Balkans and Central Europe took advantage of this opportunity. Possession of Spanish papers would become vital during the relentless roundups and deportations of the 1940s.

During the 1930s, many Jews fleeing Germany found their way to Spain. By 1936 the Spanish Jewish population reached 6,000, but following the chaos and fear that descended upon Madrid and Barcelona at the outbreak of the Spanish Civil War, many fled. Some unfortunates returned to Germany, only to be immediately imprisoned. The collapse of the Spanish Republic and the outbreak of World War II ushered in a period of profound uncertainty for the Jews of Spain as General Franco vacillated between nonbelligerence and loyalty to the Axis countries. By 1943, as the tide of war was turning against Germany, Franco took a neutral stance and it became possible for the Allies to encourage Spain to act on behalf of Jewish lives. Down to the present, the story of Spain's checkered rescue efforts has been distorted for political reasons. The truth about her actions provides a parameter of Spanish ambivalence toward Sephardic nationals.

In the first stages of the war, while Franco was trying to remain within the Axis camp but also pursue an independent policy, the Spanish Ministry of Education inaugurated an Institute of Hebrew Studies (Escuela de Estudios Hebraicos) in Madrid for the purpose of exploring the nation's Sephardic legacy. While seemingly innocuous, the establishment of such an institute, along with its scientific journal *Sefarad,* was a statement of some political significance, articulating an interest in the "gracious and noble Sephardim" entwined with the national heritage, as distinct from the Ashkenazim. Yet even as the study of Spain's Jewish legacy was recognized as legitimate, the rescue of Jewish lives was to be problematic. This distinction between Jewish culture and the bearers of that culture has continued to mark the policies of Spain.

During the war, the country confronted the Jewish question

head-on in two arenas. First, there was the provision of a temporary refuge for Jews fleeing Axis-occupied Europe. But tens of thousands of these refugees would be unsuccessful in trying to enter Spain. When Madrid was confronted with a potentially massive immigration problem after the fall of France, her reaction to Jewish refugees was extremely negative: those without proper papers were barred entry and turned back at the borders, imprisoned as they crossed, or, at best, hastily pushed through Spain to Portugal and North Africa. One of the most famous refugees rejected in this way at the Franco-Spanish border in 1940 was Walter Benjamin, a German Jewish philosopher widely acknowledged posthumously as one of the foremost literary critics of the twentieth century. He took his life in despair at not gaining permission to pass through Spain. From the outset, the country had adopted a policy of granting the temporary papers for such passage only sparingly.

Second, there was the entirely separate issue of the safety of foreign Jews who carried valid Spanish passports. During the harrowing years of Nazi occupation, a Spanish passport provided one of the few possible means of escaping Hitler's Final Solution. But Spain decided to make repatriation of one group of such refugees contingent upon evacuation of another, so that the country would never hold more than a few thousand Jews at any one time. This policy was inflexibly pursued throughout the war. In addition, the number of Jews who carried Spanish papers was quite small, not much more than 4,000.[8] During the entire World War II period, no more than 800 persons with Spanish citizenship were repatriated to Spain.

On April 9, 1941, when the Germans entered Salonika, there were 511 Spanish nationals among the Jews of the city (according to a list drawn up on German orders a year later). Their fate provides an interesting subtext to the larger story of the Holocaust. The case of Salonika presented Spain's government with a test of its responsibility for the Sephardic Jews who carried Spanish papers. During the fateful months of 1942, the Nazi murder machinery was in full gear in occupied Europe. Deportations of Jews from every corner of the continent were fueling the crematories in Poland. Even as these millions were being annihilated, the fate of the Sephardim in Salonika with Spanish passports became the subject of long and tedious negotiations between Madrid and Berlin. When Spain asked that her nationals not be deported to Poland, the Nazis, though resolute in clearing Greece of Jews, devised an interim solution for the 367 Jews with Spanish passports who were still under direct German control. (Some 150 had escaped from Salonika to Athens in the Italian military zone.) They were held aside throughout the months of deportations until August 2, 1943, when they were shipped to Bergen-Belsen in Germany. Upon their arrival on August 13, they were held separately in special quarters to keep them from seeing the horrors, in case Spain should repatriate them. In the prolonged negotiations that followed, Madrid refused to accept these Jews in groups larger than twenty-five and wanted assurances that other Jewish detainees who had arrived from Paris the same month would first be removed from Spanish soil. Repatriation was thus excruciatingly protracted. The first group, which arrived in Spain in February 1944, were cared for by the American Jewish Joint Distribution Committee, then transferred in June to Casablanca before being taken to Palestine. As Allied troops approached Bergen-Belsen on April 6 of the following year, the German commanders and guards placed the Spanish nationals still awaiting repatriation together with 2,200 other prisoners on railroad cars that wandered aimlessly through Germany until the Americans finally rescued them, more dead than alive. Among those Jews bearing Spanish passports who survived the death camp were several members of the Abrabanel family who live now in Israel.

In the meantime, the 150 Spanish nationals who had made it to Italian-occupied Athens faced imminent destruction. As Spain procrastinated, Jürgen Stroop (the general responsible for the destruction of the Warsaw Ghetto) took over Jewish deportations in Athens on the orders of Adolph Eichmann. He had all foreign Jews arrested. While Spain continued to maintain that she could not save one group of Jews until another had left her soil, the Spanish Jews in Athens disappeared, presumably because they were sent to Auschwitz. Consequently, not even this small number of Spanish nationals holding proper papers was repatriated. The records clearly reveal that Spain's humanitarian words were never matched by deeds. To be sure, her consuls who actually saw the horrors being perpetrated within the occupied zone tried their utmost to help but met with continuous bureaucratic stalling in Madrid. Those who became too zealous, like Julio Palencia, consul in Bulgaria, were forced to relinquish their posts.

Even so, the myth that Spain worked diligently to rescue Jews is still alive, fueled by official circles and by the outside world's faulty memory. Consider the following boast in a pamphlet produced by the Spanish government in 1949:

Spain, imbued with its universal Christian spirit of love for all the races on earth, contributed to the rescue of Jews, and acted more for spiritual than for merely legal or political reasons. Our government's aid was extended not only to Spanish Jews dispersed throughout the continent, but also whenever the opportunity presented itself, to all Jews irrespective of their nationality or their place of residence.[9]

In fact, the number of stateless Jews allowed refuge at any given moment in Spain never exceeded 2,000. The nation actually protected only its nationals, and even them with some hesitations and delays. In many cases, the government claimed the property of nationals sent to Auschwitz. Spain quite strictly defined who could be helped; when the Sephardic Jews of France sought protection, they were refused. The argument frequently made that Spain provided transit visas in many cases during the first years of the war rings somewhat hollow, especially since the Nazis often did so too during that period. But Spain's record of diplomatic protection was better with Jews who did not need actual repatriation. In the final hours of the Hungarian Jews' agony in 1944, after prodding by the United States, Spain protected 2,795 of them. Scholars have estimated that the number of Jews saved through Spanish diplomatic intercession in Bulgaria, Greece, Hungary, and Rumania was 3,235 out of a total Jewish population of almost two million in that region (including 160,000 Sephardim).

By the end of World War II, only 600 Jews remained in Spain, and movement toward religious toleration in the postwar period was slow. In the Statute of the Spanish People (*Fuero de los Españols*) promulgated July 17, 1945, Catholicism was declared the official religion. All others were to be private. The law of May 17, 1958, that defined the Principles of the National Movement went even further, terming Catholicism the "very essence and singularity of the Spanish people and state." Only in 1965 did General Franco even hint at the possibility of extending the rights of non-Catholics.

But Vatican II paved the way for a new relationship between Spain and the Jewish people. Finally, in December 1968, the Spanish government issued a statement granting full recognition to the Hebrew Congregation of Madrid, and the edict of expulsion was revoked. After the ceremonial opening of the first officially sanctioned synagogue in more than 600 years, several significant symbolic gestures followed. When Jews were imprisoned in Egypt during the Six-Day War of 1967, Spain adopted a visible role in arranging for their release. In 1976, Queen Sophie paid a visit to the Madrid synagogue, accompanied by the auxiliary bishop of the city and the leaders of the Spanish Reformed, Baptist, Lutheran, and Mormon churches. Finally, in May 1978, a new Spanish constitution was ratified that guaranteed "freedom of ideology, religion, and worship for individuals and communities" and declared that "there shall be no State religion" (Article XVI).

Today, the Jewish community in Spain remains small and inconspicuous, but its 20,000 souls, concentrated principally in Barcelona and Madrid, are conscious of their role as guardians of a glorious past. The members of the handful of congregations derive predominantly from refugees from Morocco and Argentina. In preparation for the commemorative events of 1992, a few of the extant Sephardic monuments have been restored, and the Sephardic museum of Toledo has been refurbished. Several Spanish scholars have made it their life's work to retrieve the Sephardic past from oblivion, and the volume of fine scholarship on Sephardic civilization produced in Spain keeps growing. For the Spanish people, the ultimate sign of recognition of Sephardic involvement in the national culture was the bestowal in 1991 of the Asturias Prize, the country's highest honor, upon the Sephardic diaspora. But for many observers, it was Spain's eventual recognition of the State of Israel in January 1986, that closed a circle and began a reconciliation between two peoples.

Immediately after World War II, it would have been difficult to anticipate that France would soon be dotted with dozens of new Jewish communities or would become the largest Sephardic settlement outside Israel. The native community, traumatized by the horrors of the conflict, was haunted by memories of Vichy collaboration with Nazism and by the zealous participation of the French gendarmerie in the roundups and deportations. One hundred thousand French Jews had not returned from Auschwitz and the other death camps. Still, two-thirds of the community had survived.

By the mid-1950s French Jewry was undergoing a challenging test and quickening revival as Jews from North Africa began to seek asylum in metropolitan France in the closing days of French colonialism in the Maghreb. Moroccan, Tunisian, and Algerian independence brought waves of refugees eager to rebuild their lives and their cultural institutions. The Sephardim of North Africa were a youthful community,

French-speaking and fairly traditional in religious practices. Thus their influx into France in hundreds of thousands caused a veritable revolution as French Jewry assumed a North African Sephardic coloration. Areas of France that had been devoid of Jewish settlement for centuries suddenly became home to new communities. The number of Jews rose from approximately 250,000 to around 600,000 between 1945 and 1970. In the 1970s, a new Jewish activism could be discerned throughout the country. Symbolic of the transformation of French Jewry, René Samuel Sirat, born in the Algerian seaport of Boné, was elected chief rabbi in 1981.

One of the most fascinating developments of postwar French Jewry has been the emergence of a new Jewish political style. Previously, the Ashkenazic majority of the community, having painfully learned that France was not receptive of ethnicity, had avoided confrontational politics and all overt expressions of ethnic or religious particularism. But the vocal, Zionist-oriented newcomers, coming from families that had divided between Israel and France, instinctively adopted a more nationalistic, high-profile manner, demanding that the established Jewish community respond to their interests. They also required more Jewish institutions—kosher butchers, schools, cultural outlets—and sought to provide them by strengthening the community's organizational infrastructure.

During the course of the 1960s French foreign policy began to tilt markedly toward the Arabs. Finally, five months after the Six-Day War, on November 27, 1967, in a press conference replete with racial generalizations, President de Gaulle called the Jews an "elite," "domineering," and "self-assured people," using old anti-Semitic stereotypes to justify his abandonment of France's traditional ties with Israel. He linked Israeli policies and Jews in general with a tendency to "aggression" and gave a green light to Jew-baiting, claiming that Jews provoked anti-Semitism by their wealth and influence and were buying support for Israel through their domination of the press. De Gaulle's astounding remarks included a charge of dual loyalty. His successor, Georges Pompidou, made further declarations casting doubt upon the loyalty of French Jews. Perhaps not coincidentally, France was exempted from the 1973 Arab oil embargo, while its government implied that Israel was to blame for the boycott.

In March 1979, several people were killed in an assault on a Jewish student restaurant in Paris. In May 1980, *Le Monde* charged French Jews with treason. Finally, on October 3, 1980, on the festival of Simhat

Torah, unknown assailants bombed the Liberal synagogue on rue Copernic in Paris. When it turned out that three of the four fatalities in the attack were not Jewish, Prime Minister Raymond Barre expressed his regret, noting that the terrorists "intended to kill Jews, but wound up killing innocent Frenchmen instead."

The accumulation of these verbal and physical assaults on the Jews of France led to a new courage in the community. The former timidity of the old French Jewish leadership was discarded, and in April 1980, a massive pro-Israel rally was held in Paris. There, a new movement of French Jewish political activists, *Renouveau Juif* (Jewish Renewal) called for changes in strategies of Jewish behavior, denouncing as politically bankrupt both the assimilationist old ways and the universalist pieties of the "notables" of the traditional leadership. In this vein, they berated the old guard of the chief Jewish organization, the *Fonds Socials Juifs Unifiés,* challenging its Rothschild leadership to cede power to the new (Sephardic) generation. Indeed, in October 1980, the new mentality was clearly echoed in comments by Baron Alain de Rothschild, the embodiment of "old guard" leadership, after the rue Copernic bombing. He vowed publicly that Jews would never again fall into a state of "inferiority, submission, and fear."

The very concept of Jews thus asserting ethnic particularism was novel to French politics, but it should be recalled that the previous decade had seen rising social acceptance of *le droit à la différence* (the right to be different). It is perhaps not accidental that the return to Jewish heritage in France coincided with both a wider challenge to the French national tradition of cultural centralization and a new consciousness of the legitimacy of pluralism. Of equal importance was the appearance of a talented group of young thinkers of North African origin, most notably Bernard-Henri Lévy and Shmuel Trigano, who called for a return to Jewish sources so that Jews could reenter history on their own ethical foundations. Not surprisingly, one of the major themes of these intellectuals has been the rejection of the assimilationist ideologies that were so deeply ingrained in the history of French Jewish emancipation.

The Jewish revival promoted by the movement *Renouveau Juif* was further stimulated by regionalist revival movements. In 1977 President Giscard d'Estaing had declared, in a statement diametrically opposed to the tenets of the French Revolution, that there was no longer a contradiction between the aspiration to be considered a full-fledged French citizen and the desire to perpetuate one's ancestral traditions (*le droit à la différence* encapsulated this change of attitude). In addition, anti-Semitism from both the Left and the Right, along with the government-sponsored anti-Israel campaign, played a role in reversing the trends of assimilation that had followed the end of the war.[10]

Despite the verve and commitment of the activists, however, the resulting proliferation of Jewish publications, lectures, Jewish Studies courses and organized debates, and the renewal of religious practices and greater observance of *kashrut* has given new self-awareness and a new voice to only a minority of the community. The majority have moved completely out of the orbit of Judaism through intermarriage and nonaffiliation. Perhaps 82 percent of French Jewish children receive no Hebrew education whatsoever.

Thus, France's community of approximately 600,000 souls remains divided by the two contrasting trends. On the one hand, the new vitality, increased militancy, and high profile of *Renouveau Juif* are evident in the presence of highly ideological Jewish radio stations in Paris, each reflecting a heated point of view, and in the mass demonstrations against the Right, to protest cemetery desecrations, or on behalf of Israel. On the other hand, intermarriage is on the rise and communal institutions are endemically weak.

Observers of the contemporary scene are struck by the rich contribution of the Sephardic majority in all areas of French life, especially in the arts, philosophy, medicine, and finance. The uprooting of the Sephardim has become the literary motif and source of creative inspiration of the writers Albert Memmi, Albert Solal-Cohen, and Edmund Jabes (d. 1991). Indeed, Sephardic exile has been transformed into a universal metaphor for the modern postwar period of cultural deracination. It is impossible to predict which trend—the particularistic or the universalist—will prevail in this complex community. But one thing is certain: the Sephardic presence has modified generations of political behavior and challenged the long-cherished assumptions of the Jews of France.

Although the first American synagogues and organized communities were founded in the seventeenth and eighteenth centuries by Jews from Spain and Portugal, they never exceeded a few thousand people *in toto*. By contrast, in the nineteenth and twentieth centuries, the vast majority of Jewish immigrants were Ashkenazim, coming first from Germany (until the late 1870s), then from eastern Europe. Throughout this period, the major wave of synagogue and institution building was an Ashkenazic endeavor, and the Sephardic presence remained virtually invisible. But while the small Sephardic community had little in common with the massive influx of traditional, penniless Jews from eastern Europe, their sympathies lay with these refugees. It was the spectacle of this Ashkenazic immigration that inspired one Sephardic poet, Emma Lazarus, to compose her famous poem inscribed upon the Statue of Liberty, "The New Colossus."

Not until the early part of the twentieth century did Sephardic Jews again begin to gravitate to America. Most of these prewar immigrants, impelled to flee Balkan upheavals in the last days of Ottoman decline, came from Greece, Rhodes, Turkey (Anatolia), and Syria, with smaller numbers originating in Palestine or North Africa. In sum, according to U.S. government sources, 25,591 Sephardim from Muslim lands entered the United States between 1899 and 1925, a flyspeck among the more than one million Jewish immigrants arriving at the time.[11] With the adoption of the Immigration Act of 1924, which introduced a quota system based upon national origin, most Sephardic immigration was cut off. The majority of the Sephardim would settle in New York, but a few adventuresome souls moved on to found Sephardic congregations in Rochester, Detroit, Atlanta, Birmingham, Los Angeles, San Francisco, Portland, and Seattle. In addition, some were settled intentionally outside New York by the Industrial Removal Office, a Jewish organization that sought to disperse immigrants and thus relieve pressures on the city. This handful of Arabic- and Ladino-speaking Jews provided the founding corps of today's American Sephardic dispersion.

The newcomers faced special difficulties. They were not only penniless but also unskilled. Unlike the Ashkenazim, who flocked to the garment industry, the Sephardim were predominantly peddlers, grocers, bootblacks, and fruit vendors. They did not speak Yiddish, the language of the majority of the Jewish immigrants. Jewish relief agencies frequently did not understand their culture or even identify them as Jews at Ellis Island.

Much of the resettlement burden fell to America's premier Sephardic congregation, Shearith-Israel, the Spanish and Portuguese synagogue of New York. While the congregation and its sisterhood provided laudable assistance through its Oriental Committee and the settlement house it operated for Sephardim on the Lower East Side, the aristocratic old-timers had little in common socially and culturally with the immigrants from the Levant and were concerned that these new-comers from Muslim lands would also be considered Sephardic. Iron-ically, many of the Turkish immigrants were lineal descendants of the exiles of 1492, while most of the congregation of Shearith-Israel, the name notwithstanding, were Ashkenazic. Yet even though issues of pride and independence cropped up in the dealings between the two dissimilar groups, the congregation provided many needed services rit-ually and in helping the unskilled arrivals find employment.

At first, only the coffeehouses frequented by Sephardic men pro-vided some avenue of sociability and escape for the hard-pressed im-migrants from the Levant, but soon they formed social clubs and societies based upon geographic origins. While it was true that all immigrant groups tended at first to divide along such lines, Sephardim kept to these divisions much longer, despite repeated efforts in the 1920s to form a federated organization. In 1941, the Sephardim did succeed in establishing the Central Sephardic Jewish Community of America, an umbrella organization for the sharply divided community.

The new emigrants could also find help in the Ladino press that was soon flourishing in New York, for newspapers like *La Vara* (1922–48) and *La America* (1910–23) provided advice, comfort, and news of long-lost relatives. Like the Yiddish press, they also served as an instrument for Americanization, offering practical guides to acculturation and help-ing the immigrant generation gain an understanding of the new world in which they found themselves. Unfortunately, the Judeo-Spanish press would be a victim of its own success, ceasing publication in 1948 after most of its readership had become Americanized.

Only the Syrian Sephardim, who mainly hailed directly from Syria, were able to create a network of institutions that formed a comprehen-sive community. Most of them had originated from Aleppo, the largest wave coming between 1911 and 1920. They settled together in one neigh-borhood of Brooklyn, New York, and their community was later joined by about 10,000 Jews from Egypt. Over the years, they have risen above their modest origins and now form an affluent, closely knit community numbering approximately 35,000, including many prosperous business-men and some professionals. They tend to marry among themselves or within the greater Syrian community of Mexico City or Israel, and have built a solid base of schools, a community center, a summer resort where their children can socialize exclusively within the community

(Deal, New Jersey), and rabbinical institutions to assure the perpetuation of their culture. Coming from a learned community that boasted generations of rabbis in Syria, they have established several day schools where almost 90 percent of their children study. Until recently, the older generation still spoke the Arabic-Jewish dialect of Aleppo. Their continuing identity as a close-knit subgroup within the American Jewish community down through the third and fourth generation defies the assimilating trend of this country's immigration history. In addition, they have tended to remain religiously traditional in a cluster of their own synagogues.

The American Sephardic community began to grow dramatically following World War II, when the post-Holocaust refugees arrived, followed by Jews from Muslim lands fleeing the wave of nationalist fervor. Beginning in the 1970s, Sephardim seeking wider opportunities than they could find in Israel also began to emigrate from there to the United States. Today, most Sephardim belong to Sephardic congregations or to the American Sephardi Federation, which was founded in 1972 as part of the World Sephardi Federation. In New York, the pride of the community has been the Sephardic Home for the Aged in Brooklyn.

Sephardic congregations, in keeping with their historic background, have been either traditional or orthodox, and they have organized themselves along geographic lines of countries of origin—Moroccan, Greek, Iranian, Afghani, Yemeni, or Syrian. These divisions have tended to detract from efforts at united action to further Sephardic education; nonetheless, at Yeshiva University, a new generation of spiritual leaders is being trained to carry on the Sephardic ritual.

Many Sephardim have entered the mainstream American Jewish community where, though they are a minority within a minority, they do not seek a separate institutional identity. Their pronunciation of Hebrew, which is much closer to the ancient and original pronunciation of Hebrew, has become accepted as the norm for all Jews. Their religious practices are part of normative Judaism but, owing to the influence of the cultures of the countries where they lived, their cuisine and liturgical tunes are distinctive. In addition, Sephardim are distinguished by several nuances of difference in ritual. Since the influence of emancipation came much later to the Sephardic Jews, their traditional way of family life, including celebration of festivals among extended families, has broken down only slowly. Indeed, Sephardic Jewish religious expression is overwhelmingly familial. Some customs, such as

naming children after living grandparents, differ from those of Ashkenazim, and respect for elders is especially important.

Outside the United States and France, smaller Sephardic communities can be found in almost every place that Jews have chosen to settle.
Sephardim constitute 10 percent of Argentina's Jewish community of
350,000. Out of Brazil's 165,000 Jews, approximately 50,000 are
Sephardim. About a tenth of Uruguay's 50,000 Jews are Sephardic, as
are 35 percent of Mexico's 50,000 Jews. Almost all of the 5,000 Jews in
Panama are Sephardic. The patterns of migration to these communities
resemble those in twentieth-century America. That is to say, whether in
Montreal, Toronto, Mexico City, Buenos Aires, Johannesburg, Brus-
sels, or Caracas, the Sephardic diaspora today tends to consist of refugees who came from the disintegrating Ottoman Empire before World
War I and were joined by immigrants from Muslim lands after World
War II.

What binds them together, if anything, is the sense of a shared past
as Jews from Ottoman lands and a sense of group identity and pride,
though with diminishing substantive content. As their own religious
observance breaks down with the third and fourth generation, and
marriage with Ashkenazim increases, Sephardic identity in the Americas is weakening. The Sephardic congregation that has only Sephardic
members is becoming a relic of the past. If they join Ashkenazic congregations, the young generation of Sephardim tend to know nothing
about their history and culture. Present-day Sephardim in America
reveal two tendencies—a minority that wants greater activism and identification, a majority that aims to diminish cultural distinctiveness and
blend with the wider Jewish community. Only a major campaign of
community building will reverse the effects of homogenization that
have affected all American Jews. Although the community of over
200,000 Sephardic Jews in America is widely dispersed, the task of
building Sephardic cultural institutions in the form of more schools,
publications, and libraries is not beyond the material means of the
community. However, there is no indication that its members are moving in that direction.

The reestablishment of the Jewish state in 1948 galvanized the Sephardic
people like no other event since the messianic frenzy for Sabbetai Zevi

three centuries before. No other story in their past 500 years equaled that of their homecoming, in terms either of drama or sheer human fortitude. The return has been virtually total, accomplished in a series of daring and frequently heroic rescue operations that included clandestine evacuations, smuggling of the young and elderly across deserts, secret departures by boat at night from Moroccan shores, and the rescue of Moroccan children behind the facade of sending them to summer camp in Switzerland and France. Entire communities found themselves thrust penniless from countries they had inhabited for thousands of years, then made their way into an old-new land still caught in the throes of a war for survival. The cosmopolites from Alexandria, the commercial, legal, and medical establishment of Baghdad, North Africans from crowded slums and luxurious villas—all found themselves congregated in temporary tent cities as Israel's population of 600,000 Jews doubled within three years.

In the course of the past forty years, almost one million Sephardic Jewish refugees from Muslim lands and the Balkans have arrived in Israel, making it the Sephardic community *par excellence* today. But the homecoming was by no means free of internal conflict: settling in this new land and its culture has required some of the most challenging adjustments and improvisations necessary in the long history of Sephardic wandering.

Unfortunately, one myth of modern Zionism that is still widely believed is the alleged absence of Sephardic participation in the Zionist revolution. In fact, Sephardim were always Zionists in the sense that many of them have lived in Palestine for centuries while others continued to migrate there over the past 1,000 years. Moreover, since the country formed an integral part of the successive empires in which they lived, they could hardly regard it with idealistic religious sentiment as some remote, almost mythical land to be redeemed in God's own time by the arrival of the Messiah. In other words, the relationships of the Sephardim with the land of Israel—unlike those of other Jews—were intimate, long-standing, and concrete.

While Jews in northern Europe were cut off, the Sephardim throughout the Islamic world were able to enjoy an ongoing dialogue with representatives from the Palestine community. Especially after the Spanish expulsion and the subsequent revival of Sephardic settlement in the Holy Land, the emissaries (*sheluhei Eretz Yisrael* or *shadarim*) of the holy cities of Safed, Hebron, Tiberias, and Jerusalem would periodically make their way to all corners of the Sephardic diaspora in order to raise funds for their communities and share news of the latest intellectual currents at home. These itinerant fundraisers and preachers were treated with the utmost reverence, listened to with rapt attention, entertained in the homes of notables, and offered positions as spiritual leaders. If the fundraiser happened to die on one of his missions to North Africa, his grave would become the site of pilgrimage and "miracles."

There were other strong ties to Palestine in the daily lives of Sephardic Jews. In the sixteenth century, for example, the North African community (Maghrebis) began to build its own nexus of institutions there. The spiritual innovations of the rabbis in the Holy Land, such as Lurianism or the movement led by Jacob Berab to reinstate *semikhah* (rabbinic ordination), echoed throughout North Africa.

In addition, the tradition of emigration to the Holy Land (*aliyah*) was actively practiced among the Sephardim, quickening in the early part of the nineteenth century. Jaffa and other somnolent cities were revived by the entrepreneurial descendants of this wave of immigration. In fact, by the middle of the century, the majority of gainfully employed Jewish settlers in Palestine were Sephardic, living by commerce and agriculture rather than being supported from abroad.

Moreover, the first summonses to the Jewish people to return to Zion were issued by the Sephardic leaders Rabbi Yehuda Alkalai (1798–1879) and Rabbi Yehuda Bibas, a native of Gibraltar who served as rabbi of Corfu in the early nineteenth century. Rabbi Bibas was profoundly influenced by the Greek uprising against the Turks in 1821, which he saw as a model in many ways of how Jews should redeem their destiny: i.e., take up arms themselves and wrest Palestine from the Ottomans. A strong advocate of the view that new Jewish settlement in the Holy Land ought to be self-supporting, Bibas interpreted the traditional Judaic notion of *teshuvah,* or repentance, to imply its literal meaning of "return."

His colleague, Rabbi Alkalai, who was born in Sarajevo, probably spent his youth in Jerusalem and began his rabbinical career in Semlin, the capital of Serbia. By 1834, perhaps in response to the wave of nationalism then sweeping through Greece and beginning to be reflected in the aspirations of Serbs and other Slavs, he proposed in *Shma Yisrael,* his first printed book, the creation of Jewish settlements in the Holy Land in preparation for national redemption. But, like his most famous successor, Theodor Herzl, Alkalai recognized that resettlement of large numbers of Jews would require the development of a modern economy. He pleaded with Western Jews for assistance, proposing such schemes as a Jewish National Fund, and traveled widely to publicize his ideas. He won numerous supporters, including Herzl's grandfather, Simon Loeb Herzl.

One of the most important traits of Sephardic Zionism was that its adherents responded and spoke in the language of traditional Judaism. Like Bibas, Alkalai also believed *teshuvah* implied return to Israel, and he was especially hostile to reform rabbis in Europe and America who disavowed the historic connection between Jews and the Holy Land. At the time of the Damascus Blood Libel, he was not among those who calculated that the Messiah was going to come immediately. Instead, he urged Jews to save themselves and eliminate such outrageous acts by emigration. Thus, for its day, Sephardic Zionism was revolutionary precisely because it blended Jewish activism with traditional Judaic religious precepts. By contrast, the ideology of the Socialist Zionists of Europe required that Jews find redemption by abandoning their religion. Consequently, it was Alkalai's brand of Zionism that tended to fuse with traditional leadership rather than encourage a splintering into a welter of parties and organizations. Along with Bibas, he placed a strong emphasis on gaining political support for the Zionist venture.

Alkalai's words often strike a surprisingly "modern" tone:

> If you wish to fulfill the commandment of settling in the land, do this and you will succeed: Speak to the wealthy people and ask them to build a house in Israel. . . . There are wealthy Jews in the diaspora who own houses and property for rental. Let them also build houses in Israel to rent to whomever they please, and they will provide shelter for the poor and the rich. . . . The righteous Jews who love the land should each send one of their children or workers to settle in Israel. . . . Let everyone visit Israel from time to time. . . . The Jews are satisfied with too little, we don't sense the need to seek a great holiness. . . . Agricultural work is the first commandment in settling the land, for it provides sustenance for the poor. The first settlers will be poor. . . . The commandment of settling the land will hasten the redemption.[12]

For its day, this approach was particularly unusual for a rabbi to adopt.

In 1858, decades before the rise of Zionism as a political movement in Europe, yet another Sephardic leader became an active proponent of the return. Rabbi Israel Moshe Hazan (1809–63), who was born in

Izmir and held rabbinical posts in Jerusalem, Rome, Corfu, and Alexandria, urged European Jews to purchase land from the Arabs in Palestine and to that end established a fund, which he called *keren kayyemet*.

Sephardic lay leadership in the nineteenth century also displayed an unusual sympathy for Zionism. Sir Moses Montefiore, who was so active in the affair in Damascus, was only the most conspicuous of a number of prominent Sephardim to encourage modern Jewish settlement in Palestine.

Like the Ashkenazim, an activist minority of Sephardic Jews was drawn to Zionist organizational activities. The first Zionist societies to educate youth were created in Bulgaria by Joseph Marco Baruch in 1895. In Morocco and Tunisia as well as Greece, early adherents to the movement struggled to make an impact upon their modernizing communities. They faced other difficulties as well. The directors of the *Alliance* schools, a major force in the Near Eastern communities, tended to oppose the Zionist movement entirely. Inevitably, the Zionists in Muslim countries found it difficult to organize a mass movement because of the decidedly negative view of their aims taken by their fellow citizens and rulers. Even so, when the first Zionist congresses were convened in Europe at the turn of the century, representatives of Zionist groups in Egypt and Algeria appeared among the delegates. Eventually, the strongholds of Zionism in Muslim lands would be Morocco, Tunisia, and, to a lesser degree, Libya.* Even among the first waves of the European so-called *aliyot* (waves of immigration to Palestine), a large number of recruits were Sephardim. Sephardic Jews comprised one-sixth of the pre-1949 Jewish population of Palestine although they were less than one-tenth of the world's total Jewish population.

Local hostility was not the only obstacle to the spread of Zionism in the world of Islam. In addition, European Zionists paid such scant attention to their depressed brethren in the East that they did not bother to send out emissaries or publish their materials about grass-roots organization building in the languages of the Sephardim. More-

* Moroccan Jews comprised 3 percent of the population of their country at the end of World War II. In Tunisia, Jews were less than 1 percent of the population, and Libya's 35,000 Jews also constituted only a fraction of a percent of the country's population.

over, few French-speaking Zionists were trained to work with the increasingly gallicized communities of North Africa. Another obstacle was the hostility or indifference of the families of notables who dominated the communities. In some cases, as in Algeria, opposition sprang from assimiliationist ideology and indeed total identification with the cause of France. Elsewhere, many of the *Alliance*-trained alumni in particular were antagonistic to Zionist activities, as they were to any ideology that suggested Jewish particularism. Finally, some *Alliance* leaders were opposed on the grounds that Zionists might be working in tandem with British designs, since it was Great Britain that had granted the Jews the possibility of return to Palestine in the Balfour Declaration of 1917.

In contrast with their European colleagues, Sephardic rabbis tended to be supportive of Zionism from the outset, for the movement was a natural form of expression of Sephardic Judaism. In any event, the reality of Jewish life under Muslim rule was that communities were ethnically autonomous. Therefore, theories about Jewish nationalism could hardly sound strange or incomprehensible. But not only were Eastern Jews accustomed to thinking of themselves as citizens of a separate Jewish nation, they also, at least in Morocco and Tunisia, espoused a Zionism tinged with a strongly messianic fervor.

As the Jewish situation worsened in Muslim countries after World War I, the Zionist movement became more attractive to the timid Jewish masses. Given the increasingly precarious nature of their daily lives, it is understandable that Jews in the East would be tantalized by the Zionist dream; but as we have seen, any sign of identification with Palestine *Yishuv,* could be dangerous. Several Arab countries banned all contact with or espousal of Zionism; Jewish leaders were often forced to disavow publicly any association with Zionist aspirations. Still, as the situation of the Sephardim continued to deteriorate after the war, the Jewish masses in the East became increasingly sympathetic to the call of Zion.

After the Second World War, the state of crisis was only more severe. In tandem with the Arab-Jewish conflict in Palestine, violent acts against Jews escalated in virtually all of the Muslim lands. Various Arab newspapers carelessly disseminated false rumors about Jewish "atrocities" against Palestinian Arabs, thus sparking pogroms in Libya, Aden, Egypt, and Iraq. Meanwhile, the wartime experience of Nazi occupation and potential annihilation helped transform the Jewish masses into Zionists; in other words, reality totally discredited the assimilationist ideals of the *Alliance Israélite Universalle*. In addition, contact with Jewish soldiers from Palestine in the British army as well as the stepped-up activity of *Yishuv* emissaries augmented the cultural activities of the Zionists, and more and more Jewish youth turned their eyes toward Palestine.

Even without these external factors, there is no question that Sephardic Jews *were* Zionists. Their special blend of practical messianism and historic sentiment was fervent, whether in Yemen, Yugoslavia, Greece, Libya, or Bulgaria. Once given the opportunity to join the emergent Jewish state, almost the entire Sephardic world rose up to participate in the return. Faced with the same option, most Ashkenazim stayed where they were in their lands of dispersion. They voiced their sympathies for the *Yishuv* with charitable donations, not by engaging in mass migration.

Israeli society was transformed by the 1948–51 wave of immigration, which put enormous strains on the fledgling state as almost one million impoverished refugees, including Sephardim and European Holocaust survivors, joined the resident population of only 600,000. In addition to the penniless Sephardim, something like 250,000 more Jews came from hideouts in the forests and concentration camps of Europe. These were unimaginably difficult circumstances for the tasks of state building and immigrant absorption.

The ethnic landscape of Israel, then and now, is generally described simplistically, even by serious students of Israeli society, as a split between Ashkenazim and Sephardim. The truth is a great deal more intricate. From the outset, the reception of immigrants was determined by a few guiding principles. On the one hand, there was *mizug hagaluyot*, the principle of integrating the exile communities. Basically, the assumption was that a melting pot of all the exile cultures would produce a new Israeli personality completely different from those typifying the different traditions. The principle was to apply to all groups, not just Sephardic Jews. On the other hand, the cultural ideal projected by the European Jews who had formulated the Zionist ethos before the founding of the state was heavily socialist, anti-religious, and reflective of the needs and goals of European Jews. In other words, the Zionism of the founding Labor Party was at odds with some of the most treasured values of the Sephardim. Israel demanded a renunciation of the past, even when the immigrant had not necessarily disavowed his patriarchal, familial, and traditional ties and beliefs.

The resulting crisis of homecoming was far-reaching. The social, ideological, and cultural background of Middle Eastern immigrants was very different from that of the main veteran population of Israel. In that country's society, as in all immigrant societies, the importance of seniority (*vetek*) in arrival was critical in sharing the limited economic pie. Since the Ashkenazim had arrived earlier, they could help their postwar relatives and friends and ease their adjustment by giving them a boost up the economic ladder.

By the early 1960s, inevitably, a serious cleavage had developed between the two groups. The Sephardim tended to have larger families and to remain concentrated on the lower rungs of society in low-prestige occupations, living in disadvantaged neighborhoods or development towns. They rarely succeeded in leaving these towns, originally established to disperse the entire immigrant population and thus protect the new borders, but designed with little consideration for providing employment opportunities. Coming from Muslim countries with less advanced economies, their skills were often limited and their per capita income and educational attainment were typically, and strikingly, inferior to Ashkenazic levels. (To be sure, while 90 percent of those living in poor neighborhoods are Sephardim, "only" 30 percent of all Sephardim live in conditions of overcrowding and substandard housing.) But whatever the explanations for these divergences, and even though they were not the result of an official policy of discrimination, by the early 1960s sociologists were talking about the "two Israels," recognizing that the absorption process still had a long way to go before the creation of a new egalitarian society.

The wide gap between Ashkenazim and Sephardim in Israel has been exacerbated by the sense that many Sephardim shared of being somehow dispossessed of their past and their self-respect. Many felt a sense of cultural loss in the urban, industrialized, dynamic Israeli society and tended to idealize their past. Coming on the heels of the profound identity crisis many of them had undergone in the last years of the colonial regimes, their sense of loss was especially profound. Indeed, all too many Sephardim accepted the Ashkenazim's low estimation of their way of life and tried to change their identity.

Perhaps one of the most moving descriptions of this process can be found in Shulamith Hareven's novel *City of Many Days,* which describes life in Jerusalem prior to and immediately after the establishment of Israel. One day the heroine's son comes home from school with a radical proposal to disavow his identity. As the novelist makes clear, his crisis is not unique to Sephardim, yet acculturation in Israel was particularly painful for them:

> He felt as if some part of him had been altered, and one morning, as though under duress, he asked Sara what she thought of changing their last name to Amir. It sounded more Hebrew, he said to her, embarrassed. Sara agreed right away. Since her grandfather's death, the name Amarillo no longer meant much to her. She saw little of Gracia, who had since returned to Jerusalem, or of her pudgy mother-in-law, Allegra, who had occasionally sent them jars of olives and olive oil from Tiberias, to say nothing of all her *tias* and *tios* scattered throughout Jerusalem. Hillel was enthusiastic about the change. By the standards of the Ashkenazi school he now attended, Amir was certainly a nicer name than Amarillo. His teacher Tzippora thought so, too. Botanically derived names were in fashion that year, and Amir, which meant "treetop," was right in keeping with style.[13]

The assault on Sephardic culture came from all quarters—the kibbutzim, youth groups, residential Youth Aliyah programs, and even the religious schools, which were perhaps the principal agents of social adjustment. If "Amarillo" was to be discarded, so be it. What did it matter that the name had been borne by generations of Eastern Jewish scholars, including three chief rabbis of that quintessentially Sephardic city Salonika, the "Jerusalem of the Balkans"?

This kind of pressure and the unintentional slights and mistakes of the first generation of Israeli state builders were legion. For example, Sephardic youngsters were removed from school after the seventh grade and enlisted to serve as agricultural workers with the heavily Zionist explanation that they would be redeemed through manual labor. The strong anti-religious bias of the bureaucrats and social workers entrusted with assisting the new immigrants made deep inroads on the faith of the Sephardic community. Loss of tradition among the younger generation entailed a breakdown of the family structure. Dispersion into different communities also produced a sense of malaise. To take another example, the advice of some of Israel's emissaries to potential Sephardic immigrants had been to leave their precious Judaica behind because such objects would not be needed in the new state. Such mistakes have been ruefully acknowledged by the new generation of Israelis, who have accordingly modified their policies toward subsequent immigrants. These unfortunate policies were counterbalanced by a uniform system of employment and other social benefits in Israel. Certainly, Sephardim never had to face any kind of legal discrimination.

By 1967, the Sephardim outnumbered the Ashkenazim, particularly among the young. Once they comprised more than 50 percent of the population, they began to exert their electoral muscle and in the late 1970s finally ousted the Labor Party, which had been in power since 1948. Their virtually revolutionary election of the Likud Party was the result of demoralization and the sense that they had not received their fair share. While Labor in their eyes was the incarnation of Ashkenazic privilege, they felt that the leader of Likud, Menachem Begin, personified the outsider to the system, the strong nationalist who respected Sephardic tradition and the Sephardim themselves. Up to the present, they have tended to maintain their support for Likud.[14] With the recent massive Soviet immigration, the weight of the Sephardim in Israel is decreasing. It is too early to tell whether Sephardim will move up in society as menial jobs are filled by the Russian newcomers, or whether they will be bypassed by the new arrivals with superior education and skills.

The Sephardim were caught between a nostalgia for the old world and the notion that the emergence of a national identity is a total experience that supplants the diaspora Jewish identity. During the 1960s and 1970s Sephardim thus became uprooted and disconnected from their past as they undertook to establish their roots and become part of something new. Recently, as all Western societies have experienced a new appreciation of pluralistic interests and diverse cultures, ethnic diversity has become a byword in Israel as well. There is a new acceptance of ethnic festivals of the Sephardic communities, and elements of the diverse Jewish heritages have been introduced in all the elementary and secondary school curricula. Many courses on Sephardic civilization have been introduced in the universities. Cultural and ethnic activities have grown in popularity with immigrants from specific locations or communities, which have organized associations to renew their ethnic festivals and publish their own cultural materials. The most prominent example of this renewal is the revival of the Moroccan festival of the *mimouna*. Formerly an at-home celebration on the last day of Passover for families and friends to visit and dine together with much festivity, the *mimouna* in Israel has become a national Israeli and Moroccan holiday of picnicking and celebration during which even Ashkenazic politicians pay homage to the secular and religious leaders of the nation's Moroccan community. In the annual *mimouna* festival Moroccans have become, as it were, hosts to all the other populations of Israel. Similarly, Kurdish Jews have revived their festival of the *seherrana* and the Persian Jews, in turn, have recently gathered to celebrate their special festival known as the *Ruz-e-begh*.

More than a tolerance of diversity is at issue. The ethnic revival in Israel has been a dynamic creative force for new celebrations that combine aspects of the old with the new. Perhaps the most notable such cultural development is the explosion of pilgrimages (*hilloulot*) to graves of pious leaders. An especially meaningful rite in North Africa, the *hilloula* was one of the expressions of Judaism that was publicly observed by multitudes on the anniversary of the death of a saintly personality. The pilgrimage combined study of mystical texts with visits to the grave of the venerated figure. Jews of the Maghreb believed that their prayers at the gravesite could be especially efficacious and that the commemorated person would intercede with God on behalf of the petitioner. About ten years after the end of the mass immigration of North Africans to Israel, their custom of *hilloula* was revived. Sometimes, the revival seemed almost spontaneous, when a pious "saintly" deceased figure "miraculously" appeared in a dream to advise his simple follower to restore the visits to a gravesite or other designated spot. Initially, some of the rabbinical authorities frowned upon the custom, citing the boisterous behavior of the participants and the intermingling of men and women. Beginning as modest affairs, the *hilloulot* have become larger with each passing year, drawing thousands of Jews to the Israeli towns of Beersheba, Ashkelon, Hatzor, and Netivoth (all development towns with predominantly North African immigrant populations), either where the tombs of great rabbis of Tunisia and Morocco were located or where ancient gravesites have been appropriated for modern purposes. The fascinating transfer of this custom has not only provided an opportunity for ethnic renewal but also occasions for reunions of extended families and kinsmen from the same towns in the old country.

At the same time that ethnic festivals and traditional cuisine have been revived, Sephardic writers such as Shimon Ballas, Amnon

Shamosh, Eli Amir, Ada Aharoni, and Sami Michael have sensitively recorded the loss of the Middle Eastern universe they left behind in their migration. Their depiction of the rich life of the Sephardic exile in Muslim lands is a transitional literature of a group not yet quite "at home."

How the Sephardic heritage will ultimately shape the still-evolving Israeli culture is an open question. Whether that heritage will find its voice before it is drowned out by the competing voice of the most recent and vastly talented Russian immigration remains to be seen. What has become most apparent in the 1990s is that the former split between Sephardim and Ashkenazim has begun to fade among the new generation of Israeli youth. They are neither one nor the other, in the sense that their parents or grandparents were during the diaspora. With their homecoming, bittersweet as it may have seemed to the immigrant generation, a new chapter in the long history of the Sephardic Jews is beginning.

APPENDIX 1
The Edict of Expulsion

Don Ferdinand and Doña Isabel, by the grace of God King and Queen of Castile, Leon, Aragon, Sicily, Granada, Toledo, Valencia, Galicia, Mallorca, Sevilla, Sardinia, Cordova, Corçega, Murcia, Jaén, the Algarve, Algeciras, Gibraltar, and the Canary Islands; [to the] Count and Countess of Barcelona and the lords of Biscay and Molina, Dukes of Athens and Neopatria, Counts of Rosellon and of Sardinia, Marquees of Oristan and of Gociano; to the Prince Don Juan, our dear and beloved son, and to the Infantes, prelates, dukes, marquees, counts, masters [of military orders], priors, wealthy men, knight-commanders, governors of the castles and strongholds of our kingdoms and seignories, and to the councils, magistrates, mayors, constables, royal judges, cavaliers, official shieldbearers and good men of the very loyal city of Burgos and of the other cities and villages and places of its bishopric, and of the other archdioceses and bishoprics and dioceses of our reigns and seignories, and to the *aljamas* [communities] of the Jews of the said city of Burgos, and to all the cities and villages and places of our said reigns and seignories, and to all the Jews and their singular persons, thus men and women of whatever age and to all the other persons of whatever legal status, dignity, or preeminence or condition to which that contained below in our letters appertains or may appertain in any manner, health and grace [unto you].

SOURCE: Luis Suarez Fernández, *"Documentos Acerca de la Expulsión de Los Judíos,"* Consejo Superior de Investigaciones Cientificas, Patronato Menendez Pelayo, Valladolid, 1964; quoted by David Raphael in *The Expulsion 1492 Chronicles* (N. Hollywood, California 1992).

You well know or should know that, because we were informed that in these our kingdoms there were some bad Christians who Judaized and apostatized from our holy Catholic faith, this being chiefly caused by the communication of the Jews with the Christians, in the Cortes that we held in the city of Toledo in the year 1480, we ordered that the said Jews be separated in all the cities, villages, and places of our kingdoms and seignories, and that they be given *juderías* [Jewish quarters] and separate places where they could live, hoping that this separation would remedy [the problem]. Moreover, we have sought and given the order that an inquisition be conducted in the said kingdoms and seignories which, as you know, has been done and is continuing, and on account of it, many guilty individuals have been found, which is notorious. According to which, we are informed by the Inquisitors and by many other religious persons, ecclesiastical and secular, it is evident and apparent that the great damage to the Christians has resulted from and does result from the participation, conversation, and communication that they have had with the Jews, who try to always achieve by whatever ways and means possible to subvert and to draw away faithful Christians from our holy Catholic faith and to separate them from it, and to attract and pervert them to their injurious belief and opinion, instructing them in their ceremonies and observances of the Law, holding gatherings where they read unto them and teach them what they ought to believe and observe according to their Law, trying to circumcise them and their children, giving them books from which to read their prayers, and declaring the fasts that they ought to fast, and joining with them to read and teach them the histories of their Law; notifying them of Passover before it comes, advising them what they should observe and do for it, giving them and taking unto them the unleavened bread and the [ritually] slaughtered meats with their ceremonies, instructing them on the things they should stay away from, thus in the foods as in the other matters, for observance of their Law, and persuading them as much as they can there is no other law nor truth besides it. This is evident from the many declarations and confessions, [obtained] as much from the Jews themselves as from those perverted and deceived by them, which has redounded to the great injury, detriment, and opprobrium of our holy Catholic faith.

Notwithstanding that we were informed of most of this beforehand, and realizing that the true remedy for these injuries and inconveniences was in breaking off all communication of the said Jews with the Christians and to eject them from our kingdoms, we sought to content ourselves in ordering them out of all the cities and villages of Andalusia where it appeared they had done great damage, believing that this would be sufficient, so that the other cities and villages and places of our kingdoms and seignories would cease to do and commit the aforesaid.

And because we are informed that neither that, nor the punishments meted out to some of those said Jews found culpable in the said crimes and transgressions against our holy Catholic faith, will suffice as a complete remedy to obviate and to terminate such great opprobrium and offense to the Christian religion; because every day it is found and made apparent that the said Jews increase their evil and injurious activities where they live and converse, and so as not to grant them more space within which to further offend our holy faith, as much in those whom God has protected as in those who have fallen, but have amended and returned to the Holy Mother Church, which, according to the weakness of our humanity and the diabolical suggestion that continually wars against us, which easily could come to pass, unless the principal cause of it be removed, which is to eject the said Jews from our kingdoms. Because whenever some grave and detestable crime is committed by some persons of a group or community, it is right that such a college or community be dissolved and annihilated, and that the minors be punished for the elders, one for the other; and that those who pervert the good and honest living of the cities and villages, and that by contagion could injure others, be expelled from among the peoples, and even for other lighter causes that are harmful to the states, and how much more so for the greatest of the crimes, dangerous and contagious as is this one.

Therefore, we, with the counsel and advice of some prelates, grandees, and cavaliers of our kingdoms and other persons of knowledge and conscience of our Council, having had much deliberation upon it, resolve to order all and said Jews and Jewesses out of our kingdoms and that they never return nor come back to any of them. Concerning this, we command this letter [Edict] to be given, whereby we command all Jews and Jewesses of whatever age they may be, who live and reside and are in the said kingdoms and seignories, natives and non-natives alike, who by whatever manner or whatever reason may have come or are to be found in them, that by the end of July of the present year, that they leave the said kingdoms and seignories with their sons and daughters, male and female servants and Jewish domestics, both great and small, of whatever age they may be, and that they dare not return unto them, nor be in them, nor be in any part of them, neither as dwellers, nor as travelers, nor in any other manner whatsoever, upon punishment that if they do not thus perform and comply with this, and are to be found in our said kingdoms and seignories and have come here in any manner, they incur the penalty of death and confiscation of all their belongings for our treasury, and such penalties they shall incur by the very deed itself without trial, sentence, or declaration. And we command and maintain that no one in our said kingdoms of whatever status, conditions, or dignity they may be, dare to receive, harbor, defend, either publicly or secretly and Jew or Jewess after the said deadline at the end of July has passed, henceforth and forevermore, neither in their lands nor in their homes nor in any other part of our said kingdoms and seignories, under pain of losing all their belongings, vassals, fortresses, and other landed properties and, moreover, to lose whatever sums they may have from us for our treasury.

And so that the said Jews and Jewesses, during the said time until the end of the month of July, may better dispose of themselves, their belongings, and their estates, we hereby take and receive them under our security, protection, and royal guardship; and we assure them and their belongings that, during the said time period until the said day, the end of the said month of July, they may go about in safety, and they may enter, sell, barter, and transfer all their movable and immovable goods, and dispose of them freely at will; and that during the said time period, no evil, injury, or offense be done to their persons nor unto their goods contrary to justice, upon punishment of that which befalls and is incurred by those who transgress our royal security. In like manner, we give permission and authority to the said Jews and Jewesses that they may take out their goods and estate from our said kingdoms and seignories, by sea or by land, provided they do not take out gold, silver, minted money, or other items prohibited by the laws of our kingdoms, except for non-prohibited merchandise or exchange bills.

And, moreover, we command all the councils, justices, governors, cavaliers, shieldbearers, officials, and good men of the said city of Burgos and of the other cities and villages of our kingdoms and seignories and to all our vassals, subjects, and natives that they observe and comply and cause this, our letter and all that is contained in it, to be observed and complied with; and that they give, and cause to have given, all necessary support and help, upon [threat of] punishment by our grace and the confiscation of all your goods and benefits for our treasury. And so that this may come to the notice of all, and no one may pretend ignorance, we command that this letter be proclaimed in the plazas and customary places of that said city and of the principal cities and villages and places of its bishopric by a public crier and before a public scribe. Neither one nor another should do the contrary by whatever manner, upon punishment by our grace and the loss of your offices, and the confiscation of the belongings of whoever does the contrary. And we further command the person who shows them this letter, that they are summoned to appear before us in our court, wherever we may be, within the fifteen days following the day of our summons, upon [threat of] the said punishment, and concerning which we command whichever public scribe was called upon to do this, that he show you signed testimony with his signet in order that we may know how our command is complied with.

Given in our city of Granada at XXXI days of the month of March, the year 1492 of our Lord Jesus Christ. I the King, I the Queen, I, Juan de Coloma, secretary of the King and Queen, our Lords, which I have written upon their command.

APPENDIX 2
Immigration Tables

	1948	1990
Morocco	265,000	12,000
Algeria	140,000	
Tunisia	105,000	
Libya	38,000	
Egypt	75,000	300
Iraq	135,000	
Syria	30,000	4,000
Lebanon	5,000	
Yemen	55,000	1,000
Aden	8,000	
Iran	100,000	35,000
Turkey	60,000	25,000
Afghanistan	5,000	
Total	1,021,000	77,300

Appendix 2

IMMIGRANTS TO ISRAEL
By Period of Immigration and Previous Continent of Residence
(*In Thousands*)

	Total	Asia	Africa	Europe	America/Oceana
1948–1982	1721.4	350.4	409.3	793.3	143.0
1948–1951	686.7	237.3	93.9	326.8	5.1
1955–57	164.9	8.8	103.8	48.6	3.6
1961–64	228.0	19.2	18.0	23.4	2.0
1969–71	116.5	19.7	12.0	50.6	33.9
1972–74	142.8	26.8	102.8	6.8	6.3
1975–79	124.8	11.8	6.0	77.2	29.3
1980–82	46.8	5.4	3.7	23.9	13.6

SOURCE: Statistical Abstract of Israel, 1983.

APPENDIX 3
Maps

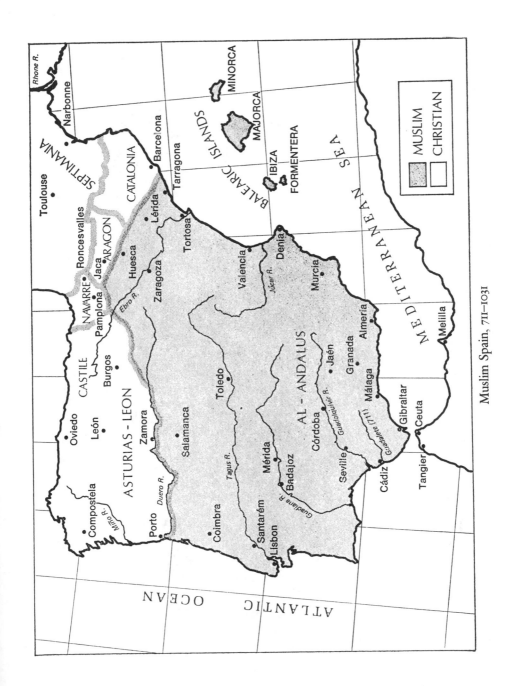

Muslim Spain, 711–1031

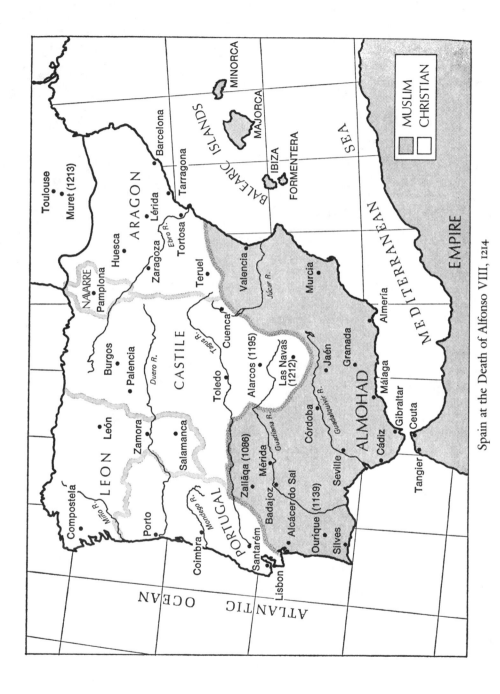

Spain at the Death of Alfonso VIII, 1214

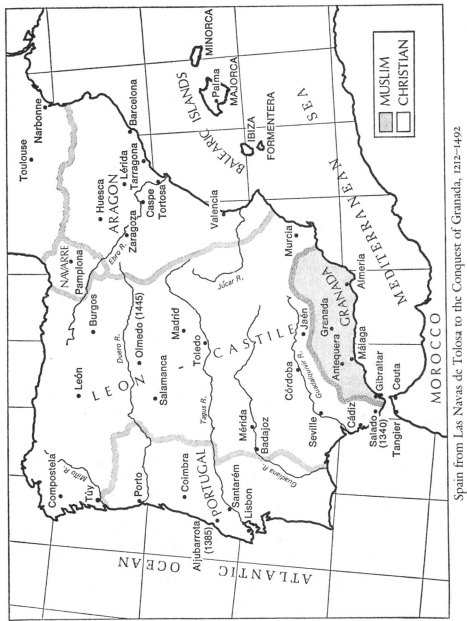

Spain from Las Navas de Tolosa to the Conquest of Granada, 1212–1492

MUSLIM
CHRISTIAN

ATLANTIC OCEAN

MEDITERRANEAN SEA

BALEARIC ISLANDS

MINORCA
MAJORCA
Palma
IBIZA
FORMENTERA

MOROCCO

Toulouse
Narbonne
Barcelona
Tarragona
Lérida
Huesca
ARAGON
Caspe
Zaragoza
Tortosa
Valencia
NAVARRE
Pamplona
Burgos
Olmedo (1445)
Madrid
Toledo
CASTILE
Júcar R.
Ebro R.
Duero R.
León
L E O N
Salamanca
Tagus R.
Compostela
Miño R.
Túy
Porto
Coimbra
PORTUGAL
Santarém
Lisbon
Aljubarrota (1385)
Mérida
Badajoz
Guadiana R.
Seville
Córdoba
Guadalquivir R.
Jaén
Murcia
Granada
GRANADA
Antequera
Málaga
Almería
Cádiz
Salado (1340)
Gibraltar
Ceuta
Tangier

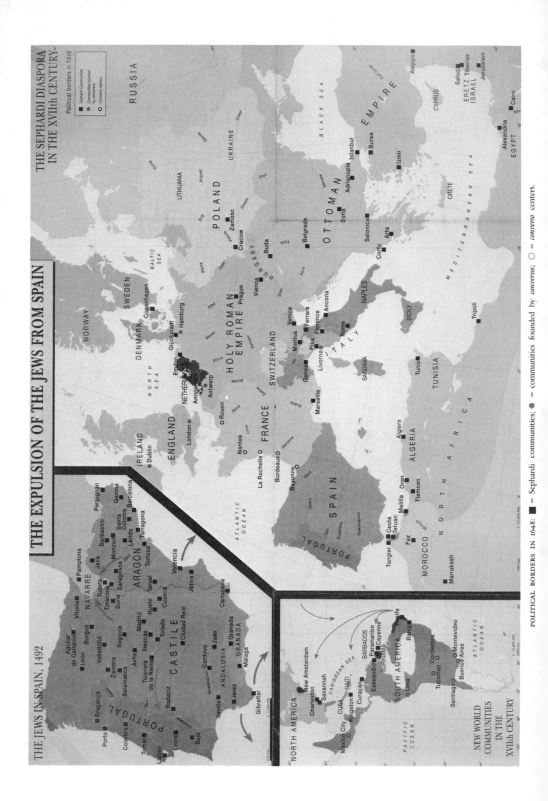

THE EXPULSION OF THE JEWS FROM SPAIN

THE JEWS IN SPAIN, 1492

THE SEPHARDI DIASPORA IN THE XVIIth CENTURY.

Political borders in 1648

■ Sephardi Communities
◉ Communities founded by conversos
○ Converso centers

NEW WORLD COMMUNITIES IN THE XVIIth CENTURY

POLITICAL BORDERS IN 1648: ■ = Sephardi communities; ◉ = communities founded by *conversos*; ○ = *converso* centers.

298

NOTES

Introduction

1. Zacuto's fate would be typical of Jewish life in Spain at the close of the fifteenth century. Although he would be allowed to carry on scientific studies for the bishop of Salamanca until 1480 and afterward for the grandmaster of the Order of Knights of Alcantara, even he was forced to flee in 1492. Unable to find a haven in Portugal or Tunis, he died in Turkey after years of fruitless wanderings.
2. Fernando Columbo, *Historia del Almirante Don Cristobal Colon* (Madrid, 1892), chap. 2.
3. Isaac Abrabanel, *Mayanei ha-Yeshua* (Stettin, 1860), Introduction quoted by Marc D. Angel, *Voices in Exile* (New York, 1991), p. 4.

Chapter 1. Volatile Origins

1. John G. Gager, *The Origins of Anti-Semitism: Attitudes towards Judaism in Pagan and Christian Antiquity* (New York, 1983), chapter 6.
2. L. Garcia Iglesias, *Los judios en la Espana antigua* (Madrid, 1978), pp. 69ff. For another translation see Jacob R. Marcus, *The Jew in the Medieval World* (New York, 1960), pp. 101–2.
3. An extensive body of literature on the theological roots of anti-Semitism in Western civilization has emerged since World War II and especially since Vatican II. See, for instance, Alan Davies, ed., *Anti-Semitism and the Foundations of Christianity* (New York, 1978); Franklin H. Littell, *The Crucifixion of the Jews: The Failure of the Christians to Understand the Jewish Experience* (New York, 1965); and Rosemary Reuther, *Faith and Fratricide* (New York, 1974). For a recent study which includes pagan attitudes, see Gager, *The Origins of Anti-Semitism* and Gavin I. Langmuir, *Toward a Definition of Anti-Semitism* (Berkeley and Los Angeles, 1990).
4. Salo W. Baron, "Graeco-Roman Association," in *The Jewish Community* (Philadelphia, 1942), I: 75–117. The multiplicity of institutions designed to take care of all needs of the community were remarkably similar in many countries through the ages. Spain's self-governing community, later known as the *aljama*, controlled many aspects of the inner life of the Jews.
5. Bernard Lewis, *Race and Slavery in the Middle East* (New York, 1990). On the slave trade in Roman times, see Baron, *A Social and Religious History of the Jews* (New York and Philadelphia, 1957), IV: 187–96; Simha 'Assaf, "Slavery and the Slave Trade among the Jews in the Middle

Ages" (in Hebrew), *Zion* (1938–39), pp. 91–125. For a theoretical discussion see Boaz Cohen, *Jewish and Roman Law: A Comparative Study*, 2 vols. (New York, 1966), esp. I: 159–278.

6. Bernard S. Bachrach, "A Reassessment of Visigothic Jewish Policy, 589–711," *American Historical Review* 78, no. 1 (1973), p. 12

7. James Parkes, *The Conflict of the Church and the Synagogue: A Study in the Origins of Antisemitism* (Philadelphia, 1961). p. 354.

8. Solomon Katz, *The Jews in the Visigothic and Frankish Kingdoms of Spain and Gaul* (Cambridge, Mass., 1937) for a discussion of the oscillations of Visigothic policy. Bernard Bachrach balances the various theories of historians in his "Reassessment," pp. 12–13, and suggests these correlations.

9. A summary listing of legislation affecting Jews from 300 to 800 CE, the formation centuries during which anti-Jewish policies developed, can be found in Parkes, *The Conflict of the Church*, pp. 379–88. For illustrative texts of the required oaths of abjuration, see pp. 394–401.

10. Bernard Lewis, *The Muslim Discovery of the West* (New York, 1982), especially the extended analysis in chapter 2.

11. An extensive body of literature exists on Muslim-Jewish relations at the time of Muhammad and in the early centuries of Islam. For a summary of this literature see Mark R. Cohen, "Islam and the Jews: Myth, Countermyth, History," *Jerusalem Quarterly* 38 (1986), pp. 125–37. Selective passages on the Jews from the Koran and early Muslim tradition are available in Norman Stillman, *The Jews of Arab Lands* (Philadelphia, 1979), pp. 113–51.

12. Hava Lazarus-Yafeh, "Minorities under Islam and Islam as a Minority," in *Perspectives on Israeli Pluralism*, ed. Kitty O. Cohen and Jane S. Gerber (New York, 1991), pp. 23–33. For text of Abu Yusuf, see p. 23.

13. For discriminatory clothing in Morocco, see Jane S. Gerber, "The Pact of 'Umar in North Africa: A Reappraisal of Muslim-Jewish Relations," *Seminar on Muslim-Jewish Relations in North Africa* (New York, 1975), pp. 40–50. For anti-Jewish literary expressions of outrage at signs of Jewish affluence, see Bernard Lewis,"An Ode against the Jews," in *Islam in History* (New York, 1973), pp. 158–65. This ode was composed in eleventh-century Granada.

Chapter 2. The Birth of Sepharad

1. Thomas F. Glick, *Islamic and Christian Spain in the Early Middle Ages: Comparative Perspectives on Social and Cultural Formation* (Princeton, 1979), pp. 55ff. and p. 323, n. 12.

2. Franz Kobler, ed., *Letters of Jews through the Ages* (Philadelphia, 1978) I: 100–101.

3. S. D. Goitein, *A Mediterranean Society* (Berkeley and Los Angeles, 1967), I, for a meticulous and exhaustive discussion of the economic foundations of the medieval Islamic empire. While Geniza material is heavily weighted toward North Africa and Egypt, Goitein has amassed and translated enough evidence to interject Spanish material in many of his detailed discussions. Spain forms an integral part of the medieval tableau depicted by the Cairo Geniza.

4. Ibid., I: 157.

5. Kobler, *Letters of Jews*, I: 142.

6. On the ambiance in which the poet worked, see Raymond Scheindlin, *Wine, Women and Death: Medieval Hebrew Poems on the Good Life* (Philadelphia, 1986), "Introduction."

7. See Jacob R. Marcus, *The Jew in the Medieval World* (New York, 1974), pp. 374–77, for the text of a typical medieval Jewish curriculum in Andalusia. The text is reproduced in Norman Stillman, *The Jews of Arab Lands* (Philadelphia, 1979), pp. 226–28.

8. See Gerson D. Cohen's excellent discussion of the courtier-rabbi, "The Typology of the Rabbinate," in his critical edition of Abraham ibn' Daud's *Sefer ha-Qabbalah: The Book of Tradition* (Philadelphia, 1967), pp. 263ff. Cohen analyzes the mentality as well as the world of the Jewish grandee in Spain. See also J. Shirmann, "The Function of the Hebrew Poet in Medieval Spain," *Jewish Social Studies* 16 no. 3 (1954), pp. 235–52.

9. al-Tha'alibi, *Fiqh al-Lughra* Cairo, 1284), as quoted by Bernard Lewis in *The Middle East and the West* (Bloomington, 1965), p. 86.

10. The central motif of Ross Brann's book is precisely this duality of the Spanish poet, the *bon vivant* who nevertheless felt compunctions about enjoying life so much. See *The Compunctious Poet: Cultural Ambiguity and Hebrew Poetry in Muslim Spain* (Baltimore, 1991) for an extended analysis of this phenomenon in both Muslim and Christian Spain.

11. E. Ashtor, *The Jews of Moslem Spain* (Philadelphia, 1973), I: 155–227 for a detailed description of the career of Hasdai ibn Shaprut.

12. Cohen, "The Typology of the Rabbinate."

13. For Hasdai's correspondence with the King of the Khazars, see *Miscellany of Hebrew Literature*, trans. A. I. K. D. (London, 1872), I, pp. 92–93.

14. Numerous messianic pretenders arose among the Jews in the first several centuries of Islam. Salo Baron's chapter on "Messianism and Sectarian Trends" in volume 5 of *A Social and Religious History of the Jews* (New York and Philadelphia, 1957), pp. 138ff., provides important interpretive comments on the medieval messianic movements. For a general overview, see Abba Hillel Silver, *A History of Messianic Speculation in Israel* (Boston, 1959).

15. This parallel between the Spanish and Babylonian models of Jewish community organization is suggested by Gerson Cohen in "The Story of the Four Captives," in *Studies in the Variety of Rabbinic Cultures* (Philadelphia, 1991), p. 179.

16. M. Perlmann, "Eleventh-Century Andalusian Authors on the Jews of Granada," in *Proceedings of the American Academy for Jewish Research, XVIII,* (1948—49), pp. 269–90; also see Bernard Lewis, *Islam in History* (New York, 1973), pp. 159–61.

Chapter 3. The Golden Era

1. The two most recent discussions in English depicting the poetic milieu are Ross Brann, *The Compunctious Poet: Cultural Ambiguity and Hebrew Poetry in Muslim Spain* (Baltimore, 1991) and Raymond Scheindlin, *Wine, Women and Death: Medieval Hebrew Poems on the Good Life* (Philadelphia, 1986), "Introduction." Also see Abraham Halkin, "Judeo-Arabic Literature," in *Great Ages and Ideas of the Jewish People,* ed. Leo Schwarz (New York, 1956) for an overview of the literature.

2. The interweaving of new forms with traditional religious themes and the embellishment of these themes with new and daring motifs is the subject of Raymond Scheindlin's *The Gazelle* (Philadelphia, 1991).

3. Franz Kobler, ed., *Letters of Jews, through the Ages* (Philadelphia, 1978), p. 163.

4. Scheindlin, *Wine, Women and Death,* "Introduction."

5. For a sensitive discussion of the wine motif in medieval Andalusian poetry, see ibid., p. 20.

6. Leon Weinberger, *Jewish Prince in Moslem Spain: Selected Poems of Samuel ibn Nagrela* (University, Alabama, 1973), p. 106 and David Goldstein, *Hebrew Poems from Spain* (London, 1965).

7. Goldstein, *Hebrew Poems from Spain,* p. 115.

8. Scheindlin, *Wine, Women and Death,* p. 119.

9. T. Carmi, *The Penguin Book of Hebrew Verse* (Philadelphia, 1981), pp. 353–54.

10. Scheindlin, *The Gazelle,* pp. 97–101.

11. Scheindlin, *Wine, Women and Death,* p. 152.

12. Carmi, *Hebrew Verse,* pp. 286–88.

13. Ibid., p. 347.

14. This famous responsum is quoted by Scheindlin in *Wine, Women and Death,* p. 182, n. 30.

15. *Judah Halevi's Book of Kuzari* ed. H. Hirschfeld (New York, 1946).

16. Brann, *The Compunctious Poet,* chapter 4, "A Way with Words or Away with Words? Judah Halevi" on Halevi's sojourn in Egypt and S. D. Goitein, "The Last Phase of Rabbi Judah Halevi's Life in the Light of the Geniza Documents" (Hebrew), *Tarbiz* 24 (1954), 36–37.

17. Carmi, *Hebrew Verse,* pp. 350–51.

18. Ibid., p. 352.

19. Abraham Joshua Heschel, *Maimonides* (New York, 1982), p. 247.

20. Abraham Halkin and David Hartman, eds., *Crisis and Leadership: Epistles of Maimonides* (Philadelphia, 1985), pp. 31–33.
21. Courtesy of Dr. Daniel Miller, Strang Clinic, Cornell Medical Center.
22. Kobler, *Letters of Jews, I:* 194–96.
23. Isadore Twersky, *A Maimonides Reader* (New York, 1972), p. 236.
24. Heschel, *Maimonides,* p. 240 and Kobler, *Letters of Jews,* I: 215–16.

Chapter 4. The *Reconquista*

1. See Joseph F. O'Callaghan, *A History of Medieval Spain* Ithaca, 1975), pp. 467–69, for a discussion of the interrelationships between the military orders and other institutions in Spanish society.
2. Robert I. Burns, *Muslims, Christians and Jews in the Crusader Kingdom of Valencia* (Cambridge, 1984), pp. 161–66, and Appendix 3, documents on pp. 292–303.
3. Dwayne E. Carpenter, *Alfonso X and the Jews: An Edition of and Commentary on 'Siete Partidas 7.24 De los judíos'* " (Berkeley and Los Angeles, 1986), p. 30. On the role of the Jews in Alfonso X's court, see Americo Castro, *The Structure of Spanish History* (Princeton, 1954), pp. 479–91; Yitzhak Baer, *A History of the Jews in Christian Spain,* 2 vols. (Philadelphia, 1978), I: 113–30.
4. The best discussion on the persistence of Arab technologies in agriculture can be found in Thomas F. Glick, *Islamic and Christian Spain in the Early Middle Ages: Comparative Perspectives on Social and Cultural Formation* (Princeton, 1979).
5. Salo Baron, *A Social and Religious History of the Jews* (New York and Philadelphia, 1957), VII: 154.
6. On the schools of translators in Toledo, see Castro, *The Structure of Spanish History,* pp. 479ff.; Evelyn S. Proctor, *Alfonso X of Castile: Patron of Literature and Learning* (Oxford, 1951), pp. 113–39; David Romano, "Le opere scientifiche di Alfonso X e l'intervento degli ebrei," in *Oriente e Occidente nel Medioevo: Filosofia e Scienze* (Rome, 1971), pp. 677–711.
7. Jeremy Cohen, *The Friars and the Jews: The Evolution of Medieval Anti-Judaism* (Ithaca, 1982). Cohen argues that the Dominicans and the Franciscans had far-reaching designs to delegitimize the Jews and Judaism in Europe. The religious dispute was merely one weapon they used to pursue their program. Robert Chazan counters Cohen's thesis in *Daggers of Faith: Thirteenth Century Christian Missionizing and Jewish Response* (Berkeley and Los Angeles, 1989) with a close study of the Disputation of Barcelona. For an earlier study of the personality of Nahmanides, see Solomon Schechter, *Studies in Judaism* (Philadelphia, 1896), pp. 99–141. Extracts from the debate are included in Oliver Shaw Rankin, *Jewish Religious Polemic* (New York, 1970), pp. 157–210.
8. Cohen, *The Friars and the Jews,* p. 89.
9. The notion of Jews as "serfs of the chamber" who belonged to the king was widely held throughout medieval Europe. It was amplified by Frederick I and Frederick II of the Holy Roman Empire and was fully elaborated in the twelfth and thirteenth centuries as vigorous popes attempted to increase their own control over the emperors. For a discussion of these competing forces, see Solomon Grayzel, *The Church and the Jews in the Thirteenth Century* (Philadelphia, 1933). An extensive discussion of the competition between pope and emperor can be found in Salo Baron, " 'Plenitude of Apostolic Powers' and Medieval 'Jewish Serfdom' " and "Medieval Nationalism and Jewish Serfdom," in Leon A. Feldman, ed., *Ancient and Medieval Jewish History: Essays* (New Brunswick, N.J., 1972), pp. 284–307, 308–22.
10. Cohen, *The Friars and the Jews,* pp. 247ff.
11. See Chazan, *Daggers of Faith,* p. 96, for a discussion of Nahmanides' interpretation of rabbinic *aggadot.*
12. See Benzion Halper, *Post Biblical Hebrew Texts* (Philadelphia, 1921), pp. 178–81, for the text of the epistle prohibiting anyone under the age of twenty-five from studying philosophy.
13. On the emergence of irrational forces and demonic images of the Jews, see Joshua Trachtenberg, *The Devil and the Jews* (New Haven, 1943), esp. pp. 57–155. On suspicion of Jews as

poisoners, see Carpenter, *Alfonso X and the Jews*, p. 34, for the text of *Siete Partidas*, 7.24.8.
14. Trachtenberg, *The Devil and the Jews*, pp. 47ff.
15. Baer, *History of the Jews,* II: 95ff. Hasdai Crescas's succinct account is supplemented by Cecil Roth," A Hebrew Elegy on the Martyrs of Toledo, 1391," *Jewish Quarterly Review* 39 (1948), pp. 129ff. and the detailed account of scholars who converted in Baer, *History of the Jews,* I: 468ff., no. 4.

Chapter 5.   Path to Expulsion

1. Solomon Alami (c. 1370–1420), *Igerret Mussar,* as quoted by Yitzhak Baer, *The Jews of Christian Spain* 2 vols. (Philadelphia, 1961–66), II: 239–42.
2. H. Z. Hirschberg, *A History of the Jews in North Africa,* 2 vols. (Leiden, 1974–80), II: 320, from *Responsa* by Isaac ben Sheshet No. 60.
3. B. Netanyahu, *The Marranos of Spain,* 2nd ed. (New York, 1966). Netanyahu explores the criteria set by the rabbinical authorities during the first crusade for determining the Jewishness of the forced converts of the Rhineland and applies these criteria to the situation in Spain following 1391. He also analyses the statements and rulings of the fifteenth-century rabbinical authorities (primarily in North Africa) and determines that the *conversos* were becoming increasingly detached from Judaism in the course of the fifteenth century.
4. See Baer, *The Jews of Christian Spain,* II: 35–84, on the decline and communal tensions preceding 1391 and pp. 244–79 on the aftermath of 1391.
5. Abundant details on *marrano* Jewish observances are available in English, Spanish, and Hebrew studies. See expecially H. Beinart, *Records of the Trials of the Spanish Inquisition in Ciudad Real* and *Trujillo: A Community in Extremadura on the Eve of the Expulsion from Spain* (Jerusalem, 1980). On practices in Majorca, see Baruch Braunstein, *The Chuetas of Mallorca* (New York, 1936); also Carlos Carrete Parrondo, *Proceso inquisitorial contra los Arias Dávila segovianos: un enfrendamiento social entre judíos y conversos. Fontes iudaeorum regni castellae,* vol. 3 (Salamanca, 1986).
6. Baer, *The Jews of Christian Spain,* II: 175ff.
7. See Louis Finkelstein, *Jewish Self-Government in the Middle Ages* (New York, 1964), pp. 348–75, for the rulings and ordinances (*Takkanot*) of Valladolid of 1432.
8. See A. Sicroff, *Les Controverses des statuts de pureté de sang en Espagne du XVe au XVIIe siècle* (Paris, 1960), for a full discussion of the genesis and vicissitudes of the laws of *limpieza.*
9. See Cecil Roth, *The Spanish Inquisition* (New York, 1964), as well as the classic study of the Inquisition by Henry C. Lea, *A History of the Inquisition in Spain* (New York, 1906), vol. 1, for a discussion of the genesis of the institution and the atmosphere of conspiracy which it introduced. "Signs" of Jewish practices were circulated and intimidation and fear were widespread.
10. E. Capsali, *Seder Eliyahu* ed. A. Shmuelevitz (Jerusalem, 1975), chapter 58.
11. See Fernández Luis Suárez, *Documentos Acerca de la Expulsión de los Judíos* (Valladolid, 1964), for a collection of primarily sources shedding light on the protective policies of the monarchs as well as the text of the expulsion decree. See pp. 116–17.
12. Baer, *The Jews of Christian Spain,* II: 398–423. Even today the story of the Holy Child of la Guardia appears in Spanish history books as a matter of fact. The tale inspired a play by the great Spanish dramatist Lope de Vega, significantly entitled *El Niño Innocente de la Guardia.*
13. Capsali, *Seder Eliyahu,* chapter 69.
14. *The Expulsion 1492 Chronicles,* ed. David Raphael (North Hollywood, Calif., 1992), p. 186, from Luis de Páramo, *On the Origins and Advances of the Holy Office of the Inquisition* (De Origine et Progressu Officii Sanctae Inquisitionis, Madrid, 1598).
15. See Suárez, *Documentos,* passim.
16. Capsali, chapter 67, quoted by Raphael, *Chronicles,* p. 13.
17. Joseph Hacker, "New Chronicles on the Expulsion of the Jews from Spain, Its Causes and Consequences" (in Hebrew), *Yitzkah F. Baer Memorial Volume, Zion* 44 (1979), pp. 201–28.

18. Solomon ibn Verga, *Sherbet Yehudah,* ed. A. Shohat (Jerusalem, 1947), the forty-fourth conversion.
19. See expulsion degree in Appendix.
20. Leo W. Schwarz, ed., *Memoirs of My People* (New York, 1943), pp. 46–47.
21. Isadore Loeb, "Un convoi d'exilés d'Espagne à Marseilles en 1492," *Revue des Etudes Juives* 9 (1884), pp. 66–76, and Agostino Guistiniani, *Annali della Republica de Genova illustrati con noe dal Cav. G.B. Spotorno,* 2 vols. (Genoa), II: 566.
22. Raphael, *Chronicles,* pp. 71–72, from Andrés Bernáldez, *Historia de los reyes Católicos Don Fernando y Isabel* (Seville, 1869).
23. Samuel Usque, *Consolation for the Tribulations of Israel,* ed. and trans. Martin A. Cohen (Philadelphia, 1964), pp. 201–2.

Chapter 6. Return to the Islamic World

1. See F. Kohler, *Letters of Jews through the Ages,* 2 vols. (Philadelphia, 1951), I: 283–85, for text of the letter attributed to Isaac Zarfati. This attribution has been questioned by Joseph Hacker in a masterful study of Ottoman Jewry. See J. Hacker, *Jewish Society in Salonica and its Environs in the Fifteenth and Sixteenth Century* (in Hebrew). PhD. dissertation, Hebrew University, 1978.
2. E. Capsali, *Seder Eliyahu,* ed. A. Shmuelevitz. (Jerusalem, 1975) chapter 70.
3. Samuel Usque, *Consolation for the Tribulations of Israel,* ed. and trans. Marvin A. Cohen (Philadelphia, 1964), p. 200.
4. Solomon ibn Verga, *Shebet Yehudah,* the fifty-second conversion, quoted by David Raphael, ed. *The Expulsion 1492 Chronicles* (North Hollywood, Calif., 1991), p. 97.
5. Judah ibn Hayyat, *Minhat Yehuda,* quoted by Raphael, *Chronicles,* p. 114. On resettlement in Morocco, see Jane S. Gerber, *Jewish Society in Fez 1450–1700* (Leiden, 1980) and bibliography there.
6. Capsali, *Seder Eliyahu,* chapter 81.
7. Ibid., chapter 83. See Yosef H. Yerushalmi, *Zachor: Jewish History and Jewish Memory* (Seattle, 1982), on the messianic mood of the sixteenth-century historians, the majority of whom were Sephardim.
8. Quoted by Leah Bornstein-Makovetsky, "Structure, Organization and Spiritual Life of the Sephardi Communities in the Ottoman Empire from the Sixteenth to the Eighteenth Centuries," in *The Sephardi Heritage: The Western Sephardim,* ed. R. D. Barnett and W. M. Schwab (London, 1989), p. 316.
9. Salo Baron, *A Social and Religious History of the Jews* (New York and Philadelphia, 1957), XVIII: 467, n. 20.
10. On the career of Rabbi David ibn Abi Zimra, the RADBAZ, see Israel M. Goldman, *The Life and Times of Rabbi David Ibn Abi Zimra* (New York, 1970).
11. Bornstein-Makovetsky, "Structure, Organization and Spiritual Life," p. 317.
12. High Holiday prayerbook of the Bevis Marks synagogue of London.
13. Bernard Lewis, *The Jews of Islam,* (Princeton, 1985), p. 135.
14. Ibid.
15. The dramatic account by Cecil Roth in *The House of Nasi: Dona Gracia* (Philadelphia, 1947) is still the standard biography of Dona Gracia. A more refined and detailed interpretation of the boycott of Ancona can be found in Marc Sapirstein, "Martyrs, Merchants and Rabbis: Jewish Communal Conflict as Reflected in the Responsa on the Boycott of Ancona," *Jewish Social Studies* 43 (1981), pp. 215–28. See also Isaiah Sonne, *From Paul IV to Pius V* (in Hebrew), (Jerusalem, 1954), pp. 146–59 and Baron, *A Social and Religious History of the Jews,* XIV: 35–43.
16. See Gershom Sholem, *Major Trends in Jewish Mysticism* (New York, 1961) and his exhaustive biography of the messianic pretender, *Sabbetai Sevi: The Mystical Messiah* (Princeton, 1973). The best introduction to the community of mystics established in Safed is Solomon Schechter,

"Safed in the Sixteenth Century," *Studies in Judaism* (New York and Philadelphia, 1958), pp. 231–97. On the interpretation of Zevi's aberrant behavior according to messianic and Lurianic doctrines, see G. Scholem "Redemption through Sin," in his volume of collected essays, *The Messianic Idea in Judaism* (New York, 1971), pp. 78–141.

Chapter 7. The Westward Journey

1. Moses A. Shulvass, *From East to West* (Detroit, 1971), pp. 25–50.
2. Cecil Roth, *History of the Jews in Venice* (New York, 1975); B. Ravid, *Economics and Toleration in Seventeenth-Century Venice* (Jerusalem, 1978). On the Sephardic and Levantine synagogues in Venice, see Roberta Curiel and Bernard Dov Cooperman, *The Venetian Ghetto* (New York, 1990); on music, see I. Adler, *La Pratique musicale savante dans quelques communautés juives en Europe au XVIIe et XVIIIe Siècle* (Paris, 1966). For discussion of the Levantine Jews in Venice, see B. Cooperman, "Venetian Policy towards the Levantine Jews in Its Broader Italian Context," in *Gli Ebrei e Venezia*, (Milan, 1987), pp. 65ff.
3. Quoted by Cecil Roth, *The History of the Jews in Italy* (Philadelphia, 1946), p. 346.
4. On migration from Italy to Holland, see Miriam Bodian "Amsterdam, Venice and the Marrano Diaspora in the Seventeenth Century," in *Dutch Jewish History*, ed. Jozeph Michman (Jerusalem, 1989), pp. 47–65 and Jonathan Israel, "The Jews of Venice and Their Links with Holland and Dutch Jewry (1650–1710)," in *Gli Ebrei e Venezia*, pp. 95–116.
5. For a lengthy discussion of factors motivating return to Judaism and the difficulties of penetrating the psyche of the New Christian, see Yosef Hayim Yerushalmi, *From Spanish Court to Italian Ghetto: Isaac Cardoso. A Study in Seventeenth-Century Marranism and Jewish Apologetics* (Seattle, 1971). Yerushalmi provides a probing investigation of the "signs" of Jewishness and steps toward the embrace of Judaism in the life of Isaac Cardoso.
6. See Yosef Hayim Yerushalmi, *The Lisbon Massacre of 1506 and the Royal Image in the Shebet Yehudah* (Cincinnati, 1976), for a discussion of the actions of King Manuel of Portugal as well as of ibn Verga's appraisal of the king's behavior.
7. See Yosef Kaplan, *From Christianity to Judaism: The Story of Isaac Orobio de Castro* (Oxford, 1989) for a brilliant account of the intellectual odyssey of this important figure in Jewish apologetics.
8. Quoted in ibid., p. 329.
9. Quoted by Frances Malino, *The Sephardic Jews of Bordeaux: Assimilation and Emancipation in Revolutionary and Napoleonic France* (University, Alabama, 1978) p. 3 and p. 117, n. 1. For further considerations of demography, see Soza Szajkowski, "Population Problems of Marranos and Sephardim in France, from the 16th to the 20th century," *Proceedings of the American Academy for Jewish Research* 27 (1958), pp. 83–105; also Michel Rolland Francisque, *Les Portugais en France, les Français en Portugal* (Bordeaux, 1882), p. 187.
10. On the vicissitudes of *marrano* life in France presented in dramatic though somewhat dated fashion, see Cecil Roth, *History of the Marranos*, 4th ed. (New York, 1974). On the number of Jews remaining outside the Jewish community, see Gérard Nahon, "The Sephardim in France," in *The Sephardi Heritage: The Western Sephardim*, vol. 2, ed. Richard D. Barnett and W. M. Schwake (London, 1989), pp. 46–74. Nahon argues convincingly that the majority of the *conversos* were indeed crypto-Jews while Szajkowski in "Population Problems" asserts that many new arrivals simply sought greater security and had no intention of reentering the Jewish community.
11. Quoted by Herbert I. Bloom, *The Economic Activities of the Jews of Amsterdam in the Seventeenth and Eighteenth Centuries* (New York, 1937), p. 8.
12. Quoted by J. Meijer, "Hugo Grotius' Remonstrantie,'" *Jewish Social Studies* 17 (1955), pp. 91–104.
13. Bloom, *Economic Activities*, p. 49.
14. George Alexander Kohut, "Jewish Martyrs of the Inquisition in South America," *Proceedings of the American Jewish Historical Society* (1894), pp. 132–34

15. On the complex personality of de Barrios and his friendship with Isaac Orobio, see Kaplan, *From Christianity to Judaism,* pp. 222ff.
16. See Miriam Bodian, "The Portuguese Dowry Societies in Venice and Amsterdam," *Italia* 6 (1987) and the unpublished paper by the same author "The Shaping of Converso Identity in Early Modern Europe," University of Maryland, April 1991.
17. Yirmiyahu Yovel, *Spinoza and Other Heretics: The Marrano of Reason* (Princeton, 1989), p. 40.
18. Ibid., p. 3.
19. David S. Katz, *Philosemitism and the Readmission of the Jews to England 1603–1655* (Oxford, 1982), chapter 1.
20. Ibid., pp. 43ff.
21. For the traditional story of the admission of the Jews to England, see Cecil Roth, *A History of the Jews in England* (London, 1964) and Lucien Wolf, *Menasseh ben Israel's Mission to Oliver Cromwell* (London, 1964). Newer source analysis has considerably revised the standard view. See Ismar Schorsch, "From Messianism to Realpolitik: Menasseh ben Israel and the Readmission of the Jews to England," *Proceedings of the American Adademy of Jewish Research* 45 (1978), pp. 187–208; for a discussion of Menasseh's Messianic politics, see Harold Fisch, "The Messianic Politics of Menasseh ben Israel," in *Menasseh ben Israel and his World,* ed. Yosef Kaplan et al. (Leiden, 1989), pp. 228–390.
22. Todd M. Endelman, *Radical Assimilation in English Jewish History 1656–1945* (Bloomington, Ind., 1990), p. 10.
23. Morris Schappes, ed., *A Documentary History of the Jews in the United States 1654–1875* (New York, 1971), document 1 (September 22, 1654).
24. Quoted by Jacob Rader Marcus, *United States Jewry 1776–1985* (Detroit, 1989) p. 77, n. 53.
25. Yerushalmi, *From Spanish Court,* p. 44.

Chapter 8. Encounter with Modernity

1. Stanford J. Shaw, *The Jews of the Ottoman Empire and the Turkish Republic* (New York, 1991), p. 207.
2. Edward W. Lane, *Manners and Customs of the Modern Egyptians* (London, 1954), p. 559.
3. Germaine Mouette, *Histoire des conquestes de Mouley Archy* (Paris, 1683). Reprinted in *Les Sources inédites de l'histoire du Maroc: Archives de France,* ser. 2, (Paris, 1924) II: 177.
4. William Lemprière, *A Tour from Gibraltar to Tangier, Sallee, Mogadore, Santa Cruz, Tarudant, and thence over Mount Atlas, to Morocco: Including a Particular Account of the Royal Harem* (London, 1791), p. 188.
5. David Porter, *Constantinople and Its Environs* (New York, 1835), 2 vols., I: 167, as quoted by Mair José Benardete, *The Hispanic Culture and Character of Sephardic Jews* (New York, 1982), p. 138.
6. C. J. Wills, *Persia as It Is* (London, 1887), p. 231.
    For a more general discussion of discriminatory legislation, see Jane S. Gerber, "Anti-Semitism and the Muslim World," in *History and Hate: The Dimensions of Anti-Semitism,* ed. David Berger (Philadelphia, 1986), pp. 73–93.
7. Cevdet Pasha, *Tezakir,* ed. Cavid Baysun (Ankara, 1963), I: 67–68. Quoted by Benjamin Braude and Bernard Lewis in *Christians and Jews in the Ottoman Empire* (New York, 1982), I: 30.
8. Quoted by Jane S. Gerber, "The Damascus Blood Libel—Jewish Perceptions and Responses," *Eighth World Congress of Jewish Studies* (Jerusalem, 1982), Division B, pp. 105–10.
9. Isaac Leeser, *Persecution of the Jews in the East: Proceedings of a Meeting in Philadelphia 1840,* in *Beginnings: Early American Judaica,* introduced by Abraham J. Karp (Philadelphia, 1975), p. 46.
10. Quoted by Jonathan D. Sarna, *Jacksonian Jew: The Two Worlds of Mordecai Noah* (New York, 1981), p. 125.
11. *Minute Book of the Board of Deputies,* IV: 106.
12. Aron Rodrique, *French Jews, Turkish Jews* (Bloomington, Ind.: 1990), p. 22.
13. Ibid., p. xi.

14. Ibid., pp. 71–72.
15. Ibid., p. 145.
16. Quoted by Shaw, *Jews of the Ottoman Empire,* p. 190.
17. "Report of American Jewish Committee," in *American Jewish Yearbook,* 5654, (1914) and subsequent yearbooks for 1915, 1916, and 1917 (Philadelphia, 1915–1917) and 1936, 1937.
18. For a detailed study of the career of Rabbi Nahum, see Esther Benbassa, *Un Grand Rabbin Sepharade en politique 1892–1923,* (Paris, 1990) and especially her dissertation "Haim Nahum Effendi, dernier grand rabbin de l'Empire Ottomane (1908–1920), son rôle politique et diplomatique," unpublished thesis, Université de Paris III, Sorbonne Nouvelle, 1987.
19. See a discussion of oscillating policy of Bulgaria toward its Jews during World War II in Frederick B. Chary, *The Bulgarian Jews and the Final Solution 1940–1944* (Pittsburgh, 1972) and Nissan Oren, "The Bulgarian Exception: A Reassessment of the Salvation of the Jewish Community," Yad Vashem Studies VII (1968), pp. 83–106.
20. Michel Abitbol, *Les Juifs d'Afrique du Nord sous Vichy* (Paris, 1983), pp. 146–55 and Marcel Aboulker, *Alger et ses complots* (Paris, 1945). See further notes in Norman Stillman, *The Jews of Arab Lands in Modern Times* (Philadelphia, 1992), p. 134.
21. Stillman, *The Jews of Arab Lands,* p. 431.
22. Albert Memmi, *Pillar of Salt* (New York, 1953), p. 272.
23. The *farhud,* denoting a massive breakdown of law and order, was the name which Iraqi Jewry bestowed upon the pogrom. On the events themselves, see Elie Kedourie, "The Sack of Basra and the Baghdad *Farhud,*" in idem, *Arabic Political Memoirs and Other Studies* (London, 1974), pp. 283–314.

Chapter 9. Revival and Return

1. Pre-war census figures do not break down the Jewish population into Sephardim and Ashkenazim. In the case of France, the names of victims in detailed deportation lists and memorial books reveal that many were of Sephardic origin. It has been suggested that approximately 35,000 Sephardic Jews resided in pre-war France and 20,000 in Holland.
2. R. de Felice, *Jews in an Arab Land: Libya 1835–1970* (Austin, Tex., 1985), p. 206.
3. Ibid., p. 209.
4. Harvey Goldberg, *Jewish Life in Muslim Libya: Rivals and Relatives* (Chicago, 1990), pp. 97–122, contains a cultural analysis of the riots which claimed dozens of Jewish lives.
5. Quoted by C. C. Aronsfeld, *The Ghosts of 1492: Jewish Aspects of the Struggle for Religious Freedom in Spain 1848–1976* (New York, 1979), p. 5.
6. Ibid., pp. 8–9.
7. Ibid., p. 13.
8. Haim Avni, *Spain, the Jews and Franco* (Philadelphia, 1982), p. 92. Avni estimates that 640 Jews in Greece held Spanish passports, 130 in Bulgaria, 100 in Rumania, less than 50 in Hungary, and perhaps 25 in Yugoslavia. In addition, there were 3,000 Jews with Spanish papers in France, along with a few dozen elsewhere. According to Avni (p. 162), no more than 800 of these Jews were repatriated during the Nazi years.
9. Quoted in Ibid., p. 179.
10. See Shmuel Trigano, *La République et les Juifs* (Paris, 1982) and Bernard-Henri Levy, *L'idéologie française* (Paris, 1981) for cogent expressions of the new outlook of Jewishly engaged French intellectuals.
11. Marc D. Angel, "The Sephardim of the United States: An Exploratory Study," *American Jewish Year Book* (Philadelphia and New York, 1973) pp. 77–138. For the post–World War I period, see p. 87, n. 21.
12. Yehudah Alkalai, letter to Moses Sachs from 1866 to *Kitvai ha-Rav Yehudah Alkalai,* ed. Isaac Rafael (Jerusalem, 1974), II: 678ff.
13. Quoted by Daniel J. Elazar, *The Other Jews: The Sephardim Today* (New York, 1989), pp. 185–86.

14. One fascinating reflection of the continuing Sephardic sense of distinctiveness is the creation of a separate Sephardic religious political party in Israel in the 1980s (Shas). While its leadership has been trained in Ashkenazic yeshivot (institutes of rabbinical studies), followers tend to see Shas as an expression of Sephardic identity. Preliminary breakdowns of election results of the June 1992 election reveal that the majority of Sephardim still lean toward Likud as well as to Shas. It is still too early to predict what the future political clout of Sephardim will be since the immigration of Soviet Jews continues, although on the scale of approximately only 4,500–6,000 per month in 1992.

A NOTE ON
FURTHER READING

The suggested readings that follow are intended for the English-speaking reader who is interested in learning more about Sephardic Jews, but may not have the necessary linguistic tools to explore further readings also available in Hebrew, Spanish, or French sources. Omission of suggested Hebrew readings, in particular, does not mean to suggest that the works of Schirmann, Beinart, Ben Sasson, Benayahu, and the many other significant Israeli scholars who have been publishing important studies during the past several decades are not essential for the more serious student. A major problem confronting the novice is that no single-volume study on the Jews of Spain or the Sephardic diaspora exists. Works of a general nature tend to ignore the history of the Jews, while specialized Jewish studies frequently treat their Jewish subject without due recognition of the broader historical currents. Perhaps the most useful introductory work is the volume of collected essays *The Sephardi Heritage,* ed. Richard D. Barnett, vol. 1 (London, 1971), describing Sephardic civilization until 1497 and *The Sephardi Heritage:, The Western Sephardim,* ed. R. D. Barnett and W. M. Schwab, vol. 2 (London, 1989). An absorbing, if sometimes romantic, study of selective aspects of Jewish life during the Muslim period, drawing heavily upon Arabic sources, is E. Ashtor's *History of the Jews in Muslim Spain* in three volumes, translated from the Hebrew by Aaron Klein and Jenny Machlowitz (Philadelphia, 1973–1984). A two-volume history by Yitzhak Baer, *The Jews of Christian Spain* (Philadelphia, 1961–66), is the standard work on Christian Spain. With the expulsion and dispersion of the Jews in 1492, the literature on Sephardim tends to be subsumed under general studies of each diaspora community.

Studies of individual aspects of Jewish life in Spain, such as poetry, mysticism, linguistics, and philosophy, can be found in Salo W. Baron's monumental *A Social and Religious History of the Jews,* 2d ed., vols. 3–8 (New York and Philadelphia, 1957–58). His later volumes (9–18) include invaluable and comprehensive treatment of the Sephardic diaspora until 1650. Especially relevant are vol. 12 ("Economic Catalyst"), vol. 13 ("Inquisition, Renaissance, and Reformation"), vol. 15 ("Resettlement and Exploration"), vol. 17 ("Byzantines, Mamelukes and Maghribians), and vol. 18 (The Ottoman Empire, Persia, Ethiopia, India and China). While his work is not intended for the beginner, his extraordinary notes frequently furnish hard-to-find information.

Sephardic Jews were shaped by more than a millennium of residence in Christian Europe where questions of religious dissidence formed a major part of the Jewish-Christian encounter. Spain was often the site of religious debate and forced conversion. A growing body of literature exists on the theological roots of anti-Semitism in Western civilization. Studies providing helpful insights on the complex subject include Alan Davies, ed., *Anti-Semitism and the Foundations of Christianity* (New York, 1979); Franklin Littell, *The Crucifixion of the Jews: The Failure of Christians to Understand the Jewish Experience* (New York, 1965); and Rosemary Ruether, *Faith and Fratricide* (New York, 1974). For a creative and sophisticated discussion which distinguishes between Christian anti-Judaism and anti-Semitism, combining history and social psychology, see Gavin I. Langmuir, *Toward a Definition of Anti-semitism,* (Berkeley and Los Angeles, 1990). His volume *History, Religion and Anti-semitism* (Berkeley and Los Angeles, 1990) is an original presentation of the irrational forces behind the blood libel accusation. It supplements the older, but still excellent, pioneering study of popular attitudes toward Jews represented in the literature, art, and architecture of medieval times in Joshua Trachtenberg, *The Devil and the Jews* (New Haven, 1945). The case of the infant of La Guardia, the notorious Spanish blood libel of 1491–92 which fueled popular anti-Jewish sentiments on the eve of the expulsion, is discussed by Sanford Shepard in "The Present State of the Ritual Crime in Spain," in *The Blood Libel Legend: A Casebook in Anti-Semitic Folklore,* ed. Alan Dundes (Madison, Wis., 1991), pp. 162–79.

The waves of persecutions that engulfed the Jews in Visigothic Spain in the sixth and seventh centuries are among the least well documented in Jewish history. For a useful discussion of Visigothic anti-Jewish policies, see Bernard S. Bachrach, *Early Medieval Jewish Policy in Western Europe* (Minneapolis, 1977) and Solomon Katz, *The Jews in the Visigothic and Frankish Kingdoms of Spain and Gaul,* (Cambridge, Mass., 1937). Bachrach has a useful summary and analysis of the Visigothic persecutions in "A Reassessment of Visigothic Jewish Policy, 589–711," in the *American Historical Review* 78 (1973), pp. 11–34. Sample texts of oaths imposed upon Jews forcibly converted to Christianity can be found in James Parkes, *The Conflict of the Church and the Synagogue* (Philadelphia, 1961).

The Muslim conquest of Spain in 711 inaugurated a new chapter in the history of the Jews of the Iberian peninsula. The best single source for reconstructing the life of the Jews in medieval Islam is the rich documentary horde of documents that were preserved in a storage attic in a synagogue in Cairo, known as the Cairo Geniza. The master of Geniza research, S. D. Goitein, has produced a monumental five-volume study from the tens of thousands of Hebrew and Arabic fragments which he deciphered. Even when Spain is not specifically mentioned, the Geniza is the essential source of information on the shared civilization of all Mediterranean peoples in medieval times. Goitein's magisterial *A Mediterranean Society* (Berkeley and Los Angeles, 1967–88) throws light on the social, economic, and family life of the Jews throughout the Mediterranean world. His collection of representative Geniza letters in *Letters of Medieval Jewish Traders* (Princeton, 1973) gives voice to the pious and intrepid personalities who plied the seas on commercial ventures during medieval times. Many of their casual comments illuminate specific trade conditions the Spanish merchants confronted.

A growing body of literature exists regarding the Jewish status in the world of Islam. Numerous studies by Bernard Lewis offer a balanced approach to the subject. In *The Jews of Islam* (Princeton, 1985) Lewis clearly presents the attitude of Islam toward other religions in general and the Jews in particular, detailing the discriminatory regulations as well as the positive aspects of intergroup relations. Norman Stillman's *The Jews of Arab Lands* (Philadelphia, 1979) includes an excellent discussion of early Islamic attitudes toward Jews and a useful collection of sources documenting the complex subject of Muslim-Jewish relations in the vast Muslim empire. Mark R. Cohen surveys the current schools of thought on Muslim-Jewish relations in a thoughtful essay "Islam and the Jews: Myth, Countermyth, History," in *The Jer-*

usalem Quarterly 38 (1986), pp. 125–137. Jane Gerber gives an overview
of the fluctuations in Muslim attitudes toward Jews and Judaism in
"Anti-Semitism and the Muslim World," in *History and Hate: The Dimensions of Anti-Semitism,* ed. David Berger (Philadelphia, 1985). Ample
documentary evidence of Muslim discrimination against Jews can be
found in Bat Ye'or, *The Dhimmi: Jews and Christians under Islam* (Ruth-
erford, N.J., 1985).

Medieval Jewish culture was heavily indebted to Muslim interests
and literary tastes. A brief, yet comprehensive, presentation of the history of Islamic Spain that specifically treats the cultural milieu is *A
History of Islamic Spain* by W. Montgomery Watt (Edinburgh, 1965).
Abraham S. Halkin's essay "The Judeo-Islamic Age," in *Great Ages and
Ideas of the Jewish People,* ed. Leo W. Schwarz and S. D. Goitein's *Jews
and Arabs: Their Contacts through the Ages,* 2d ed. (New York, 1974)
offer clear and concise overviews of the background in which Jewish
literature flourished.

The Hebrew poetry of medieval Spain is the subject of several excellent
recent studies. For a fine general survey of the poetry of the Golden
Age, see Shalom Spiegel's essay "On Medieval Hebrew Poetry," in *The
Jews: Their History, Culture and Religion,* ed. Louis Finkelstein, 3d ed.
(New York, 1960). Raymond P. Scheindlin's *Wine, Women and Death:
Medieval Hebrew Poems on the Good Life* (Philadelphia, 1986) and *The
Gazelle* (Philadelphia, 1991) provide masterful translations and com-
mentaries on selected Hebrew secular and religious poetry of the
Golden Age of Spain. A sophisticated theoretical discussion of the
creative tensions that the Sephardic poet experienced can be found in
Ross Brann, *The Compunctious Poet* (Baltimore, 1991). Translations of
several of the poets are available in David Goldstein, *Hebrew Poets from
Spain* (London, 1965) and T. Carmi's *Penguin Book of Hebrew Verse*
(New York, 1981). Leon Weinberger treats the unusual career of the
courtier-poet-statesman Samuel ibn Nagrela, providing a wide sam-
pling of his poetry in *Jewish Prince in Moslem Spain: Selected Poems of
Samuel ibn Nagrela* (University, Ala., 1973).

Poetry was one component of a broader cultural milieu that included the study of medicine, the contemplation of philosophy, and a
courtly life-style. The best introduction to this milieu is analyzed by

Gerson D. Cohen in his translation and notes on *Sefer ha-Qabbalah: The Book of Tradition* (Philadelphia, 1967). The study of philosophy was as important to the courtier-rabbis as was poetry. A good edition (abridged) of Yehudah Halevi's *Kuzari* is Isaak Heinemann's (Oxford, 1947). The best introduction to Moses ben Maimon's (Maimonides') writings is Isadore Twersky's *Maimonides Reader* (New York, 1972). For a very readable and human portrait of Maimonides, see the biography of Abraham J. Heschel, *Maimonides* (New York, 1982). Maimonides' epistles are the subject of a fine translation by Abraham Halkin, with significant introductory essays by David Hartman, in *Crisis and Leadership: Epistles of Maimonides* (Philadelphia, 1985).

The Christian reconquest of Spain began in 1085 and continued until the fall of Granada in 1492. During the centuries of reconquest, Spanish life underwent major changes and subtle reconfigurations. The transition from Muslim to Christian rule was accompanied by significant societal and institutional changes, analyzed in two excellent studies, Thomas F. Glick's *Islamic and Christian Spain in the Early Middle Ages* (Princeton, 1979) and Robert Burns's *Muslims, Christians and Jews in the Crusader Kingdom of Valencia* (Cambridge, 1984). Both historians offer insights into Jewish participation in the period of cultural transition from the perspective of general Spanish history. A rabbinic leader who bridged the two civilizations, Meir ha-Levi Abulafia (Ramah), is the subject of perceptive analysis in Bernard Septimus' *Hispano-Jewish Culture in Transition: The Career and Controversies of Ramah* (Cambridge, Mass., 1982).

As the Christian kingdoms gained greater control of the Iberian peninsula, they promulgated new laws to regulate the position of the Jews. A useful English translation of the laws of Alfonso the Wise contained in his *Siete Partidas* is available in Dwayne E. Carpenter, *Alfonso X and the Jews: An Edition and Commentary on Siete Partidas 7.24 "De Los Judios"* (Berkeley and Los Angeles, 1986). Internal social and economic developments in the Jewish community from the thirteenth through the fifteenth centuries are examined in the dated, but still useful, study of Abraham A. Neuman, *The Jews of Spain,* 2 vols. (Philadelphia, 1942).

For two significant and contrasting views of the origins and scope of the missionary efforts aimed at Jews (and Muslims) in the thirteenth century, see Jeremy Cohen, *The Friars and the Jews* (Ithaca, 1982) and Robert Chazan, *Daggers of Faith: Thirteenth-Century Christian Missionizing and Jewish Response* (Berkeley and Los Angeles, 1989). Both studies suggest new ways of regarding the phenomenon of the religious disputation in thirteenth-century Spain.

The complexity of the last century of Jewish life in Spain is reflected in rich archival sources and Spanish monographic studies. The events surrounding the expulsion are included in several contemporary Hebrew, Spanish, and Portuguese chronicles. A very handy anthology of extracts from these chronicles as well as the text of the expulsion decree are contained in a volume by David Raphael, *The Expulsion 1492 Chronicles* (North Hollywood, Calif., 1991). For Abrabanel's perceptions of the events unfolding in fifteenth-century Spain, see B. Netanyahu's biography, *Don Isaac Abravanel, Statesman and Philosopher,* 2d ed. (Philadelphia, 1968).

One of the most controversial issues of Sephardic historiography is the question of the Jewishness of the conversos. Haim Beinart's lifelong study of Inquisition records leaves little doubt about the authenticity of faith and tragedy of martyrdom of the *conversos.* See *Inquisition at Ciudad Real,* 4 vols. (Jerusalem, 1974–85), and *Conversos on Trial,* (Jerusalem, 1981) for a thorough discussion of the *modus operandi* of the Inquisition and the plight of its Jewish martyrs. The classic study of the history, methods, techniques, and chief actors of the Spanish Inquisition is Henry Charles Lea, *A History of the Inquisition in Spain,* 4 vols. (New York, 1906–8). For a provocative and sharply contrasting study of the Jewishness of the *marranos,* based upon a close reading of rabbinic responsa, see B. Netanyahu's important *The Marranos of Spain,* 2d ed. (New York, 1966). Still useful and very readable is Cecil Roth's *History of the Marranos* (Philadelphia, 1932).

The causes of the expulsion are the subject of lively discussion among contemporary authorities. Most of these debates are not available in English. For a fine study of the expulsion of the Jews from Navarre in 1498 which touches upon broader questions of the expulsion in 1492, see Benjamin R. Gampel, *The Last Jews on Iberian Soil: Navarese Jewry 1479/98* (Berkeley and Los Angeles, 1989).

The exiles of 1492 who departed from Portugal were soon confronted by a brutal forced conversion from which there was no reprieve. Popular wrath against the Portuguese New Christians erupting in 1506 is the subject of a fine reconstruction of data from the chronicle of ibn Verga by Yosef H. Yerushalmi, *The Lisbon Massacre of 1506 and the Royal Image in the Shebet Yehudah* (Cincinnati, 1976). Yerushalmi's brilliant reconstruction of the life of Isaac Cardoso in *From Spanish Court to Italian Ghetto* (Seattle, 1971) and his eloquent study of Jewish historiography (including the sixteenth-century Sephardic authors) in *Zachor: Jewish History and Jewish Memory* (Seattle, 1982) shed new light on the psyche of the generation of the expulsion.

The exiles of 1492 who returned to the world of Islam revitalized moribund communities or established new centers of Jewish life. On Morocco, see Jane S. Gerber *Jewish Society in Fez* (Leiden, 1980); on Turkey, see Morris Goodblatt, *Jewish Life in Turkey in the XVI Century: As Reflected in the Legal Writings of Samuel de Medina* (New York, 1952). On North Africa, the best overall survey is H. Z. Hirschberg, *A History of the Jews in North Africa,* 2 vols. (Leiden, 1974–1980). Hirschberg is especially strong on the political history of the Jews. Cecil Roth's highly readable biographies of Don Joseph Nasi and Dona Gracia Mendes, two sixteenth-century Sephardic personalities who dominated Jewish life and played crucial roles in Ottoman diplomacy during its era of expansion, have recently been reissued (Philadelphia, 1992). Important studies of Israeli scholars like Joseph Hacker await translation in English. Stanford J. Shaw's *The Jews of the Ottoman Empire and the Turkish Republic* (New York, 1991) should be used with some caution, but is very strong in areas such as demography and residential patterns.

The intellectual upheaval caused by the expulsion and its aftermath emerges in the vivid essay of Solomon Schechter, "Safed in the Sixteenth Century," in his *Studies in Judaism* (New York, 1970). Highly recommended for its enormous erudition and wealth of data is the biographical history of the messianic movement of Sabbetai Sevi by Gershom Scholem, *Sabbetai Sevi: The Mystical Messiah* (Princeton, 1973). Marc D. Angel's *Voices in Exile* (New York, 1991) discusses little-known thinkers from the Sephardic diaspora in a timely and useful volume for a general audience.

The Sephardic diaspora in Amsterdam is the subject of an old, but still useful, history of Solomon H. Bloom, *The Economic Activities of the Jews of Amsterdam in the Seventeenth and Eighteenth Centuries* (New York, 1937). For an excellent study of the intellectual climate in the Portuguese *marrano* community, see Yosef Kaplan, *From Christianity to Judaism: The Story of Isaac Orobio de Castro* (Oxford, 1989). On the career and thought of Baruch Spinoza, see the fine study of Yirmiyahu Yovel, *Spinoza and Other Heretics: The Marrano of Reason* (Princeton, 1989).

Few English studies are available on Sephardic migration in the New World. A. Wiznitzer's *Jews in Colonial Brazil* (New York, 1960) can be supplemented by more up-to-date articles of Anita Novinsky in collected volumes and journals for greater understanding of that community. The single best work on the secret Jews of New Spain is Martin Cohen's *Martyr: The Story of a Secret Jew and the Mexican Inquisition in the Sixteenth Century* (Philadelphia, 1973). For a very useful survey of Sephardim in America from colonial times to the present, containing important information on the twentieth-century immigration of Sephardic Jews, see Marc D. Angel "Sephardim in America," *The American Jewish Yearbook* (New York, 1973).

The story of modernization of the Sephardic Jews has yet to receive the kind of scholarly attention that has been devoted to Ashkenazic Jews. For a suggestive approach to the decline of Jewish life in the Ottoman Empire, see Bernard Lewis's discussion in *The Jews of Islam* (Princeton, 1985) and the introductory essay in Norman Stillman's *The Jews of Arab Lands in Modern Times* (Philadelphia, 1991). The role of the *Alliance Israélite Universelle* as the major instrument of modernization and Westernization is the subject of an important archival study of Aron Rodrigue, *French Jews, Turkish Jews* (Bloomington, Ind., 1990). Shlomo Deshen analyzes the blend of tradition and change in Moroccan Jewish society in incisive fashion in *The Mellah Society: Jewish life in Sherifian Morocco* (Chicago, 1989).

The history of the destruction of the Sephardic Jewish communities of Greece and the Balkans has not yet received proper treatment in English. The little-known story of Spain during the Holocaust and its ambivalent attitude toward rescue of Jews can be found in Haim Avni's carefully researched *Spain, the Jews and Franco* (Philadelphia, 1982). The North African chapter of the Holocaust is subjected to close study from archival sources in Michael Abitbol's *The Jews of North Africa during the Second World War* (Detroit, 1989). On contemporary Yugoslav Jewry and its rich past, with special emphasis on demographics, see Harriet Pass Friedenreich, *The Jews of Yugoslavia* (Philadelphia, 1979).

A growing library on Sephardim in Israel is now available in English. Most of the authors are anthropologists and sociologists concerned with the adaptations of a traditional ethnic group or geographically defined community to the new Israeli policy. Among the best studies are Shlomo Deshen and Moshe Shokeid, *The Predicament of Homecoming* (Ithaca, 1974); Moshe Shokeid, *The Dual Heritage: Immigrants from the Atlas Mountains in an Israeli Village* (New York, 1971); Alex Weingrod, *The Saint of Beersheba* (Albany, N.Y., 1990); and Yoram Bilu "Dreams and Wishes of the Saint," in *Judaism Viewed from Within and Without*, ed. Harvey Goldberg (Albany, 1987). The latter two explore the religious revival of North African Jewish traditions in pioneering analyses. Specialized studies on the largest immigrant group, the Moroccans, include the controversial volume *Ethnic Integration in Israel: A Comparative Case Study of Moroccan Brothers Who Settled in France and Israel* (New Brunswick, N.J., 1977), by Michael Inbar and Chaim Adler. In a symposium "Israel: State and Society: 1948–1988," in *Studies in Contemporary Jewry*, vol. 5 (Jerusalem, 1989), Pnina Morag-Talmon offers a more optimistic view, based on the latest data, on the integration of Sephardic Jews into the Israeli economy and Israeli society. For a comprehensive overview and provocative analysis of the contemporary Sephardic situation, see Daniel J. Elazar, *The Other Jews: The Sephardim Today* (New York, 1989).

With the current expansion of research institutes devoted to the study of Sephardic history and civilization in Spain, Israel, and the United States, further works should become available in the near future. It is also entirely possible that the topic will eventually become a subject of serious inquiry in the Arab world. Both peoples share an Iberian past of grandeur in Sepharad and al-Andalus. Both were expelled from Spain in her Golden Age; their lost civilization in Iberia is part of a larger legacy of common traditions.

INDEX